Adventuring in the
San Francisco
Bay Area

Adventuring in the San Francisco Bay Area

COUNTIES OF
SAN FRANCISCO
MARIN
SONOMA
NAPA
SOLANO
CONTRA COSTA
ALAMEDA
SANTA CLARA
SAN MATEO

Third Edition

PEGGY WAYBURN

SIERRA CLUB BOOKS • SAN FRANCISCO

The Sierra Club, founded in 1892 by John Muir, has devoted itself to the study and protection of the earth's scenic and ecological resources—mountains, wetlands, woodlands, wild shores and rivers, deserts and plains. The publishing program of the Sierra Club offers books to the public as a nonprofit educational service in the hope that they may enlarge the public's understanding of the Club's basic concerns. The point of view expressed in each book, however, does not necessarily represent that of the Club. The Sierra Club has some sixty chapters coast to coast, in Canada, Hawaii, and Alaska. For information about how you may participate in its programs to preserve wilderness and the quality of life, please address inquires to Sierra Club, 85 Second Street, San Francisco, CA 94105.

www.sierraclub.org/books
Copyright © 1987, 1995, 1999 by Peggy Wayburn

LIBRARY OF CONGRESS CATALOGING-IN-PUBLICATION DATA
Wayburn, Peggy.
    Adventuring in the San Francisco Bay Area: counties of San Francisco, Marin, Sonoma, Napa, Solano, Contra Costa, Alameda, Santa Clara, San Mateo / Peggy Wayburn.—Completely rev. and updated.
      p.   cm.—(The Sierra Club adventure travel guides)
    Includes bibliographical references and index.
    ISBN 0-87156-951-5 (alk. paper)
    1. San Francisco Bay Area (Calif.)—Guidebooks. I. Sierra Club. II. Title. III. Series.
    F868.S156W39 1999   917.94'60453—dc21   98-51160

Second revised edition: 1999

Maps by Hilda Chen

Printed in the United States of America on acid-free paper containing a minimum of 50% recovered waste paper, of which at least 10% of the fiber content is post-consumer waste

10 9 8 7 6 5 4 3 2 1

*To all those people who gave so generously of themselves
to gain protection for the Bay Area's lovely lands
and open space; and, in particular,
to Edgar Wayburn, who initiated, led, and saw through
so many of the battles that won for everyone
a priceless treasure of parklands*

Acknowledgments

Many people have most generously shared their time and knowledge with me as I have researched the material for this book. To them all goes my sincere appreciation. In particular, my thanks go to Jim Cohee, Paul Kaufmann, Gladys Hansen, Mala McGee, Susan Smith, Monica Bjorkman, Doris Sloan, James P. Delgado, Burchard Thomsen, Michael J. Ellis, Dave Shuford, David F. DeSante, Jim Locke, Robert Nuzum, Katie Wiggins, George Ellman, David Pesonen, David Wm. Hansen, Mary Lee Jefferds, Bob Berman, John Steiner, Jim Latte, Kevin Murphy, Gary Arsham, Tony Look, Thom and Susan McDannel, Philip Hocker, David Christy, Brian O'Neill, Volker Eisele, Ted Chandik, Ned McKay, Herbert Grench, Bob Doyle, John Sansing, Mary Burns, Jana Sheldon, Robert Augsberger, Malcolm Smith, Doug Nadeau, Bob Stewart, Tim Lillyquist, William Davoren, and the California Wine Institute.

My friend Connie Parrish has been invaluable in gathering information for the revision of this book. My talented copyeditor, Mary Anne Stewart, has added consistency and cohesiveness to my text. My husband, Edgar Wayburn, has been, and remains, my pillar of strength; my gratitude to him goes beyond words.

Considering the magnitude of the help I have received, this book should be flawless. However, I know that such is never the case, and I am, of course, responsible for any and all errors. I welcome suggestions and corrections from my readers, who, I hope, will gain as much information and pleasure out of this book as I have gained in the writing of it.

Contents

V • East Bay

VI • South Bay

• Appendixes

PART I

The San Francisco Bay Area

Introduction

San Francisco Bay is embraced in part by nine counties—Marin, Sonoma, Napa, Solano, Contra Costa, Alameda, Santa Clara, San Mateo, and San Francisco. Added together with the magic body of water as their heart, these counties constitute the Bay Area, one of the world's most special places. It is beautiful—and much more: it has a delightful climate; it was at the center of California's history; it has become the focal point of northern California's commerce and culture and has inspired some unique efforts for environmental protection; it has a lovely, varied, and, in places, remarkably unspoiled landscape; and it has the extraordinary bay itself—with a freshness and vitality to spark the spirit of anyone who stands beside it or ventures onto it, or just looks at it. This remarkable piece of geography, not surprisingly, also offers an exceptional spectrum of recreational opportunities. People who love the out-of-doors will find it an ideal place to explore and enjoy.

This book is meant to supply such people with information that will add to their pleasure in exploring the San Francisco Bay Area. In the belief that we enjoy most the things that we know something about, the book provides background information on the geology, the weather, the natural history, and the human history of this unique area. It also offers some specific information on the many kinds of outdoor adventures to be enjoyed here and how best to go about enjoying them. Where are the best places to stroll along the waterfront, for instance? Or to hike in the open countryside of the Bay Area counties? What about kayaking in the bay? What special aspect of the Bay Area climate makes it the second-best place on earth for windsurfing, and where is the best place to watch this beautiful sport? What about interesting geological sites to be visited? Which are the best historical and natural history museums? How do the counties of the Bay Area differ, and what unusual recreational opportunities do they each offer? How can you make the most of a foggy day? Where is the United States' only congressionally designated "wilderness" in the heart of a metropolitan area? You will find answers to these and to many other questions in the following pages.

As I went about selecting and gathering material for this book, I soon realized that I had undertaken something of a Herculean task. The San Francisco Bay Area is "so full of a number of things"—there is so much to see and do here, so much history, and so much fine outdoor adventuring to enjoy—that it is manifestly impossible for one small volume to cover the full scope of every subject I might want to include. Furthermore, there are a great many books that have already been written on different aspects of the Bay Area. This book, then, would have to be personal, reflecting my own views and experiences, and so it is. It would also entail hard choices, and so it has. I have had to be arbitrary in deciding what to put in and what to leave out. I have been guided throughout, however, by certain goals: first, I have tried to give the reader a feeling for the Bay Area as a whole, and its extraordinary natural assets. Secondly, I have tried to include information about the uncommon devotion of Bay Area people to preserving their beautiful environment—and how this has paid off for everybody. Thirdly, I have tried to supply comprehensive "hard information" that might not be available elsewhere between the two covers of a single book. And, finally, I have tried to answer the questions that I have found especially important or intriguing. I have also, in the Bibliography, referred readers to other sources and to excellent books that supply more detailed information than I have the space, or the knowledge, to provide.

In organizing my material, I have grouped the nine Bay Area counties into four regions: thus, there is a section on the North Bay (Marin, Sonoma, Napa, and Solano counties); one on the East Bay (Alameda and Contra Costa counties); one on the South Bay (San Mateo and Santa Clara counties); and one on the city and county of San Francisco. There is also an introductory section offering general background information; a section on the pleasures of San Francisco Bay; appendixes with detailed information on natural history, parks, museums, and other places to go or stay, including addresses and telephone numbers; a bibliography; and an index.

Each Bay Area county is unique, and I have tried to reflect this in my text: San Francisco, for example, is a wonderful city for walking, and I have detailed two long walks (which can be taken in shorter sections) with informative notes. Solano County, on the other hand,

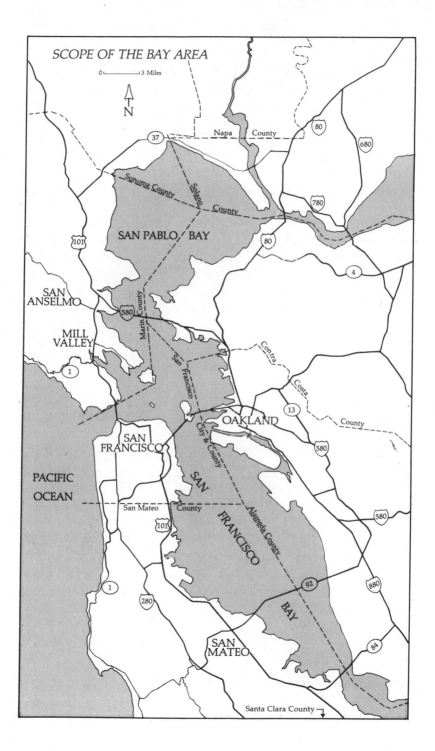

SCOPE OF THE BAY AREA

0 — 3 Miles

N

is notable for its fascinating history; Marin County has officially designated "wilderness" and, in West Marin, some of the choicest hiking; Alameda and Contra Costa counties have a marvelous, many-faceted regional park system, while the South Bay counties have wonderful county parks and regional open space; Sonoma and Napa counties are the Bay Area's wine country, and so forth. Such diversity, I felt, called for the diverse approaches that I have used.

As much as possible, I have stayed away from giving the kind of information that is subject to change at any time: for example, I have not included the routes or numbers of buses in the various counties but have, instead, supplied phone numbers where the reader can get the latest information. However, it has not been possible to omit a great many bits of information that are extremely useful, but which may change—even before the book is in print. For this unavoidable fact, I am sorry. I will appreciate readers sending me updated information—indeed, sending me any pertinent information at all.

Hopefully this book will give you some of the thrills of discovery that writing it has given me. Hopefully, too, it will add to your insight into the multiple pleasures of the Bay Area, surely one of the finest places in the world for outdoor adventuring.

Circle of the Year

There are real seasons in coastal mid-California, although it is sometimes hard to convince an easterner of this when roses can be seen blooming at Christmastime. Here are a few notes to give you an idea of what to look for and what to expect as the Bay Area moves around the circle of the year.

January. There are mild, hazy days. The sky is peach colored at sunset, the evening star impossibly bright. (Is this the one the air traffic controller tried to call in? Is it really making shadows?) Spring is starting tentatively to touch the land: the first wild iris blooms bravely by itself, and the first poppy. Some of the manzanitas are covered with creamy pink bells. A kestrel hovers at eye height above the meadow, breasting a thermal, fluttering its gray wings with beautiful economy of motion to hang poised in one exact spot while it searches the greening grasses for insects. Narrow white ribbons of water lace the mountainside. Distant mountains are like blue shadows on the sky. The gray whales are passing: the Point Reyes Lighthouse is a wonderful spot from which to watch them fountaining their way to the south. No rain for weeks, but there are chilly fogs.

One day late in the month, the sun wears a soft halo; rain is coming. A cold storm from the north drives through, washing down the world, cleaning out the trees of their old leaves, renewing the streams and setting them to singing again; now the mountains once more resound. The storm leaves behind a clear, bright morning, with crisp frost in Golden Gate Park. Delightful weather for walking (kayaking, too, my friend says).

February. There are brilliant, cold days; the air is so crystalline the coast is visible from Point Reyes to Pigeon Point, with Mount Hamilton dark on the southeastern horizon. The mimosa bursts into a mist of creamy yellow blooms. There's a round, cool, metallic moon. Daffodils, narcissus blossom. Red-tailed hawks decorate the tops of telephone poles. The surfers are out in crowds. The hills have a soft green haze beneath the pale brown of the last year's grasses that still linger in the meadows. Owls call at twilight.

A low-growing ceanothus (mountain lilac is a more apt name) is beginning to unfold its deep blue blossoms; the lighter clouds of blossoms—those that match the sky—will come on the later-blooming variety, the *Ceanothus thyrsiflorus.*

Sandhill cranes are in the Central Valley now, in the levee country of the Sacramento River, only a few hours away. The South Bay is full of avocets. Bolinas Lagoon is crowded with ducks. A flock of shorebirds wheels above them, now flashing white, now mysteriously disappearing; it is as though the birds were illuminated in bursts by some distant, brilliant searchlight. There is the first soft, plaintive song of the mourning doves, and the first gentle peep-peeping of the phoebes. Small brown fox sparrows execute their little dances as they search for food in the garden. The whales still travel southward.

There are suddenly fields of iris, deep purple, lavender, beige, pale blue, gray, white, in the coastal hills. Wild strawberry and wild cucumber vines open their white flowers. The wild mustard glows like sunshine between the dark, even rows of vines in the Napa Valley. We have a few warm, windy days.

One night, the moon is a slim silver scimitar, outshining even the evening star in a pale evening sky with a band of deep blue above the horizon. The next day, winter returns with a dramatic storm, brewed in Hawaii. It brings heavy, warm rains, then distant drumbeats of thunder, then rainbows.

March. The winds increase; the Pacific High is slowly but surely approaching. The fog creeps in, invading the bay like an insubstantial ocean; there are fog waves, then fog swells, and streams of fog breaking against the Berkeley hills.

The egrets are winging into Bolinas Lagoon, trailing elegance in their nuptial plumage; Audubon Canyon Ranch is open for views of the treetop nesters.

Comes the season for sailors, for hang-gliders, and for wind-surfers, now that the westerlies have returned. Windsurfers consider themselves members of an exclusive club; they have a late and leisurely lunch and lounge around until the breeze is just right. Then wind-borne, they skim the water ecstatically, their bright wings back-lit by the western sun.

A blue-shadowed near-full moon looks transparent in the pale afternoon sky. The evening sky is colorless. Clouds come; a full night moon moves through a sky now thick and dark, now gauzy with mist. The waves roll moon shadows before them.

Days begin to grow longer. Low, deep purple lupine paints the road cuts. A storm is promised and does not come. Another storm is promised and arrives, fierce, full of hail and torrents of cold rain. The calla lily blossoms hang like torn white flags, but most of the daffodils and tulips are unexpectedly tough and emerge unscathed.

April. The tip of every Douglas fir branch is tasseled with new chartreuse green needles—like Christmas tree decorations, a child once remarked. The new oak leaves are as pink as flowers. The madrones show off their new growth in gold-green clusters, like fancy bows. The soft rains continue, and the hills are radiantly green: some say like Ireland, but others see Scotland in the rolling ridges and meadows.

Who could wish for lovelier music than that of the mockingbird?

Or a nicer Easter gift than having this performer choose the top of a pine tree nearby to pour out his songs? In one afternoon, he mimics the robin, the scrub jay, the pygmy nuthatch, the bushtit, the wrentit, and the California quail. (One of Point Reyes Bird Observatory's chief ornithologists has heard a mockingbird mimic species that do not occur nearby, which raises intriguing questions: evidently, the male mockingbird's repertoire is limited only by his auditory experiences, but where did he hear these songs? Was it from an older family member? Is there a racial mockingbird memory? Or was he just a widely traveled bird?) The females hang around this songster, listening, waiting for something to happen. Monarch butterflies arrive in crowds. Hummingbirds do their roller-coaster flights, the bejeweled male showing off for the quiet little female, who will have to do all the work of nest building and parenting the young while himself sips nectar instead.

This is a month for birds. Crossbills fill every branch and twig of a small Douglas fir (as do primitive artists crowd their trees with birds in their paintings and carvings). Great blue herons stalk the marshes. Shorebirds come through like clouds of confetti. The osprey nesting on Inverness Ridge fish all day off the Marin coast for their young. The pelicans glide along the shores. There are bluebirds in the meadows.

The sky is flawless; no cloud is in sight. The sea is blue, quiet, the sun pouring onto everything. The bush lupine forms huge bouquets of soft lavender blue. There are buttercups and goldfields and lotus, crowds of golden poppies, clusters of blue-eyed grass, mariposa lilies—everything rich and glossy and full of life. A gentle, cool breeze is a delight—for hikers, surfers, kayakers, all sailors, for loungers in meadows, and for people who like to stand on the tops of mountains. Mount Tam, Mount Diablo—even Sweeney Ridge—promise fields of wildflowers and distant views of other mountains like mirages on the blue horizons.

May. The clear days with their westerlies continue. The bay is filled with crowds of white sails. The hang-gliders swoop like wildly colored prehistoric birds. The hills begin slowly to turn golden brown. The buckeyes are polka-dotted with sunbursts of pale white blossoms. The fog pours in and lingers through the morning, then burns off: wonderful views of it moving through the Golden Gate may be had from the East Bay hills. Brodea stars the inland meadows; the taller deep purple lupine grows in dry places; poison hemlock like a cloud of pale lace marks the damper spots. The very last iris, finally fading to the palest blue, still lingers. Wild honeysuckle, morning glories, and the mimulus (the orange monkey flower with its sensitive pistil that closes tightly at a touch and its lush golden blossoms that ornament marshy streamsides) all decorate the trails. The yellow lupine illuminates the Point Reyes meadows and the hills above Baker Beach. Marsh hawks balance in the sky.

June. The days are dry and windy on the bay. Wind whips sharply around the downtown buildings, but it is gloriously hot inland and down the Peninsula. The bracken grows green among the gold dry grasses. The monkey flowers are in full bloom, with the cheerful dandelions; these are welcome blossoms in the fading meadows. The greasewood has already gone ghost, its dark leaves turned gray. The beetles are busy among the dried grasses of the open meadows. There are still small flames of Indian paintbrush here and there. The irises are gone.

Cool fog comes in to sheathe the ridges. It makes for delightful hiking. The forests are deep and mysterious in the soft, wet mist that drips from the eucalyptus and redwoods like gentle rain. On the longest day of the year, all 15 hours are fog filled.

July. Almost imperceptibly, the days begin to shorten. The parched meadows seem to ache for rain, but it will not come soon unless we have a freak thunderstorm. Not likely. Seeds are already attaching themselves to hikers' socks. Windsurfers fill the Gate, crowd the Foster City marina, scud away from the Alameda shore. Surfers, their black wetsuits shining like the wet fur of seals, sport along the coast. Clear nights are velvety and star filled. The last of summer's daytime low tides bare offshore tidepools.

August. The fog lifts higher and hangs in balance over the bay, putting a gray lid on the world. East of the Berkeley hills, a narrow band of light along the horizon shows that the sun is shining there. The strong winds continue, strong enough to have congregations of sailors and championship meets of windsurfers, who come from all over the world. The birds are fewer; it is a time of quietness along the Pacific Flyway. The salmon begin to run.

September. The golden month unfolds one gorgeous day after another. Comes the hottest weather of the year; our Indian Summer. The sun feels like a warm and loving hand on a hiker's back. Its light still floods the hills with color at evening. The nights, subtly longer, bring a hint of coolness.

There are lingering bursts of poppies brightening the wheat-colored fields. Wild cucumber vines begin to turn yellow. The bay laurel trees are decorated with little green berries; the coffee bushes have fruit like dark, lustrous marbles. In San Francisco, the first big leaves drift from the elm trees that line the streets.

The salmon are still running. Crowds of anchovies swarm in the shallow offshore waters with brown pelicans and Heermann's gulls (by the thousands, it would seem) fattening on them. The osprey are gone, but other raptors are journeying southward. Shorebirds are gathering along the Pacific Flyway; moving in flocks of hundreds, they scud just above the water, flying as though they were only one organism, turning in perfect synchronism, now appearing, now fading into cloudlike bursts of motion.

This is the month to visit the wine and apple country. The grapes are heavy on the vines and the harvest is on. Proud vintners show off their huge vats brimming with the new crush. Apples perfume the warm air. There is fresh-pressed cider to be had, as sweet as honey.

The winds are lessening, but sailors still take to their boats and their boards, and the sky-travelers strap on their wings and soar.

October. The skies are deep blue at midday, fading to the palest mauves and apple greens as night comes. Clouds mask the setting sun. Scarves of fog wreathe the hills, ghostlike. The full moon is the biggest, the brightest, the most burnished of the whole year. It spills its light on the ocean, first in a pathway and then in a full, rich flood of molten gold-silver. The waves are quiet, marked by their moving shadows.

Flocks of brown pelicans fly out into the twilight, heading south. (Why does one lone bird turn and return as though it had left something behind?) There are many raptors passing through. Two red-tailed hawks circle high above a mountain ridge calling to one another, their cries as harsh as the sounds of rusty hinges.

Pumpkins glow on the coastal fields. The blueberries are ripe and luscious beside the forest trails; vine maples make sunshine in the shadows. All the broad-leafed trees are losing their green; like high torches, the poplars burn gold. The first falling leaves make soft patterns on the ground. There are still monkey flowers blooming, and a few hummingbirds remaining. The world is slowing down, waiting for the rains to come.

November. One day starts with a rush of rain, so loud and constant, it drowns out the sound of the sea. The sea creams against the shore in a wide white band. The rain stops, and the voice of the sea returns. Clouds fill the sky, but here and there is a splash of sun or a wisp of blue sky. Clouds lift from the mountains; there is a soft light on the water. A rainbow arches against the hills and stays, intensifying, fading, growing more brilliant, for more than an hour.

Bird-watchers along the flyway count ten species of wildfowl resting and feeding in the flooded marsh: bufflehead, wigeon, pintail, mallard, gadwall, teal, ruddy duck, shoveler, scaup, surf scoter. The wigeons upend themselves to fish; they have a gentle whistle—*whew, whew*—and are pretty to boot. Along the shore there are killdeer, kingfishers, great blue herons, snowy egrets, a Cooper's hawk, Forster's terns, pelicans, cormorants holding out their wings to dry, and, wonderfully, a black-shouldered kite.

The bright red toyon berries glow as though lit from inside. The forests are fresher and greener for the rain; the low, feathery branches of the Douglas fir are lacy in the late sun; the trunks stand in strong silhouettes. Small redwood-colored newts find their way along the trail, moving purposefully, as though they know just where they are going. Silky seed pods decorate the chaparral.

At sunset, gray clouds billow up in the north; they become golden and their light falls onto the sea. Stripes of clouds move across the low sun. The clouds grow icy gray as the light fades. Dark comes on very quickly. The cities shine and shimmer like skeins of jewels. The next morning is intensely clear. The view from Mount Diablo must be staggering—all 45,000 square miles of it.

December. Wet trails are printed with the tracks of deer and hikers. The days seem to grow shorter ever more quickly until the solstice brings the shortest day of all, with less than nine hours of sunlight. A wrentit fills the chaparral with its Ping-Pong-ball song; a hawk cries out as it spirals skyward. Flocks of white gulls fly out to sea. There are nuthatches traveling head-down on the trunks of the pine trees.

The green of new life glows more and more on the hills, the dead grass fading into small puffs of gray here and there. A dandelion is a burst of unexpectedly bright color. The laurels are decorated with tiny green-yellow blossoms. Mushrooms make little gray parasols stuck into the cold, damp forest floors.

At the times of the frailest and the fullest moons, the tides surge the highest, dashing the waves into high fountains against the rocky shore; and they draw down the sea the farthest, too, baring the secrets of the underwater coastal world. On sandy beaches, the ocean spreads scallops of white surf on dark, gleaming, satiny sand.

Storms move over the Bay Area; one leaves a frosting of snow on the higher mountains to glitter in the morning-after sun. There is a general exodus from the cities to the mountaintops. Sleds appear miraculously: children and birds are everywhere; people shout; would-be sculptors work seriously on snowmen; there are royal snowball fights. But even as snow transforms the Bay Area world, it begins to melt. By afternoon, it is becoming thin and tattered as the wet, brown earth emerges. By the next morning, the snow is gone. From high ridges, however, the snowy Sierra beckons from the east.

The willows are growing golden and rosy with new buds. Thus does the end of the year bring its promises of spring.

Geology and Weather

Weather and landscape are so closely interdependent that they are like the proverbial two faces of the same coin. Weather shapes the land, and the land returns the compliment. Nowhere is this more graphically illustrated than in the San Francisco Bay Area. To understand the unusual—and delightful—climate of this region, it may help to start with its geology.

Geology is a science as dynamic as the earth it studies. It also requires smart detective work based on evidence that is frequently, and literally, fragmentary, and sometimes millions—billions—of years old. With these givens it is intriguing to consider the latest geological theory, known as plate tectonics. (*Tectonic* comes from the Greek word *teknos,* meaning "builder.") More intriguing still is the fact that the plate tectonic theory helps explain the Bay Area landscape as it has not been explained before.

Until recently, geologists thought that the insides of the earth were encapsulated in more or less of a rock shell, the lithosphere, on which rested the oceans. A favorite geological analogy, in fact, likened the earth to a soft-boiled egg: it had a liquid core (the yolk), a somewhat firmer mantle (the white), and around it all was a crust (the shell). The core was known to be largely molten, still seething after the planet's formation from the dust of stars; the mantle was cooler and less liquid, but plastic nonetheless; the crust was the coolest, lightest component of all. And while known to be fractured in places with earthquake faults, punched through in places by the upwelling of lava, and wrinkled in places by inner pressures, the crust was considered to be a relatively fixed, continuous integument. Furthermore, it was believed that while continents could be uplifted and depressed, they stayed pretty much in the same place, so that the sequence of their rock formations could give a good idea of their geological history in situ. This left a lot of things unexplained: there were bothersome questions that had no clear answers (but perhaps there always will be).

In the past decades, however, geologists have found and accepted startling (and exciting) new evidence that has changed not just geological theories, but the fundamental beliefs of the science. Some geologists compare this breakthrough in geology to the discovery of evolution in biology. While the earth's core and mantle are probably much as they were thought to be, the new theory goes, its outer casing is not a structured shell. Rather it is fractured, being made up of several huge pieces—or plates—that interact continually and dynamically with one another. (*Terra,* it seems, is not really *firma.*)

The earth's plates, it is believed, are kept in motion by a kind of bubbling up—and circulation—of magma propelled by heat from deep in the earth. Seaming the midocean floors are giant rifts, or cracks—known as spreading zones—through which the magma escapes as molten lava to form new crust. Then, to make way for its more or less continuous replacement, this new crust inches away from the spreading zone (at a rate of 2 to 20 centimeters a year, a centimeter being about 0.39 inch). Thus the ocean floor, to put it simplistically, is basically composed of dynamic plates moving away from each other. Some geologists compare the eruption of midocean lavas to water boiling up in a kettle; others liken the ocean floors to enormous conveyor belts being continuously replenished with new crustal material that they carry off to make new land. In any case, continents are now seen, as one geology text puts it, as "mats of foam, drifting in the eddies of a stream."

Given the shape of the earth, the plates moving away from one midocean rift must inevitably meet other plates moving away from other spreading zones. (All of this takes millions of years, of course.) Ocean plates most frequently collide with continental plates, which are not only lighter, floating higher on the earth's mantle, but more rigid and static than ocean floors. When collision occurs, the heavier plate (the ocean floor) is pulled downward under the lighter plate by gravity in a process known as subduction. Eventually the heavier plate returns its material into the furnace of the earth to be recycled; the continental plate is usually shoved higher, as though by a giant bulldozer. Such subduction encounters are the scenes, literally, of earthshaking events: as one plate meets another, the land shudders convulsively, great cracks form in its surface, rocks and sediments are stuffed against each other and upthrust into mountains, and volcanoes erupt. Ultimately, a gigantic trench is formed offshore where the ocean floor is dragged back into the depths.

A classic demonstration of plate tectonics at work is the Ring of Fire that rims the Pacific Ocean. (The Ring of Fire is a circle of volcanoes that roughly outlines a pattern of seismic activity as well as vulcanism.) Running asymmetrically roughly northeast-southwest along the Pacific Ocean floor is a ridge of submerged volcanoes that spew out new material into the cool depths. From each side of this spreading zone, the ocean floor is pushed in a generally east or west direction to start its slow travel toward the continents and islands that circle the Pacific, to there be subducted. The active subduction zones are marked by vulcanism (as in Alaska and Indonesia and, closer to home, Mount Saint Helens in our Cascade Range), earthquakes (as in Alaska and Japan), mountain building (as in the Andes), and the formation of deep, offshore trenches (as in the Aleutian Trench).

When active subduction along a particular continent slows down or stops—which it does from eon to eon in this dynamic global process—the collision courses of the two plates involved may be deflected. Then, instead of meeting head-on, the ocean plate and the

Black Mountain in the Monte Bello Open Space Preserve; note the San Andreas Fault in the upper right. PHOTO BY DAVID HANSEN.

continental plate begin to grind past one another laterally, creating a giant tear, or transform fault, in the earth's surface. When this occurs, an ocean plate may carry off a piece of the continent that has stuck to it during earlier subduction. Thus do bits and pieces of the earth get rafted, at times great distances, to show up hundreds or thousands of miles away from their birthplaces, perhaps millions of years later.

How does the California coast, especially the Bay Area, fit into this picture? It provides textbook examples of plate tectonics. This region was for over 100 million years (starting perhaps 200 million years ago) an active subduction zone where the ancestral Pacific Plate plunged underneath—in a generally easterly direction—the North American Plate. This encounter resulted in the crushing, scraping off, and piling up of vast amounts of crustal materials from both plates. The mix thus created not only contained all of earth's building materials—volcanic, sedimentary, and metamorphic rock—but rock formed only under specific conditions—at spreading zones underwater, for instance, or in zones of subduction under immense pressures. It was out of this extraordinary mix (now known as the Franciscan Complex) that much of the Bay Area landscape was subsequently formed. Thus people interested in geology can study rocks on and around Mount Tamalpais or Mount Diablo, for example, for first-hand evidence of ancient plate tectonic action.

Furthermore, plate tectonic activity in the Bay Area did not stop when subduction, quite literally, ground to a halt. Although no longer meeting head-on, tectonic plates continued to collide in this region, eventually thrusting up the Coast Ranges and Mount Tamalpais, squeezing up Mount Diablo, and creating volcanic areas that still steam in Sonoma County. And, indeed, plate collisions continue actively in the Bay Area today: now the Pacific Plate is thrusting generally northwestward, while the continental plate resists its inexorable push. This grinding encounter is producing a system of lateral transform faults before our very eyes. One of these is, of course, the San Andreas Fault, which went into action plus or minus 15 million years ago; another is the Hayward fault, which slices through the South and East Bay. Both are active, as the Hayward fault demonstrated so dramatically in 1989, and either can quite literally cut loose at any time.

Meantime, the Point Reyes Peninsula (named aptly by author Harold Gilliam an "island in time" in his book of that title) is being unobtrusively but firmly dragged generally northwestward along the central California coast at the rate of somewhere around 1 inch a year; it is part of the Salinian Block (Pacific Plate), having been picked up millennia ago and rafted northward. Some of its rocks match those of distant mountains more than 300 miles to the south. (So do the rocks of the Farallon Islands, 20 miles to sea; these once formed the mountainous tip of a mainland peninsula, most of which was drowned at the end of the last ice age when floods of meltwater raised earth's oceans some 400 feet.) The San Andreas Fault marks the rift in the earth's crust where the Pacific Plate grinds past the North American Plate; it forms the Olema Valley in West Marin County, through which runs Highway 1. To the west of Olema Valley, the land has been shoved up into Inverness Ridge (part of the Point Reyes Peninsula "island"), and to the east, it has been upthrust into Bolinas Ridge, an arm of Mount Tamalpais and part of the "mainland."

Not surprisingly, the topography of the nine Bay Area counties reflects the immense geologic forces that shaped—and continue to shape—this restless portion of the earth's mantle. Each county (even Solano) has its mountains, upthrust by the massive collision of tectonic plates meeting long ago. Each county has its own fault system. (A map of the earthquake faults that have been identified in the Bay Area may remind you somewhat of the crackled pattern that you find on some pottery; two major faults, however, predominate—the San

Andreas and the Hayward, both trending northwest-southeast.) Each county can expect another good shake-up at some time during the next hundred years. And each county has some special feature— hot springs, sag ponds, vernal pools, vulnerable groundwater sup- plies, evidence of volcanic activity, massive landslides—that marks it as having evolved in an active geological zone. Furthermore, two counties—Marin and San Mateo—offer unusual chances to observe how a great fault shapes the landscape. (See Point Reyes National Seashore and Los Trancos Earthquake Trail.)

Stand on the top of San Francisco's Twin Peaks on a clear day and look northward; you will see the Indian maiden waiting for her lover, the sun (or the Sleeping Lady, as another legend has it)—Mount Tamalpais, Marin's own magic mountain, part of the Coast Ranges that edge the Pacific. It offers excellent displays of rocks formed in the process of subduction—serpentine, chert, graywacke among them. Cross to the summit of Mount Tamalpais and look northward again, and you will see Mount Hood and Mount Saint Helena mark- ing Sonoma and Napa counties; these mountains are also part of the Coast Ranges. You may not see as well, however, the series of gener- ally parallel valleys—the Sonoma Valley, the Napa Valley, Berryessa Valley (now flooded by the Monticello Dam)—that trend northwest and southeast between the folds of hills. To the northeast, Solano County's less impressive mountains, the Twin Sisters northwest of Fairfield—sometimes touched by snow—may not be visible, for they are not so grand (but they are cherished by the county's lowlanders just the same). Looking eastward from almost any one of San Fran- cisco's higher hills, your view of Mount Diablo will be obstructed in part by the high ridge of the Berkeley-Oakland hills (which delineate the Hayward fault), but that wonderful mountain still presides over the landscape around it. To its south lie other mountains of the so- called Diablo Range—Mission Peak and Sunol Peak among them. Southwestward, however, the mountains that you see when you fly into San Francisco are more members of the Coast Ranges, usually referred to as the Santa Cruz Mountains. And, of course, in the mid- dle of all this, there is that body of water that marks the power of moving waters to sculpt the landscape almost as vigorously as seis- mic activity—San Francisco Bay.

San Francisco Bay is a product of both the local geology and the weather. Lying to the east of it, across the great Central Valley, is the high wall of mountains, the Sierra Nevada (marking another fault system). Lying to the north of the Bay Area are the southern slopes of the Cascades (part of the Ring of Fire). And to the north and south are the eastern slopes of the Coast Ranges, the bay's own mountains. These three mountain ranges form the great watershed of the bay; all three intercept the rain clouds borne off the Pacific Ocean, and all three channel their waters into the rivers that feed the bay. Some estimate that over 50 percent of California's water once flowed past Carquinez Straits on its way to the ocean. The bay itself is the ancient river valley of the Sacramento River, which was flooded, like the rest of the Bay Area landscape, by meltwaters at the end of the last ice age. But for the critical gap provided by the old river mouth, now called the Golden Gate, there might be a marshy inland lake where the bay now lies.

Along with the seascape, the bayscape, and the landscape, certain physical laws shape the Bay Area weather, and it may be helpful to review these briefly (and simplistically) as well: warm air is lighter than cool air; air, like water, seeks its own level, i.e., equalization of temperature; moist air condenses when chilled; the continental land mass heats (and loses heat) more rapidly than the ocean; as the earth spins in space, the Coriolis force (named for its French discoverer) swings the winds and waters of the Northern Hemisphere always clockwise, i.e., to the right; as our planet makes its annual orbit around the sun, the sun moves to the north in the summer and to the south in the winter (or so it seems to us).

And there is a mass of cold air (something like a great frigid volcano) that sits in the mid-Pacific and spews out cool winds in all directions: this is known as the Pacific High. For reasons not entirely understood, the Pacific High seems to travel with the sun, moving northward in the summer and southward in the winter. (Perhaps it is a function of the jet stream, but ask several different meteorologists to explain the Pacific High, and chances are you will get several different answers.)

All of these—geology, meteorology, and physics—produce the Bay Area weather. While generally equable, this is a varied climate with surprisingly different miniclimates (the temperature can vary from one spot to another nearby by 20 degrees on the same day). What makes for this is, of course, the fog. Without the fog, this would be just another coastal region of mid-California, not as hot and smoggy as it is to the south, but with predictable cool winters and hot summers. But you can count on the fog: expect it during the late spring

and summer months, whether it comes in at night and is burned off
by the next morning's sun (which does happen), whether it comes in
for a week at a time (which it sometimes does), whether it stays
around for several weeks (which it has been known to do), or
whether it is low or high. This natural air-conditioning not only
influences Bay Area living, it is likely to play an important part in any
Bay Area outdoor experience.

The foggy season tends to start some time around the March
equinox when the sun, moving steadily to the north, drags the Pacific
High with its cool and steady westerly winds ever closer to the mid-
California shore. As these winds scud across the surface of the ocean,
they tend to push the warmer surface waters in front of them. This
allows the cool ocean water to well up from the depths and to travel
shoreward, too. The Coriolis force, however, bends these waters
inexorably to the right so that as the days go by an increasingly wide
river of cold water begins to flow southward along the shore. (Swimmers take note: this makes for chilly ocean water, around 55 degrees
Fahrenheit, for most of the summer; the water off the northern
Sonoma coast may actually be warmer in the winter than it is in the
summer.) It is this mass of cold water that forms the nucleus of the
fog; when the warmer moisture-laden air above it is blown across it,
the moisture begins to condense.

Meantime, as spring brings longer days, the Bay Area grows
warmer. The earth begins to soak up the sunshine, and the difference
between the temperature of the land and that of the sea increases.
One lovely sunny day, a faint whiff of fog appears at sea, like the
barest wisp of a fluffy cloud. (Fog actually meets the definition of a
stratus cloud: it is engendered by horizontal movements of the air.)
Then the cloud begins to swell and grow and push shoreward. The
winds pick up as the fog starts to flow beneath the Golden Gate
Bridge and creep up the bay. The foghorns start their songs. People
downtown who brought their coats are glad to button them up;
those without coats shiver and move faster. The fog is in.

Were it not for the Golden Gate—and the other gaps and passes
through the Coast Ranges—the fog might simply continue to pile up
along the mountainous shore, held effectively at bay. But the Golden
Gate ushers the cool mass through to meet another inexorable force
that will keep it moving even further inland: the warm air of the interior valleys pulls the fog inland even as the westerlies push it from
behind.

Those first springtime fogs are often highly picturesque, surging through the Gate, swirling over Angel Island, crowning Alcatraz, and making grand fog-falls over the Marin Headlands—one of the unique and thrilling natural phenomena of the bay. (There are great opportunities for photographers. Try the view from Vista Point, just across the Golden Gate Bridge in Marin County.)

A good heavy fog may travel through the Central Valley as far as Sacramento or Stockton, but more often it will stop short, burned off by a hot morning sun. Interestingly enough, however, the fog's own influence will eventually mitigate the inland heat, cooling things off to the point where the pull of warm air is no longer strong enough to suck in the moist, cool air pushing against the coast. In a word, the fog "self-destructs," as Harold Gilliam puts it in his book *Weather of the San Francisco Bay Region,* and retreats to the west. But then, of course, the whole process commences all over again.

As the summer solstice comes and passes, the fog pattern may undergo an interesting flip. Having established itself, the mass of cool surface air may begin to shove the layer of warmer air (that has been basking in the warm sun) above it, lifting it until the two layers stabilize in dynamic balance above the bay. The resultant inversion sometimes persists for days—or even weeks. This can cause fog to form on the interface of the cool and warm air, thus forming summer's high fog.

Another interesting event is waiting to occur as the autumn equinox passes and the sun begins its long march to the south, with the Pacific High dutifully following. Days begin to grow noticeably shorter; the westerlies begin to weaken; the inland valleys grow cooler. Since the land loses heat more rapidly than the ocean, the ocean gradually becomes the warmer of the two. Then the push-pull effect begins to reverse; the warmer ocean air begins to pull the cooler inland air toward the coast. The westerlies no longer have the strength to stop the process, and the wind pattern does an about-face. The fog flows out to sea, and the inland air floods the Bay Area. This brings the glorious days of September and "Indian Summer" when the sun can pour down unobstructed. (This may also allow for smog if the inversion still persists.)

Coastal mountains play a major part in the distribution of the fog. Not only does the Golden Gate act as a huge funnel, the smaller gaps in the hills perform similar functions, allowing smaller streamers of fog to flow through them. At the same time, the higher ridges cast "sunshine shadows," and communities directly behind them may bask in the heat while neighboring sections shiver. A graphic illustration of this phenomenon may be had at Point Reyes National Seashore, where Bear Valley headquarters can be in full, hot sunlight when fog is thick on the coast less than 5 miles away: in between, of course, is Inverness Ridge forming a 1,000-foot-plus barrier.

The bay itself not only influences the fog patterns but nourishes the fog with its own moisture. And, like any large body of water, it influences local weather as well, freshening the air on smoggy days, and acting as a neutralizer of extreme temperatures, thus stabilizing the day-to-day climate. It influences the impact of the seasons, too, its waters helping to absorb the violence of winter storms. Summer days would be degrees hotter without it, forgetting all about the wonderful fog.

An interesting side effect of that wonderful fog is the contribution it makes to the annual rainfall: this is known as fog drip. Fog drip is caused by the gathering of the fog's moisture onto the leaves and needles of trees (or, indeed, any surface exposed to the elements). The moisture forms into diamondlike drops (which may tip every needle of a pine or redwood) and then falls to the ground. (Watch out when you walk through stands of trees on foggy days.) Fog drip may amount to 10 inches in summer in an area like the Berkeley hills. And it may even add up to an extraordinary 80 inches in a heavily forested area over a year. It is what nurtures the coastal redwoods during the critical month of August.

First People

Because their way of life differed from ours and did not include our technical niceties, we sometimes consider the Stone Age people who settled America before us as crude, uncultured heathens. This is a mistake. Theirs were very real cultures, as important to them both socially and artistically as ours is to us. Their religion was as deeply ingrained and as commanding (and demanding) as any contemporary religion. And although they kept no written record of their history, it shaped them even as our history has shaped us. Moreover, evidence also suggests that the Stone Age people who first colonized the Bay Area—the Coast Miwoks, Ohlones (or Costanoans), and Wintuns—achieved a social order that was both stable and successful, and workable enough to serve them well for thousands of years. During these years, they destroyed neither one another nor their environment nor their own or each other's culture.

Thus, we might have learned much from these "uncivilized" people. But the Europeans who discovered them, while remarking on their ready friendship and generosity, still considered them inferior savages. The Spanish, in fact, thought the Bay Area Indians sinfully lazy and indolent heathens: they called them *bestia*—"beasts"—while they called themselves *gente de razon*—"people of reason." The later comers—English, Scandinavian, American, and so forth—held the native people in such low esteem that they took their land and lives without conscience or compunction. And so the Bay Area natives, like other aborigines in the Americas, dwindled in number until they were all but gone, a sorry end for people whose ancestors preceded ours in this pleasant place by thousands of years.

It is believed, in fact, that these ancestors first started moving into California 10,000 or more years ago; some anthropologists insist it was 20,000. They were wanderers, hunters, and gatherers, and they came as they did elsewhere, in little bands or family groups, following—or seeking—the animals and the environments that could provide them with subsistence. They probably crossed the Bering Land Bridge (now the Bering Strait) from what is now Russia and made their way southward. It seems likely that some of those people, members of the Penutian family and speakers of the Penutian language, found the Bay Area so much to their liking that they stayed and put down their roots here to evolve a sort of cul-de-sac culture. (Others of those wanderers went on to the south to evolve other cultures—Incan, Mayan, and Navajo among them.)

Lacking a written record, we turn to the mute shell mounds the early people left to tell us part of their story before the Spaniards came. Bits more of knowledge have been gleaned from the random observations of the Europeans who arrived on the scene some 200 years ago. And the few survivors of the first comers have added insights and recollections of their own. From this evidence, anthropologists have managed to put together a picture, however incomplete, of the way the Bay Area's first people lived with the world around them, and with one another.

Archeologists counted 425 shell mounds around the shores of San Francisco Bay at the turn of the twentieth century, and there were others in nearby places. As they sifted through the ashes, fragments of bone, bits of obsidian, and clam and mussel shells, they gathered some interesting and some curious facts. As might be expected, the aboriginal diet was rich and varied in the Bay Area. The people ate all kinds of seafood, deer and elk, birds' eggs, birds, small rodents, insects, greens, roots, and berries. Through the centuries that they lived in this bountiful environment, they prospered. They improved their tools, fashioning their mortars and pestles to be increasingly efficient, for example, and adding bows and arrows to their hunting regalia so that they broadened their food base. (Sir Francis Drake's party remarked on the great skill of the Coast Miwoks with bow and arrow.) They increased in number, and as they did so, they evolved a society of tribelets or villages of 100 to 200 people. Thus, from a wide-ranging nomadic existence, they settled into a comfortable pattern of living, wintering in one area and summering in another nearby.

Notably, the evidence suggests that, once established, the same basic pattern of existence persisted through the millennia; customs appear to have stayed much the same. If there were no great cities built—but only tule shelters—there were no great battles fought either. From generation to generation, life went on much the same. Thus, the native people who greeted the Spanish with such friendship and generosity were very likely the descendants of pioneer families who had arrived on the scene thousands of years before, and they were carrying on family traditions from the distant past.

In the late eighteenth century, these native people are believed to have numbered many thousand, and the tribes and tribelets had developed many different patois, or sublanguages, out of an earlier common language. Some of these sublanguages, in fact, were unintelligible to other members of the same overall tribe. Tribelets, however, lived in a kind of balance with one another, staying at arm's length for the most part, yet intermarrying (by tribal law). This kept the gene pool varied and healthy. It is likely, too, that social pressures and taboos, rather than disease or starvation, kept the population in balance. For example, among the Ohlones, nursing mothers abstained from intercourse with their husbands for the two years following the birth of a child; a man refrained from taking a second wife until he could support an extended family. Whatever the reason, these people had relatively few children—enough to keep a healthy society going, but not enough to bring on the problems of overpopulation.

These first people led highly structured lives. Rituals, such as those marking adolescence, were cherished, adhered to, and passed on faithfully. The roles of men and women were clearly defined; an integral part of the social fabric, they were functionally different. The men were the hunters; the women were the gatherers and the preparers of the food. Together they reared the children, and with great affection. Homosexual couples were accepted in tribelet life, with one partner assuming the role of a woman. Children were taught early to revere the older tribal members for their wisdom. The families took loving care of the elders, who participated in family activities to the best of their abilities. Expert weavers (the Coast Miwok feathered baskets are among the most beautiful in native American art), the women taught the girl children their craft. Fine toolmakers and arrowhead knappers, the men taught the sons their skills. Men and boys had their own lodge. Women and girls had their own (smaller!) as well. There was a useful, traditional place for every member of the family in this society.

The Bay Area Indians built their spiritual beliefs around some-times-quixotic animal gods—Coyote, for instance, was the principal Miwok deity. Coyote created them out of sticks, feathers, and mud, they told their children. He sent Hummingbird to the sun to steal fire for the people, hence the bird's bright red neck feathers, stained when she tucked the flame under her chin to carry it away. Coyote's grandson was a falcon, Wek-Wek, who was married to Frog-Woman, Kotola. Not only creatures but certain places and natural phenomena had special religious significance, too. And dreams were considered to be as real as "reality." Dance and song were integral parts of religious expression and religious experience as well as social pleasures. There was a religious reason—or taboo—to explain everything.

Underlying the religious and social customs of these people was a basic belief or philosophy. Lowell J. Bean describes it this way:

> To the California Indian, humanity was seen as one of a number of cooperating beings who shared in the working of a universe that was an inter-acting system. All parts of this system were reciprocal, and humanity had obligations to the rest of the universe and its creatures.

Thus the people honored the stone, the plant, or the animal they took for their own use. And, even as they skillfully hunted and fished, they made certain that the fellow creatures they killed were not destroyed as species; they treated the land itself with the same respect. (They had a surprisingly modern explanation for how the land came to be: it began as rock, they said; rains came—like people all over the world, they had the "great flood" in their legends—and washed off bits of rock to make soil; plants grew and created more soil, deepening it; trees grew and created still more soil as they dropped their leaves, needles, and cones; just look at a cross section of the forest floor and see if this is not true!)

It is noteworthy that the Bay Area native people—long, long before Christians found them—had invented and lived by the precept that it is more blessed to give than to receive; the more a family gave away, the higher it rose in the social echelon. People did not encumber themselves with material possessions. When a person died, her or his belongings were burned with the body, and friends and relatives added some of their own possessions to the funeral pyre.

Because of the benign Bay Area climate, the native people lived and worked much in the out-of-doors. It is estimated that they spent perhaps half their time hunting, gathering, and preparing their food; thus they were intimately acquainted with the land and the life around them. Although they established territories, they drew no strict boundaries on those lands. And even as they shared in the demanding task of hunting, they shared in the food from the hunt.

Thus did the Coast Miwoks, Ohlones, and Wintuns live—simple, stable lives that were deeply enriched by their religious beliefs and their traditions. And because they were in harmony with their world and generally with one another, they were without the constant dread of war.

"Uncivilized"? Their conquerors thought they knew the answer. And certainly those first people were no match for the sword and the cross—for the Christians who tried to "save" them and to bend them to different ways.

Malcolm Margolin pays a poignant tribute to these native people in his book *The Ohlone Way:*

> Beyond doubt, [they] had been settled for an extremely long time before the arrival of the Europeans, and it was during these many centuries that they achieved something quite rare in human history: a way

of life that gave them relative peace and stability, not just for a generation or two, not just for a century, but probably for thousands of years.

It is too bad that the people who found them did not bother to learn
their secret.

Throughout the Bay Area, there are faint traces left by the first
people. There are also museum exhibits that give an idea of the way
these people lived. Perhaps most interesting of all is the Coast Miwok
village, Kule Loklo, in Point Reyes National Seashore, which is an
attempt to recreate the Coast Miwok way of life as it once was. The
following list offers a few suggestions as to where you will find further information about these early people:

California Academy of Sciences, Golden Gate Park, San Fran-
cisco; telephone 415-221-5100
Coyote Hills Regional Park, Fremont; telephone 510-795-9385
Kule Loklo, near Bear Valley visitor center, Point Reyes National
Seashore; telephone 415-663-1092
Marin Museum of the American Indian (also archaeological site),
Box 864, Novato; telephone 415-897-4064
Oakland Museum of California, Tenth and Oak Streets, Oakland;
telephone 510-238-3401

Some Facts About the San Francisco Bay Area

San Francisco Bay is located at longitude 122 degrees, 31 minutes—
three hours east of the international date line—and latitude 37
degrees, 48 minutes—in the same range with Athens; Seville; Washington, D.C.; and Tokyo.

The bay is fed by 16 rivers, the largest of which are the Sacramento, the Pitt, and the San Joaquin. In 1850, San Francisco Bay received 27.5 million acre-feet of fresh water per year; in 1980, it received 10.3, the other 17.2 million acre-feet being siphoned off into water diversion projects. The bay has 276 miles of shoreline, of which 100 are rimmed with hills, some rising right out of the water. It covers 420 square miles, being approximately 50 miles long and 1 to 12 miles wide. (It has lost 40 percent of its area to fill since gold was discovered at Sutter's Fort in 1848 and sediment began to be washed from the mines; deliberate filling of tidelands and marshlands greatly accelerated the process.) The bay contains 2 trillion gallons of salt water, the surface of which is under the aegis of the Twelfth U.S. Coast Guard District. The inflow and outflow of its water rushes through an 0.7-mile opening, the Golden Gate. It has ten islands and three embayments—Richardson, San Pablo, and Suisun bays.

San Francisco Bay reflects the tidal pulls of the sun and, especially, the moon with two tidal cycles a day. Its mean tidal range is 4 feet, and its maximum range is 9 feet. The North Bay is subject to great and variable currents, being influenced strongly by the tides—which account for 80 percent of the action—and by the inflow of river waters—which account for the other 20 percent. The waters of the South Bay move something like water being sloshed in a tub, oscillating north-south in a standing wave; nonetheless, they have the highest and the lowest of the bay's tides. The effect of the Coriolis force keeps the level of the South Bay slightly higher than that of the North Bay.

When California became a state in 1850, it claimed all of San Francisco Bay, although San Francisco—under the aegis of Major Kearny—had been selling waterfront and underwater lots since 1847. After taking over, the state began to dispose of its treasure. Today, approximately 50 percent of San Francisco Bay remains in state hands, 23 percent belongs to the cities and counties around it, 22 percent is in private hands, and 5 percent is owned by the federal government. There are seven bridges across the bay and more than a dozen cities around it.

The bay has been used for, among other things, salt production (Leslie Salt operates on 40,000 acres of it and has taken millions of tons of salt out of the bay waters), cement making, sand mining, sport fishing, duck hunting, pleasure boating, surfing and windsurfing, swimming, garbage disposal—both solid and liquid—waste irrigation waters and industrial waste, commercial fishing, shellfishing, shipping, a naval base, heavy industry, airports, ferry boats, a race-track, a federal prison, a world's fair, a parking lot for a racetrack, condominiums and other residential subdivisions, and, last and least, parks and preserves. It was once a prime "nursery" for ocean marine life but is now contaminated by as much as 330 tons of potentially toxic trace metals a year—along with other poisons. It is still one of the great estuaries on the Pacific Flyway, being used by approximately 1.5 million migratory wildfowl per year. (A century ago, the skies were darkened with migratory birds; San Mateo history tells how they were shot and hauled out by the wagonload.)

San Francisco Bay acts like a giant thermostat, controlling the climate of the Bay Area. In winter, it stores the sun's heat to warm the air; in summer, while the land around it swelters, it "keeps its cool," sending lovely onshore breezes to bring down the temperature. (A difference of some 20 degrees was once measured one August day between a San Mateo hilltop—which was close to 90 degrees—and the bay shore just a few miles away—which was in the 70s.)

Until February 17, 1965, the date on which the San Francisco Bay Conservation and Development Commission (BCDC) was officially set up, there was no overall planning for San Francisco Bay. Diverse public agencies and private parties did with their portions pretty much what they pleased. The result was alarming. And it inspired the commitment of Bay Area people, spearheaded by the Save San Francisco Bay Association, to bring about change. On August 7, 1969, BCDC was made a permanent commission. While it does not have power to fully control bay conservation and development, it has put the brakes on many destructive projects, and it provides a forum for continued public involvement.

But, despite much of its history, and above all else, San Francisco Bay is beautiful. Harold Gilliam, one of its most eloquent lovers, once wrote

It is a mirror of the sky, reflecting the sun, the gray summer fogs and white clouds, the crimson and purple twilight, the jeweled amber lamps of its long arching bridges, the shimmer of moonrise above the eastern mountains. . . . [It] shapes in countless ways the lives of [5] million people who live and work on its shores.

And, it may be added, it can shape in countless happy ways the lives of those who visit it.

A Comparison of Counties

The nine Bay Area counties share unequally in beautiful San Francisco Bay, as the accompanying table indicates. Note that the two largest counties, Sonoma and Santa Clara, have the smallest share of all: Sonoma has about 8 miles of bay frontage, and Santa Clara only about 6 miles. San Francisco County, on the other hand, is more than half water.

County	Total Area* (in square miles)	Water Area*
Sonoma	1,521.2	18.6
Santa Clara	1,315.9	13.9
Solano	872.2	45.2
Alameda	825.4	92.4
Contra Costa	797.9	63.9
Napa	796.9	38.9
Marin	588.0	68.0
San Mateo	530.8	76.8
San Francisco	91.1	46.1

* Areas include lakes and rivers. Source: California State Department of Water Resources

Some Remarkable Bay Area Parklands and Preserves

The San Francisco Bay Area has not only a treasure of regional, district, and county parks and open spaces, but three federal reserves that are unique in such a well-populated area. It has two major park units (which are contiguous in places) administered by the National

Park Service—71,000-acre Point Reyes National Seashore and the 76,500-acre Golden Gate National Recreation Area, which includes Muir Woods National Monument. It has two large Fish and Wildlife Service refuges that are open to the public—14,000-acre *San Pablo Bay National Wildlife Refuge* and 21,500-acre *Don Edwards San Francisco Bay National Wildlife Refuge.* (Each of the above administering agencies belongs to the United States Department of the Interior.) It also has a marine sanctuary administered by the National Oceanic and Atmospheric Administration—the near-948-square-nautical-mile Gulf of the Farallones National Marine Sanctuary (which includes the Cordell Banks). All of these federal parklands and reserves protect irreplaceable natural environments and ecological communities. And they all offer unique and wonderful outdoor experiences to Bay Area residents and visitors. In fact, they are used and enjoyed by literally millions of people from all over the world.

Point Reyes National Seashore and the *Golden Gate National Recreation Area*—This book contains much information about these two beautiful national parklands—Point Reyes National Seashore and the Golden Gate National Recreation Area (GGNRA)—which together give the Bay Area some 150,000 acres of magnificent wilderness and open space right next door. However, mention should be made of the two late Bay Area congressmen who were primarily responsible for the establishment of these exceptional parks.

Marin County's Congressman Clem Miller authored the legislation for Point Reyes National Seashore and was its most effective advocate. He saw his park bill signed into law by President Kennedy in September of 1962, but he did not live to see the park dedicated by Ladybird Johnson in 1966; in October of 1962, he was killed in a small-plane crash while campaigning for reelection. His ashes rest on a promontory near Bear Valley within the park. Congress designated 32,730 acres—the heartland of the seashore—as legally protected "wilderness."

San Francisco's Congressman Phillip Burton made the establishment of the Golden Gate National Recreation Area one of his top priorities. Although a "city boy," he had a strong sense of the need of urban dwellers for open space and the natural scene. He believed, as well, that urban parks should be accessible and available to everyone: it is not an accident that the GGNRA charges few fees and that most of the activities within it are free. In an unprecedented action,

Congress voted unanimously to dedicate the Golden Gate National Recreation Area to Burton after his death in 1983, and several of its units now bear his name. More recently, Congress again recognized Burton's great contribution to the preservation of the Bay Area's beautiful landscape by naming the wilderness area in Point Reyes National Seashore the *Phillip Burton Wilderness.*

Don Edwards San Francisco Bay National Wildlife Refuge and *San Pablo Bay National Wildlife Refuge*—The 35,500 acres of San Francisco Bay wetlands protected by the San Francisco Bay and San Pablo Bay National Wildlife Refuges (established by Congress in the early 1970s) are scraps—though extremely important ones—of an extraordinary bayshore resource that, in a hundred years, had been considered wasteland and thoughtlessly degraded or destroyed. These bay wetlands—and, indeed, all coastal wetlands—are, in fact, among earth's richest habitats. The salt-marsh plants that grow here—cordgrass (*Spartina foliosa*) and pickleweed (*Salicornia* spp.) among them—are exceptionally efficient in converting the sun's energy into nutrients that are readily available to myriad forms of life. Thanks to these plants, a double handful of San Francisco Bay mud may be home to 40,000 miniscule living creatures. Many larger creatures of the sea shelter in the tidelands that also serve as nurseries for their young. The bay refuges provide sanctuary and/or breeding places, as well, to at least 250 species of birds. It is perhaps significant that one-third of the country's threatened or endangered species are wetlands dwellers; a wildlife refuge is literally that.

The *San Pablo Bay National Wildlife Refuge* is oriented primarily to wildlife management and is almost entirely undeveloped for general public use. Limited access by boat is possible, however, and birding (often excellent) can be enjoyed by people willing to walk a little; it is a minimum of 5½ miles (from Highway 37) to the best birding area and back. There is no camping, no dogs are allowed, and parts of the refuge are sometimes closed entirely to visitors. Fishing and controlled hunting—allowed in many national wildlife refuges as part of wildlife management—are permitted during the state's legal seasons. It is well to note that the shores of San Pablo Bay become one huge mud flat at low tide: if you want to visit this refuge, get a tide table first (at a sporting goods store) and use it. For information, write San Pablo Bay National Wildlife Refuge, Box 2012, Vallejo, CA 94592; telephone 707-599-1404.

In contrast, the **Don Edwards San Francisco Bay National Wildlife Refuge** (the headquarters for both bay refuges) welcomes public use of its well-developed educational facilities and its quite extensive hiking trails, which tie in with those of Coyote Hills Regional Park in Alameda County. There is an excellent visitor center near Newark, where displays provide important wetlands facts and figures and where you can get information about the refuge's facilities, interpretive programs, and trail systems. The refuge also conducts scheduled activities, such as flower walks, photography outings, birding—and even astronomy sessions—virtually every weekend of the year, an unusual and valuable wetlands resource. You can get a three-month refuge program, issued quarterly, at the visitor center.

If you are interested in birds or in wetlands generally, a walk through this refuge can be highly rewarding. On a late February afternoon, for instance, you may see hundreds of black-legged stilts probing the marshland, or an equal number of avocets straining the rich marshland "soup" with their gracefully upturned bills. Or you may watch willets flash their showy wings and listen to their plaintive calls. Ducks of many kinds may delight you as they scud across the water. Raptors, such as marsh hawks (now known as northern harriers) and the small, swift kestrels, will likely patrol the ground from above, swooping for their unwary prey. If the weather is warm, which it very well may be, you may admire the early lupine and the crowds of poppies brightening the nearby hills. And, any time of the year that you come, you can experience some of the mysterious force of tidal water, watching the marshlands slowly drain and slowly (and surely) flood. (Note that the cordgrass can keep its feet in salt water for 21 hours of the day's 24, whereas pickleweed can only survive 3 hours of such immersion and so must—and does—locate itself on higher ground.) You will find good interpretive signs placed along the 1½-mile Nature Walk.

The San Francisco Bay National Wildlife Refuge has a second center in Alviso on the southern side of the bay, just off Highway 237. This is used primarily for environmental education classes and field trips, but is open to the public on weekends. It is also a fine place for birding and shares its quarters with the San Francisco Bay Bird Observatory. Its parking lot and trails are open every day until 4:30 P.M., when the gate is locked.

There is no camping in the refuge, and parts of it may be closed to visitors at times to protect sensitive wildlife populations. No dogs are allowed. The usual national wildlife refuge hunting and fishing regulations apply here, i.e., both sports are allowed and both are controlled. The refuge is open from 7:00 A.M. to sunset seven days a week except for major federal holidays. The visitor center hours are 10:00 A.M. to 5 P.M.; closed Mondays and federal holidays. The refuge is easily reached by car from the eastern terminus of the Dumbarton Bridge: the refuge turnoff is well marked on Highway 84. For further information write: Don Edwards San Francisco Bay National Wildlife Refuge, P.O. Box 524, Newark, CA 94560; telephone 510-792-0222.

Note: There are no food facilities in the refuge. Plan to eat in nearby Newark if you want a delicatessen or restaurant meal, or bring your own food.

Gulf of the Farallones National Marine Sanctuary—Bay Area fishermen, among others, are fortunate to have this 948-square-nautical-mile sanctuary: over a third of the area's total fish catch (recreational and commercial) is taken from the protected waters of this extensive national marine sanctuary, first established in 1981 and renamed in 1987. The boundaries of this important reserve take in the Farallon Islands, encircling these drowned mountains (which, incidentally, mark the edge of the continental shelf) for 12 nautical miles. Elsewhere they stretch from Bodega Head (in Sonoma County) to Rocky Point (south of Stinson Beach in West Marin County) and extend 6 nautical miles offshore. Within these boundaries is a large section of the Gulf of the Farallones, Bodega Bay, Tomales Bay, Drake's Bay, Bolinas Lagoon, and Duxbury Point. The sanctuary also protects the estuaries, salt marshes, sandy beaches, surf-swept rocky sea cliffs, kelp beds, and the intertidal zones, as well as the depths of the ocean floor.

The highly nutrient-rich waters within the sanctuary (among the most productive off California's coast) are important not only to the local fishery resource (imagine San Francisco without Dungeness crab, salmon, and sea bass!) but to 25 species of pinnipeds and cetaceans, among them harbor seals, elephant seals, sea lions, dolphins, porpoises, and the gray whales that pass through this part of the ocean each year on their migratory travels. Of equal interest and importance is the bird—as well as the marine mammal—life protected on the Farallon Islands. Here the Point Reyes Bird Observatory (PRBO) (see Point Reyes Bird Observatory) is in charge of protecting and studying the over 300,000 birds—murres, cormorants, puffins, gulls, and rhinoceros auklets—that live and breed on the islands. Many stray birds also use the islands, and PRBO has chalked up a list of resident and visitor birds that totals more than 350 species. The elephant seals, once all but gone from these waters, are also under the aegis of PRBO: they have repopulated the islands in recent years with great success: more than 400 pups a year have been born and successfully reared on the rocky, wave-swept shores. (PRBO is associated as well with a one-of-a-kind study of white sharks, which breed in Tomales Bay and congregate around the Farallones in larger number than perhaps anywhere else on earth.)

The Gulf of the Farallones National Marine Sanctuary is under the aegis of three federal agencies: the Farallones themselves are administered by the U.S. Fish and Wildlife Service; the shores of the sanctuary are the responsibility of the National Park Service; and the sanctuary's waters are the province of the National Oceanic and Atmospheric Administration. For further information about the sanctuary, address: Gulf of the Farallones National Marine Sanctuary, Building 201, Fort Mason, CA 94123; telephone 415-561-6622. Rejoice, when you look across the shining waters of the Pacific to the rugged silhouette of the Farallones against a setting sun, that this priceless resource is protected for you to enjoy as well as for its own, very special sake.

It is possible to visit the Farallon Islands by boat out of San Francisco, but for the protection of the birds and animals as well as the safety of visitors, landing on the steep rocky shores of the island is not permitted. However, this daylong trip gives unexcelled opportunities for observation and photography. (See appendixes for nature outings.) *Note:* The nonprofit Farallones Marine Sanctuary Association raises funds for public education programs (address is The Presidio, Box 29386, San Francisco, CA 94129; telephone 415-561-6625).

The *Central California Coast International Biosphere Reserve,* dedicated in 1989, takes in much of the parklands and preserves noted above. (A Biosphere Reserve, established by the United Nations, is an area of special ecological and social concern, to be studied and protected.) Involving a unique mix of federal, state, county, and private partners, this is the only Biosphere Reserve in the world located next to a heavily populated urban area, and the only one in the world whose geography is terrestrial and estuarine as well as marine. Including the marine (with such units as the Gulf of the Farallones National Marine Sanctuary and the Cordell Banks), it embraces nearly 2 million acres, taking in parts of four Bay Area counties—San Mateo, San Francisco, Marin, and the tip of Sonoma. It has the largest seabird and marine bird breeding colonies south of Alaska in the United States. Needless to say, it has wonderful and remarkably varied opportunities for recreation. This Biosphere Reserve is a model of a well-balanced approach to protecting and enjoying our priceless natural resources.

Note: The **Bay Area Ridge Trail,** which is being spearheaded by the Bay Area Ridge Trail Council, is a 400-mile trail that, when complete, will link more than 75 public parks and open spaces on the ridges overlooking the bay. It's a multi-use trail, for hikers, bicyclists, and equestrians. The Bay Trail began with a plan by the Association of Bay Area Governments (ABAG), mandated by the state legislature. When complete, the Bay Trail will link all nine Bay Area counties and 42 shoreline cities by 400 miles of pathways for hikers, runners, bicyclists, and nature lovers. The San Francisco Bay Trail Project is coordinating this effort. The Ridge Trail is marked by a light blue dot on trail markers; the Bay Trail logo is a distinctive dark green and light blue and orange. Both organizations can supply you with detailed maps and descriptions of the trails that have been officially designated as part of these trail systems and open for public use. (For a bit of history about these trails, see East Bay Regional Parks.)

Words to the Wise

Wind. While the San Francisco Bay Area's fogs are justly renowned, its winds are not as well advertised. Yet this coastal region frequently feels the westerlies engendered at sea, and when storms come in, they may bring nor'westers or sou'westers as well. Wind is quite often a part of the Bay Area experience. (This applies to downtown as well as the coast or the countryside: the maze of canyons between downtown skyscrapers can quickly turn into a maze of wind tunnels when the breezes begin to blow.) Those who plan to enjoy the Bay Area out-of-doors should thus be prepared: a light windproof jacket or parka is usually enough protection, especially when you have other layers handy to reinforce it.

Tides and Ground Swells. As in any coastal area, tides are a concern, especially in the winter. Although the average tidal range is around 6 feet, this can vary considerably. If you're planning to be on the beach at any time, consult a tide table: you can buy one for very little money at any sporting goods store or National Park Service visitor center. (A beach walk can turn into a wade as the tide rises.) Also ask the park service people what to expect along their coastal areas. Be aware that ground swells—waves swollen offshore to twice or three times their usual size—can be dangerous on coastal cliffs as well as on beaches: unsuspecting picnickers on the Marin Headlands bluffs have been swept away by a ground swell when they chose a spot too near the water.

Other Ocean Caveats. The beautiful blue waters of the Pacific Ocean with their creaming surf usually look good enough to swim in. But be aware that those waters are cold—their average temperature is about 55 degrees Fahrenheit the year round. Those lovely waves, too, may mask strong currents and undertow. Swim only at beaches designated as safe, preferably when there is a lifeguard on duty; even though a nine-year-old boy once swam the Golden Gate (see San Francisco History), only strong, experienced swimmers should venture any distance from shore.

Trail Etiquette. Although Bay Area wilderness is rarely wild, being as well known as it is, it does have a few hazards, like poison oak and, in a very few places, rattlesnakes (see Some Pesty Problems, below). For your own safety and comfort, it is wise to stay on trails. For the sake of the land itself, it is even more important not to wander or take shortcuts: despite its sometimes lush character, the Bay Area countryside is fragile and particularly subject to erosion (see Unstable Soils, below). Please use it gently and carefully. And, of course, take along any trash you engender in your adventuring and dispose of it in a trash container; most public land agencies provide same at parking lots and trailheads as well as picnic areas.

Unstable Soils. Bay Area geology is not only fascinating, it also poses problems—quite aside from earthquakes! Belonging to the Franciscan Complex, many Bay Area soils are loosely compacted, almost rubble: they move easily, especially when exposed, in steep cliffs (of which there are plenty) or when waterlogged. Landslides are frequent, both inland and along the coast. This means it's a good idea to stay away from the edge of cliffs and to watch where you put your feet, particularly in steep places. Also, be aware that water-saturated coastal bluffs can slump onto beaches below them; during rainy periods, try to avoid narrow beaches with unstable cliffs above.

Drinking Water. Don't be tempted to drink from Bay Area streams, even when they look as fresh and clear as mountain waters. The natural waters of the Bay Area—and, alas, of the mountains, too—are apt to be contaminated with the protozoan that causes giardiasis, a particularly unpleasant intestinal disease. (Like infectious mononucleosis, it can leave you feeling like a wet dishrag for weeks.) Most public land agencies provide good drinking water. Use it, or carry your own canteen.

Animals. Coming into contact with wild animals in the Bay Area— with harbor seals, bobcats, foxes, coyotes, deer, or others—is a wonderful and unusual privilege. Never touch them, however, no matter how adorable they may look: they may carry a disease or be less friendly than they appear. Wild should wild remain: photograph, by all means, but never pet. (Rabies is endemic in parts of California and has been found in the Bay Area. It is highly unlikely that you will encounter a rabid animal, but in the remote chance that you are bitten by a small mammal, say, a skunk or a bobcat, get help immediately. If you are in a park, any park personnel will assist you; if you are elsewhere, find the nearest doctor, humane society, or even veterinarian. The animal should be examined, and you may need medical attention. The treatment for rabies has been improved and is highly effective.)

Dogs are generally not allowed on national park or state park trails. There are, however, exceptions; check with the nearest ranger or visitor center for canine rules and regulations.

Horses are allowed on specified trails; again, best to check with park personnel. Commercial stables will also steer you in the right directions.

Fog. Bay Area fogs are sometimes very wet. Indeed, if you walk beneath a eucalyptus or Douglas fir tree in a heavy fog, you might think it is raining. (See Geology and Weather re fog drip.) A light raincoat or parka is good to have along when you go adventuring in this part of the world. Some people, including hikers, like to keep an umbrella handy as well.

Some Pesty Problems. Although the Bay Area is generally mosquito-less and gnatless, it does have ticks in its countryside. These little arachnids (relatives of the spider, of course) frequent the brushy chaparral as well as meadow grasses during the wet months of the year; they are particularly apt to lurk in the beautiful wild lilac (ceanothus) bushes. Ticks are not choosy in selecting a host and will fasten onto any available warm-blooded animal, including humans. They are usually easy to find, and a tick hunt is in order after a hike during the winter months. If you do get a tick under your skin, grasp it with tweezers and ease it out; wash the resultant little wound well with soap—or detergent. Tick-borne Lyme disease is a health concern in the United States. It is carried by the Western black-legged tick, which is most common in moister areas, such as the Marin and Sonoma coasts. A physician, expert on tick-carried Lyme disease, estimates that a relatively small percentage of local ticks carry the disease, but prompt removal of ticks is the prudent way to avoid what can be a debilitating illness.

Always keep a sharp eye out for poison oak, *Toxicodendron diversilobum.* This handsome plant has an oily substance in its glossy dark green leaves and in its stems, as well, to which most people are highly allergic. Even an ankle-brush against a leaf may result in a miserable skin rash. (Some people are so sensitive to *Toxicodendron diversilobum* that they must avoid smoke from its burning leaves.) Poison oak is easy to identify, being generally bushlike, or vinelike and draping itself on bushes as it matures, and bearing its shiny leaves in clusters of three. It turns beautiful shades of red and crimson in the fall and has little white berries (about the size of the blisters it might raise on your skin). It is a tough plant and grows almost everywhere—in forests, among meadow grasses (where it is scrub-size), and along trails. Although other plants present their leaves in clusters of three, a good rule is: leaves of three, let it be. Its leafless branches in winter can be toxic, too, so it's a good rule to hike in jeans rather than shorts on most Bay Area trails to avoid contact with this ubiquitous pest. Should you encounter it despite your precautions, wash well with detergent—dishwashing type is good—to remove all traces of its oil: take a shower, not a bath. *Note:* Dogs can carry poison oak on their coats, and your own coat, shirt, or jeans, your car handles, or other people's hands can also pick up the oil. Handle items accordingly and be sure to wash your hands well with detergent to avoid contamination. Poison oak is not transmissible once the oil has been washed off.

Other plants to avoid are nettles (a tall, soft-looking, droopy-leafed plant with a thick growth of tiny needlelike thorns) and thistles (there are several varieties of this stiff, pointed-leafed exotic with the beautiful red and rose sunburst blossoms). Avoid both plants and thickets wherever possible. Again, jeans provide better protection than shorts. *Note:* The visitor center at Point Reyes National Seashore has good exhibits on poison oak and nettles.

Rattlesnakes are indigenous to the Bay Area, but almost all of them have been eradicated. The few that have survived prefer warm, dry places, like rocks and rocky ridges, where they can sun themselves. Your chances of coming across one are minute, but try to stay away from nooks and crannies when you're scrambling in rocky areas, especially on hot days. Should you meet up with a rattler, it will probably snake away quickly, being more frightened than you. Its bite is, of course, poisonous, but rarely fatal if medical care—usually readily available in the Bay Area—is obtained. Some park districts post warning signs in rattler territory.

Fire. Fire is essential to the life cycle of many Bay Area plant communities—the redwood forest and the chaparral being prime examples. California state park people and the National Park Service therefore may practice controlled burning as part of their management program. In this populated metropolitan area, however, uncontrolled burning can be a disaster: during the dry months of summer and autumn, the countryside can be a tinderbox, and wind-driven fire can travel with amazing and deadly speed. Please be careful accordingly.

Wildflowers. Those lovely blue and lavender lupines and the golden poppies you admire are protected by California state law: it is illegal to pick these or any other wildflowers. This is a sensible regulation since California's wonderfully colorful native flowers are a joy that everyone should be able to share in. Besides, wildflowers wilt almost immediately when picked.

Safety Tips. Outdoor people usually enjoy one another's company. It's also fun at times to solo: it's a good idea in the Bay Area, however, as it is everywhere, to let someone else know if you want to take a turn at, say, windsurfing, on your own. (And, of course, you will know the skills your sport requires and how to handle any emergency that might come up in connection with it.) There are very few really isolated places in the Bay Area, and as you travel around, you are often within calling distance of someone else: still, it's fun to share your outdoor experience and to hike in pairs or in a group. (See Environmental Organizations appendix for information on local group activities.)

Bay Area cities—like cities all over the world—have would-be purse-snatchers and, occasionally, muggers. No need to tempt fate: don't be careless with handbags and wallets; avoid dark streets and alleys at night; don't leave valuables lying in the open in your car, even if it's locked. Again, when possible, enjoy the company of a friend as you adventure around the city.

To Take Along. A pair of field glasses and a hand lens will both enrich your outdoor experience. The latter not only is good for seeing the beautiful details of flowers but comes in handy when you're looking for minute fossils in rocks. Sunglasses are also recommended, along with a broad-brimmed hat. Since drinking water is not always available, it's a good idea to carry a canteen.

Access Guide

San Francisco Bay is encircled almost completely by freeways. Its west side is rimmed north-south by Highway 101, the heavily used freeway that links San Francisco to San Mateo and Santa Clara counties to the south, and (via the Golden Gate Bridge) to Marin and Sonoma counties to the north. The northern bay is bordered by Highway 37 (two lanes, in places), which runs generally east-west and joins I-80 just east of the city of Vallejo, in Solano County. (Taking off northward from Highway 37, Highway 121 provides access to Sonoma and Napa counties.) Turn south on I-80 at Vallejo to cross Carquinez Straits into Contra Costa and Alameda counties. I-80 funnels into the Bay Bridge from Oakland to San Francisco, where it joins Highway 101. Continue south of the Bay Bridge in Oakland, and I-80 becomes I-880, which joins Highway 101 at San Jose. Thus the circle is closed.

Most of the following directions to various parts of the Bay Area refer to one or another of the highways described briefly above, and this book also provides maps showing the location of these and other key roads. It is also a good idea for travelers by car to get a detailed Bay Area road map (the AAA provides the best), which may lead to further adventuring. Here are thumbnail sketches of the easiest access to points of interest in the nine Bay Area counties, along with an estimate of the driving time (from San Francisco) required. Most of the places described in this book are within an hour's drive of San Francisco; some may take an hour and a half or two to reach. Note that in California, the AAA is the California State Automobile Association, CSAA.

West Marin—The Southern Section. Marin Headlands, Tennessee Cove, Muir Woods, Mount Tamalpais, Muir Beach, Stinson Beach, Audubon Canyon Ranch, Point Reyes Bird Observatory, Palomarin, Olema Valley, Bolinas Ridge, Inverness Ridge, Five Brooks, Olema.

Allow a half hour to get to Rodeo Lagoon in the Marin Headlands. Tennessee Cove is about 20 minutes from San Francisco, Muir Woods half an hour, Muir Beach 45 minutes, Stinson Beach 55 minutes, and Audubon Canyon Ranch about an hour. Add 10 to 20 minutes to reach the other destinations; to Olema (Olema Inn, Jerry's Farm House), it is some 90 minutes from downtown San Francisco when approaching from the south.

The southernmost part of West Marin (the Marin Headlands) can be reached by taking the first Sausalito exit right off Highway 101 north of the Golden Gate Bridge onto Alexander Avenue. (Be sure not to turn into the Vista Point viewing area.) You then turn left immediately, drive under the freeway, and turn right directly onto Conzelman Road into the Golden Gate National Recreation Area. Traveling to the south on Highway 101, you can turn right just short of the Golden Gate Bridge; follow the signs to the GGNRA.

For Tennessee Cove, take Highway 1 north of the last Sausalito turnoff. Continue westward (where Highway 1 makes a right-angle turn) on Tennessee Valley Road to reach the Tennessee Valley trailhead. To reach Muir Woods or the top of Mount Tamalpais, stay on Highway 1 until you come to Panoramic Highway, signed Muir Woods and Mount Tamalpais; turn north on Panoramic Highway (a real hairpin of a turn) and follow signs to Muir Woods or Mount Tamalpais State Park trailheads at Mountain Home, Bootjack, Pan Toll, and the top of the mountain.

To reach Muir Beach, Stinson Beach, and Audubon Canyon Ranch, cross the Golden Gate Bridge on Highway 101, turn west on Highway 1, and stay on Highway 1. To get to Point Reyes Bird Observatory (PRBO) and the Palomarin trailhead, continue north from the Stinson Beach stop sign 4.5 miles to the northern end of Bolinas Lagoon. Here, at highway marker 17.00, turn left at the *unsigned* crossroad and keep following the lagoon to your left (highway markers indicating C 122 will let you know you're on the right road, signed finally as the Olema-Bolinas Road somewhat farther on) until you reach a stop sign at Mesa Road, just short of Bolinas. Here turn right for about 4 miles to PRBO and another short mile to the Palomarin trailhead. Olema Valley starts at the north end of Bolinas Lagoon and runs north about 9 miles to Olema; Bolinas Ridge lies east of the valley, Inverness Ridge to the west. Five Brooks trailhead is in the valley about 5.6 miles north of the intersection of Highway 1 and the Bolinas-Fairfax Road. *Note:* It is possible to reach

Muir Beach from Muir Woods; turn west exiting Muir Woods and stay on the Frank Valley Road (also called Muir Woods Road), which dead-ends at Muir Beach and the Pelican Inn.

West Marin—The Northern Section. Olema, Inverness Ridge, Point Reyes National Seashore headquarters (Bear Valley), Limantour, Point Reyes Station, Inverness, Heart's Desire Beach, Drake's Beach. Allow 60 minutes from downtown San Francisco to Olema when approaching it via Sir Francis Drake Highway. It is another good 30 to 40 minutes to the tip of the Point Reyes Peninsula and the Point Reyes Lighthouse.

To reach the northern part of West Marin, cross the Golden Gate Bridge and stay on Highway 101 to the Central San Rafael exit. Turn left at Third Street, the first one-way street to the west (second traffic light), and continue westward to San Anselmo, where Sir Francis Drake Boulevard comes in. Sir Francis Drake will lead you to Olema. (Alternative: Cross the Golden Gate Bridge and stay on Highway 101 to Sir Francis Drake Boulevard; turn west and continue to Olema. Sir Francis Drake between Highway 101 and San Anselmo can be slow going, though.) Turn northward at Olema and, almost immediately, turn west on Bear Valley Road and follow the signs to Point Reyes National Seashore headquarters; this is where the visitor center, Earthquake Trail, Morgan Horse Farm, and Kule Loklo, the Coast Miwok Indian village, are located. It is also the trailhead for Bear Valley, Mount Wittenberg, the Old Pine Trail, and the coast. Allow 60 minutes from San Francisco to Point Reyes National Seashore. The chapter map indicates other points in the northern part of the seashore (i.e., Limantour, Drake's Beach, Point Reyes Lighthouse, Heart's Desire Beach, etc.); en route northward, you can pass through Inverness or take a short side trip to visit—and perhaps dine in—Point Reyes Station, a picturesque and historic town. Or you can continue north on Highway 1 to Bodega Bay and Sonoma County's lovely coast.

East Marin. Vista Point, East Fort Baker (GGNRA), Sausalito, China Cove, Marin Civic Center, Highway 37. Cross the Golden Gate Bridge to the north and follow the road signs. Allow 20 minutes to the Vista Point, East Fort Baker, and Sausalito (Alexander Avenue exit) turnoff, just north of the Golden Gate Bridge; 35 minutes to the Marin Civic Center and China Cove turnoff; 40 minutes to Highway 37.

Sonoma County—Central Section. Petaluma historic site, Santa Rosa. Take Highway 101 north and follow the road signs. Allow 45 minutes to Petaluma; 55 minutes to Santa Rosa.

Sonoma County—Eastern Section. Wine country, historic sites, state parks, Sonoma, Glen Ellen, Kenwood. Proceed north on Highway 101 to Highway 37. Follow 37 eastward to Highway 121; turn north on 121 and take Highway 116 north at the junction. Continue north on 116 for Glen Ellen, many historic wineries, and Jack London State Park. Allow 60-plus minutes to reach Glen Ellen. For more wineries, Sonoma historic sites, Mission Solano, and Boyes Hot Springs, stay on Highway 121 to its junction with Highway 12; turn north on Highway 12, which passes through Santa Rosa en route to the coast. Allow 50 minutes to Sonoma; another 10 to 15 to Glen Ellen and Jack London State Park; another 10 minutes to Sugarloaf Ridge State Park.

Sonoma County—Western Section. Wine country, apple country, Armstrong State Park. Take Highway 101 north to Highway 116. Turn left on Highway 116 and continue to Guerneville; follow the road signs to the park. Allow an hour to an hour and a half for leisurely exploring.

Sonoma Coast. Historic sites (Russian), state parks. Take Highway 101 north to Highway 1. Follow Highway 1 north as far as desired. Allow two and a half hours to Jenner. (Alternative: Stay on Highway 101 to Santa Rosa; thence take Highway 118 west to Highway 1.)

Napa County. Wine country, Silverado Trail, state park, Calistoga. Take Highway 101 north to Highway 37, thence to the east and the junction with Highway 121. Follow Highway 121 north to Highway 12 and continue on the two routes into Napa. Here you can take the "main drag" north (Highway 29) past historic wineries, Saint Helena (museum and eating places), Bothe-Napa Valley State Park (good camping and Robert Louis Stevensoniana), and Calistoga. Allow one and a quarter hours to Calistoga. The Silverado Trail (turnoff is just north of Napa) parallels Highway 29, which can be joined at several crossroads along the way as far north as Calistoga. There are several smaller wineries along the Silverado Trail, as well as lovely countryside.

Solano County. Benicia historic sites, state recreation area, birdwatching in fine marshes, roadside fruit stands (in season), Vallejo. Benicia can be reached via Highway 101 and Highway 37 along the northern edge of the bay; turn south on I-80 to I-680 and follow the road signs. For Suisun Marsh, take Highway 21 out of Benicia and follow the road signs to Grizzly Island. Allow an hour and 15 minutes to Benicia. (Alternative: Take the Bay Bridge to Oakland, then I-80 to the north. Follow road signs to Benicia. Allow an hour to reach Benicia or Vallejo.)

Alameda and Contra Costa Counties. East Bay Regional Parks and Mount Diablo. Cross the Bay Bridge and take I-80 north for Contra Costa County and Pinole Point. Allow 45 to 50 minutes to reach Point Pinole. For Mount Diablo, follow the signs to Walnut Creek from the Bay Bridge. You will be on Highway 24 east into Walnut Creek, where you pick up I-680 south to Alamo or Danville. Follow the road signs to Mount Diablo. Allow an hour to reach the state park. To reach Alameda County and the East Bay Regional Parks headquarters at 2950 Peralto Oaks Court, Oakland, cross the Bay Bridge and take I-580 south to the 106th Avenue, Oakland, exit. Cross under the freeway; turn right on Peralto Oaks Court (first cross street); this dead-ends at the headquarters parking lot. Allow 50 minutes to the regional parks headquarters.

San Mateo and Santa Clara Counties. County parks, state parks, open-space preserves, historic sites, wineries. You can travel south to "the Peninsula" on Highway 101, I-280 (called the most beautiful freeway in the United States), Skyline Boulevard (Highway 35), or Highway 1. There are connecting roads between these generally north-south routes, enabling you to make a loop trip down and up the Peninsula. Highway 1 accesses the coast and coastal state parks; allow an hour to the Pescadero turnoff and Portola State Park; allow 20 to 25 minutes more to Año Nuevo Point. Montebello Ridge and its wineries can be reached via I-280 and Stevens Canyon Road; allow a good hour. Los Trancos Preserve, with its edifying San

Andreas Fault Trail, is reached via I-280 and Page Mill Road. Allow an hour to get there. The bayfront parks—Coyote Point, Palo Alto Baylands, and Mountain View—are accessed via Highway 101. Allow 30 minutes to Coyote Point, 45 to 50 minutes to Palo Alto Baylands, and 50 to 55 minutes to Mountain View.

PART II

The Pleasures of
San Francisco Bay

Introduction

San Francisco Bay offers many pleasures, the most obvious of which are its visual charms. It is a joy to look at the bay from almost every angle. It is also delightful to walk beside it (see GGNRA and Crown Beach walks). Furthermore, it has three islands to be explored (one on foot, one on foot or bike, and one by car) and a bridge to be walked (or driven) across, for new and different—and delightful—perspectives. The bay also has audible charms—the sound of its surf along the shores of the Golden Gate, the deep-voiced calls of its ships, and the haunting sounds of its foghorns. And it has particular historic structures that tell of its colorful past, including the fortifications that rim it (see Fort Point, in GGNRA Walk 2, and Marin Headlands) and the lighthouses that mark its more dangerous spots. Add to all of these the pleasures of being on the bay (you can even go dining on it)—and, under certain circumstances, in the bay—and you come up with a veritable treasurehouse of special outdoor experiences.

Islands of the Bay

Alcatraz—There can hardly be a more beautifully located island anywhere—or one more desolate to live upon. Alcatraz—named by Spanish sailors when the birds of the island (probably cormorants, not pelicans) evoked nostalgic memories of birds near their homes—has fascinated explorers since they first found the bay. They soon found that this rocky peak of a drowned mountain was not very livable, except for birds. It has no fresh water, and it is surrounded by

Looking north down Hyde Street toward the bay, Alcatraz, and Angel Island. PHOTO BY RICHARD FREAR, NATIONAL PARK SERVICE.

cruel, swift currents that effectively isolate it from ready human approach. (Nonetheless, practiced bay swimmers have made the round
trip from the San Francisco shore.) Furthermore, Alcatraz is one of
the first places to feel the impact of the westerly winds and the rush
of fogs that surge through the Golden Gate. It is easy to understand
why it has never become a playground for Bay Area residents—nor
been developed as a sort of Tivoli à la Copenhagen, which one pro-
moter once optimistically proposed.

Instead, Alcatraz has become storied as the Rock, the federal maximum-security prison where the most desperate criminals were interred during three grim decades and where a group of them once held the place under siege for days. It has also made headlines as a symbolic piece of homeland that was occupied by American Indians in one of the more bizarre and tragic human rights gestures of the 1960s. (The daughter of the Indian leader died as a result of a fall off of one of the buildings.)

Today Alcatraz is a popular and much-visited unit of the Golden Gate National Recreation Area (GGNRA). It offers an interesting half-day outing for anyone wanting a pleasant (perhaps windy) ferry ride and a visit to a spot of somewhat infamous history. The park service provides ranger-led interpretive tours of the prison buildings, or you can wander around the notorious island on your own. Photographers will find wonderful views of the bay and its metropolitan environs. The temperature as well as the atmosphere on Alcatraz is apt to be chilly, so dress warmly if you elect to visit it. (See Public Transportation appendix for ferry information.)

Angel Island—Another unit within the GGNRA, Angel Island State Park also offers exceptional views of San Francisco. This somewhat more than 1-square-mile island also offers some excellent biking on its dozen or so miles of old military roads and equally good hiking: there's a 5-mile loop around the island on Perimeter Road, or you can climb to the top of Mount Caroline Livermore—named for a Marin County conservationist who helped turn this island into a state park during the 1960s—for a superb overview of the bay. Riding the ferry to Angel Island (the only way to get there unless you go by small boat)—from San Francisco (and Vallejo) on the Red and White Fleet, or from Tiburon on the Tiburon–Angel Island Ferry Company—is one of the special pleasures of visiting it; you can take your bike aboard for a small fee. (*Note:* The Alameda-Oakland Ferry serves Angel Island on weekends.)

Angel Island is believed to have been discovered by Don Juan Manuel de Ayala, the first European to have sailed into San Francisco Bay; he is given credit for naming it Isla de los Angeles. He found it occupied by Coast Miwok people, who for generations had taken advantage of its many trees and its good freshwater streams. Later, in 1839, it was granted to Antonio Maria Osio by the Mexican governor, Juan Alvarado. Osio dammed a stream to water his cattle and farmed and ranched the island for the next 20 years. In 1859, however, he lost his grant to the United States, and soon afterward the U.S. Army took over and started building fortifications and garrisons. During the next century, Angel Island served not only the military (it was used as a detention camp for "enemy" aliens, including a German consul, during the two world wars), but the Immigration Services and the Public Health Service, which until 1936 here screened all ships entering the bay for contagious diseases. Many old buildings remain as mementos of days past, including the Angel Island State Park ranger station (and visitor center) at Ayala Cove, where you can look at a model of the island and pick up a map; there are interpretive programs put on by the park and docent-conducted walks. (The Angel Island Association is an active volunteer support group.) During the summer months, you may also be able, for a fee, to ride around the island in an open-air tram.

Angel Island is a nice place for a picnic, and there are picnic facilities at Ayala Cove. There's also a small restaurant there in case you don't want to pack in your own food (open on spring weekends and in summer). (*Note:* When the fog is pouring through the Golden Gate, the south side of the island can be cold and gusty and gray, but you may be able to sunbathe on the grassy lawn at Ayala Cove.) The best times of year to visit the island are spring and fall, although the ferry service may not be as good during these seasons. The late Clyde Wahrhaftig in his book *Streetcar to Subduction* gave a good description of what to look for on Angel Island in the way of interesting rocks—including blueschist—if you're geologically inclined. (See Public Transportation appendix for ferry information.) *Note:* There are nine "environmental" (meaning there are no amenities) campsites on the island where you can overnight.

Yerba Buena Island and *Treasure Island*—Belonging officially to the city and county of San Francisco, 198-acre Yerba Buena Island is notable for the number of names it has gone by, a somewhat mild military history, and, more obviously, for providing the principal anchor point for the San Francisco–Oakland Bay Bridge. The island was first named by José de Canizares in 1776; he called it Isla del Carmen. Later, in 1838, it was granted to José Castro, and 5 years later it was claimed by José Limantour. Then, in 1850, when assigned to San Francisco County, it was given the name of Yerba Buena—the Spanish for "good herb." But locals called it everything from Wood

Island and Bird Island to Goat Island, so the U.S. Geographic Board dubbed it Goat Island in 1895. Less than 40 years after it did this, the same board gave the island back its Yerba Buena identity, and so it remains today.

From 1866 to 1898 the island was an army post, but it was turned over to the navy in 1898, and part of it was used by the navy for officer housing. In 1933, Yerba Buena Island was the site of a highly ambitious building project—the construction of the double-decker tunnel that would link the two spans of the 8½-mile San Francisco–Oakland Bay Bridge. Fifty feet high and seventy-six feet wide, this was the largest bore tunnel in the world at the time the bridge opened on November 12, 1936; Clinton Construction Company of San Francisco did the job.

Earlier in 1936, construction of a 407-acre island to the north, adjacent to Yerba Buena Island, got under way. This man-made island—5,520 feet long by 3,400 feet wide—was created specially for the 1939–1940 Golden Gate International Exposition—which was meant to celebrate the completion of the Golden Gate and Bay bridges. Its name—Treasure Island—was inspired in part by Robert Louis Stevenson's book of the same name, and in part by the intention that the island was to be "glamorous, beautiful, almost fabulous" as it displayed the treasures of the world—with emphasis on the Pacific Rim—in the gala fair that was planned. It required more than a year of dredging to obtain adequate fill for Treasure Island and the causeway that links it to Yerba Buena, and its seawall—containing 287,000 tons of quarried rock—still stands as a monument to its builders' skills. Most of the cost of this ambitious project—$3,799,800—was paid by the Works Progress Administration. (Imagine what it would cost today!)

The Golden Gate International Exposition took place, all right, but, in a war-torn world, it was never the smash hit its backers had hoped it would be. Its 400-foot-tall Tower of the Sun and virtually all of its other wonderful art deco buildings—some designed by the period's famous architects, Arthur Brown, Jr., and Timothy Pflueger—are now no more. One building, complete with an Avenue of Palms in front of it, did survive to become the terminal of the fabled *China Clipper,* the 12-passenger amphibious plane that made weekly trans-Pacific flights from 1939 through 1946. It cost $1,000 to ride the *Clipper,* which also carried tons of mail. During World War II, it flew only to Hawaii and back.

In 1941, Treasure Island, too, was turned over to the navy. Happily, the navy converted the exposition-relic *China Clipper* terminal into a museum, which you can visit, free, any day of the year (except Thanksgiving, Christmas, and New Year's Day) from 10:00 A.M. to 3:30 P.M. You'll find an interesting permanent exhibit on Yerba Buena Island, the history of the Bay Bridge and the 1939–1940 exposition, a model of the *China Clipper,* and the crystal lens of the Farallon Island lighthouse (it was the most brilliant of its kind when it was in use).

To reach Treasure Island, take the Bay Bridge and the Treasure Island exit. The museum is just inside the gate; you can park next to it. There are no picnic facilities, but there are wonderful views of the city and the surrounding seascape.

Three acres of Yerba Buena Island are presently occupied by the U.S. Coast Guard, which there operates a dual service: a vessel traffic service and a search-and-rescue station. The vessel traffic service operates five radar screens and has two controllers present at all times. It performs some, but not all, of the functions that a control tower provides: vessels in the bay can call in here to report their own location and learn of the location of other bay traffic. The service does not, however, prescribe a course for vessels, which, being informed, are then on their own. It does monitor distress calls and works closely with the search-and-rescue unit, which is the third-busiest search-and-rescue station in the world. This is the command post for an area that stretches from the Gualala River in the north to Point Piedras Blancas (off San Simeon) in the south, extends up to two hundred miles to sea, and takes in all of the bay, the delta, and Lake Tahoe. The reason for its great activity is the easy accessibility of the local waters for almost any kind of boat and the often unsuspected unpredictability of these waters. While most people think of the south bay as being as calm as a bathtub, it is actually subject to giant swells—as much as 10 feet high—when a strong wind pours through, say, the Guadalupe gap in the Coast Ranges. Several Coast Guard craft—including a 180-foot cutter that maintains local buoys—are docked at this station, ready to be pressed into service.

Both of these Coast Guard facilities are reached by taking the Yerba Buena Island exit off the Bay Bridge, and both of these interesting operations can be visited—free—if you call ahead. For the vessel traffic service, telephone 415-556-2760; for search and rescue, call 415-399-4400. *Note:* Views from Yerba Buena Island are also spectacular.

A Hike over San Francisco Bay

Walking the Golden Gate Bridge

For a special "only in the San Francisco Bay Area" outdoor adventure, consider this walk across the Golden Gate Bridge. It can take a pleasant morning or afternoon (it's about 1½ miles one way—8,981 feet, to be precise), or it can be stretched into a day's outing if you want to continue your walk through East Fort Baker and Sausalito (another 2½ miles). You'll probably want to start from the south end of the bridge, and since the parking plaza there has a time limit on its meters, you might find it easier to get there by bus. Both the San Francisco Muni and Golden Gate Transit serve the bridge's toll plaza, and, of course, Golden Gate Transit serves Sausalito. Before starting across the bridge, you can take the pedestrian subway beneath the toll plaza to the Golden Gate Bridge headquarters to pick up a pamphlet presenting bridge facts and figures. (There is also a public telephone here.)

As a general rule, walkers are routed on the east walkway at all times; bicyclists use the east walkway on weekdays but the west walkway on Sundays and holidays. There is no fee. It is not a good idea to walk across the Golden Gate Bridge during rush hours. Even in light traffic, you'll probably notice the fumes from passing cars. The bridge is also apt to be both windy and chilly, so bring along a sweater, a snug cap, and a light windbreaker. Whatever its drawbacks, however, this bridge walk is worth it, for it will give you perspectives on the bay, the ocean, and the surrounding lands that you can get nowhere else. A particularly good time to take this walk is when there's a sailboat regatta or any other bay "occasion," such as a windsurfing race. The *San Francisco Chronicle* runs a calendar of outdoor events in its Monday sporting section at least once a

Golden Gate Bridge and the city of San Francisco seen from the Marin Headlands.
PHOTO BY RICHARD FREAR, NATIONAL PARK SERVICE.

month, or you can consult the Sunday *Examiner* (which includes the *Chronicle*).

Before starting, you might want to visit the statue of Joseph B. Strauss in the view area to the east. (Strauss was chief engineer for the bridge project and is given—or took—credit for making it a reality. However, local accounts now say that two others deserve recognition as well: engineer Charles Ellis, who did the actual design, and San Francisco architect Irving Morrow, whose painter's sense of scale, perspective, and color refined Ellis's work into the elegant structure you see today. Strauss did, however, carry forward the idea of the bridge despite the dire predictions that "it couldn't be done.") And if you want to look at Fort Point up close (you'll get a bird's-eye view from the bridge), you can go down the hill here to this historic structure. Once on your way on the bridge, you can enjoy the panorama of San Francisco Bay spread out literally below your feet. From the Marin Headlands to the Berkeley-Oakland hills to the magic city, it's all there for you to marvel at. If a cruise ship or tanker steams through the Gate below you, you'll have an extra fillip to the show. Note the high wire fence above the railing at the south end of the bridge; it was put in place to deter would-be suicides. It may give you a shiver to realize that many hundreds of people have jumped from here, despite—or perhaps because of—the beauty of this particular place on earth.

Just before you come to the north tower, you will enter Marin County, and whether or not you're going to continue your walk to Sausalito, you may want to visit the Vista Point area ahead of you to see the classical view of the San Francisco skyline that has been immortalized by so many photographers. (*Note:* There's an even more photogenic view of the city, including the sweep of the bridge, to be had from East Fort Baker below you.) If you do turn back, you will now have the advantage of facing the oncoming traffic. You'll also have a whole new perspective of the bay.

To continue to East Fort Baker, take the dirt road that runs northeast from the north end of the viewing area just before the reentry point onto Highway 101. Follow it downhill; it will go under the bridge once, then join a paved drive. Follow this back under the bridge and down the hill to Horseshoe Bay, where you'll undoubtedly see some fishermen, and where you'll get that special view of the city. You can then visit East Fort Baker, named for the silver-tongued orator and friend of Abraham Lincoln, Colonel Edward D. Baker, who eulogized Senator David Broderick so eloquently. (Baker is also remembered by Baker Beach and Baker Street in San Francisco.) This old army post is notable for its handsome parade ground, its period architecture, and the Bay Area Discovery Museum; 415-487-4398. This is a unique children's—really family's—museum, with hands-on activities that challenge and involve the visitor. Highly recommended for a family outing.

To reach Sausalito (meaning "little willow group" in Spanish), follow Murray Circle in either direction around the parade ground to East Road. East Road, which almost immediately joins Fort Baker Road, is the fort's principal access. Follow this road for about a mile to join Alexander Avenue. Turn to your right onto the shoulder of the highway and in not too many steps you will come to a sidewalk that will lead you on into Sausalito. Here you'll find a picturesque village (originally subdivided out of William Richardson's grant in 1868) with gorgeous views, a number of good eating places, and what seems like hundreds of shops to tempt you with their charming wares. To return to San Francisco, you can either take the romantic way—the ferry, which docks at the Ferry Building on the Embarcadero—or you can pick up a Golden Gate Transit bus, which may carry you closer to your destination.

Foghorns and Lighthouses

Although San Francisco Bay is renowned for its foghorns, its first foghorn was not a horn at all. It was a retired army sergeant setting off an old cannon.

The year was 1855, and Sergeant Pat Maloney, having done his stint in the military, was looking for a nice, easy job. And, indeed, he thought he had found it when he signed up to become a foghorn. The army donated an old cannon, which was hauled from Benicia Arsenal and hoisted up to the top of Point Bonita on the north side of the Golden Gate. Maloney had to supply his own powder, and he was charged with firing the 24-pound cannon "every half hour during fogs at the entrance to the Bay, whether they occur at night or in the day, the firing being made at hours and half of San Francisco mean time."

Pat Maloney reported for work happily on August 6, but the poor man had figured without the plenitude of fog that rolls in through the Golden Gate during the summer months, or perhaps August and September of 1855 were unusually foggy. Whichever it was, after two months of firing his cannon faithfully, he managed to get a message back to the government: "I cannot find any person here to relieve me, not five minutes," he wrote plaintively. "I have been up three days and nights, had only two hours rest, I was nearly used up. All the rest I would require in the twenty-four hours is two, if only I could get it." His boss, ensconced in the "Monkey Block" Building, then on the San Francisco waterfront, sent out a substitute for Maloney, who thereupon hastened back to the city, stepped ashore, and promptly disappeared, never to be seen again. So much for the job of being a foghorn.

Evidently Maloney's relief fared better than he, and the cannon continued to be fired for the next two and a half years. It was an expensive undertaking, however, and was thought to be too dear to continue after March 18, 1858. According to information supplied by the U.S. Coast Guard in Alameda (where the cannon, lovingly restored, now stands), the cannon was fired 1,390 times during the first year "with the exception of 88 foggy days . . . for want of powder. . . . Excluding the pay of the gunner, it cost $1,487 and 5,560 pounds of powder to keep [it] in action."

The cannon was on display in 1915 at the Panama Pacific International Exhibition and again in 1939 and 1940 at the Golden Gate International Exposition.

Foghorns and other signals became mechanized well before the turn of the century, and one popular model was a large bell with an automatic clapper, which a lighthouse keeper would activate when the fog poured in. History has it that the Angel Island bell broke down in a real pea-souper of a fog in 1906, and the heroic woman lighthouse keeper banged the bell herself for nearly 21 straight hours.

Fog-signaling devices have proliferated mightily in the Bay Area since those early days; a survey in 1978 counted more than 90 foghorns, sirens, and bells. Today, although that number has probably increased, the U.S. Coast Guard cannot easily keep up with it, since private boatyards and marinas—and even waterfront residences—may set off a fog signal of their own if they wish.

Until recent years, there was a fine spine-tingling foghorn on the Golden Gate Bridge. It was the only diaphone left of the several that once made San Francisco Bay so memorable to visitors on foggy nights. Driving across the bridge in the fog, you used to hear the two-tone diaphone emit a huge, tumultuous moan—*Ohhhhhhhhhhhh-Huh*—that blasted passing boats almost out of the water and that could be heard at least 5 miles away. Now, alas, all the bay foghorns you hear are the diaphragm type. The diaphragm horns work something like an automobile horn, only they are a great deal louder. They are distinguishable one from another by their pitch, by how many times they are sounded in sequence, and by the frequency with which they are sounded. Although they would be more efficient if tuned to a higher note, people would probably go crazy listening to the lot of them, since such a sound is hard on the eardrums; instead, these foghorns let out fairly mellow bellows that sailors of all kinds soon come to recognize. (They play it by ear.) There are two diaphragm horns on the base of the Golden Gate Bridge's south tower, which are synchronized to sound in the intervals of quiet between the great moans of the bridge's diaphragm.

Fog sirens are something like king-size fire engine sirens that can be effectively pitched and turned on and off to form an easily recognized audible pattern. The other fog signal is the bell—always a loud one—that is pitched and sounded, again, in a sequence of gongs that makes it readily identifiable.

The bay's foghorns are now automated, some completely—requiring no human hand—others being activated by the press of a button several miles away. (The profession of lighthouse keeping has become, alas, obsolete, bell-ringing heroines no longer being required.) The bells and sirens on the Bay Bridge, for example, are entirely mechanized. It is the Coast Guard at Fort Point, however, that decides when it's time to start up the signals on Yerba Buena Island and the Port of Oakland. And the responsible signal sounders at the Golden Gate Bridge set off their foghorns when Mile Rock and the Marin shore disappear in the soup.

When heavy fog presses on the waters of San Francisco Bay and all the foghorns, sirens, and bells get going, it can be quite a symphony. So thought local composer Ingram Marshall, whose work *Fog Tropes* was once performed by the San Francisco Symphony with Marshall himself conducting. San Franciscans in the audience looked wisely at one another, each one appearing to recognize immediately the foghorns being "set off." The composer was applauded roundly for capturing music that so many had been listening to for so many years.

San Francisco Bay has its share of lighthouses as well as foghorns. Some of these you can visit; others you will have to settle for simply seeing.

The Mile Rock's Light was decapitated a few years ago, leaving only a platform (a helicopter pad) and the light that marks the southern entrance to the Golden Gate.

Fort Point has the relic of an iron-sided light tower that was decommissioned in the thirties. (It is the only standing bay lighthouse not in use.)

The Lime Point Light identifies the north tower of the Golden Gate Bridge.

Alcatraz Island's concrete tower warns of its rocky shores.

The East Brother Light leads ships through San Pablo Strait. Its wonderful old Victorian buildings have been restored into a neat and popular bed-and-breakfast inn. You reach it via boat out of Point San Pablo. You can also visit it by day, for a fee; it's a fine place to take a picnic. Telephone—in advance—510-820-9133. This unique operation is run by a nonprofit organization.

Point Bonita is where the bay's first foghorn was set up in 1855. Now it is part of the Golden Gate National Recreation Area, and you may be able to visit the lighthouse (by trail, tunnel, and bridge) at specified times. Telephone 415-331-1540 for the latest information. Photographers take note: a sunset from Point Bonita can be spectacular.

(Point Reyes Lighthouse, one of the Bay Area's most interesting and accessible lighthouses, is in Marin County. See Point Reyes National Seashore for more information.)

Note: Lighthouses can be identified by the patterns of their flashes, even as foghorns are identified by the audible patterns of their calls.

On the Bay

An especially good way to enjoy San Francisco Bay is to take a jaunt on a ferry or tour boat, or you can go forth on a marine nature excursion (see Nature Outings appendix). If you're looking for a more intimate experience with the salty blue waters, however, you can choose from even more nice possibilities: you can take a brisk sail, surf the lively waves, or feel the winds and spray from a sailboard; you can venture out in a bluewater or oceangoing kayak; or, if you're so-minded, you can go sculling. And you can even take a swim (it will help if you really like really cold water). Each of these activities offers a different dimension in Bay Area outdoor adventuring, a unique way to view the surrounding bay cities, and a special chance to explore the different moods of the bay.

Most of these activities call for a particular set of circumstances— wind, or lack of it, calm waters, or rousing surf, etc.—for special equipment, and for expertise in what you're doing. Happily, the Bay

Area offers almost any nautical gear you can think of—to rent or to buy. It also offers expert instruction in the various marine sports. And if you're excursioning, you can expect a comfortable experience.

It goes without saying that you need to know what you're about—as well as what you're getting into—when you venture onto or into the bay firsthand. It is helpful to have a knowledge of how tides and currents work, for San Francisco Bay is a dynamic body of water, especially around its several straits, such as Raccoon, Carquinez, and the Golden Gate. Anyone who supplies you with equipment or instruction should be able to give—or show—you what to look out for. There are also good manuals to be had: some sporting goods stores carry them, or you might try Armchair Sailor Books and Charts, 42 Caledonia, Sausalito; telephone 415-332-7505. You can also pick up a "Light List" at the U.S. Government Printing Office (on Second and Harrison streets) in San Francisco. Another useful publication is the *Coast Pilot,* available at marine sporting goods stores. It goes without saying that a tide table, also available at sporting goods stores, is essential. A major resource is the United States Army Corps of Engineers Bay Model in Sausalito. You can study tides and currents here as nowhere else, and you can get an invaluable overview of the bayscape. (Call 415-332-3870 for visiting hours.)

Sailing and surfing in the Bay Area are well-established sports, but recently they have been challenged in popularity by kayaking and windsurfing. Herewith is a brief rundown of what you may expect in bluewater kayaking and windsurfing.

Kayaking. Bluewater kayaking—or sea kayaking—is not the same as whitewater kayaking, as any aficionado of the sport knows well. And sea kayaking outdates river kayaking for sport by probably thousands of years. Alaska's Aleut people are believed to have invented the *bidarka* (or kayak) for ocean hunting at least 5,000 years ago. Bidarkas and the larger skin-boats, the umiaks, became the principal—and the unifying—means of transportation that gave rise to an Arctic culture that extended from Greenland to the Beaufort Sea, or Arctic Ocean. Some anthropologists believe the Arctic people also indulged in racing their beautifully designed crafts. In contrast, the first use of the kayak for sport probably dates back no farther than something over a century: one John "Rob Roy" McGregor built a wooden kayak 15 feet long and a little over 2 feet wide in

England the year the Civil War ended and engendered a somewhat short-lived enthusiasm for kayaking on such rivers as the Nile. Then, in the first decade of the twentieth century, Johann Klepper came on the scene with his classic *faltboot* kayak. Other foldboats followed, and recreational kayaking, especially the whitewater variety, was on its way; in recent years, it has become one of the all-time popular wilderness sports.

The seagoing kayak differs from the rivergoing kayak in basic design, requiring, for example, a broader, flatter keel for increased stability. There are more than 100 different versions of this craft presently available on the North American continent: these weigh anywhere from 28 to 89 pounds; they may be 15 to 20 feet long, and have a beam from less than 2 feet to almost a yard wide. You can find singles, doubles, and even triples, and you can choose between a rigid frame (less expensive, lighter, ready to go, and, importantly, more readily rolled—as in the Eskimo roll, an essential technique for righting a capsized kayak) and the folding type (easier to carry around, and possibly more comfortable and quiet).

Bluewater kayaking in San Francisco Bay has been enjoyed by a few individuals for many decades (see below), but it has been a commercial enterprise only since October 1982. It is now a flourishing business, and what is especially nice about it in the Bay Area is that a novice can rent the proper gear and receive expert instruction (and supervised experience) for a relatively modest outlay. This means that almost any prudent person in reasonably good shape—this includes many people with handicaps—can enjoy what is one of the great San Francisco Bay experiences. Keep in mind, however, that ocean kayaking requires certain learned skills, and it also requires, as Bay Area aficionado and author Will Nordby puts it, "respect for and understanding of the sea." Training is essential, and, happily, the bay offers relatively sheltered places where beginners can safely learn. Chances are that you'll get very wet—that's the penalty of the Eskimo roll—and you'll have lessons in reading the waves and understanding the tides. You'll also find out the best time for bay kayaking—when the wind isn't blowing, when a storm isn't brewing or breaking—and how to dress to be comfortable.

What are the rewards? You might get to see the sun come up over the Berkeley hills and spill its golden light all over the bay (dawn is a prime time to be on the water); or, equally, you might witness a moonrise that floods the bay world with silver. You might get to see a harbor seal or California sea lion close up. You would, for sure, get a different perspective on the San Francisco skyline. There's more, too: listen to the words of the late Paul Kaufmann, who was known affectionately as the Old Man of the Bay, not because he was ancient, but because he was one of the very first to discover and articulate the mystique of bay kayaking (he made over 630 kayak trips on the bay and wrote a gem of a book, *Paddling the Gate,* about it all):

> I'm in a different world. . . . The firm realm of land and dock has been exchanged for the realm of the depths—far less secure, but infinitely more peaceful. The soothing calmness from the water flows right through my body, and I can feel the sea inside, nourishing some hungry spaces.

Another sea kayaker, John Ince, puts it this way: "To voyage in a kayak is to connect with the great rhythms of nature, the afternoon winds and the evening calm, the steady pulse of an oceanborne swell, the rise and fall of the tide." Bon voyage.

Windsurfing. In great contrast to kayaking, windsurfing—or sailboarding—was not invented until the middle of the twentieth century. A number of people claim that they originated this beautiful sport, but the first sailboard to be patented in the United States was designed by Jim Doyle and Hoyle Schweitzer and launched in 1968. (In 1984, England declared that an odd-looking contraption put together in 1951 by Peter Chilvers was, in fact, the first sailboard, thus making England the original home of windsurfing and Chilvers the original inventor thereof.) Whatever its beginnings, windsurfing has taken off with a great spray and splash and has become the darling of athletic people on wave-washed coasts the world over. It achieved Olympic status in 1984—record time for any sport to be so recognized.

A sailboard has more parts than a kayak—the board itself, the sail, and the rigging (which includes the mast, the boom, and footstraps). As the sport has become more and more sophisticated, there have been improvements and refinements of earlier designs (although the original Schweitzer Windsurfer, as it was christened, is still considered a very acceptable all-around recreational board), and there is now quite a range of boards and sails to choose from. The kind of windsurfing you are going to do—racing, jumping, or just plain sailing—will determine your choice.

Windsurfing in San Francisco Bay, particularly across the Golden Gate, is considered by many to be truly world class, second, in fact, only to windsurfing in Hawaii. (The best place to see windsurfers in action is off Crissy Field in the GGNRA.) The reason for this, aside from the configuration of the bay, is the dependable westerly wind that begins to blow sometime in March and can be counted on to continue more or less steadily for the next six months. The wind has a pattern of coming up—"the fan turns on," as one windsurfer puts it—soon after noon and becoming progressively weaker after 6:00 P.M. Thus, contrary to kayaking, which is usually best in the morning, windsurfing in the bay is an afternoon (or "stockbroker's") sport. Windsurfers are sometimes accused of being elitists who like to gather for a late lunch, loll in the sun a while, and then man their boards when the breeze becomes just right.

Windsurfing requires more physical effort than kayaking—it involves virtually every muscle you are equipped with—and, arguably, more skill. It certainly demands lessons and an understanding of the bay's tides and currents before it is undertaken. It also has a few other requirements, according to one of the finest windsurfers on the bay:

1) Be prepared to leave your ego on the shore. You'll fall down a lot, and you might as well be resigned to it.
2) Be friendly with the water; understand that bay water will be "quite bracing."
3) Always wear a good wetsuit, one that is designed for cold water and plenty of movement.
4) Perfect your technique: it is more important than brute strength. (Experts say that there is no such thing as being too old to learn the sport.)
5) Develop a sense of the wind. (Without wind, standing on a sailboard is like "balancing on a basketball.") Never allow your sail to get between you and the wind.

As with kayaking, windsurfing is a burgeoning business in the Bay Area. You can practice it in the East Bay regional parks, the North Bay (Larkspur is a favorite spot), the South Bay, Benicia, Alameda, Redwood City, and so on. There are many surf shops that can outfit you completely, including wetsuit, and teach you the necessary know-how to take off into the wind. They will also supply you with maps that indicate the spots that are good for boardsailing, as many call the sport since *windsurf* has become a patented word. Consult the yellow pages of a San Francisco phone book for information. (Keep in mind that this sport may not require exceptional strength or sailing experience, but you must know how to swim.)

The San Francisco Boardsailing Association is a volunteer, non-profit group dedicated to promoting the safety of boardsailing, to organizing and taking part in boardsailing activities, and to obtaining and providing information about the state of the sport in the Bay Area. With over 1,500 members (as of this writing), the association publishes a quarterly newsletter. If you are interested in boardsailing in the Bay Area and need more personal information, you can write to the association (which, incidentally, welcomes new members; the membership fee is exceedingly modest). Address is San Francisco Boardsailing Association, 1592 Union Street, Box 301, San Francisco, CA 94123. There is presently no telephone, there being no paid staff to answer one.

Sailing. If you're a more traditional type and want to go sailing on the bay, again, look in the Yellow Pages of the phone book: there are dozens of outfits eager to get you onto the water.

Sculling. Another sport on the bay is sculling. This was once limited to boat club members, but now there's an Open Water Rowing outfit (at 85 Liberty Ship Way, Sausalito, CA 94965; telephone 415-332-1091), which will rent you a shell (a lighter, longer craft than a rowboat, and with sliding seat and oarlocks on riggers to make rowing easier) and give you lessons, if needed. Rowing on the bay is much better than an exercise machine, and a great way to sightsee as well. *Note:* You can rent equipment only if your sculling skills are certified or if you complete a four-hour (two two-hour lessons on two days) novice program.

Excursions on the Water. One of the most pleasant ways to see the sights of San Francisco Bay is from the deck of a boat. You can do this, of course, on a tour boat if you're interested in having an informative spiel along with your viewing. If you like to go it on your own, however, you can take a ferryboat ride. Happily, after decades of being considered "obsolete," ferries are once again plying the bay's blue waters. You might plan to take one to Vallejo to visit Marine World there, or try an on-the-water trip to Tiburon for a seafood meal complete with waterfront views. Or simply take a ride to Larkspur and back. (See Islands of the Bay: Angel Island and Alcatraz, too.) You might choose one of the Bay Area's unusual scorchers to take such an outing: there's no better way to beat the heat.

Whalewatching expeditions offer a wonderful bay experience as well as the thrill of venturing out to sea, for the expedition boats sail from the San Francisco piers or small harbors. Thus, as you sail toward the Golden Gate, you can take in the landscapes and cityscapes of the bay itself. You will get fine views of Fort Point under the Golden Gate Bridge (also thrilling when viewed from directly below) and Point Bonita with its picturesque lighthouse on the tip of the Marin Headlands. (The same holds true, of course, for excursions to the Farallon Islands.) Whale-watching trips can take up half a day or a whole one, and you may need to bring along your lunch. As you venture seaward, you should also expect cool breezes and, sometimes, rough waters, so dress and plan accordingly, especially if you are prone to seasickness. Be sure and take along binoculars!

More information on ferries, tour boats, natural excursions on the bay, and whale-watching is in the Nature Outings and Public Transportation appendixes.

Dining on the Bay. What more delightful way to see the sights of San Francisco Bay than on a comfortable boat—while you're enjoying a delicious brunch, lunch, or dinner? The Blue and Gold Fleet offers dinner dancing seasonally. The *California* sails year-round; it has quite elegant dining accommodations (including fresh flowers and full bar) in its spacious dining salons and serves dinner—with live music—year-round, as well as lunch on weekdays and brunch on Sundays. These are large ships. For a smaller, more informal ship, choose the sloop *Ruby.* Menus vary according to the meal, of course, and the price (reasonable enough compared to most restaurants), and you can suit your palate with everything from caviar to barbecued chicken.

Routes of the ships depend upon conditions in the bay and the pleasure of the ship's captain, but you can count on one and a half to three hours aboard, depending upon the meal you choose. You can count on those great views, too. Reservations should be made two or more weeks ahead and are, of course, essential. Here are addresses and telephones:

Blue and Gold Fleet, Pier 39, San Francisco, CA 94133; telephone
    415-705-5555.
California, Hornblower Yachts, Pier 33, San Francisco, CA
    94111; telephone 415-394-8900.
Ruby, China Basin Charter, 1129 Folsom Street, San Francisco,
    CA 94103; telephone 415-861-2165. *Note:* The *Ruby* is
    docked at the foot of Mariposa Street.

PART III

San Francisco

San Francisco History

At first glance, it seems incomprehensible that the early seafaring explorers of California sailed merrily past the Golden Gate without, apparently, having the slightest idea that it opened into one of the world's most magnificent harbors. Such expert Spanish sailors as Juan Rodrigues Cabrillo, Bartolome Ferrelo, Sebastián Rodrigues Cermeño, and Sebastián Vizcaíno—and almost certainly the Englishman Francis Drake—all made this interesting mistake. Perhaps it was heavily fogged in when these intrepid men encountered this part of California, but more likely they missed the Golden Gateway simply because they were prudent navigators who kept well out to sea along an unknown coast with its forbidding headlands and mountains that plunged into the sea. Seen from a short distance away, say, just beyond the infamous shallows known as the Potato Patch, the East Bay shore may appear to be part of the Golden Gate, and even Angel Island can look deceptively close.

Whatever the reason, it was left to a handful of Spanish foot soldiers to blunder onto the great bay, and they were not exactly thrilled by their discovery. They were intent on finding Monterey Bay, which happens to lie nearly a hundred miles to the south, and it was a bitter disappointment to find that they had come too far.

The year was 1769, a time when the European powers, seeking to enlarge their empires, were looking to the west, even as Russia was looking to the east. From its vantage points in Mexico and Baja California, Spain was particularly anxious to cinch ownership of as much of the New World as it could. Especially, it wanted to "get there first" in the largely unexplored land it considered Alta California. From past experience, Spain had learned the pacifying—and economic—advantages of pairing the cross with the sword, and so it was that Don Gaspar de Portolá (first governor of the Californias, Baja and Alta) set forth from Loreto with the Franciscan father Junípero Serra to explore, claim, and settle the enticing unknown territory to the north for their Catholic king, Charles III. Portolá commanded a 300-man party on this four-pronged "holy expedition"—two ships and two groups of land travelers. He had only a sketchy guide to navigation prepared by Cabrero Bueños more than a century earlier to go by, and the lyrical descriptions of Monterey Bay provided by Vizcaíno. Bueños's map showed a bay at San Diego as well as at Monterey, and one just south of Point Reyes on the very spot where Drake is believed to have put ashore. In 1595, Cermeño, following Drake by a few years, may have removed the traces of the English when he claimed the place for Spain. At any rate, he named the small bay (now known as Drake's Bay) for the seraphic Saint Francis of Assisi. Monterey Bay, however, was Portolá's ultimate goal, and he was pledged to find it.

Only half of the "holy expedition" survived to reach San Diego, and the two ships got no farther. But there Portolá and Father Serra did establish the first of the California missions, of which 21 in all would be built in the next few decades. Portolá then took 63 of his strongest remaining men (including Father Juan Crespi) and continued northward on the search for Monterey Bay.

The going proved to be rough along the coast, and the party was forced inland around the Santa Lucia Mountains. It is probable that they regained the shore near Monterey Bay, but from the land they failed completely to recognize the bay and pushed onward. On the last day of October, they bivouacked somewhere near the present town of Linda Mar and climbed the promontory to the north. It must have been one of those crisp, clear autumn days, for they could see the great sweep of the coast all the way to Point Reyes. Alas, this was clearly not Monterey Bay. It must be Cermeño's "San Francisco Bay"! They had overshot their mark.

Nonetheless, Portolá sent out a party of scouts led by José Ortèga to take a closer look, and to find an overland route to Point Reyes. Ortèga left camp on November 1. The next day, two deer hunters who had stayed behind discovered an "immense arm of the sea . . . [extending] inland as far as they could see." When Ortèga returned on November 3 to describe finding a bay ("like unto a securely locked chest") with an estuary that had blocked his way, he corroborated their story. The next morning—November 4, 1769—the whole party climbed a ridge to the northeast and were brought up short by one of the great views of the world: there at their feet lay a bay so grand that Father Crespi, perhaps their best reporter, noted that "this port of San Francisco . . . could [contain] not only all of the armadas of our Catholic Monarch, but also all those of Europe." (The beautiful rise they climbed is now known as Sweeney Ridge; happily it was added to the Golden Gate National Recreation Area in 1983.) This, they all mistakenly agreed, must indeed be Cermeño's "San Francisco Bay," so that was what they called it. Then Portolá turned his back on the magnificent view—and the extraordinary possibilities of the newly christened harbor—and, being a remarkably single-minded fellow, marched his party off to the south, still seeking the elusive Monterey Bay. (He did find it the following year, but after that Portolá's name disappears from the story; he left California.)

Who, then, actually saw the mighty harbor first? In the reams of reports that this expedition (and other Spanish expeditions) produced, this tidbit of information was not included. Although Portolá often gets the credit (and he was leader of the expedition), many historians reason that it must have been Ortèga. It seems likely that he viewed the Golden Gate, at least, from the Punto de los Lobos Marinos (Point Lobos) the same day he left camp. (One historian, Zoeth Skinner Eldredge, even sets the exact time that Ortèga took his first look: according to this scribe, it was between two and two-thirty on the afternoon of November 1, 1769.)

For the next half dozen years, the Spanish explorers with their doughty Fathers returned again and again to San Francisco Bay to chart its waters and map its shores. The magnitude of their great discovery became increasingly clear to them. Don Juan Manuel de Ayala, captain of the *San Carlos*, the first ship to enter the bay, was another helpful reporter. He wrote that "this port is good not only for the harmony that [it] offers to the view . . . but [it also has] good fresh water, wood and ballast—beautiful in abundance." To this he added that "the heathen Indians" around the bay were "constant in their good friendship . . . and gentle in their manners. . . . [Their] friendship was a great comfort to us." This area of California obviously could accommodate two missions, if not more. And Father Serra voiced a dream of the Franciscans when he later planned for the founding of a particular mission to honor *"nuestro Padre en su Porto"*—"our Father in his port."

In 1776, a momentous year on several counts, the port got its presidio, and Saint Francis got his mission. Don Juan Bautista de Anza, after an especially grueling expedition, chose the site of the present Fort Point for the military outpost (it was later moved to the site of the present Presidio), and Father Pedro Font gave it his blessing. They found a fine location for the mission some 3 miles to the south and east in a well-watered and sheltered place where the wild violets grew in profusion. Because the day was the Friday of Sorrows, the mission would be named Dolores, for Our Lady of Sorrows (the Mission Dolores is San Francisco's oldest intact building and its principal link to its beginnings). Father Font bestowed his blessing once more, and then, being a practical man, he saw to it that seed was broadcast in anticipation of the mission's garden. Perhaps the good Father was feeling a little homesick when he noted in his diary that if San Francisco Bay could only be "settled like Europe" there would be no lovelier place on earth.

It would be many moons before Father Font's dream came true, and homesickness was not the only problem those first Spanish pioneers—especially the presidio soldiers—had to contend with. Although the soldiers had brought their families and their stock with them (along with the promise of a land grant after ten years of service), the mission claimed most of the best land. Their windy, sandy, flea-ridden outpost proved to be so remote that they had almost no contact with the outside world, let alone adequate supplies. Even their pay was held up for years. (When Captain George Vancouver sailed the first non-Spanish ship into the bay in 1792, he commented on the sad state, and the ineffectualness, of the presidio and its men.) There was almost nothing to keep the men busy except an occasional rounding up of the Indians who ran away from the mission. The post had to turn to the mission for food, and the Fathers insisted upon proper requisitions before they meted out bare-bone rations. (Imagine a San Francisco that offered nothing but boredom and skimpy meals!)

The Indians, of course, fared far worse. Herded into barracks, the women separated from the men by the careful Fathers, they proved to be frighteningly susceptible to the white man's diseases. When Otto von Kotzebue sailed his Russian ship, the *Rurik,* into San Francisco Bay in 1816, he was shocked and saddened by the squalor in which he found the Indians living, and by the "great" mortality rate of the people—some 30 percent per year. (As late as 1837, it was reported that 60,000 North Bay native people fell victim to smallpox—carried in by one Mexican officer.) Their spirits were too often bent and broken, too, by the yoke of the industrious white man's culture. (Louis Choriz, who chronicled in watercolors von Kotzebue's expedition, noted, "I have never seen one laugh.") The missionaries, of course, were intent on making good frontier housewives out of the women, and prudent husbands and ranch hands out of the men—and God-fearing believers of them all. Those who tried to flee the mission were treated like criminals and often flogged and shackled. And, as von Kotzebue noted succinctly, both men and women were made to "labor hard." The ways of the generous and friendly "heathen" were thus erased and discarded, never mind they had sustained a people for thousands of years.

Although the missionaries did best of all in the new colony, these cultured European men led no easy lives. Believing sincerely in their calling, they had to seek out as many inhabitants of "heathendom" as they could and take on the hard task of saving their souls. They, too, had come with cattle and sheep and now turned to farming and ranching, with the Indians providing free labor. In time, many of the missions became successful ranchos producing most of the hides and tallow that were eventually traded in the bay area. (The Fathers were resourceful as well as practical. When they had no incense for their services, they were known to have the nearby soldiers fire their muskets so that the gun smoke could be used instead.)

As the two small settlements around the presidio and the mission took root, the place came to be known as Yerba Buena, for the good-smelling herb that grew in such places as the presidio itself. (You can still find this aromatic plant in the Strybing Arboretum's Garden of Fragrance in Golden Gate Park.)

At the turn of the century, this scene of "peaceful solitude," as one historian described it, began to liven up. By then, ship traffic in the Pacific was increasing, and Yerba Buena and Sausalito both offered snug harbors. Early in the 1800s, the Russians sailed into San Francisco Bay in search of sea otters. Camping on the Farallon Islands, they found a rich supply that by 1811 they had pretty well finished off. (In 1809, they took 2,000 of these beguiling, unfortunately valuable, creatures—most of them in the bay.) They had their own free labor supply—the Aleuts they had pressed into service in Alaska (and whose bidarkas, or kayaks, they brought along for efficient trapping). The whalers followed, and by 1826, so many were dropping anchor in Sausalito that it became known as El Puerto de los Balleneros—"whalers' harbor." Around this time, the hide and tallow deal-ers began to ply their trade. They sailed in loaded to the gills with needed goods, like floating department stores, and exchanged their cargos for the local products.

The first non-Spanish white settlers were few and far between. In 1813, a young Scot named Gilroy landed in Monterey Bay and set himself up about halfway between tiny Yerba Buena and not-much-larger Monterey. He did well enough to leave his name on a thriving town but contributed little to San Francisco's history. William Richardson, however, was another story. He sailed into San Fran-cisco Bay on the whaler *Orion* in 1822, when he was 26 years old. One look around and he decided to stay. (It is reported that his cap-tain let him go but was "furious.") Tall, blue-eyed, and "clipper built" (and a new face, to boot), he was welcomed into presidio soci-ety. In 1823, he converted to Catholicism, and two years later he married the beautiful Maria Antonio Martinez, eldest of the several beautiful daughters of Ignacio Martinez, commander of the presidio. Now William Antonio Richardson, he next renounced his English citizenship and pledged his alliance to Mexico, thereby completing the steps that other sons-in-law would take to become proper Cali-fornians.

For a time after his marriage, Richardson explored southern Cali-fornia. He then returned to San Francisco and was soon made cap-tain of the port. He proved to be one of the best pilots and traders around. By 1840, he had become Don Guillermo Antonio Richard-son, and his name was not included in that year's official list of "San Francisco Bay foreigners": he was no longer considered such.

In 1835, Richardson put up the first nonmilitary, nonmission home in Yerba Buena: it was a large tent, described as being "sup-ported by four redwood poles and covered by a ship's foresail." The next year, he received the first properly conveyed lot in the tiny town, and there he built his adobe Casa Grande, the largest house in Yerba Buena. It stood on the Calle de la Fundación (later DuPont Street, now Grant Avenue) between what are now Washington and Jackson streets and was the scene of many local events, both official and social. Thus Richardson was the first "civilian" settler of the place that would be San Francisco.

Despite all this, Richardson managed to acquire a land grant that encompassed most of southern Marin County, and in 1838 he moved his family to Sausalito. There he provided such good service to visiting ships—replenishing their food and water, and offering notable hospitality as well—that the new Yerba Buena customs officer complained that he was stealing business away.

Another early arrival to the San Francisco area was John Reed. By 1826 he had built himself a shelter in Sausalito and had initiated the first ferry service in the bay, rowing his passengers back and forth between Sausalito and Yerba Buena.

Jacob Leese came a few years later, married Rosalia, sister of General Mariano Vallejo, after completing the necessary steps of initiation, and fathered the first "civilian" child to be born in Yerba Buena—a daughter who was named for her mother. In 1836, Leese also got himself a lot on the Calle and built a house and store next to Richardson. These two men were the nucleus of the tiny, slow-growing town.

The year before William Richardson arrived in San Francisco Bay, Mexico had seceded from Spain, and in 1824 the country became a republic. A new era commenced. One of the first changes was the secularization of the missions, which was achieved during the mid-thirties. This made some of the richest lands available. Not only did lots in little Yerba Buena begin to go, but lush acreage was granted around the bay, in what would later be the Bay Area counties. Some of the land grants were enormous: Richardson had nearly 20,000 acres. One John Marsh (who became Juan Maria Marsh) acquired closer to 50,000 acres in 1837 in what is now the East Bay. This property was known as Los Meganos—"the dunes"—and had originally been granted to José Noriega. Marsh's stone house still stands on Marsh Creek Road near Brentwood.

A kind of halcyon lifestyle evolved on the great ranchos—for the rancheros, that is. (The Indians, cut loose to fend for themselves, and with no vestige of their former culture remaining, became cowboys where they could—they were the famed vaqueros—or semislaves on the ranchos; most were not so "fortunate.") The sunny days of living leisurely and continually partying—dancing and feasting—became renowned, as did the hospitality the rancheros dispensed. *"Mi casa es su casa"*—"my house is your house"—was their courteous greeting—which some of the Yankees later took literally.

Meanwhile, Mexico found it harder and harder to support its northern colonies. At the same time, the young United States was inching westward. By 1835, San Francisco Bay had become well enough known to tempt President Andrew Jackson to offer Mexico a half million dollars for it (and the rest of northern California); ten years later, President James K. Polk upped the offer to $40 million—80 times as much. Needless to say, neither offer was accepted. But during the 1840s more and more Americans began to find their way west. Once there, some went through the formalities of getting land grants, some bought parts of established ranchos, and some just squatted. (Juan Maria Marsh was murdered by squatters on his land.) Word of California and its colonies spread more and more. Richard Henry Dana had visited the bay in 1835 (and found both the presidio and the Mission Dolores in a wretched state) and in 1840 published his famous *Two Years Before the Mast*. Soon afterward, Captain John C. Frémont hit town and gave the Golden Gate its name (inspired by Istanbul's Golden Horn). About the same time, a man named John Augustus Sutter acquired land near Sacramento and founded New Helvetia, a kind of beneficent personal domain.

It was Frémont who helped instigate the Bear Flag Revolt, a smallish explosion of American patriotism and colonialism. He and his band of adventurers joined with a handful of American settlers led by Robert B. Semple (who later founded Benicia) and William B. Ide (whose adobe is now a state historical park at Red Bluff) to evict General Mariano Vallejo, Mexican governor of Alta California, from his fort in Sonoma. They imprisoned this man who had provided the Yankees with much generous hospitality and, on June 14, 1846, hoisted a somewhat bedraggled flag (complete with grizzly bear) to proclaim the founding of the California Republic.

Meanwhile, a more official war finally erupted between Mexico and the United States, and, at eight o'clock on the morning of July 9, 1846, the American flag was properly raised over the Presidio of Yerba Buena. Captain John B. Montgomery, on orders of Commodore John S. Sloat, officiated at the ceremony while his ship, the *Portsmouth*, stood offshore. Two days before, he had rung up the flag in Monterey, and soon afterward it was floating in Sacramento, San Jose, and Sonoma. Alta California was on its way to becoming a territory of the United States, which it did in 1848; two years after that, it became a state. (Montgomery and Sloat bequeathed their names to important San Francisco streets, and the pleasant plaza in dusty Yerba Buena became Portsmouth Square, and still is.)

In 1847, the population of the San Francisco Bay Area stood at somewhere near 500, thanks to the arrival of a Mormon party of over 200 people a year earlier. At that time, the town of Yerba Buena boasted a "large frame building" tenanted by the Hudson Bay Company, a couple of other stores, a billiard room and a bar, a blacksmith's shop, a few houses, and other outbuildings, described by Lieutenant Charles Wilkes a few years earlier as "few in number [and] also far between." Sam Brannan, the Mormons' flamboyant leader, had already established himself as Yerba Buena's most aggressive and outspoken citizen, having launched the *California Star* in January 1847. (This was the town's first newspaper and California's second.) He had fought the change of name decreed by alcalde (mayor) Lieutenant Washington A. Bartlett that same month, but he had not prevailed, and Yerba Buena was now known as San Francisco. (See Solano County.) No one in that windy, sand-blown, rechristened little harbor town dreamed that a man named James Marshall would, on January 24, 1848, stoop to pick up a nugget of gold in John Sutter's millrace and so change the history of California and make famous worldwide the name of San Francisco. Father Font, long since departed, might have been pleased.

The impact of the gold rush on San Francisco is hard to imagine. From a small, sleepy little town it turned overnight into a jam-packed, noisy, dirty, bustling tent-and-shanty city, with canvas flapping in the windy fog and sand cut loose from the new-carved streets gusting into everybody's eyes. Ships by the hundred crowded the harbor, which a few months before had held only a half dozen vessels or less. Many vessels rocked empty on the waves, the entire crew gone with the passengers on the mad search for El Dorado. (The several hundred abandoned ships served many useful purposes: one was pressed into service for the city's first jail; many others were used for landfill, and some were even converted into buildings.)

People poured through the Golden Gate, dazed and ecstatic to set foot on solid ground, especially after a four-to-eight-month, often turbulent voyage from the East Coast, or a fever-ridden sickening trip across the Isthmus of Panama and then six to eight weeks on the tumultuous sea. Doctors, lawyers, cowhands, carpenters, cooks, shopkeepers, poets, thieves, madams, aristocrats, beggars—the city made room for them all. (Until 1880, by far the majority were men; early on, a French visitor noted the high cost of spending the night with "a woman of easy virtue"—as much as $400. He then added succinctly that there were a few honest women in San Francisco, "but not very many.") They had come from all over the world: from the East Coast of the United States; from Germany, France, England,

Ireland, Spain, and Mexico; from Peru and Chile, Hawaii, Australia, and China. They were people of every race and every color. By 1850, half of the 200,000 people who had flooded California in search of gold were stretching the seams of San Francisco.

The city soon had more than its share of characters. There was Sam Brannan, who managed to ride the great tide of the gold rush with the expertise of a Hawaiian surfer. Sometimes called the Paul Revere of the Gold Rush, he was the one who yelled the news to the world, running through Portsmouth Square with a bottle of nuggets in one hand and his fancy beaver hat in the other (he was a great dandy), screaming, "Gold! Gold! Gold from the American River!" (This was after he had thoughtfully stocked a store at Sutter's Fort with tents, pickaxes, shovels, and other mining requisites, so the rumor went.)

Brannan had already left the Mormon church after being accused of funneling church funds into his own pockets. Challenged by a furious Brigham Young to give an accounting, he replied that he would be happy to do so—when the Lord signed the request. He soon became one of the wealthiest, most influential—and loudest—men in the new San Francisco. A prudent gambler, he was also a shrewd real estate dealer, the owner of a flour mill, the publisher of the city's leading newspaper, and, later, a founder of a telegraph company and an express firm. His fortune was said to have totaled $5 million.

Brannan was the principal organizer and president of San Francisco's first Vigilante Committee in June 1851. He helped to hang one John Jenkins—an unfortunate and unsuccessful thief who tried to steal a safe and got caught—in Portsmouth Square. He was not above taking the law into his own hands and once orated, "We are the mayor and the recorder. We are the hangman and the law." As his biographer, Josiah Royce, put it: "Mr. Sam Brannan, the lion-hearted, [was] a man always in love with shedding the blood of the wicked."

As time went on, Brannan's gifts seem to have failed him. He tried to make a Saratoga out of hot springs in Napa County north of San Francisco, which he dubbed Calistoga, but he lost the proverbial shirt on this endeavor. (Sam Brannan once explained how he came by the name of Calistoga: "I was saying . . . 'Someday, I'll make this place the Saratoga of California,' but my tongue slipped and what I said was, 'I'll make this place the Calistoga of Sarafornia.' " And so the name has remained.) Others of his investments went sour, and

Brannan turned to drink. He died in Escondido in 1889. Brannan
Street is his memorial in San Francisco. (Originally, it was only two
blocks long and partly underwater.) For several years, ships unloaded
their passengers (many of whom were Chinese) and their cargos
directly onto it.

Another noteworthy character was Henry ("Honest Harry")
Meiggs. Born in New York's Catskill country, he came to San Francisco with his family in July 1849, just after his thirty-eighth birth-
day. He was blond, blue-eyed, culture loving, and evidently loaded
with charisma. He was also a clever businessman and had the fore-
sight to bring with him some $50,000 of lumber, which he promptly
sold at a pretty profit. During the next five years he built up a splendid fortune (he was known as "the richest man on the coast"),
became one of the city's leading socialites and civic leaders, and was
elected to the city council.

A lumberman at heart, his first business venture was to build a
lumber mill. Soon he was involved in the logging off of the Contra
Costa redwoods. Next he turned to the forests around Bolinas. When
these were finished and San Francisco and most of the structures his
redwoods had built went up in flames, Meiggs found an untapped
supply of redwoods in Mendocino.

With some of his lumber, he constructed a 2,000-foot-long wharf
to dock ships and to accommodate their crews. (Meiggs' Wharf, as it
was known, is now Fisherman's Wharf.) And, as a member of the
city council, he managed to get the city to build streets to serve his
new enterprise. This was the beginning of North Beach.

Generous and public spirited, so all of San Francisco thought,
Honest Harry was enormously popular and garnered high accolades
for building a music hall, promoting concerts, and donating a fine
organ to Trinity Church.

He may have been the richest man on the coast, but the 1853–
1854 crash wiped him out. Abysmally in debt (to the tune, it was
later said, of having to pay $30,000–$40,000 interest a month), he
kept his bankruptcy to himself. And, being a resourceful fellow, he
turned to the city's till, forging municipal warrants or promissory
notes. Kindly historians believe that he did this to pay back money
borrowed from his friends. Whatever his motives, he managed to
help himself to an estimated $365,000 of the city's money before he
fled San Francisco with his family under cover of darkness on September 24, 1854. An angry crowd is said to have sailed after him

down the bay, screaming imprecations as the distance widened between his ship and theirs.

Meiggs took with him the evidence of his thievery, the proceedings of the board of aldermen from 1850 to 1854, and the city never recovered these valuable papers. He went on to a new life in Peru, recouped his fortune, helped to beautify the city of Lima, and built an 800-mile railroad, importing Sonoma redwood for its ties, to the delight of that county's entrepreneurs. Before he died in 1877, he is said to have tried to make restitution, sending money even to his enemies, and also to St. Luke's Church in the Catskills.

And then there was James Lick, an eccentric piano tuner from Pennsylvania who managed to arrive in San Francisco just 17 days before gold was discovered. He parlayed a few thousand dollars into millions, largely through his expert real estate dealings. Although he lived like a pauper, he built one of the city's first plush hotels, and he left a home in San Jose that still stands. When he died, still single, he left his millions to a variety of good causes: among others, for the establishment of the observatory on Mount Hamilton that bears his name; for a school of mechanical arts; for public baths; for the Mechanics' Institute; and for a statue of Francis Scott Key, which still stands in Golden Gate Park.

Although Bayard Taylor, the *New York Tribune* reporter who captured so much of the gold rush spirit in his early writings, observed that "the rashest speculators were the most fortunate," this did not always hold true. Joshua Abraham Norton was a case in point. Norton came to San Francisco from South Africa in 1849 and in four years built up a modest fortune. In 1853, however, he wagered all of it on an effort to corner the rice market (cornering the market was a popular form of speculation), and when this failed, he evidently lost his mind and left town. When he returned a few months later, he presented himself to the *San Francisco Bulletin* as the "Emperor of the United States and Protector of Mexico" and issued the first of what would be a long line of proclamations (which were often witty and sometimes wise). The *Bulletin* ran his story straight, and in a city noted for its tolerance of the different and even the absurd, Norton was accepted at face value.

For the next 27 years, the Emperor Norton was the darling of just about everybody in town. He was a familiar sight on city streets, proceeding in a dignified manner with his two faithful dogs, Lazarus and Bummer, always at his heels. Decked out in royal (epauletted) finery that local tailors had supplied, he honored the local bars with his presence and accepted the free lunches as his due. The town's business fathers sat him down at their board meetings and listened to him gravely. As the historian Tom Cole puts it, "He gave good value for the newspaper space, the free lunches, and the self-conscious generosity of his subjects."

He died in 1880, the year that his privately printed promissory notes—honored everywhere—came due. He was given a fittingly royal funeral, and more than 10,000 of his grieving subjects turned out to mourn his passing. Norton was one of San Francisco's nicest folk heroes; the city's newspapers have rarely had such good local copy since.

By 1853, San Francisco had grown to be what Taylor described as "an actual metropolis." It was already noted for its wonderfully high living. A contemporary writer, Hinton Helper, itemized some of its virtues as "purer liquors, better seegars, finer tobaccos, truer guns and pistols, larger dirks and bowie knives, and prettier cortezans." San Francisco was also enamored of things cultural, especially the theatre. Lola Montez and, later, Lotta Crabtree were particular favorites and played to standing room only when they came to town. (Lotta's Fountain, a bequest of the actress, who died in 1924, can still be seen on the corner of Kearny and Market streets: see Geary Walk 1.) The city prided itself on its excellent restaurants, such as Delmonico's and the Old Poodle Dog, and the number of places where liquor could be bought was noteworthy: that year, the *Christian Advocate* counted 573. With all of its boomtown attributes, however, San Francisco was evolving a solid core of respectable citizens who could afford to live in "well-built houses," although many still occupied flimsy and frigid tents that were no match for the bone-chilling winds and fogs.

The year 1853 ushered in some momentous changes. The seemingly inexhaustible cascade of gold from the Mother Lode was at last beginning to dry up; in that one year the volume shrank $30 million. People stopped pouring into California. Real estate values plunged. One of San Francisco's most respected banks closed its doors. Merchants were suddenly confronted with slow sales and stacks of unsold goods.

Young San Francisco had never been the safest place to live. (If the hoodlums didn't get you, Sam Brannan might.) Among other forms of violent death—such as hanging—dueling was still considered in order. By 1856, two prominent San Franciscans—lawyer George T. Hume and state senator W. J. Ferguson—had both gone to their fate on the field of honor. (As late as 1859, California's United States Senator David D. Broderick—already the survivor of an earlier duel when his life was saved by a heavy pocketwatch—was mortally wounded at Lake Merced in a duel with California Chief Justice David Terry and died soon after at Fort Mason.) But that year, with crime on the increase, two blatant murders shocked San Franciscans to the core. Charles Cora, a professional gambler, shot down United States Marshall William R. Richardson (no relation to Guillermo) "in cold blood" over an unkind comment about his girlfriend. And an irate city councilman, James P. Casey, fired his gun into the curmudgeon editor of the *Evening Bulletin,* James King of William, as he sat at his desk—for King's exposure of him as an ex-convict.

Reenter the Vigilantes, this time under William Tell Coleman (Sam Brannan was along), and this time 5,000 men strong. They strung up Cora and Casey after a cursory "secret" trial and gave notice to the town's wrongdoers that they could expect no better. (The Vigilantes were last heard from on July 18, 1856, when they marched in a final, triumphant parade as a prelude to disbanding.)

From the time of the gold rush, California—especially San Francisco, which was, of course, the state's business and population center—had been a kind friend of labor. Indeed, as the ill-fated David D. Broderick pronounced in his maiden speech before the United States Senate in 1858, "There is no state in the Union, no place on earth, where labor is so honored and so well regarded." Printers had organized in San Francisco as early as 1850. And by 1856 teamsters, draymen, lightermen, riggers, stevedores, bakers, bricklayers, caulkers, carpenters, brickmasons, blacksmiths, plasterers, shipwrights, and, by no means least, musicians all had banded into infant unions. With an Eight Hour League and insistence on $16 a day (the value of an ounce of gold), these artisans and skilled workingmen—many of whom were European born and already familiar with the emergence of labor as a force to be reckoned with—had established high standards of work and high rewards for themselves. They had also set the stage for what would prove to be the phenomenal growth of the labor movement.

As the 1850s drew to a close, San Francisco's population had shaken down to around 50,000 souls, and the city had become as respectable as it would ever be, more like an eastern seaboard port than a budding Wild West metropolis. The times had slowed down, and fortunes were declining. But 1859 changed all that. Once again, the city's streets were jammed with would-be miners eager to stake their claims and walk away with their millions. Only this time, it was not gold they were after, but silver. And this time it was not Placerville they were headed for, but Virginia City, the Queen of the Comstock.

As it turned out, the great silver rush was very different from the storied gold rush of the decade before. The silver did not lie around on the ground or in streambeds waiting to be picked up. It had to be smelted out of a heavy blue muck that comprised a good part of Sun Mountain (later Mount Davidson) in what is now Nevada. When someone looked twice at this strange mud and decided to have it assayed, a Grass Valley assayist estimated that it would yield almost $4,000 of the precious metal per ton.

What was needed here was obviously not pans and pickaxes nor "windy no gooders" like Henry T. P. Comstock, who let his stake in the world's richest silver mine slip out of his hands. What was needed was competent mining engineers, mechanized mining equipment to build the tunnels that would honeycomb Sun Mountain (and celebrate Adolph Sutro's engineering genius), foundries to extract the ore—and, more than anything else, capital. There proved to be no shortage of any of these. A few wily capitalists (the Rothschilds among them) made Croesuses out of themselves during the next couple of decades. And, before it was all over, an estimated half billion dollars worth of silver was wrung out of the Comstock lode.

During this period, an emerging labor movement began to gain strength and momentum. Small unions began to consolidate into larger councils and federations. (By 1901, San Francisco's City Front Federation was being called the most effective trade union in the country.) The early labor leaders were canny as well as dedicated. When, struck by boilermakers and molders in 1864, iron works employers tried to import strikebreakers from the East Coast, paying their way west, members of the striking unions met the strikebreakers in Panama, convinced them of the rightness of their cause, and escorted them into San Francisco as fellow union members.

As had happened during the gold rush, San Francisco became the operating headquarters for the new mining endeavors. (Virginia City was considered its "essential suburb.") And, as they had a decade earlier, new characters emerged to leave their names in the history of the time. One of the most colorful was William C. (Billy) Ralston, who was known by his contemporaries as "California's great empire builder" and "the financial autocrat of the Pacific." (More recently, historian Tom Cole epitomized him as "San Francisco's all time No. 1 mover and shaker.")

A Mississippi river hand in his youth, Ralston had managed to come west as a (one-time) captain of a steamship that sailed from Panama to California in service of the forty-niners. Good-looking, Scotch-Irish, and with a brilliant streak of financial savvy, he was, like the miners, seeking his fortune. He decided to settle in San Francisco in the mid-1850s and go into business. With one partner, M. O. Mills, he founded the Bank of California. With another, William Sharon—"a little man with little black beady eyes"—he set out to buy up a controlling share of the Comstock. (This was accomplished in part by offering loans with rock-bottom interest rates to the miners and then picking up their stock when they defaulted, as many did.) Before his career was over, Ralston also owned woolen mills, a carriage factory, a furniture factory, and a watchmaking business. For a while, everything he touched seemed to turn to, well, if not gold, silver.

Ralston thought big. He bought for his bride, San Francisco belle Lizzy Fry, a gorgeous estate in Belmont (south of the city), landscaped it with fabulous gardens, and built her a palatial 80-room mansion with stables paneled with mahogany inlaid with mother-of-pearl. The harnesses of his horses were mounted in silver.

Ralston was renowned for never asking the price of anything. When he built the California Theatre, he is said to have instructed his architects to find out the size of the largest theatre in the country, and to make his "ten feet bigger." He built one luxury hotel for the city, and then a second—the Palace—perhaps his most fitting monument, although it burned in the 1906 fire. The Palace occupied 2½ acres and, with its 7,000 bay windows, was the largest hotel in any American city. Ralston saw to it that it had its own water supply—four wells—and that it was sumptuously furnished. He imported 30,000 pieces of French china and purchased Irish linens by the ton. For furniture, he induced New York's elegant W. and J. Sloane to open a San Francisco branch. (It was one of San Francisco's landmark stores for well over a century.) Ralston even had a 100-piece solid-gold service made for his hostelry.

A civic leader, Ralston was one of the prime movers behind the establishment of Golden Gate Park. He also promoted the transcontinental railroad, which was completed in 1869. He was convinced that the railroad would bring business and commerce to his beloved city. Ralston, for all his grand ideas, was a modest man, the story goes. He declined the honor of having a new Central Valley community given his name. Instead, it was called Modesto—still in his honor.

Unfortunately, the railroad, which stopped short of the Bay Area, in Sacramento, proved to be no bonanza for San Francisco, although it did make enormously wealthy—and powerful—business moguls out of Charles Crocker, Mark Hopkins, Collis Huntington, and Leland Stanford, whose empire was dubbed The Octopus and whose names still ring in the city. While the cross-country trains hauled in more and more goods manufactured in the East, they brought little business with them. In 1869, San Francisco went into another depression.

This was just the beginning of the end for Billy Ralston. Five years later, four shrewd Irishmen who came to be known as the Bonanza Kings (John W. Mackey, William O'Brien, James Fair, and James Flood) gained control of what proved unexpectedly to be one of the richest of all the Comstock properties: they made the proverbial millions. Meantime, Ralston's Comstock holdings were running out. Deeply in debt—to his bank as well as to other creditors—Ralston managed to forestall one run on the Bank of California, but not a terrible second. After a hasty meeting of the bank's directors on the morning of August 27, 1875, Ralston was asked to resign. He did, and then, being a regular swimmer in the bay, he took his final—and fatal—swim, from present-day Aquatic Park. Whether he deliberately gave himself up to the sea or was the victim of a stroke was never ascertained. It was just two months later that his fabulous Palace Hotel opened its doors, and carriages of San Francisco's elite drove into its seven-story-high atrium to discharge the friends—and foes—of the departed Billy Ralston for an evening of impressive revelry at which "the process of absorption went gaily forward until near midnight."

William Sharon died ten years later. He had built a mansion on Nob Hill that boasted the first hydraulic elevator on the West Coast and whose window drapes were supposed to have cost $2,000 a window. Later a United States senator from Nevada, he passed away in the midst of a scandal that titillated the press for over two years.

Miss Sarah Althea Hill—the "Rose of Sharon," of course—was the lady involved, and although she failed to prove her claim that Sharon had married her, she married the same David Terry who had dispatched Senator David Broderick with a bullet from his dueling pistol some 16 years before.

So much of San Francisco has been paved over, built on, or deliberately gardened that it is hard to picture the way it was when it was being settled. Then, there were sand dunes everywhere, downtown as well as in the "Outside Lands"—the northern and western parts of the city (which were owned by the state until 1903). There were, of course, the many and precipitous rocky hills. And there were streams and ponds and marshes. This landscape dictated where the city first grew—on the relatively flat, accessible places—but not how, and the good old grid pattern of streets slowly emerged.

The streets themselves were dreadful. The first paving was planks. (The first direct route between Yerba Buena and the Mission Dolores was a planked toll road—25 cents per horse was the charge—with a pontoon bridge across Seventh Street.) As time went on, basalt squares replaced the planks, but they were not much better. Everybody swept dirt and sand between the cracks, and when the winds came, the dirt and sand blew out in clouds, giving the city a billowy appearance. Cobbles were the next step in pavements, but they were hard on the feet of paraders—and parades were a favorite pastime—and of horses.

Horse-drawn vehicles, of course, were what moved people around. There were buckboards, victorias, and carriages of all kinds, and until the late 1870s, the city's traffic—heavy much of the time—was largely powered by the "hay burners." (There were a couple of steam locomotives that clattered along Market Street, belching coal dust and smoke, and preceded by a man on horseback, ringing a bell loudly and yelling, "Look out for the train!")

The first public conveyances went into service in the early 1850s, and tracks were soon being laid for horse-drawn streetcars. Ponds had to be filled and sand dunes sliced through—and then the sand had to be continuously shoveled off the tracks. Some of the cars were marvels; one line (to the enormously popular Woodward Gardens, a sort of super amusement park and zoo on Misson at Fourteenth Street) had a Street Palace, an elegantly furnished car with murals that was strictly for "ladies"; "disgusting pipe or cigar smoking" was not allowed, nor were unescorted gentlemen. Then there were the "balloon cars," oval shaped and with a kind of built-in swivel that enabled the car to be pivoted around and obviated the need of hitching and unhitching the horses. Some cars were powered by one horse, others by two or more, and it was not uncommon on hills for extra horses to be added, or even for passengers to get out and walk to lighten the load.

Horses had a hard time of it and were frequently injured, especially on the steep cobbled hills when it was wet. It is said that Andrew S. Hallidie, the ex-miner and expert cable-maker, witnessed a particularly nasty accident on a rainy day, when two horses pulling a load of 40 people slipped and were dragged backward down a hill. This determined Hallidie to make his dream of a mechanical cable car a reality. He succeeded, and on August 1, 1873, his miraculous invention ran up Clay Street from Kearny to Powell, and then back down.

That year, San Francisco had eight different private horsecar companies vying to transport the city's 188,000 people over 8 miles of single track. Hallidie's Clay Street Hill Cable Car Company signaled the beginning of the end for the horse-drawn cars. It also signaled the opening up to development of large areas of the city that had previously been inaccessible. Leland Stanford, the ex-merchant who became a railroad tycoon, California's governor, and builder of a fine mansion on Nob Hill, promptly organized a group of his wealthy neighbors to form the California Street Cable Car Company for door-to-door service to their Montgomery Street businesses. Soon more tracks were laid into the city's outskirts—to the increasingly popular Golden Gate Park and to other parts of the "Outside Lands." The cable cars proved to be not only efficient for their time and place, but fun to ride. Among the early thrills was the unforgettable trip down Fillmore Street from Broadway to Lombard (a 24-degree slope); the weight of the descending car was used to pull another car up the hill, and it was said to be a moment of great excitement when the two cars passed.

As the Victorian era unfolded into full flower during the last decades of the 1800s, life in San Francisco continued on its upward spiral. Despite the bust of the Comstock lode in the late 1870s and periods of depression and hard times, the city continued to grow: it added more than 100,000 people to its population to top 300,000 by the turn of the century.

For the handful of shrewd—or lucky—men who struck it rich in the gold or silver mines, or the (perhaps more lucrative) Southern Pacific Railroad, the century's last decades were years of incredibly ostentatious wealth. In a kind of mad game, the newly minted multi-millionaires—some erstwhile bartenders, grocers, or shopkeepers—vied with one another to see who could spend the most money in the most spectacular way. They spared no expense for their enormous 60-or-more-room dwellings: when Crocker forked up $2 million for his mansion, Hopkins produced $3 million for his—and their dollars were worth perhaps 20 times as much as ours. Flood's residence on Nob Hill took two years to complete and was set off by a $60,000 handwrought bronze fence around the entire property. Fine horses were very much a status symbol: James Ben Ali Haggin built not only a palatial house but stables so sumptuous he entertained in them. Stanford had statues of his horses—he thought nothing of paying $500 for one—placed on their graves. (See San Mateo and Santa Clara Counties.)

These men sought out the most expert and expensive architects to make their dream houses come true, and the tycoons, along with their wives, did not lack in imagination. The Floods and the Crockers, the Haggins and the Hopkinses, the Fairs, Sharons, and Stanfords—a partial listing—all added to the marvelous and monumental outcroppings atop Nob Hill. Wood was specially painted to suggest marble: columns, porticoes, towers, turrets, and special statuary (and for the interiors, fine art and ready-made libraries) were indulged in a burst of instant culture.

Edgar Kahn, in his *Cable Car Days,* describes the gingerbread, "villa," and wedding cake creations delicately as "belonging to no one style of architecture . . . [but] having a distinctive individuality in keeping with the influence and personality of their owners." Architect Willis Polk was not as kind: he dubbed the Crocker house, for example, "the delirium of a wood carver."

The wives were just as eager to outdo one another in showing off their gorgeous décolletages and their jewelry. Society writers titillated their readers with descriptions of who wore what and delighted in detailing the diamond tiaras, the blazing 2-inch-wide "dog collars" of pearls and diamonds, and the costly gems on hands that had recently been much more at home in washtubs.

More modest San Franciscans contented themselves with a simpler life. They built themselves less spectacular—but still wonderful—Italianate and Victorian houses, choosing their ready-made frosting, curlicues, and spindles from mail-order catalogues, and indulging their taste for round towers, arched windows, bays, columns, and porticoes. They crowded their houses together on the city's standard 25- by 75-foot (or 100-foot) lots, and contented themselves with handkerchief-size backyard gardens. (One, an undertaker by the name of Nicholas Young, made the mistake of choosing a lot on Nob Hill before the mass influx of millionaires. His lot stood in the way of Charles Crocker, who wanted to acquire an entire block for his estate: when Young refused to sell, Crocker erected a 40-foot-high spite fence around three sides of the poor man's property, effectively consigning him to living inside a well of darkness.)

Many of San Francisco's wealthy Victorians carried on the city's tradition of civic-mindedness. Adolph Sutro was one. A Prussian businessman, entrepreneur, and engineer, he succeeded in building a remarkable tunnel through the Comstock lode (to drain the mines and protect the miners) and was clever enough to sell the tunnel just before the silver ran out. He chose the northwest corner of the city, Sutro Heights, for his magnificent estate, which was noted especially for its gardens. He designed and built an extraordinary complex of baths with six tanks of salt water for swimming in various temperatures, an immense dome of stained glass, and lush tropical flora and fountains, veritably "California's Tropical Garden." He also engineered a funicular railroad around Land's End. Then, believing that all San Franciscans should be able to enjoy Ocean Beach as well as these "amenities," he managed to get a 5-cent fare for the trolley that ran the length of Geary Boulevard. This, incidentally, made the Cliff House—which he also happened to own—accessible. Along with combining his business with popular pleasures, he instituted, on California's first Arbor Day, a tree-planting program for which he provided 45,000 seedlings for schoolchildren to plant. Along with the estimated 250,000 trees he planted on his own properties, he left the city a fine heritage of (mostly Monterey pine and cypress) forests. Some of Sutro's forests still stand. Sutro left his name on a city park, all that remains of his estate, and even on a mountain. (See GGNRA Walk 2.)

Leland Stanford also left lasting legacies. He founded the university that bears his name, memorializing a son who died at 15. He became governor of California early on and during his time in office had the forethought to wrest San Francisco's piers out of the hands of the "robber barons" who owned them and to convey them to the state. Traffic on the high seas was flourishing in those years, and San Francisco—with the only publicly owned docks on the West Coast—became known as the Queen Port of the Pacific. By 1890, it had become the eighth-largest city in the United States.

It was closer to number one when it came to its legendary high living. The Palace Hotel's great bar—with its 30 bartenders—was a popular place to gather. Fine restaurants proliferated: some, such as Jack's, Sam's, and Maye's Oyster House, are still going strong. The Barbary Coast flourished, and added to it there were nests of opium-shrouded vice in mysterious Chinatown.

During this period, the written word flourished in San Francisco in several forms. San Francisco is said to have had more newspapers than any other American city in the 1860s. William Randolph Hearst, son of another Comstock tycoon, established his "Monarch of the Dailies," the *San Francisco Examiner,* and at first was an articulate champion of liberal causes. The de Young brothers, M.H. and Charles, began publishing the *San Francisco Chronicle,* another crusading daily newspaper. (You will find both of these papers on today's newsstands.) In unhappy city tradition, Charles de Young was killed by the son of a Workingman's Party candidate whom the *Chronicle* had criticized, and M.H. nearly suffered the same fate (but managed to survive) a few years later at the hands of a furiously insulted sugar baron, Adolph Spreckels. A Scottish shepherd named John Muir fell in love with the Sierra Nevada, and his eloquent prose awakened two United States presidents—Grover Cleveland and Theodore Roosevelt—and the whole country to the beauties and significance of the natural world. His legacy: Yosemite National Park and the Sierra Club, both of which he fathered. Jack London enchanted readers with his gift for storytelling. And Hubert Howe Bancroft—who may not have been much of a writer himself—invented his extraordinary literary "factory," where he paid a battery of scribes to turn out a massive history of the West that was called "the greatest . . . since Thucydides."

The city stayed afloat during the great depression of 1893 and celebrated its survival in 1894 with a Midwinter Exposition in Golden Gate Park that infuriated its "resident genius," John McLaren. It almost went under a few years later during a pioneer general strike in 1901. Having helped launch the labor movement, San Francisco was an obvious arena for the movement to flex its muscles. This strike, started by railroad employees, eventually idled thousands of sympathetic workers and left some 200 ships untended in the bay. Governor Henry T. Gage threatened to call out the National Guard and place the city under military law before the strikers made their point.

For all the city prided itself on its cosmopolitan tolerance and liberal outlook, in the later 1800s it indulged itself in a sorry outburst of racism. Part of the rancor felt against its Celestials—as the Chinese were known—stemmed from times of unemployment when, with jobs scarce and money short, the Chinese would work for almost any wage and for unlimited hours. Part of it may have stemmed, too, from an irrational fear of the alien and unknown culture that was thriving in the heart of the city. But people like Dennis Kearney (for whom the downtown street is not named), a silver-tongued orator who helped establish the Workingman's Party, were among the first to rail against the exotic Chinese. Known as the Cicero of the Sandlots, Kearney was thick in the fight for restrictive and exclusionary immigration laws (which, shamefully, were passed) and for the vindictive action that landed many innocent (and voteless) Chinese in jail, where it was a routine humiliation to cut off the men's pigtails.

With all its faults, however, San Francisco was then, as always, a city of culture where drama and art and music thrived. Such performers as Enrico Caruso and John Barrymore could be sure of sold-out theatres and enthusiastic audiences. As it happened, both of these performers were in town that momentous April 18, 1906—just a few years after Queen Victoria had died and a new century had gotten under way. Caruso had sung the role of Don José in Bizet's *Carmen* the night before and, a guest in the sumptuous Palace Hotel, was enjoying the sleep of a satisfied artist when the earth went into one of its most massive convulsions—an earthquake later estimated to have been at least 8.3 on the Richter scale (which had not yet been invented). History has it that when Caruso picked himself up, he found he had lost his voice. When finally able to speak, the shaken tenor declared, "I never come back to this city!" He was later seen aboard a garbage wagon heading for Golden Gate Park. And true to his word, he never sang in San Francisco again. (It is not reported what Barrymore, said to have been ensconced in a hotel room with an unknown inamorata and several bottles of champagne, remarked; he may have slept through the entire great event.)

Caruso and Barrymore survived the monumental shake, but more (possibly many more) than 700 others perished as the city shuddered and then went up in flames. Among those who were lost was the city's fire chief, Dennis T. Sullivan, who had been trying unsuccessfully for years to get the city to upgrade an obsolete fire department.

Whether any fire department, no matter how well equipped, could have stopped the fire storm that engulfed the shaken city is moot. As it was, some 28,000 buildings were destroyed (including Crocker's mansion, his spite fence, and Young's house). In the hours between 5:15 A.M. of April 18 and 3:00 P.M. of the following day, an estimated $444 million in damage was done—80 percent of it caused by fire. Most of downtown was devastated, and of Nob Hill's magnificent mansions, only James Flood's survived. It is today the Pacific Union Club on the corner of Mason and California streets: the bronze fence still stands as well, a memento of a bygone time.

Around the turn of the century, San Francisco's city fathers had been intrigued with the "city beautiful" idea, then popular throughout the country, and they had employed city planner and designer Daniel ("Make no little plans") Burnham to come up with blueprints for an ideal San Francisco. Burnham's imaginative master plan—produced after two years of studying the city from a cottage on Twin Peaks—was in hand at the time of the 1906 holocaust, but the golden opportunity to take advantage of it was lost as the city's business community rushed to rebuild "while the ruins were still smoking," as a contemporary writer put it. In less than three years, San Francisco was celebrating its "instant city" rebirth—and the pattern of city streets was locked into its original mundane grid. Still, by 1909, the downtown area could boast millions of dollars worth of new steel-frame and concrete-reinforced buildings, and most of the nearly 30,000 buildings destroyed in the quake and fire had been replaced. What better way to celebrate this extraordinary Phoenix-from-the-ashes feat than with an international exposition?

As early as 1904 the city had begun laying the ground for being the official site for a world's fair to celebrate the completion of the Panama Canal—a logical enough move since so many early San Franciscans had reached their mecca via Panama. The canal was scheduled to be finished in 1915, and in 1910 the city won out: the state legislature and the United States Congress both gave their blessings to a Panama Pacific International Exposition in San Francisco, and $4 million of stock for the great event was sold out almost as quickly as it was issued. Plans got under way forthwith: hotels (including the Clift) started building, and a good part of the city's northern shore was soon being filled to provide space for the fairgrounds. (Coincidentally the city launched its symphony orchestra under Henry Hadley—another great event for the culturally minded.) A fairyland of pavilions, including the Tower of Jewels— with 100,000 hand-polished mirror-backed glass jewels—and the Palace of Fine Arts, was created for what turned out to be one of the world's all-time most successful expositions. The buildings, however, were constructed for only temporary use, and when the fair closed on December 4, 1915, after a smashing nine months' run, all but one were demolished and so lost to posterity. The Palace of Fine Arts, designed by Bernard Maybeck as a monument to the "mortality of grandeur," was just too beautiful to tear down and was restored a half century later. (See GGNRA Walk 2.) Most of the exposition grounds were cleared and subdivided for choice residential lots, and the city sold them for a tidy profit. The area became the Marina district, and the yacht harbor and the Marina Green became cherished city amenities. (A late-afternoon stroll along Marina Boulevard can be a particular pleasure during December when boat riggings and picture windows are festive with Christmas lights and decorations.)

Being the Queen City of the Pacific Coast, San Francisco was not surprisingly a goal for many aviators in their pioneering flights during the late teens and early twenties. In 1917, Katherine Stinson made a record long-distance nonstop flight of 619 miles from San Diego to San Francisco; it took her 9 hours and 10 minutes. Two years later, after the trauma of the war that was to make the world safe for democracy, the Presidio dedicated Crissy Field as the official army airport (it would serve as this for nearly two decades). In 1920, ten army planes made the first transcontinental group flight from New York to Crissy Field and back. The following year, the first transcontinental airmail flight from New York was completed at Crissy Field. Soon civilian airmail pilots were flying regularly between San Francisco and New York: they thought they were doing well when their flight time was 34 hours.

It was during the second decade of the twentieth century that two events set back the cause of the labor movement and sharpened the growing differences between employers and union members: one was the 1910 bombing of the *Los Angeles Times*, when 21 people were killed; the second was the Preparedness Day Parade disaster in San Francisco, when 10 were killed by a bomb on July 22, 1916, as they marched down Market Street to the Ferry Building in a labor demonstration. The ensuing incarceration of labor leader Tom Mooney became a cause célèbre that lasted until he was finally released from prison more than two decades later.

In 1927, at the height of the Roaring Twenties, San Francisco and the country were basking in prosperity and good times, and the city was basking under the leadership of its perennial good-time mayor, "Sunny Jim" Rolph, who wore his polished cowboy boots on every occasion, even when he dressed up in baseball mufti to throw out the first ball of the San Francisco Seals' season. That year, with air traffic sufficient to warrant the opening of an official municipal airport, the city dedicated Mills Field. Soon afterward, daily passenger and express service was established between San Francisco and Los Angeles. And even in the depths of the Depression that followed a few years later, Pan Am launched a regular, transoceanic clipper service from San Francisco, first to Hawaii and then to New Zealand. The overwater flight between San Francisco and Honolulu took upwards of 18 hours.

Even though San Francisco had to tighten its belt along with the rest of the country during the thirties, the city remained a choice and charming place to live, particularly toward the close of the decade, when things began to look up. Rents were wonderfully cheap, and gourmet meals might cost 35 cents—or 50 cents with wine. Perhaps best of all, the city managed to make it through these worst of times without lowering its sights or losing its exuberance. It was during this decade that the War Memorial Opera House was opened (1932); that Coit Tower was built on Telegraph Hill and dedicated (1933); that the Bay Bridge was completed, linking San Francisco to the East Bay and setting new engineering—and cost—records (1936); that the Golden Gate was spanned by one of the world's most beautiful bridges, and a crowd of a quarter million people walked across it the day it opened (May 27, 1937); that a horse named Blackie swam across the Golden Gate in 23½ minutes (1938); that Frank Fuller flew from San Francisco to Los Angeles in 1 hour, 31 minutes, and 7 seconds and then from San Francisco to Seattle in 2 hours, 31 minutes, and 41 seconds (1938); that President Franklin Delano Roosevelt visited the city (1938); that Tom Mooney (the labor leader accused—probably falsely—of setting off the bomb that killed ten in the 1916 protest parade) was at last pardoned by California governor Culbert Olson and released from prison (1939); and that the Golden Gate International Exposition, another world's fair, this one "A Pageant of the Pacific," opened for the first time on Treasure

Island on land dredged from the bay and pumped up as fill (1939). (The fair was opened again and closed, finally, in 1940; although it attracted upwards of 17 million visitors, it was a financial flop.)

It was also during the thirties, it may be noted, that San Francisco's powerful labor leaders made headlines all over the world by bringing off an unprecedented general strike in which an estimated 127,000 workers walked off their jobs (this following the shutting down of ports the length of the West Coast and the subsequent clubbing, gassing, and killing of two workingmen in the Bloody Thursday confrontation between the International Longshoremen's Association [ILA] and the San Francisco police on July 5, 1934).

On December 8, 1941, Japan bombed Pearl Harbor, and at 6:15 P.M. that evening, sirens wailed to signal the first blackout in San Francisco's history. This initiated nearly four years of feverish war activity for the city that was to serve as the principal gateway to the action in the Pacific Theatre. More than 1.5 million servicemen poured into—and out of—San Francisco between 1942 and 1945, jamming sidewalks and hotels, crowding restaurants, bars, and the dance floors of nightclubs and USO centers, and packing what accommodations there were so cram-full that barracks had to be erected in Civic Center. Billions of pounds of war materials were stacked on the city's piers to sail out of the Golden Gate. The city's factories and its shipbuilding industry all but went crazy, and thousands of workers flowed in from all over the country: San Francisco's labor force nearly tripled. Local citizens did their bit collecting tin cans and other metal, and scrap drives highlighted each war year. The shores of the Golden Gate, heavily fortified off and on ever since the city was settled, bristled anew with mortars and antiaircraft guns. The armed forces strung a huge net across the Golden Gate to snag any enemy submarine that dared try to sneak into the bay.

As the war began to wind down in 1945, San Francisco was chosen to host the United Nations conference, and here in June, in the War Memorial Opera House, 51 nations signed the newly drafted United Nations charter. The Cathedral Grove in Muir Woods and the United Nations Plaza in Civic Center are fitting reminders of this epic event. When hostilities finally ended on August 16, the city went crazy and rioted along Market Street to celebrate the great occasion.

World War II brought profound changes to the Bay Area and San Francisco—as well as to the world—and none was more profound than the great influx of immigrants. Tens of thousands of the servicemen from other regions who had passed through San Francisco had discovered the beauties of the Bay Area and had been determined to return. And return they did, tripling the population around the bay, replacing artichoke fields with housing tracts, orchards with shopping malls and parking lots, and dirt roads with freeways, and bringing an ever more diverse ethnic mix to this already cosmopolitan area. (In 1980, the census confirmed that the San Francisco Bay Area had the most diverse ethnic mix in the United States, with 67 major ethnic groups living in the nine Bay Area counties.)

During the 1950s, San Francisco boomed. It opened its International Airport in 1954, and two years later, while entertaining President Dwight D. Eisenhower, it hosted the Republican Convention. In 1957, it joined in taking first steps toward a regional approach to regional problems: a five- (later to be three-) county Bay Area Rapid Transit District was set up by the state legislature, and San Francisco was one of the principals. (The city and county of San Francisco share the same boundaries, thus making less-than-50-square-mile San Francisco County the smallest in the state.) As though celebrating this rational approach, the Municipal Railway updated itself and replaced its two-man streetcars with one-man cars in 1958. But in what was later seen as steps backward, the San Francisco–Oakland ferry made a last run on July 29 of that year, and buses replaced the Key System trains at about the same time. In this somewhat star-crossed decade, the House Un-American Activities Committee held hearings in the city; *Sputnik* moved silently across the San Francisco night sky, and Bay Area educators reacted by tightening up public schools' curricula; television became a fact of life; and a nine-year-old boy named Dick Pee swam the Golden Gate.

San Francisco has always been known for its live-and-let-live attitude, for its willingness to experiment, and for the fact that it is frequently the crucible for new ideas and movements that spread nationwide. In the fifties, the beat generation of poets and artists moved into the city's North Beach district and made it a mecca for anyone who shared their relaxed and nonconformist attitudes toward life—and for curious tourists, too. Lawrence Ferlinghetti's City Lights Bookstore, a monument to the beatnik era, is still going strong on Columbus Avenue, and there is now a Ferlinghetti Street in San Francisco.

In the sixties, the civil rights movement came to life in San Francisco, and the city was one of the first in the country to bus students to attain a racial balance in its schools. The flower children and the hippies came along with their message of peace and love—and blatant disregard for authority and establishment values. Thousands of them gathered for an enormous Be-In celebrating their idealism in Golden Gate Park. Thousands of other San Franciscans marched against the Vietnam War and for peace, up and down Market Street, in Golden Gate Park, and in the Civic Center. San Francisco State University was gripped in student rebellion and had three presidents in one year before the final choice—no-nonsense semanticist and later senator S. I. Hayakawa—managed to restore order. In a spirit of rebellion of their own, San Franciscans managed to keep Golden Gate Park intact from freeways and voted to cut short freeway construction already under way in the city, thus leaving huge ramps empty above the Embarcadero, going nowhere. (These were later felled as a result of the 1989 earthquake.)

In this same decade, people woke up to the fact that San Francisco Bay was a finite and shrinking resource—40 percent of it had been filled in since the Spanish arrived on its shores—and the Save the Bay Association was formed by concerned citizens to come to the rescue. Another regional body, the nine-county San Francisco Bay Conservation and Development Commission, was authorized by the state legislature in 1965 to help direct development around the bay while perpetuating the bay's incomparable values. The BCDC, as it came to be known, soon became a model for similar agencies in other parts of the country. San Francisco remained the star attraction of the Bay Area, but by 1969, Oakland, in a fine exhibition of one-upsmanship, had converted its port facilities to handle containers, and the Queen of West Coast Shipping went into a period of decline. It is only now partially recovered, having finally converted some of its port facilities. Meantime, however, it has made the most of some of its abandoned piers, converting at least one of them, Pier 39, into what some people describe as a sophisticated tourist trap, and the best seal-viewing spot in the city.

The seventies saw the establishment of another (incomparable, too) urban amenity, the Golden Gate National Recreation Area (GGNRA) with what would grow to be nearly 77,000 protected acres in San Francisco, Marin, and San Mateo counties. The lovely old Conservatory in Golden Gate Park was made both a city and a California state historical landmark. Early in the decade, the Bay Area Rapid Transit System (BART), child of the Bay Area Rapid

Transit District, holed through its last subway tunnel link, and two years later the first train navigated the transbay tube to arrive at Montgomery Street Station. The Golden Gate Bridge finally paid off the last installment on its $35 million debt. All West Coast ports were closed—and then reopened—by the International Longshoremen Workingmen's Union (ILWU, descendent of the ILA). The city's bus drivers went on strike and nearly paralyzed the place. With no way to go but up, San Francisco's downtown continued to grow skyward; Transamerica and the Bank of America erected buildings of record height. San Francisco's gay community emerged as a social and political force. With a return to the mindless violence of gold rush days, President Gerald Ford was shot at in downtown San Francisco, and Mayor George Moscone and Supervisor Harvey Milk (the first elected representative of the gay community) were shot and killed in their City Hall offices.

During the eighties, San Francisco's population increased for the first time in decades to top 700,000 once again. (In 1950 there were more than 775,000 San Franciscans, the greatest number ever.) The number of automobiles in the city nearly doubled (but parking spaces did not!). Although its port was perking up, tourism was recognized as the city's biggest business: the cable cars got a $2 million redo, and new hotels continued to rise despite empty rooms. The cost of living was the highest in the country. The Democratic Convention nominated Walter Mondale in Moscone Center, San Francisco's new convention center, named for its slain mayor. A downtown plan setting some limits on growth was passed by the board of supervisors, hailed by then-mayor Dianne Feinstein (later a United States senator), but decried by many city aficionados as being too little, too late. The span of the Golden Gate Bridge was flattened (but sprang back) by a crowd of more than 1 million celebrants of its fiftieth anniversary.

As did cities across the country, San Francisco also saw an influx of homeless people during this decade, a problem with which it is still dealing. And while the most outrageous occurrence during these years was the attempted murder of President Ronald Reagan by John Hinkley, the biggest event—both literally and figuratively—of the eighties was the October 1989 earthquake. This not only killed more than 60 people in the Bay Area, but with its accompanying fire, it devastated much of San Francisco's Marina district. It also crippled the Bay Bridge as well as many of the city's freeways.

Around the turn of the century, San Francisco is being impacted by the vastly increased population of the whole Bay Area. Freeways serving the city are apt to be congested anytime during the day and evening. It is hard to go anywhere in the city without finding someone who is down on his (or her) luck. During the mid-nineties, the number of cars exceeded the number of parking spaces by a good 40,000. Still, San Francisco continues to have the talent to go easy when times are tough and to pick up where things leave off. It is a resilient city, and its special spirit endures.

The city has been called many things by the famous and the infamous: the city of romance and destiny, the most sophisticated city in the country, a marvel of nature, the genius of American cities, the city where nobody thinks, the cool, gray city of love, the queen of the Pacific Coast, the Athens of the United States, west as all hell, exciting, moody, exhilarating, marvelous, so clean, unique, and without parallel.

It has also been called a world to explore and the gateway to adventure. Outdoor-minded people will search far to find a more pleasant city to explore and to enjoy.

Street Names

From Market Street to Presidio Avenue, Geary Street/Boulevard crosses 26 streets (see Geary Walks 1 and 2), traversing some of the most historic parts of San Francisco. All of these cross streets were named in the first decade of San Francisco's existence, and each name represents a person or place that was important, one way or another, to the young city. As you cross these streets, you can learn a little early local history and get some idea of the kind of people who made it. You may also get something of a feel for the way pioneer life was lived in San Francisco nearly a century and a half ago. Keep in mind the fact that when most of these streets were named they were "the worst . . . succession of mud holes masquerading as street[s] in the United States," as William Tecumseh Sherman said of Montgomery Street during the gold rush.

When John White **Geary** arrived in San Francisco in April 1849, he brought with him sacks of mail instead of a pickax and shovel. The young city's first postmaster, he never succumbed to gold fever, but he did become both active and successful in real estate speculation. He was, in fact, a remarkably versatile young man: a civil engineer, lawyer, surveyor, farmer, and railroad worker, he became a colonel in the Mexican War and was given his postmaster's job as a political plum. He was also a very sturdy fellow, being one of the first, and probably last, people to march 3,000 miles from Mexico City to Pittsburgh, Pennsylvania, his home.

Geary was elected the sixth and last alcalde (mayor) of San Francisco in August 1849, and the following year, the city's first mayor. He helped draft the charters of both San Francisco and California and was influential in excluding slavery from the brand-new state. An ardent unionist, he became a close personal friend of the dynamic Rev. Thomas Starr King.

During the critical year that Geary was San Francisco's mayor, the city got not only its first charter but its first circus, its first hospital, its first steamboat connection with Sacramento, and its first jail—the abandoned brig *Euphemia*.

Never too happy in the raw young boomtown, Geary followed his wife and two children back to Pennsylvania in February 1852. As a parting gift to San Francisco, however, he bestowed upon it the handsome acreage that became Union Square and saw to it that it would remain public property for all time. San Francisco responded by naming a principal thoroughfare for him. Geary went on to serve with General Sherman on his famous March to the Sea and to become governor of Kansas and, later, Pennsylvania.

Some years after Geary left San Francisco, a friend remarked to him that the property that he gave to the city could have made him a millionaire. He replied that he preferred his career in the East and the culture of Pennsylvania to the "sand and fleas" of the city by the bay.

Seven streets that cross Geary, including six between Market Street and Van Ness Avenue, memorialize men who took part in the "conquest" of California. These pioneers were among the handful of sturdy adventurers (of whom several were career army or career navy men) who seized California by force or by wile from Mexico in the 1840s during a great period of empire building in the United States. Kearny, Stockton, Powell, Mason, Leavenworth, Larkin, and Lyon— all were members of this elite tribe.

A strong-willed career army man, Stephen Watts **Kearny** (not to be confused with Dennis Kearney, the sandlot orator) was sent to California from Fort Leavenworth by the War Department in 1846. Noted for his ability to handle hostile Indians, Kearny had several bloody engagements in California and served with Commodore Robert P. Stockton for some time before the territory was adequately secured. He was appointed military and civil governor of California by President James A. Polk, and in 1847 he granted title to hundreds of underwater lots in San Francisco to raise money for the growing town. Kearny and the arrogant John C. Frémont inevitably engaged in a struggle for power: the latter was court-martialed (but later restored by the army), whereas the former simply asked to leave California. He died five months after he left, just weeks after he was made a major general.

Commodore Robert P. **Stockton** played a major role in the United States takeover of California. He arrived on the California scene in June 1846, aboard the United States flagship, the *Congress*. (The *Congress* was captained by Samuel F. DuPont, for whom the avenue now known as Grant was earlier named.) It took nine wretched months for the flagship to get from the East Coast to Monterey, where Stockton took over from Commodore John S. Sloat. Sloat had just appropriated that Spanish settlement and hoisted the United States flag over it. Stockton then managed to deceive his local Mexican adversaries (who were understandably upset) as to the size and strength of his puny forces, and he proceeded to run up the stars and stripes in other parts of the sprawling territory that would become a state in 1850.

Dr. William J. **Powell**, surgeon of the war-sloop USS *Warren*, was a member of the American armed forces who sailed in and out of San Francisco frequently during these parlous times. He is remembered chiefly for having founded a hospital for sailors.

Colonel Richard Barnes **Mason** was the fourth civil and military governor of California, taking over from Kearny. He also (with Thomas O. Larkin) helped launch California's great gold rush. He had visited San Francisco in June 1848 and found the town strangely emptied of all its able-bodied males: they had left for the Mother Lode. Following the gold-fevered mob, he was stunned at the phenomenal scene that he witnessed, and he hastened to report it in detail to Washington, D.C. (When Larkin did the same thing independently, this confirmed the extraordinary discovery, and the rush was on from all over the country—indeed the world.) As governor (Mason served from February to May 1849), he was confronted with the mass desertion of his soldiers (and sailors) to the gold fields. Thinking to send his cavalry after them, he found that most of the cavalry had deserted, too. Like Kearny, Mason requested a transfer to less turbulent territory, and, like Kearny, he too died in his mid-fifties soon after he left California.

Another physician, and man of the cloth as well, was the Episcopal Rev. Thaddeus M. **Leavenworth,** who served as a chaplain in Colonel Jonathan Drake Stevenson's hand-picked First New York Volunteer Troop, which fought under Kearny in California. Leavenworth became alcalde of San Francisco in 1848 just as the gold rush exploded, and his year in office was a tough one as crime ran high in the burgeoning little metropolis. He was perhaps better in the pulpit than he was in City Hall, for he was investigated (but not convicted) of "mismanagement" while in office.

Thomas O. **Larkin** came to California in the early 1840s in search of a half brother, whom he found in Monterey. Larkin was both bright and diplomatic and was made the first—and only—U.S. consul to Mexico in 1844. He soon became a "confidential representative" who sent intelligence to Washington, D.C. Stockton picked him to carry the United States flag to Santa Barbara and Los Angeles, hoping that he could smooth the way for the American takeover. Larkin succeeded at first, but his diplomacy failed him on his way to a subsequent rendezvous with Colonel Frémont. The Spanish captured him and held him prisoner for months but eventually released him. He returned to Monterey, where his wife had all but given him up for dead. Later, he and Jacob Leese (who married a sister of Vallejo) exchanged properties, and Larkin became a Bay Area resident. He is credited with having inadvertently created the Spanish colonial style of house, and the "Larkin House" still stands in Monterey.

Captain Nathaniel **Lyon** was a West Point graduate who served with distinction in the Mexican War. He then went on to distinguish himself further by thoroughly "punishing" the Indians at Clear Lake for the murder of Captain William H. Warner. He was thus a local hero.

Along with the heroes of conquest and war, other nameworthy leaders emerged early in San Francisco. Geary was one of them, and so were Jones, Hyde, Van Ness, Buchanan, Broderick, and Baker.

Elbert P. **Jones** was a Kentucky lawyer who arrived in San Francisco in 1848. A versatile fellow, he took over management of the city's first hotel, the Portsmouth House on Clay and Kearny, and was for a time the editor of Sam Brannan's newspaper, the *Star.*

George **Hyde,** a Philadelphia lawyer and adventurer, got himself appointed as Stockton's secretary for the miserable nine-month voyage of the *Congress.* Once ashore in Monterey, he took off (as per agreement) for Yerba Buena, convinced that California would become part of the Union. After serving as the town's alcalde, he continued to do well in the following decades as the city bloomed. He and his wife chose to build their house in the somewhat distant outskirts—the corner of Post, Market, and Montgomery streets.

James **Van Ness** became mayor of San Francisco in 1855. He is remembered for presiding over the expansion of the city into the "Outside Lands" to the west. He confirmed title to the properties owned west of Larkin Street and appointed a commission to name the streets running through the new Western Addition.

John C. **Buchanan** was one of the first immigrants to reach San Francisco via the overland route, arriving in 1846. He became a successful auctioneer and was clerk to two mayors, one of whom was Hyde.

David D. **Broderick** was a self-made man, the son of a stonecutter. He arrived in San Francisco in 1849, was elected a state senator seven years later, and went on to Washington, D.C., as a United States senator from California in 1859. He was a staunch abolitionist and was also given to dueling. In an encounter in the early fifties his pocketwatch stopped a bullet that might have killed him. He was not so lucky in his duel with David S. Terry, chief justice of the California Supreme Court. On September 14, 1859, on the shore of Lake Merced, Terry—from Virginia—fatally wounded him in a confrontation over the issue of slavery. Senator Baker eulogized Senator Broderick so eloquently that he is said to have reduced his audience to tears. You can visit the site of the duel (see GGNRA Walk 4).

Edward Dickinson **Baker** served as an officer in three wars—the Black Hawk War, the Mexican War, and the Civil War. He is remembered as a lawyer, a Civil War hero, a friend of Abraham Lincoln, a public servant, an abolitionist, and, above all, a silver-tongued orator. He left the United States Senate (he was elected from Oregon) in 1861 to enlist as a colonel in the Union forces and was killed in his first engagement, at Ball's Bluff, Virginia. He left not only a street

named for him but a beach and a fort (both in the Golden Gate
National Recreation Area).

Not all of the San Franciscans remembered on Geary's cross
streets were such notable folks. The 1855 members of Van Ness's
street-naming commission managed to take care of their own. While
Mayor **Van Ness** was their obvious first choice and they named the
city's widest street (125 feet) for him, their second choice honored
Franklin, not Ben, but Silim, a somewhat obscure businessman (who
plainly was not obscure at the time).

Gough Street still commemorates commission member Charles H.
Gough. He happened to be a popular milkman who made his rounds
among the sand dunes riding his horse. How to pronounce his name
has been a challenge for more than a century. The following, written
by librarian Minnie Elmer and immortalized in one of Herb Caen's
columns in the *San Francisco Chronicle,* may, or may not, help you:

> In San Francisco passing through
> I came upon a street named Gough;
> Allergic to a name like Gough
> I there began to sneeze and cough;
> I parked my car beneath a bough
> That overhung the street sign "Gough,"
> And rested there awhile, although
> I did not like the street named Gough.
> No, I did not like the street named Gough.
> About which this is quite enough.

Although bus drivers have been known to come up with something
different, most San Franciscans pronounce Gough to rhyme with
cough.

Gough was responsible for another intriguing street name: **Octavia**
was not the romantic heroine of a novel, nor yet a Roman matron,
but Charles's sister. And L. **Steiner,** also a hardworking and valuable
citizen, was the gentleman who delivered the water around town.

At the same time, the street namers did recognize a few illustrious
outsiders: **Webster** Street takes note of Daniel of dictionary fame,
and **Scott** Street honors General Winfield, commander of the Union
army. (Geary was wounded while fighting in his ranks.) San Franciscans also took their presidents seriously. Four of the cross streets
between Market and Presidio memorialize the men who led the
country from 1845 to 1857: James K. **Polk,** the eleventh president;

Zachary **Taylor,** the twelfth; Millard **Fillmore,** the thirteenth; and Franklin **Pierce,** the fourteenth. The name of a fifth president, Ulysses S. **Grant,** supplanted that of Captain Samuel F. DuPont, commander of the *Congress,* and DuPont's name had taken the place of the Spanish Calle de la Fundaçion. Grant Avenue is the city's oldest street and runs directly through Chinatown, where for years it was known as DuPont Gai.

San Franciscans have at intervals changed the names of several of their streets, sometimes more than once, as with Grant Avenue. Such changes may have been attempts to modernize or refine the neighborhood, but they have lost us Ghost Alley, Good Children Street, and Corned Beef and Cabbage Alley. One two-block-long street—a half block from Geary off Union Square—has had four names and a notable career: first it was Morton Street, renowned for its brothels; next it was Union Square Avenue; then it was Manila Avenue, acknowledging Admiral Dewey, whose likeness stands so bravely in Union Square; finally it became **Maiden Lane,** notable largely for its Frank Lloyd Wright building, number 140. San Franciscans have also named some 100 of their streets for women, but, alas, the identity of some of the ladies, unlike Octavia, is a mystery. Who was Caroline, and why did Harriet's name replace hers? And who, indeed, was Harriet?

Only a few of Geary's cross streets remind the traveler of San Francisco's Spanish origins. **Laguna** was named for a nearby pond that was known as Washerwoman's Lagoon. **Divisadero** marks a natural division in the city's terrain (or the name may come from the Spanish *divisar,* "to see from afar," since the street climbs a high hill). **Arguello,** actually First Avenue, immortalizes California's second Mexican governor, the father of Concepçion, whose ill-starred romance made history. And **Presidio** runs through—and south from—the city's first military post.

From Presidio to Ocean Beach, most of the street names are more recent and less noteworthy. A few are named for trees, and there are some 47 avenues that are simply numbered. At Fortieth Avenue, however, where Geary Boulevard leads into Point Lobos, there is one last reminder of the arrival of the men from Spain. **Point Lobos** is an anglicized and shortened version of the original Spanish name: *lobos* is the Spanish word for "wolves," and Punto de los Lobos Marinos is "the point of the sea wolves," for thus did the conquistadores label the sea lions who serenaded their arrival those short centuries ago.

Further anecdotes about many other San Francisco street names may be found in Lowenstein's *Streets of San Francisco,* Block's *Immortal San Franciscans,* and Gladys Hansen's *San Francisco Almanac* (see Bibliography).

Architectural Heritage

Although young as American cities go, San Francisco has in its century and a half attracted an unusual variety of architecture. This is not surprising since, twice, it has risen as an "instant city," once in the 1849 gold rush and once after the 1906 catastrophe. Furthermore, it burned five times between 1849 and May 1851. As you travel through it—preferably on foot—keep your eyes open for noteworthy structures and also for interesting details, some of which are unique to the Bay Area. Here are just a few suggestions of what to look for.

As a perceptive architect friend once remarked, San Francisco's skyline is a "strange, evolutionary thing." It started its rise heavenward when its first skyscrapers went up in 1889 (see Geary Walk 1), and it has indeed been evolving ever since with varying degrees of success. Those first high-rise buildings were greeted with cheers and pride. More recently, as the city's downtown area and skyline have become ever more crowded, the word *skyscraper* has become something of a red flag, and when a new one is proposed the developer can expect a royal battle. (San Francisco's city fathers in 1985 enacted a hold-the-lid-down city plan that attempts to control the proliferation as well as the height of new buildings.)

Once a skyscraper has stood for a few decades in San Francisco, however—no matter how controversial it was when it was built—it may become accepted and sometimes beloved. A case in point is the Transamerica Building, which points skyward on Montgomery Street between Jackson and Washington and is one of the two tallest buildings in the city. It went up amid loud cries of criticism and even anguish since it caused the razing of a wonderful old structure, the Montgomery Building, built in 1853 and known affectionately as the Monkey Block. This was not only a historic treasure but was the legendary home of bohemians and impoverished artists. It inspired strong rescue efforts but was doomed by "progress," if not by the 1906 fire and earthquake. San Franciscans immediately named the building the Pyramid and called it misplaced ("put it in any city but ours") and bizarre. The "redwood forest" (a small grove of planted redwoods) at its foot was some, but not enough, compensation. Before too long, however, feelings began to soften, the Pyramid began showing up on postcards, and more and more it became a kind of symbol of the city. Now the locals often like to show it off; it's an integral part of the scene.

The Bank of America Building on California Street between Grant and Kearny is the city's other fog-piercing monument. In designing this one, the architectural firm of Skidmore, Owings & Merrill aimed to capture the rough-hewn character of the Sierra Nevada—in color and in form. A creative approach, says my architect friend, and a building that will endure. It can be seen from virtually every hill in the city. *The Banker's Heart*—as the sculpture in its courtyard is called—is worth a second look.

Skidmore, Owings & Merrill are responsible for other buildings in the city's financial district, notably the Alcoa Building, which is evocative of the Bank of America, and the Zellerbach Building on the corner of Market and Sansome. The latter is outstanding not only for its interesting architectural qualities but for the amenity of its charming and much-used little urban park and for the gazebo-type building at its foot.

The Crocker Galleria, not far away on Market, is another attractive urban effort and offers interesting strolls past its myriad shops.

Three other fairly recent San Francisco buildings merit mention: the twin-tower edifice at 345 California Street, which inspired the *San Francisco Chronicle*'s architectural editor to heights of deprecation, and Davies Symphony Hall in the Civic Center, whose design my friend sums up as "all new and all fine." This (twice-built) concert hall has not only a fabulous organ but unusually good acoustics, making it a splendid place to enjoy the music provided by the San Francisco Symphony and other top-notch performers. There is also the outstanding new San Francisco Public Library.

The sometimes overpowering effect of many of the city's newer buildings gives a little extra appeal and interest to a number of its older survivors. Not far from the 1909 redo of the Palace Hotel on Market at Montgomery is the Pacific Stock Exchange on Pine and Sansome streets. This structure boasts "heroic statues" by Ralph Stackpole on the outside and bas-reliefs by Robert Boardman Howard as well as frescoes by Diego Rivera on the inside. If you stroll up Market a couple of blocks you will come to the Flood Building on the corner of Powell Street. This one was built a few years before the turn of the century, and there are still smoke-black traces of the 1906 fire near its entrance. A walk up Montgomery Street (turn northwest off Market) will bring you to number 720, one of the oldest survivors of San Francisco's numerous disasters. This was originally the Changeman's Building and was erected in either 1849 or 1850. Rebuilt after the 1851 fire, it was at one time or another a theatre (where Lotta Crabtree performed), an auction house, and a garment factory. It is now known as the Belli Building, having been restored by the late lawyer Melvin Belli in 1959. Not far from here is Jackson Square, where a cluster of early city buildings has been restored and put happily to use.

There are other San Francisco landmarks that are well worth seeing, and if you are interested it is recommended that you visit the Foundation for San Francisco's Architectural Heritage, which is housed in the Haas-Lilienthal mansion at 2007 Franklin Street, a magnificent Victorian survivor. This organization raises funds to rescue important buildings from demolition, publishes architectural surveys, and gives lectures, tours, and special events for the architecturally minded. Or, if your time is limited, you might stop by the San Francisco Room of the San Francisco Public Library in the Civic Center. The former main library, on the corner of McAllister and Larkin, a grand old building, was injured in the 1989 quake; it was designed by George Kelham and built in 1917. Rebuilt, it is now the home of the Asian Museum. Both the old and the new library are part of the Civic Center complex that includes City Hall. The present civic structure with its gilded dome replaced a jerry-built predecessor that was, perhaps fortunately, destroyed in the great leveling of 1906. An excellent view of City Hall can be had from the north on Franklin Street between McAllister and Grove—the courtyard between the Opera House and the War Memorial Building provides an elegant window and frame. South of Market (SOMA), the new San Francisco Museum of Modern Art at 151 Third Street is outstanding and a visit to the Ansel Adams Center at 250 Fourth Street is worthwhile. The new headquarters of the California Historical Society at 678 Mission is also noteworthy.

Among San Francisco's interesting buildings are the refugee shacks that went up after the 1906 quake and fire. Virtually thrown together out of redwood planks to house the quake's homeless victims, these bare-bone structures went up along with the tents in 11 of the city's parks. They came in three sizes, the smallest being 10 by 14 feet, the largest 15 by 25 feet—which was used for schools and social gatherings. More than 5,000 refugee shacks were constructed, and some 40 still remain. Two of these historic structures were rescued from wreckers by the U.S. Army and can be seen in back of the Presidio Museum. (See Natural History Museums appendix.) One at 1227 Twenty-fourth Avenue in the Sunset has achieved city landmark status.

But perhaps the most intriguing, and certainly the most unusual, of the city's buildings are not the smallest or the grandest ones, but the hundreds of Victorian houses that survived the earthquake and fire. You can spot these in many of the city's neighborhoods, sometimes standing alone, but more often in the company of peers. (See below for suggested areas in which to view these lovelies.) There are few finer displays anywhere of the ebullient designs that typified the Victorian period, when "gingerbread"—inside or outside a house—marked the success and status of a homeowner. San Francisco was in a period of growth and expansion during the Victorian era and, more than many cities, blossomed with Victorian homes. (In a 1976 inventory of San Francisco's Victorians, Judith Lynch Waldhorn counted nearly 13,500 houses in nine neighborhoods in the process of being restored.)

The great Victorian housing boom was made possible by the discovery of the balloon frame method of building. (It was so named by an early detractor who suggested that a house constructed by this technique might billow out and burst like a balloon.) This construction technique came about after standard mill-lengths of lumber and machine-made nails became available in 1839; it consisted of erecting a two-story frame and hanging the walls, floors, and ceilings, etc., from it. This was far simpler and required much less labor than older methods, and it meant that houses could be assembled easily and cheaply, i.e., for a minimum amount of money. (In Victorian days, the word *cheap* did not imply shoddiness or sleaze.)

Along with the balloon frame came a number of other breakthroughs in Victorian building construction. Using then-new machine techniques, it became possible to turn out easily all sorts of fancy wooden millwork, such as spindles, newel posts, balustrades, lacework, arches, sunbursts, etc. Pressed designs in metal, plaster, and wood—like rosettes, wreaths, friezes, flowers, etc.—also became easier and cheaper to produce. And, making things simple for the aspiring architect, builder, or homeowner, millwork companies published catalogues with page after page offering almost infinite choices of decorative items as well as functional pieces such as windows (arched or pedimented), doors, or even towers. Thus, any proper Victorian home builder could thumb through the pages of, say, the Townley Brothers (of San Francisco) catalogue of millwork or that of the Niehaus Brothers and Company (of West Berkeley) and select the finials, brackets, beading, dentils, cornices, turrets, porticoes—or whatever—that would make his house his own. Also available were all sorts of house-building ideas, floor plans, design suggestions, etc., in two highly influential magazines published during the latter decades of the nineteenth century, the *Scientific American Architects and Builders Edition,* published in New York and claimed by its publishers to have the largest circulation in the world in 1887, and the *California Architect and Building News,* published in San Francisco. As a result of all this, while you may find many basic similarities in the city's Victorian house designs, you will also find a wonderful explosion of imagination and individuality in the profuse ornamentation of these houses.

There follow some of the things you may want to look for as you walk past these mementos of another era: *Decorative tile* and *etched* or *stained glass* may add traceries of design and color to Victorians. Glass may actually be enameled or painted, as opposed to leaded, and sometimes there are portraits of family members, or perhaps famous people, to liven up the inside (and outside) view. *Three-dimensional faces* (stamped in plaster, wood, or metal) may be carefully interwoven into scrollwork, friezes, or other frosting. The faces may be serenely happy, pompous, sad, angry, or even demonic, and they lend their character to the houses they embellish. Note the ubiquity of *pressed sunbursts. Gables* (and *false gables*) or *French caps* (*mansards*) marked the addition of attics and were popular in the 1890s. There is a marvelous variety of *newel posts, balustrades,* and *wrought-iron picket fences.* Many houses originally had *iron lacework* garnishing their widow's walks, cupolas, towers, and turrets. *Decorative shingles* placed to make patterns and designs are another frequent Victorian feature. *Columns* varied all over the lot, from *Ionic, Corinthian,* or *composite* to the unclassified, but ever more elaborate. *Columns* and *pilasters* were favorite items in the millwork catalogues. *Pediments* above doorways and windows tended to become more sophisticated, flatter, and more geometric as manufacturing techniques became refined. You might get an idea of the relative age of a house by the classiness of its pediments. *Front doors* can tell a lot about the house's original owner: builders frequently offered a standard door for, say, $1.25, but the buyer could get a fancier one for, say, $5 to demonstrate his wealth and good taste. *Arched spoolwork "curtains"* above doors, sometimes placed eccentrically, were very popular. *Eaves* were often embroidered with wooden lacework, or what looks like tatting, or they were beaded, decorated with dentils, etc. *Vergeboards*—straight frames between eaves—gave a good opportunity for pendant designs and other ornamentation. (Looking at some Victorians, you get the idea that the designer, whether architect or builder, crammed every possible surface with frills, fretwork, and filigree, and then added more surfaces—such as vergeboards—to make even more ornamentation possible.)

Many of the hundreds of builders, architects, and contractors at work during the Victorian period in San Francisco liked to sign their work with a distinctive personal detail. When you see *"drips"*—or what look like large wooden drops—hanging from eaves or vergeboards, for example, and when you see *"donuts"*—or o's—worked into fretwork or other filigree, you are likely seeing a house built by Fernando Nelson or one of his sons: these builders accounted for some 4,000 San Francisco homes, many of which had their hallmark designs of drips and donuts, which were invented and named by Fernando. Other builders favored *swags* under the roof line, *friezes,* and *fleurs-de-lys* for their signatures. Many builders left a *cast-iron circle within a square* in the sidewalk in front of their handiwork to mark the sewer gas vent. Along the edges of the square will be the builder's name; the perforated circle is the vent.

You will see bay windows everywhere. (On San Francisco's narrow lots, it was often difficult to place houses so that occupants had enough light; a city ordinance allowing for the protrusion of bays was passed early on to help alleviate the problem.) San Francisco has been called the City of Bay Windows, and the original Palace Hotel had 7,000 of them. The early bays tended to be slanted in their placement, later bays were often squared off, or even rounded, and any or all of them might be festooned with scrolls and garlands or adorned with flowery brackets.

It is almost impossible to categorize specifically the various Victorian styles that emerged in the Bay Area, but, generally speaking, the following may be broadly identified: *Flat-front Italianate* houses are frequently topped off by high (false) fronts that may disguise a peaked or flat roof and that add to the height, and therefore dignity (it was hoped), of the narrow building. (Most San Francisco lots are 25 feet wide.) Doors and windows probably wear matched pediments of curved design (segments of arcs) or of compressed triangular shape. Porches may have Corinthian columns. This style was popular in the 1870s and early 1880s. *Italianate-with-slanted-bay* houses have added room, more embroidery, and pedimented doors and windows carried to new heights (literally). The 100 block of Guerrero and 2100 block of Bush Street have good examples. *Queen Anne tower* houses and *Queen Anne row* houses added the frostings of conical turrets on corner towers, and arches, beadings, decorative shingles, and gables. These were a fad from the later 1880s to the turn of the century and are exemplified in the house at 1701 Franklin. *San Francisco stick* houses are highly ornamented with much wood or plaster "gingerbread," and often have box bays, porticoes, pilasters, dentils, rosettes (or buttons), and newel posts. These were generally built in the 1880s and early 1890s. The odd-numbered side of Laguna Street's 1800 block shows off this style at its best.

As time has passed and styles have changed, many San Francisco Victorian houses have undergone the indignity of being modernized. Stripped of decoration, they have been recovered with stucco or (gag) asbestos shingles. Forlorn ghosts, deprived of their character and panache, they look wan and downright plain. Many others have been given tender loving care, refurbished, and painted in imaginative colors to emphasize their embellishments; it is worth nothing, however, that the original Victorians were almost always painted entirely white or cream colored.

The verve and imagination, the display of ingenious ornamentation, and the care for detail associated with Victorian buildings—all seem to have gone up in the smoke of the 1906 fire, which was fueled, in large part, by the thousands of the city's Victorian (wooden) houses that burned to the ground. The teens and the twenties ushered in more modest (and sometimes ugly) pseudo-Spanish bungalows, and then came the row upon row of identical stucco "Sunset fives," the one-story houses (with in-law apartments in their basements) that line so many of San Francisco's southwest avenues. Here and there still rise unique, inspired newer homes to punctuate the more ordinary traditionals. But the fanciful and joyful gifts of the Victorian builders remain unequaled in our time.

Good city blocks to view Victorians lie west of Van Ness Avenue, but generally east of Presidio, and extend southward past Golden Gate Park into the Haight-Ashbury district and southeast into the Mission and Bernal Heights. Clay Street, between Steiner and Scott streets, has charming Victorians (restored) facing the park across from them. On Steiner at Fulton and, again, at Fell, there are two splendid Victorian mansions. And at 2007 Franklin, there is the Haas-Lilienthal House (more properly "mansion"), one of the grandest of the survivors; its interior as well as its exterior provides a nostalgic reminder of the glories of times gone by. The Haas-Lilienthal House was built in 1886 and a century later is headquarters for the Foundation for San Francisco's Architectural Heritage, which conducts hour-long docent-led tours through it (open Wednesday, 12:00 P.M.–3:15 P.M., and Sunday, 11:00 A.M.–4:15 P.M.). The foundation also conducts Sunday walks that explore the historical and architecturally interesting neighborhood of Pacific Heights. There is a modest fee—well worth it—for tours and walks. Telephone 415-441-3000 for information.

San Francisco boasts perhaps more Victorian houses per square mile than any other American city. They may have doors that stick and windows that are hard to open, but they are delightful reminders of a time in the life of the city when a man's home was veritably his castle, and if he wanted a turret on it, he could choose it from a mail-order catalogue.

Note: There is a good sampling of interesting and historic architecture in the various Bay Area counties: reference to important buildings is made in appropriate sections of the book.

City Neighborhoods

Being one of the world's most cosmopolitan—and compact—cities, San Francisco is crammed with colorful neighborhoods. Very few people, however, can agree on their exact boundaries or nomenclature. Gladys Hansen, former city archivist, for instance, lists literally dozens of "districts" in her fascinating *San Francisco Almanac*. Gerald Adams, on the other hand, divides the city into ten "districts" plus the Presidio, and then defines several "neighborhoods" within them in his interesting *Neighborhood Guide*. Then there are the city planners, city police, and even city hall, which have been known to call the same part of town by different names—or to give the same name to different parts of town. The following catalogue, then, is strictly arbitrary, and necessarily abbreviated. A visit to the San Francisco Room in the main Public Library (telephone 415-557-4567) will offer you a shelfful of much more detailed descriptions. The Foundation for San Francisco's Architectural Heritage is as well a mine of information: it also sponsors city walks. Telephone 415-441-3000 for more information. (And see Architectural Heritage.)

Commercial Centers. San Francisco grew up as a port city, and most of its early commercial development occurred around the waterfront areas along or near the bay. Fisherman's Wharf (approach it from the northern terminus of Hyde Street, where you turn east on Jefferson Street) was formerly the center of the fishing business. Now it is the heart of San Francisco's tourist district. You can take in Ghirardelli Square (one of the best-designed redos of commercial property anywhere) along with the wharf, the neighboring Cannery (another inspired redo), and Pier 39 on the Embarcadero in a visit to this northeast part of town. Find your way up Jackson Street off the Embarcadero for a look at the city's oldest block of buildings, then walk a block over to Broadway and the old Barbary Coast. Add a trip into North Beach (once the Greenwich Village of San Francisco, still the Italian district, with good restaurants and delicatessens). Telegraph Hill tops off North Beach, and a visit there will let you hit another of the city's best-known high spots, Coit Tower. If you go west instead of east from Fisherman's Wharf, you'll be in the San Francisco Maritime National Historical Park, with its historic ships.

Continue along the Embarcadero to the south and you'll pass a parade of city piers, many now unoccupied. Admire the Ferry Building, a city landmark, and go under the Bay Bridge terminal. (Peregrine falcons have nested here!) Now you're South of Market—it used to be South of the Slot when cable cars ran down Market Street—in the sunny, breezy blocks of the warehouse, factory, and manufacturing section of the city. There's some interesting restoration and revamping of old lofts and warehouses going on here. Along the bay shore are historic basins—China Basin, named for the Pacific Mail's China clippers that docked here during the 1860s; India Basin, named for the ships from India that plied their trade here a century ago; and, in between, Central Basin, named for obvious reasons. Further south is Hunters Point, scene of World War II shipbuilding and mass public housing. At the south boundary of the city is Candlestick Park, the city's monster stadium, where the winds howl and spectators shiver when Bay Area weather is in gear.

Downtown. Inland, the northeast corner of San Francisco is full of skyscrapers containing bankers, lawyers, stockbrokers, advertising executives, and all other manner of white-collar businesswomen and businessmen. You'll find the Pacific Stock Exchange here on Pine Street at Sansome. Montgomery Street, the next block west, is San Francisco's Wall Street. Hold your hat here—the streets are wind tunnels. Nearby are posh department stores and specialty shops, flower vendors, street artists, theatres, and hotels; Nob Hill with its elegant apartments and more famous hotels, Grace Cathedral, and the Flood Mansion—lone Nob Hill survivor of the 1906 quake and now the Pacific Union Club; and there's one of the city's choice ethnic neighborhoods, Chinatown, which is oriented around historic Grant Avenue—once known to its Chinese residents as DuPont Gai. Call the western boundary of the downtown district Van Ness Avenue. Where Van Ness approaches Market Street to the south is the Civic Center with its United Nations Plaza, City Hall, Convention Center, Symphony Hall, Opera House, federal and state buildings, and main public library.

San Francisco skyscrapers and waterfront. PHOTO BY RICHARD FREAR.

South of Market Street. This part of the city has been undergoing upscale gentrification. Many businesses and organizations have moved there and it is the center of many of the city's commercial exhibits and conferences, what with the Moscone Convention Center and other exhibit halls.

Residential Neighborhoods. The rest of San Francisco is, for the most part, happily given over to small businesses, various kinds of residences and neighborhood services, and some very nice parks. There is the Western Addition, running from Van Ness Avenue to Presidio Avenue east-west, and California to Hayes north-south. (See Geary Walk 2.) To the north of it are the elegant Pacific Heights, Presidio Heights, Cow Hollow, and Marina districts. These are all pleasant areas for walking, having interesting and frequently handsome architecture. The Marina, which has risen happily from the ashes of the 1989 quake and fire, also has the GGNRA and the San Francisco Yacht Harbor. Further to the west stretches another bedroom neighborhood, the Richmond district—Inner and Outer. (Again, see Geary Walks 2 and 3.) Some of the more interesting international restaurants please the palates of the Asian and European occupants of the Richmond—and of visitors, as well. Try along Clement Street from Arguello to Fourteenth Avenue, along Geary Boulevard from Presidio to Thirtieth, or along Balboa from Thirty-second to around Forty-sixth avenues. The northwest corner of the Richmond is taken up by the Cliff House, the GGNRA, Lincoln Park, and, at its eastern boundary, the Presidio, now happily a part of the GGNRA. *Note:* The inclusion of the Presidio, a U.S. Army post that was closed in 1994, in the GGNRA was mandated by the far-sighted legislation—a monument to the late congressman Philip Burton—that established the park. This was a great gift to the American people, for the Presidio occupies some of the most beautiful land in San Francisco. The National Park Service will develop it over the years, but meanwhile it is a wonderful historical, botanical, and recreational resource, a delight to walk through and explore.

The geographical center of San Francisco is marked by an upsurge of mountains, which makes for interesting outlooks as well as attractive neighborhoods. Buena Vista City Park (on the hill of the same name) looks out over some grand old Victorians and Queen Annes as well as more recent architect-designed dwellings. It is above Haight Street between Masonic Avenue and Divisadero Street. Haight, of course, is half of the Haight-Ashbury district, famous as the home of the hippie movement in the 1960s. There's also Twin Peaks nearby, with its elegant Clarendon Heights, Parnassus Heights—which boasts such charming streets as Edgewood Avenue, as well as the University of California Medical School—and, farther to the west, Golden Gate Heights—with panoramic views of the ocean—and Forest Knolls. On the lower, wooded southwestern slopes of Mount Davidson (the city's highest peak), there are some of the city's larger homes in Sherwood Forest and St. Francis Wood, and, again, farther to the west, Forest Hill. If you don't mind up-and-down hill walking, you might enjoy strolls in any of these neighborhoods. Irving Street, at the foot of Parnassus Heights, has lots of restaurants and neighborhood shops.

Lying to the south of the city's center, the Mission district also has attractive homes (some quite grand) in its Dolores Heights neighborhood and in Diamond Heights (more modest, more recent), as well as workingmen's cottages, old and new. You'll find a rich ethnic mix in the Mission, which has attracted a diverse population—primarily Hispanic—because of its relatively lower costs and wonderful weather. (In parts of the Mission, you'll listen a long time to hear

English spoken.) Early San Franciscans knew a good thing when they saw it, too, and some of their most elegant homes were built in this warmer, sunnier part of the city. On Mission Street you can find some of the best ethnic food (with an emphasis on Latin cuisines) in the city. Try exploring this colorful street in the blocks around Sixteenth Street. You'll find Mission Dolores, the oldest building in San Francisco (with the oldest cemetery), at Sixteenth Street and Dolores.

Between the Mission district and the bay shore in Potrero Hill, settled first by Scotch and Irish shipbuilders in the 1860s and 1870s and then by Russians and Slavs, who arrived in the early 1900s. There's still a Russian community with its Orthodox church, and many charming century-old houses. Around Connecticut and Eighteenth streets, you'll find a grand variety of ethnic foods, including Thai, Italian, Greek, Chinese, and San Franciscan.

If you enjoy German, Italian, or Scandinavian food, you might want to wander through the Castro district along Castro Street around Eighteenth, and along Eighteenth Street itself in the blocks off Castro; there are lots of neighborhood shops around here, as well as restaurants and delis. This is also one of the city's gay centers.

The central section of San Francisco, which stretches west to the Pacific Ocean, is occupied by one of its largest bedroom communities, the Sunset district. Here you'll find the neat white and pastel stucco row houses that went up among the sand dunes in the 1930s and 1940s, most with in-law apartments tucked out of sight behind their built-in garages. Taraval and Judah are good neighborhood streets to explore for their food and shops. The Sunset is separated from the Richmond district on the north by Golden Gate Park, and on the south it is bounded by Lake Merced and the GGNRA's Fort Funston; it also boasts busy Ocean Avenue, the San Francisco Zoo, and Stern Grove, where free concerts take place during the summer season. The Lake Merced district was developed just before and after World War II and embraces a "model community" of apartment houses and townhouses—Park Merced—that was considered the latest thing when it was built. It's still a nice place to live when the weather's good. There's the Stonestown shopping mall, another pioneer development, nearby and the California State University San Francisco campus as well. Enclaves of more expensive homes—like Pine Lake Park—are tucked among other middle-class neighborhoods, such as Lakeshore.

Bounded on the south by Daly City, San Francisco's south-central district has a more varied assortment of single-family homes, as in Sunnyside, with its stairway street, and Ingleside, with architecture ranging from modest bungalows to quite handsome detached houses. In between, you'll find some more of the row houses, too. You'll also find John McLaren Park, one of the city's largest parks, and some varied Outer Mission neighborhoods, like the Excelsior (subdivided in 1869) and St. Mary's Park (developed in the 1930s). These back up against Bernal Heights, which is more properly in the Inner Mission, and which was "out in the country" not all that long ago.

San Francisco's Parks

San Franciscans have been park lovers from the first. The city came with a ready-made 2-plus-acre park—now known as Washington Square and Marini Plaza—the historic plaza where the American flag was raised in 1846. At the time of statehood in 1850, San Francisco's mayor John Geary gave the city another 2½-acre gem, Union Square, in the center of what is now downtown. Even as the city grew during the 1850s and 1860s (when it must have seemed that there were infinite opportunities for parklands in the surrounding areas), the city fathers set aside a few sizable preserves—such as the 27-plus-acre Balboa Park and the 15-acre Mountain Lake Park (still one of the city's loveliest). Then, in 1870, they went all out and established five parks that totaled over 1,046 acres; the crowning jewel among them was, of course, the 1,017-acre Golden Gate Park. Since that time, parks have been added steadily to the list: today there are more than 200 units, administered by the San Francisco Recreation and Park Department. Some of these are tennis courts; some are playgrounds; some are small parks—measured in square feet and often used as a color spot to brighten and delight a neighborhood; and a few are of generous acreage, like Lake Merced (700 acres), McLaren (317 acres), and Lincoln (200 acres). There is also the 75-acre zoo. In all, city parks total over 3,300 acres, a more than respectable percentage of the city's size. (There are also three park department lands outside the city: Camp Mather, San Francisco's Sierra Nevada camp; Sharp Park, an 18-hole golf course south of the city; and "the Furhman bequest," a 1,515-acre tract with a few oil wells that supply small sums for the parks' operation.)

San Francisco's parks offer the full spectrum of recreation—from arts and crafts classes to merry-go-round riding (the 62-menagerie-animal Herschel-Spillman Carrousel in Golden Gate Park dates back to 1912 and has been restored to spit-and-polish condition—it's magnificent), to jogging (there are Parcourses in five parks, including Golden Gate Park), to archery, fly fishing, and pétanque (the French version of bocce ball). There are 132 free tennis courts, 21 of which are in Golden Gate Park and many of which were built during the 1880s and 1890s, when tennis was the "in" sport. There are nine swimming pools. You can enjoy the amenities of San Francisco's smaller parks as you walk around the city. Golden Gate Park, however, offers a park experience that is well worth taking some time to enjoy. It is a beautiful park that will have flowers blooming every month of the year. Furthermore, it is an example of what vision, persistence, and human ingenuity can achieve.

Golden Gate Park—Starting in 1852, San Francisco's city fathers had been trying to "prove up" on a Spanish land claim "four square leagues" in size in the "Outside Lands" west of the city; they contended that the claim belonged to the city. It took them years of legal battles to win their case, but win they finally did, and in 1870 they set about making a park out of 1,017 acres that consisted mostly of windswept sand dunes; the park would stretch west to the beach from what was then the edge of town. They got little encouragement from experts like Frederick Law Olmsted, who declared that trees could never be made to grow on this bleak terrain. And members of the press were not helpful: "Of all the white elephants the city of San Francisco ever owned," wrote one seer, "they now have the largest in Golden Gate Park, a dreary waste of shifting sandhills where a blade of grass cannot be raised without four posts to keep it from blowing away." The *Sonoma Democrat* was even less kind, declaring that the park had "wind continually sweeping over it that would take the hair off a polar bear and a fog resting on it heavy enough to give asthma

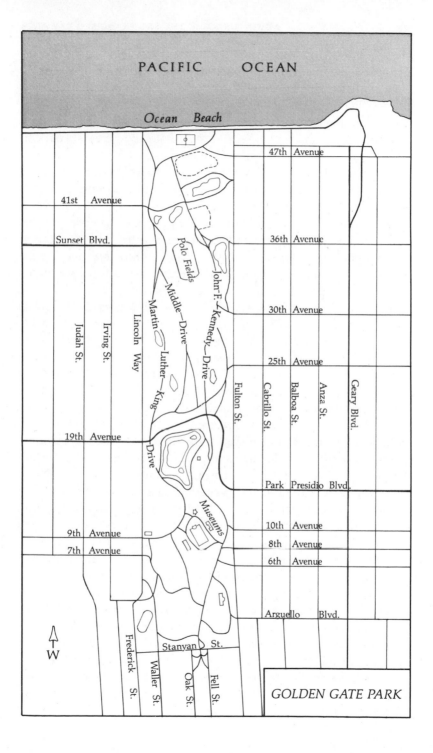

to a sea lion." Undaunted, the first park commission began by routing numerous squatters from the land (many of whom were holding
acreage for some of San Francisco's craftier businessmen). They then
hired William Hammond Hall (who had been involved in the construction of the Palace Hotel), first as park engineer and then as park
superintendent. And they gave him the go-ahead to create a park fit
for the Queen Metropolis of the Golden West.

Hall began by fencing the park against local livestock. Then he
started planting the Panhandle, the easternmost and most protected
portion of the park, where there was some semblance of native vege-
tation—although all of San Francisco's native trees had been cut for
firewood during the gold rush. From there he turned to the western
section—the real "Outside Lands"—which called into play all his
genius. How could he conquer that constantly wind-scoured sand?
How could he possibly grow parklike shrubs and flowers, let alone
trees, in this dreary, barren wasteland? The story goes, according to
Raymond H. Clary in *The Making of Golden Gate Park,* Hall happened on a spot where a survey party had camped the previous week
and found it covered with fresh barley sprouts. It seems that a saddle
horse had spilled its nose bag of soaked barley and refused to eat it
because it was covered with sand. The barley sprouts gave Hall an
idea. He took soaked barley and mixed it with soaked lupine seeds
(which had been tried alone, but grew so slowly they were covered
with drifting sand before plants took hold). The barley sprouted
quickly and protected the lupine until it was tall enough to control
the movement of the sand. In turn, the lupine—which could live at
least two years without care—protected small trees while they got
going. Hall went to work seeding large stretches, first to barley and
lupine, and then to literally thousands of trees. Most of the sand area
in the park was reclaimed in this manner over the years. However,
near the ocean, European beach grass was used, for neither barley
nor lupine would sprout on sand fresh from the sea. Along with this,
he designed and laid out the general plan of the park that we know
today. He was a park purist, and he worked to the contours of the
land, wanting a "city woodland park," not a Coney Island. He
resisted as much as he could the sometimes lavish gifts that it was
then fashionable for local tycoons to bestow: "The value of a park,"
he said, "consists of its being a park, and not a catch-all for almost
anything which misguided people may wish upon it." (He later called
Stow Lake, donated by a prominent park commission member and

ringing a central island, "a shoestring tied around a watermelon.") Hall served the park—and the city—well for more than five years before local political shenanigans prompted him to resign, presumably in disgust. By the time he left, the park had already become a magnet for San Franciscans and an increasingly popular playground. (Hall was a talented man who returned briefly a few years later to help out the park and, incidentally, to hire John McLaren in 1887.) Remarkably, there is nothing—no lake, no trail, no special spot, no monument, no plaque—in Golden Gate Park to honor, or at least to recall, William Hammond Hall, the man responsible for so much of the beauty of the park we enjoy today.

For a dozen years Golden Gate Park limped along under a succession of superintendents. (A somewhat miserly state bureaucracy funded the park until 1900, when the city took over entirely.) Once McLaren was aboard, however, the happy fate of Golden Gate Park was assured. The park was "Uncle John's" great love, and he lavished it with shrewd affection for 55 years, writing his own rules and running a show that earned for him the accolades, if not the love, of just about every San Franciscan. McLaren ruled as a stubborn but benevolent dictator: he issued driver's licenses and set up traffic courts to try—and fine—horseback riders and bicyclists who went too fast on park roads; he planted ten trees to get one, and if that one died, he planted an eleventh (he is said to have planted literally hundreds of thousands of trees); disliking statues (he called them "stookies"), he went to great lengths to place them in inconspicuous spots and to mask them with shrubbery. He paid the park gardeners with $5 gold pieces, a practice that, some wag suggested, accounted for the large number of bars that sprang up nearby. (Rumor had it that he checked everybody's breath each morning for sobriety.) McLaren had a great fondness for large rocks and was not above fabricating them when none was available: thus the obvious fake rocks here and there throughout the park, and also those across the street from the Cliff House, which were erected with highway bond money in the 1920s.

McLaren carried forward Hall's work—and added his own contribution. He was as devoted to beautifying the park with flowers and trees as was his predecessor; McLaren's specialty was rhododendrons, exotics that happen to do well in the park environment. So—as both men found out—do Monterey cypress (*Cupressus macrocarpas*), which is native to a small area in Monterey County,

Monterey pine (*Pinus radiata*), another Monterey County native, and blue gum (*Eucalyptus globulus*), a native of Australia. As a result of the efforts of these two early park superintendents, Golden Gate Park was forested with these exotics before anyone thought it would be possible: today, these three species constitute 90 percent of the park's trees. Unfortunately, many of the trees are the same age—forming an even-growth stand—and as they approach overmaturity, they must be removed. A reforestation plan is in process, and the Friends of Recreation and Parks welcomes donations for new trees; telephone 415-750-5105.

Although McLaren, like Hall, was a park purist, he was helpless before the surge of enthusiasm that sparked the 1894 Midwinter Exposition, held in Golden Gate Park. (The *San Francisco Chronicle*'s M. H. de Young was the instigator of this project.) The year 1893 had been a depression one, and the city welcomed the idea of attracting thousands of new visitors—and their money—to its beautiful Golden Gate Park. The original 60-odd acres that were selected for the fair soon swelled to 200 as buildings proliferated; one of the buildings was a 210-foot Tower of Electricity with spotlights on top, and McLaren had to dynamite it to get rid of it six months after the exposition closed. He was not so successful in ridding the park of some of the other "cultural" structures, around which the present museum complex grew up. The Music Concourse, the Japanese Tea Garden, and the Garden of Succulents also remain as mementos of the exposition.

Golden Gate Park was to inherit a number of other structures as time went on: the Portals of the Past (all that was left of the A. N. Towne mansion on Nob Hill after the 1906 quake); the Sharon Building, for which the rascal senator left the money (it was designed to be a "children's house" for nursing mothers and small children—an architectural feature that was popular before the turn of the century); and the beautiful crystal-palace Conservatory (the oldest existing building in the park), which was part of the estate of James Lick (the city actually bought this for $2,600).

There were many other early gifts to the park: the aforementioned Stow Lake, for example; the Prayerbook Cross (a memorial to the first prayerbook service held in California, by Sir Francis Drake's party on June 24, 1579); and Rainbow Falls, a gift of Herbert Fleischhacker in the 1930s. (Large gifts can no longer be easily accepted by the park, but it is possible to make a modest donation to,

The Conservatory, Golden Gate Park. PHOTO BY ROBIN LEW, SAN FRANCISCO RECREATION AND PARK DEPARTMENT.

say, plant a tree to memorialize an occasion or a person—to adopt an animal at the San Francisco Zoo—or to place a memorial bench.) The park was also used—and occasionally still is—for projects that can best be described as nonpark in character, the prime example of which is the sewage treatment plant, which was placed, and then replaced, at the western end of the park in the 1930s, then upgraded in the 1960s, and is still in use. (Poor William Hammond Hall's ghost must be whirling.) Still, Golden Gate Park has resisted many invasions successfully, perhaps the most notable being the location of a freeway through the park in the late 1950s. (The Hall of Flowers, in the south-central part of the park, just happened to be built at a crucial moment in the freeway fight, its location effectively blocking the proposed route.)

Despite John McLaren's antipathy to "stookies," there are a number of statues placed prominently in the park; some of them are noteworthy. Guarding the de Young Museum are two sphinxes that are the work of Arthur Putnam, who was also responsible for the relief sculpture on Market Street's lovely old streetlights; the sphinxes were completed in 1903 but were not placed here until 1928. A lithe cougar and a beautiful small bear have been guarding the Eighth Avenue entrance to the park since 1908; these are the work of Earl Cummings. At the east end of the Music Concourse sits Francis Scott Key in an elaborate sort of howdah minus elephant. (This was James Lick's gift and was executed by William Wetmore Story in 1885 and shipped via freighter to arrive in San Francisco in 1887.) Topping this work of art are four black eagles, one on each corner of the canopy; park officials note that pigeons carefully avoid their perches. Buried with this statue is a time capsule to be opened in 2070; it was dedicated during the park's centennial. (An earlier time capsule placed inside the base of this statue by Dr. Henry Cogswell—a public-spirited Victorian dentist, civic leader, and bluenose—was confirmed by X ray and opened with great excitement and ceremony by the California Historical Society, to whom it had been promised: its principal contents proved to be a number of treatises on temperance. Among several timely items, such as a *TV Guide* and a MUNI map, the new capsule contains a choice bottle of California wine.) As you stroll through the park you may also come upon the likenesses of Beethoven, Verdi, Cervantes, Goethe and Schiller, a doughboy, a pioneer mother, and John McLaren himself, who stands, appropriately enough, in the Rhododendron Dell opposite Sixth Avenue. Another appropriate marker remembers the Powell Street Railroad Company, which operated from 1888 to 1906, bringing passengers to Seventh Avenue and Fulton from the California Street roundhouse.

Among the unique delights of Golden Gate Park are those flowers and gardens mentioned earlier. Being a devotee of rhododendrons, McLaren not only initiated the planting of this lovely species but inspired his followers to continue the tradition; now there are more than 40 varieties of rhododendrons thriving in the park. Look for them to be in glorious bloom in a whole spectrum of colors starting in early April. Shakespeare buffs will be pleased with a garden that features 20 of the blossoms mentioned in the works of the bard. The Strybing Arboretum, owned by the city but administered by the Strybing Arboretum Society, offers a chance to savor the scent of yerba buena in its Garden of Fragrance. The arboretum, "a living library of plants"—and the oldest such institution in the United States, dating back to 1853—also has among its botanical specialties a Garden of

California Native Plants, a Moonviewing Pavilion, and a Redwood Trail. There's a Dahlia Garden, the dahlia being San Francisco's official flower; the more than 1,000 plants (totaling 250 varieties) bloom riotously in August. And there's a Rose Garden that blooms virtually all year round.

Inspiration for many of the park's gardens came from Alice Eastwood, for many years the California Academy of Sciences curator of botany. This plucky lady was a dedicated and superb botanist who managed to rescue the academy's herbarium specimens from the 1906 holocaust; the academy was located then at Market and Fourth streets, and Alice commandeered a spring wagon and hauled her treasures—barely ahead of the flames—to the bay, where she got them loaded onto a barge to ride out the conflagration safely in the middle of the water.

You will find that the Japanese Tea Garden is much more than a garden and much more than a teahouse. It dates back to the 1894 exposition, as noted above, and was primarily the work of George Turner Marsh, the oriental art specialist whose store was in the original Palace Hotel. Marsh conceived of the facility as an acre-size Japanese village; he supplied the main gate from his home in Marin County. (His first home was in the Richmond district: see Geary Walk 2.) Marsh employed a wealthy Japanese landscape gardener, Makoto Hagiwara, to design and construct the "rural style" tea garden landscape and building, where he sold his Japanese art goods during the fair. (The present pagoda is a relic of the 1915 Panama Pacific International Exposition.) Hagiwara and his family subsequently took over the operation of this popular park attraction, and the family ran it until May 1942, when they were "relocated" by the War Department. (The Japanese Tea Garden became the Oriental Tea Garden during World War II.) Credit is given the Hagiwaras for the invention of the fortune cookie. Three new gates were presented to the Japanese Tea Garden by San Francisco's sister city Osaka in 1985. The best time to visit the tea garden is in late March or early April, when the cherry blossoms should be a visual delight. (Golden Gate Park received another gift from another Oriental sister city when Taipei, in 1981, presented the city with a pavilion that now stands on Strawberry Hill in Stow Lake; it arrived in the park in 6,000 pieces and was assembled in situ; in return, San Francisco sent Taipei's Youth Park a full complement of playground equipment.)

Along with the various park attractions mentioned above, you may want to explore the Children's Playground, which was the first in the United States to be located in a public park and which has that splendid carousel. And there is the Buffalo Paddock on John F. Kennedy Drive in the western part of the park. The buffalo here—like all extant buffalo—are, of course, descendants of the buffalo that were born in New York's Bronx Zoo around the turn of the century, when the species was rescued from extinction by being bred in captivity. There is also the Beach Chalet, located on the Great Highway; this 1920s Spanish colonial revival building was the great architect Willis Polk's last work. Its roof of handwrought terra-cotta cost $60,000; it has frescoes on San Francisco life done by dress designer–artist Lucien Labaudt in the 1930s; and it is a San Francisco landmark. Closed for many years, it reopened in 1997 after a major redo. There's a Golden Gate Park visitor center on the first floor, a restaurant on the second, and a small brewery. If you visit it, you can also stop by the North, or Dutch, Windmill, built in 1902 and another San Francisco landmark; should it be springtime when you stop by, you can enjoy its Queen Wilhelmina Tulip Garden in gorgeous colorful bloom.

Birdwatchers should keep a sharp eye out for songbirds as well as waders, shorebirds, and the ubiquitous gulls in Golden Gate Park. There are 145 species of birds believed to be native to the park, although many disappeared during gold rush times when the area was denuded for firewood. It is a poignant note that one of the most popular early features of Golden Gate Park was an aviary where people could see and listen to the birds that were otherwise absent from their lives.

The best way to start a visit to Golden Gate Park is to stop in at McLaren Lodge at the eastern end of John F. Kennedy Drive. Built in 1896 during the reign of John McLaren, it was the home of the remarkable superintendent and his family until his death in 1943 (he lived to be 93, and worked for his park to the end). Now headquarters of San Francisco's Recreation and Park Department, McLaren Lodge has been extensively remodeled but still has a Romanesque flavor to it; originally, each of the principal rooms was paneled in a different wood. At McLaren Lodge you can stop by the information desk and, if you like, buy a park map published by the Friends of the Recreation and Park Department. (This organization is extremely valuable to Golden Gate Park, helping out on many fronts, including conducting interpretive walks and excursions under the aegis of their docents. You can pick up a schedule of the Friends' current events with your map.) Unfortunately, the lodge is not open on weekends, but it does have an outside map that shows two possible walks along the park's many miles of lovely trails (most paved); one is a 2-mile, the other, a 3-mile jaunt. You can get information in the Academy of Sciences, the de Young Museum, and the Japanese Tea Garden on Saturdays and Sundays. *Note:* On Sundays, the park's main roads are closed to automobile traffic, which makes it great for bicyclists, roller skaters, and skateboarders.

It should also be noted that park officials identify one of their principal problems as litter: one day out of five must be spent by park personnel—even the most expert gardeners—on clean-up duty. Volunteers supplement their efforts, but it's a monumental task to keep this heavily used park clean. Please use the trash containers supplied or pack out what you pack into Golden Gate Park, which most people agree is one of the most beautiful urban parks in the United States, one that deserves the love and respect of anyone who enjoys it.

Twin Peaks—Although they neither are at the center of the city nor include the city's highest summit, Twin Peaks are among the most prominent and central landmarks in San Francisco. The pioneer surveyor Jasper O'Farrell sighted on Twin Peaks when he laid out Market Street, the city's principal thoroughfare, in 1847, and from any spot on downtown Market, the double summits of this mountain dominate the scene to the southwest. When you stand on the top of Twin Peaks, you feel like you are in the very center of the city's universe, and, indeed, you get one of the most complete views of the metropolitan area that you can get anywhere inside or outside the city's boundaries. As an added plus, you get a very small sample of San Francisco's native flora (see the Bay Area Wildflowers appendix). Although invaded now by many exotics (park volunteers work at removing these weedy invaders) and showing a century and a half of careless use, the Twin Peaks meadows offer a beautiful show of native wildflowers in the spring and an interesting sampling of native San Francisco plants all year long.

By happy chance, most of the summit land of Twin Peaks has remained in municipal ownership throughout the city's history and, today, it's one of San Francisco's most visited parklands. Until the mid-1980s, however, nobody paid much loving attention to this unique city property. Things were not helped by the fact that several different city departments shared the care—or lack of care—of the area, or by the fact that it became an increasingly visited tourist mecca with almost no restrictions or regulations. Local public concern, however, reached city hall at long last, and a rehabilitation and beautification program was undertaken under the auspices of then-mayor Dianne Feinstein and a citizens' committee appointed by her. In a nice display of volunteer endeavor, handsome designs by two of the city's top landscape architects, Michael Painter and Kent Watson, were drawn up and implemented to accommodate the tens of thousands of people who visit this prime vista spot annually. Now the dozens of tour buses and sightseers' cars have well-defined parking areas, there are handsome walkways to follow and spacious places to stand, and there are interpretive signs to explain the landscape and cityscape visible from this top-of-the-world location. Unfortunately, some of the large bric-a-brac erected on top of Twin Peaks over the years seems to be there to stay, and in the face of no on-the-spot attendant, the predilection of too many people to treat the out-of-doors like a garbage can still make this lovely place look, at times, like the local dump.

On the other hand, there's so much to see from Twin Peaks that you can overlook the trash without too much difficulty. If you can visit this aerie in the spring, you will find mass plantings of wild iris, lupine, and wild hollyhocks, gorgeous stands of poppies, and a show of sunflowers, blue-eyed grass, and wild strawberries with their pure white blossoms hugging the rocky (chert) soil. The French broom, sweet alyssum, mustard, and brilliant magenta ice plant are, albeit beautiful, all intruders and do not belong here.

On a typical mid-April day, you may find the city spread out gloriously at your feet, basking in the spring sun, the ocean glinting to the west. By afternoon, if you are fortunate, you may be able to watch the fog gather offshore and pour into the Golden Gate, flow beneath the Golden Gate Bridge, and begin to assault, like a turbulent sea, the rocks of Alcatraz Island. And there may even be a red-tailed hawk to pose against the sky above you.

It is usually possible to get away from most of the crowd by making the short climb to the top of either the north summit (903 feet, 8 inches above sea level) or the south (910 feet, 5 inches). Since the terrain is steep, most visitors don't take the time or effort to gain these greater heights. Incidentally, the mountain to the southwest with the cross on top of it is Mount Davidson, with an elevation of 938 feet, the highest peak in the city: it is the traditional site for sunrise Easter services. And the monster antenna to the northwest is Sutro Tower, dubbed by San Francisco columnist Herb Caen "a giant roach holder."

Note: One of San Francisco's most popular landmark parks is Coit Tower, rising 180 feet above Telegraph Hill. This is the heritage of Lily Hitchcock Coit, who had a passion for the fire department. (Some people say the tower resembles the nozzle of a giant hose.) Notable for its thirties murals (wonderful) and its bay views (also wonderful), it is a tourist mecca. Best reached on foot, via Greenwich or Filbert streets (lots of stairs!).

Historic San Francisco Walks

San Francisco is a wonderful city for walking. Its geography offers an almost limitless choice of terrain, from long level stretches to gentle slopes to hills so steep that they seem to the breathless climber to be perpendicular. Virtually every part of the city provides an interesting scene, as well, and you can suit your fancy with strolls through miles of green parkland or through ethnic neighborhoods or residential sections with a range of architecture from gingerbread and San Francisco stick Victorian to turn-of-the-century beaux arts to Bernard Maybeck and Frank Lloyd Wright. You may prefer to explore the city's busy downtown streets with their sophisticated shops or to find the many view spots that open up grand vistas of the metropolis and the bay. Keep in mind that, along with all of this, two-thirds of San Francisco's beautiful waterfront is set aside in parkland, an amenity unmatched in any other of the world's first-class cities. (You can actually hike—or jog—most of 12 miles along the shores of San Francisco Bay and the Pacific Ocean without leaving the Golden Gate National Recreation Area.) While you enjoy the outdoor pleasures of urban walking and San Francisco's unique street scenes, you can also trace parts of the city's colorful history in its buildings and parks and in its place names, especially the names of its streets. And, should your appetite so dictate, you can sample some of the city's cosmopolitan cuisine.

Here are some suggestions to start you on your way.

Geary—The Street and the Boulevard

Six miles in length, Geary is San Francisco's longest east-west street. (Between Market and Gough, it is known as Geary Street; west of Gough, it is called Geary Boulevard.) It is also one of the city's oldest principal thoroughfares. Not only was it the first to link downtown to the ocean beach (it was then a toll road known as Point Lobos), but it tied almost directly into Third Street, the main artery serving "the Peninsula" (to the south) in the city's earlier days. Thus, since it was first laid out, Geary has been a natural key route for San Francisco's travelers and for its public transportation systems as well. It was along this thoroughfare that horses and then horse-drawn carriages transported San Francisco's early dandies through the seemingly endless sand dunes of the "Outside Lands" to the first Cliff House. Adolph Sutro paid his toll and, with his daughter, took his team out Geary Boulevard that fateful March day in 1881 when he discovered Samuel Tetlow's house overlooking the Pacific Ocean. (That incident changed the face of young San Francisco, for Sutro bought not only Tetlow's house but additional property and the Cliff House and then went on to open his famous gardens, to build his fabulous baths, and thereby to launch one of the city's most popular recreational centers.) Mayor James "Sunny Jim" Rolph inaugurated the city's first municipal railway system—"the people's road," he called it—when he ran a streetcar out Geary in 1912.

As you walk the length of Geary, you experience a good cross section of San Francisco. (By taking one or two short detours along the way, you can also add some extra interesting dimensions to your exploring.) No need to do it all at once: as the following notes describe, Geary divides itself quite naturally into three separate (and different) sections, each of which makes for an easy morning or afternoon—or even daylong—stroll. If you get tired along the way, you can always hop a bus.

The first walk is along Geary Street from Market to Gough. This is the oldest, most historical part of Geary, which runs through the heart of downtown, past some of the city's fine stores and hotels (with some of its better hotel restaurants) and past some of San Francisco's notable landmarks. This mile-long walk provides sometimes noisy, nearly always crowded, and always colorful street scenes and a good sampling of the city's architecture. In its first 5 blocks off of Market, Geary travels past more than two dozen buildings that went up in the feverish rebuilding of San Francisco following the 1906 disaster: these date back to 1909 or earlier. And in each of the 13 blocks between Market and Gough, there is usually at least one noteworthy structure—one actually goes back to Civil War days. Hence, the notes for Walk 1 are more detailed than for the other walks. (It is also worth noting that Geary Street from Market to Hyde has been called the spine of Dashiell Hammett's *The Maltese Falcon,* since so much of the action in this famous novel occurs here.)

The second Geary walk is the longest. Starting at Gough, where Geary becomes properly a boulevard, the walk covers the 3.6 miles to Twenty-sixth Avenue. En route, it takes you past one of the city's grand cathedrals, Japantown, some fine open space with metropolitan vistas, what was the notorious People's Temple, the city's Inner Richmond area and its Russian quarter, and some of San Francisco's most interesting ethnic eating places. An optional one-block detour off Geary Boulevard to Clement Street offers a trek through one of the city's colorful marketplaces.

The third Geary walk, 1.4 miles along the boulevard from Twenty-sixth Avenue to Ocean Beach, starts in front of an imposing Russian Orthodox cathedral, leads through a pleasant view-ful residential section (the Outer Richmond), and lands you in Sutro's charming and historical garden-park with breathtaking ocean views to the north and south and at your feet. With a short detour to the north, you can also explore what was one of San Francisco's earliest cemeteries (now a public golf course), admire some of the city's grandest old trees, and visit a fine arts museum, the Palace of the Legion of Honor. Here, you get unique views of the downtown cityscape as well as the Golden Gate Bridge (seen from the west), and the chance to see some of the museum's fine sculptures, including several Rodins, and a powerful piece of public statuary by George Segal. (This walk ties directly into GGNRA Walk 3.) Before walking the first two sections of Geary, you may want to refer to San Francisco Street Names for a rundown of the names of the 26 cross streets between Market and Presidio. These street names immortalize many of the men who made San Francisco's—and California's—early history.

Allow at least half a day for each of these walks.

Geary Walk 1—Market Street to Gough Street—Start your jaunt at the junction of Geary, Kearny, Third, and Market streets—once the most important intersection in the city. Before you get under way, it is worth taking a moment to look around.

Laid out by civil engineer Jasper O'Farrell in 1847, Market Street was purposely aligned with Twin Peaks to follow the already established route between little Yerba Buena and its nearby mission: this resulted in an unusual offset of city streets that San Francisco has lived with ever since. (Although Market runs northeast-southwest by the compass, natives tend to think of it simply in east-west terms. Thus, as you face Twin Peaks you are looking "west," and everything to your left is "South of Market.") At first, Market was lined with houses (and favored by the city's early literati); it was fashionable to promenade along its plank boardwalks. Before long, however, the houses were replaced with stores and such urban amenities as the Academy of Sciences (at Fourth Street), the city's baseball park (at Eighth Street), and the Roman Catholic Orphan Society (at New Montgomery, the site of the Palace Hotel), and the broad thoroughfare was well on its way to becoming a busy "market" street. San Francisco's first horse-drawn trolleys ran down it, the horses clopping through the blowing sand that engulfed the passengers. Not until about 1880 was the street paved, and then with basalt blocks laid directly onto the sand. Storekeepers fought a losing battle trying to sweep the sand between the cracks, and they vied with one another, and with the auctioneers, in hawking their wares with loud shouts and the fervent ringing of hand bells. When cable cars replaced the horse-drawn trolleys in 1881, they added to the general din but did not stop the street from being the chosen pathway of parades—especially Chinese parades complete with dragons—and funerals.

Lower Market Street took on a measure of scale and grandeur—and renewed fashionability—when in the mid-1870s Billy Ralston built his 2-acre-size Palace Hotel on the corner of New Montgomery. San Francisco's *Morning Call* labeled it "the finest hotel on the globe," and indeed it became world famous, attracting not only royalty but such literary luminaries as Oscar Wilde (who called San

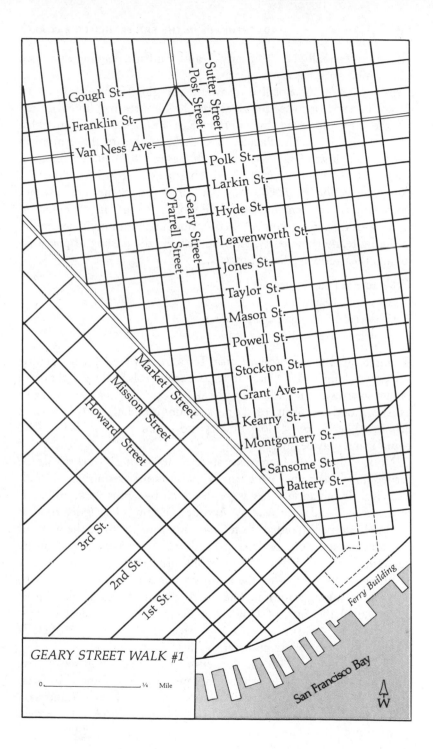

GEARY STREET WALK #1

0 _____ ¼ Mile

Francisco "a really beautiful city") and Rudyard Kipling and such performing artists as Enrico Caruso.

Billy Ralston did not live to attend the glittering opening of his Palace in 1875 or to see the rival (but less impressive) hotel opened up the street in 1877 by another San Francisco wheeler-dealer, "Lucky" Baldwin. The Palace, of course, burned to the ground in 1906 (the Baldwin Hotel went up in flames in 1898), but you can still admire Lotta's Fountain (1875), which graces the traffic island of the busy intersection where you stand. A horse trough was here first, but Lotta Crabtree presented this bronze wonder to the city to replace it. Lotta Crabtree was a winner whether dancing, strumming her banjo, or acting tear-jerking parts, and she became the darling of pleasure-loving, theatre-loving San Francisco:

> Because in Lotta we can see
> Artistic concentration
> Of sweetness, strength, and piquancy
> A pungent combination

Another favorite performer, Luisa Tetrazzini, whose great operatic career was launched in San Francisco, sang carols to the delight of an immense crowd that gathered to hear her on Christmas Eve in 1910 as she stood in front of Lotta's Fountain. This gala occasion prompted her to say: "I love no city more than this one. Where else could I sing outside on Christmas Eve!"

Notice the triple-lanterned streetlights along Market Street; turned on in 1917, they were San Francisco's first venture in outdoor electrical illumination. They were designed by Willis Polk, and their bronze relief sculpture was by Arthur Putnam. (The more modest double-lanterned streetlights on Geary are thought to be the work of the same artists.) Putnam departed radically from Victorian ideals by depicting a worn, dejected hero in his pioneer scene—called "The Winning of the West"—on the lamp standard and was roundly criti-cized for breaking tradition. These streetlights caused Market Street to be called the Path of Gold, not because of their electric light (described as "warm white") but because they were artificially bronzed and had yellow glass on the lamps.

The four buildings on the corners of the intersection where you stand are also noteworthy: all four are pioneer steel-frame structures, among the early skyscrapers that, some said, made San Francisco's Victorian skyline a rival of New York's. Number 690 Market Street, the American Savings Building immediately before you, was originally the San Francisco Chronicle Building and was long considered one of the great "architectural [triumphs and] treasures of San Francisco." It was the first of the iron-and-steel buildings erected in the city—going up in 1889, the same year that New York City, too, got its first steel-frame skyscraper. Its ten stories made it the tallest building in San Francisco (and, indeed, west of the Mississippi), and it stood through the 1906 cataclysm sturdily. Willis Polk enlarged it twice. It is said to be relatively intact behind the somewhat faceless facade of enameled metal porcelain that was placed over it in 1962.

Across the street on the northwest corner of Geary and Market stands the First Nationwide Building, constructed in 1902 and rebuilt in 1906 by its original architect, William Curlett. This limestone-clad, steel-frame structure is noteworthy for its fine vertical lines, its mansard roof, and Renaissance-baroque ornamentation. (The brick corner addition, built in 1964, echoes some of these features.)

On the southwest corner of Market and Third streets is the Central Tower, originally the Call/Claus Spreckels Building. Erected in 1898, this proved to have been exceptionally well designed and put together: it rode out the 1906 quake in great shape. The United States Geological Survey in its postquake report called it "probably . . . the best designed steel-work building in the United States." It proved strong enough to have an additional 6 stories placed upon its original 14 in a 1938 redo: the addition replaced a handsome dome, and the remodeled building now provides a good example of modern architecture.

Number 691–699 Market Street is the Hearst Building, another newspaper headquarters. (With three out of four of its corners housing newspapers, this intersection used to be referred to as "the heart of San Francisco's news.") The Hearst Building, which went up in 1909, is considered a good example of an early steel-frame building constructed to be both fireproof and earthquake-resistant.

In the decades following the installation of the Path of Gold streetlights, Market Street slowly began to fade and lose its glory. No longer a boulevard along which promenaded the city's fashionable folk, it became the haunt of the thousands of sailors from all over the world who poured into San Francisco in its heyday as a port. Peep shows, bawdy movies, and cheap penny arcades crept in. The crowds could be rough and noisy. Still favored for parades (as it is today), it was a mob scene during World War II and the scene of a near riot when San Francisco celebrated the end of that war in 1945. More and more, it became the dividing line between the city's posh downtown, centered around Union Square, and the Mission district. "South of the slot" (a hangover from cable car days), or "south of Market" was considered unfashionable, and so was the street itself.

In 1965, however, San Francisco's pride in this historic street was revived, and the city's voters authorized the expenditure of $2.5 million to beautify and restore Market Street. Part of the program was the restoration of the wonderful old streetlights. You will notice, too, the trees lining the sidewalks and a skyline of modern skyscrapers. Transportation along Market has been brought to the latest state of the art and is—usually—excellent. Both the Bay Area Rapid Transit System (BART) and the Municipal Railway (the MUNI) serve this thoroughfare.

Before leaving Market Street, take a last look around. Kitty-cornered across the street to the east you have a good view of the "new" Palace Hotel (now the Sheraton-Palace), which rose from the ashes in 1909, and next to it the Monadnock Building, which was under construction at the time of the 1906 fire. (Its builders took sly advantage of the holocaust to pick up adjacent property and so enlarge the structure.) This was considered an early typical business block. For an appropriate final view, look directly down Market Street to the east, and you will see silhouetted against the horizon the clock tower of the old Ferry Building, a fine San Francisco landmark. Built in 1895, it was modeled on Seville's famous bell tower, the Giralde: the ferry tower is the same 240 feet high but is without the 32 ramps that distinguish its Spanish inspiration.

As you walk west on Geary, you may have to look up to identify the noteworthy buildings you will pass, so many have "updated" ground floors. You will also get a better view of these buildings if you cross the street and proceed along its southern side. Be sure to notice Kearny Street as you cross. This was early San Francisco's "main drag," the site of the gambling saloons with women dealers and bouncers armed with guns. It was not far from the waterfront in those days, and Major General Stephen Watts Kearny stood on the street later named for him when he conferred rights and titles to the city's first lots, 80 percent of which were underwater. A few years later, monthly auctions were held on the corner of Kearny and Clay streets for the priceless bay tidelands. It was an extension of Kearny

that opened up the Telegraph Hill district of San Francisco and, incidentally, served the new wharf built by the rascal Meiggs in the early
1850s. The Vigilantes hung the luckless Casey near Kearny Street,
and Hallidie's first cable car took off bravely from the intersection of
Kearny and Clay.

Number 2 Geary (the four-story square building), at the corner of
Kearny and Geary, is a good example of how the early builders fitted
structures into the awkward lots delineated by the angling of Market
Street: it is nestled neatly into the Schmidt Building (number 10–12
Geary), an L-shaped structure fronting on two streets. Along with
number 28–36, these two buildings went up in 1908; number 28–36
(the Rosenstock Building) was designed by the influential, self-
trained architect Albert Pissis. Notice the progression skyward of its
ornamental columns from the simple Doric, to Ionic, to the most
complex, Corinthian. The "graceful decorum" of this treatment was
remarked by *Architect and Engineer* magazine.

The building on the southeast corner of Geary and Grant Avenue
has been a landmark at this intersection since 1912. Of steel-frame
construction finished in white-glazed terra-cotta (terra-cotta is a San
Francisco special), it was until 1948 an I. Magnin store and was
memorable, if for nothing else, for the gold-plated fixtures in the
restrooms. Note that Grant Avenue has long been the principal thoroughfare through the Chinese quarter of the city. This intriguing section of transplanted culture—so much a part of San Francisco's and
California's history and contemporary life—starts officially at Grant
and Bush Street, three blocks to the north, but unofficially at Sutter,
only two blocks away. You could spend an hour, a day, or even a
week exploring this interesting area, which is full of shops and excellent places to sample Chinese food.

The north side of Geary's 100 block has a particularly fine group
of postquake, "instant city" buildings. The sculptured masks
beneath the cornice of the building on the northwest corner are
worth noting. The Marion Building (number 108–110) and the E.
Simon Building (number 120–124), a handsome pair of brick structures, went up in 1909; each is covered with terra-cotta and ornamented in the Renaissance-baroque style. The Sachs Building next
door, also terra-cotta clad, was designed by George Applegarth and
erected in 1908. Note the rich decorative features, especially the lion
heads. A few doors up at 166 is another of the city's architectural
treasures, the Whittell Building. Since 1906, when, still under con-

struction, it was a steel skeleton looming above the ashes of downtown San Francisco, this early skyscraper has been a strong silhouette on the city's skyline. It has a particularly deep foundation, resting on hardpan, which helped it ride out both the 1906 and 1989 quakes with almost no damage.

Two of the buildings across the street date back to 1907 and 1908; they are more notable for their age than their architecture. The block is more memorable for another building that stood until quite recently as a choice survivor of the city's beaux arts days: the City of Paris (named for *La Ville de Paris,* an early floating-department-store ship), built in 1896 and remodeled in 1908, was a wonderful building with a skylit central court and a scaled-down replica of the Eiffel Tower on its roof. It was beloved by San Franciscans for over seven decades, and a spirited but losing battle was fought to save it when the Neiman-Marcus people came onto the scene in the late 1970s. Neiman-Marcus won, wrecked the building, and sold the Eiffel Tower for scrap. In deference to the civic-minded battlers—and perhaps because they recognized an architectural gem when they saw one—the new owners incorporated the skylit central court of the City of Paris into their checkered structure. It is worth stepping inside the store (on the corner of Geary and Stockton) to admire the beautiful columns and elegant stained glass that distinguish this lovely old rotunda. Note the adage spelled out in Latin on the dome: *Fluctuat Nec Mergitur.* Roughly translated, it means, "The ship may flounder but will not sink." Imagine, if you can, this four-story-high City of Paris rotunda filled up with a huge, sweet-smelling fir Christmas tree ornamented from top to bottom; this enchanted San Francisco children for generations but, alas, no more. (Neiman-Marcus does have a Christmas tree in the rotunda, but it's an artificial one, due to fire codes, and put together in sections.)

You are now at Union Square, the gift of San Francisco's first mayor, John Geary, to the young city. Although it is now the roof of a parking garage, built in 1942, it remains one of the city's choice pieces of open space, and it is decorated throughout the year with freshly blooming plants by the city's Recreation and Park Department. You may want to cross the street to enjoy this urban nicety that has been the heart of San Francisco's shopping center for decades. Its palm trees may evoke southern California, but the pigeons may remind you, instead, of London's Trafalgar Square.

While many people have an aversion to these interesting birds, pigeons play—and have played—a role in this cosmopolitan city. On the one hand, they have their dedicated critics who want no part of them, considering them a nuisance—and worse. The critics point out that pigeons have even influenced the design of several buildings—and not for the better—causing them to be designed with faceless (windowless) walls. (Prominent examples of pigeon-proof buildings are Neiman-Marcus, the old I. Magnin building (now owned by Macy's), and Macy's on Geary across the street.) On the other hand, San Francisco's pigeons have a coterie of devoted admirers who take such pleasure in their avian company that they feed them in Union Square regularly day after day. (You may find some of these pigeon lovers around.) Pigeons are, in fact, highly intelligent creatures with a lifestyle that many humans might emulate. The birds mate for life (they have a life span of 10 to 12 years), are obviously affectionate with one another, and both parents share in the care and feeding of their offspring. Their homing instincts are legendary. (See Geary Walk 2.) And they have been known to brave incredible dangers to return to their nests. Although they are no longer used by the military as they once were—one bird, Cher Ami, was credited with saving an American battalion in World War I—pigeons are pressed into service by the Coast Guard in rescue efforts at sea: these sharp-eyed flyers are far quicker and more adept at spotting survivors floating on the waves than are their human equivalents with all their radar and helicopters. Pigeons are protected by law in San Francisco, being officially recognized as part of the local wildlife. Recently, peregrine falcons have miraculously returned to keep the pigeon population in check.

The monument in the center of Union Square honors Admiral George Dewey for his 1898 triumph at Manila Bay, and the lady on top of the Corinthian column is a bronze Victory. Robert Aitken was the sculptor and Newton Tharp the architect. Paid for by public subscription, the monument was erected in 1902 and dedicated by President Theodore Roosevelt a year later. Union Square was named for a pro-Union Civil War rally, and soapbox speakers still use it.

The blocks bordering Union Square on all four sides have buildings of interest, although there's only one older structure still standing on Post Street: Bullock and Jones Men's Store was built in 1923. The Hyatt Union Square Hotel next to it is worth mention for its charming Ruth Azawa fountain (in its Stockton Street courtyard), an imaginative work depicting the people of San Francisco; it is said that when Azawa entertained while creating this work, she would present her guests with modeling clay and ask them to contribute figures of their own.

Stockton Street between Geary and Post has two buildings that are considered noteworthy: the smaller (218–222) was originally a three-story bookstore opened by A. M. Robertson in 1909. He was a legendary bookseller, publisher, and printer and very much a part of the literary scene during the first three decades of this century. The upper story of this building was the work of Willis Polk. The taller building (at 234–240) had a touch of moderne added to it when it was remodeled in the late 1930s. Between these two buildings runs Maiden Lane, and if you have the time, you might stroll up this historic byway, once the heart of the city's red-light district, to visit the architectural jewel at 140: this is a Frank Lloyd Wright building (a look-alike of New York's Guggenheim Museum) designed for V. C. Morris in 1949.

The south side of Union Square is distinguished for its pigeon-proof buildings. The erstwhile I. Magnin building was deliberately designed with smooth surfaces to discourage the birds. It is a 1946 redo of a 1905 steel structure that rode out the quake and fire. Macy's, which now owns much of this block, came along later. The 1907 building at the southeast corner of Powell and Geary has nicely detailed keystones over its windows.

The west side of Union Square is occupied by one of San Francisco's grandest and now restored old hotels, the (Westin) St. Francis. It has been called "a major monument of the city," indeed, "the architectural image of . . . San Francisco." First built in 1904, it was gutted by the 1906 fire, rebuilt and added on to in 1907, and enlarged in 1913. The 32-story tower was added in 1972 and has an outside elevator that provides some thrilling views. Note the warm-toned sandstone walls, the fine Ionic columns, the copper cornice, and the handsome streetlights. It is worth a trip into the lobby to admire the ambience of this memento of the city's splendid past. Note here the clock: "Meet me under the clock in the St. Francis" was once a legendary San Francisco phrase. The St. Francis has been a favorite of distinguished visitors since it opened. Irvin Cobb stayed here in 1920, covering the Democratic Convention, and he was terrified by the driving of the local cabdrivers who lined up in front of the hotel on Powell Street; he called one of them who drove him around "a lineal descendant of Ben Hur."

You may want to continue out Geary on the north side of the street, but note in passing the San Francisco street specialties that you'll find around Union Square—the colorful flower stands, the street performers who may be anyone from a lone bagpiper to a trio of drummers to a mime in clown makeup, and the street artists who sell everything from leatherwork to original paintings to handmade jewelry. You're likely to be treated to a concert of cable car bells as the cars approach Geary.

The Elkan Gunst Building on the southwest corner of Geary and Powell is another that dates back to 1908. Of reinforced concrete, its rounded facade provides an interesting example of corner treatment. Close by it, number 333 looks as though it should be a theatre, and so it was meant to be when it was built in 1916 by a pair of Bay Area architects (Cunningham and Politeo) noted for their dramatic structures—both literally and figuratively, it would seem. Further up the block is the Handlery Hotel, which has been standing since 1907; here stayed the legendary detective Charlie Chan in Earl Derr Bigger's 1928 thriller *Behind That Door*. On the north side of the street, a former English pub (built in 1917), the hotel at 386 (erected in 1909 as an eight-story building and remodeled extensively in 1939 into a modern structure), and the 1922 small commercial building at 383 all add to the historic flavor of this block.

The 400 block of Geary, between Mason and Taylor streets, has the Geary Theatre, a focal point of the city's extensive involvement with the performing arts since it was built in 1909. Originally known as the Columbia (its name was changed on Christmas Day in 1924), it has been played by a succession of world-famous actors and actresses; it is an official San Francisco landmark. (Hammett has one of his characters in *The Maltese Falcon* attend a performance at the Geary.) The Curran Theatre (built in 1922) next door to the west adds to the theatrical luster of this block. Note the handsome marquees of both theatres, the classic relief work on the Geary, and the Curran's beautiful copper mansard roof. The (Four Seasons) Clift, another (five-) star San Francisco hotel, was designed in 1913 by MacDonald and Applegarth specifically to accommodate anticipated visitors to the 1915 Panama Pacific International Exposition. (Many other buildings in this section of the city were built for the same reason.) The Clift houses a noted San Francisco restaurant, the Redwood Room, famous for years for its elegance, its roast beef, and for requiring gentlemen to wear ties. One architect considers this room one of the finest interiors in the country. The Clift has long been favored by visiting royalty, world travelers, and such disparate luminaries as Bertrand Russell and Sir Arthur Conan Doyle (who was more interested in spiritualism than in Sherlock Holmes when he was here in 1923). It is at least partly the model for Hammett's Alexandria Hotel.

Note that the architecture of number 459–465 (between the Curran Theatre and the Clift) echoes that of numbers 450–456 and 458–466 across the street: these were designed and built at the same time, in 1922. Other interesting buildings on the north side of the street are the three hotels: the one at 418–432 (built in 1911); that at 436–440 (built in 1912), where Alan Paton wrote the last pages of *Cry the Beloved Country* in late 1949; and the one at 490–498, also built in 1912. Notice, once again, the ubiquitous bay windows. The other buildings in this block are all old-timers that went up between 1909 and 1920. Note the rather elegant narrow building, number 486.

As anyone who has read Dashiell Hammett will recognize, you are now in the heart of Hammett's San Francisco. Hammett lived a block away up the hill at 891 Post Street, on the corner of Hyde, and he knew—and wrote wonderfully about—"his" neighborhood and "his" town, capturing the spirit (some would say "the soul") of San Francisco of the 1920s perhaps better than any other writer. Indeed, Don Herron, in his excellent literary guide to San Francisco, notes that Hammett's San Francisco can be compared to Joyce's Dublin and Dickens's London. As of this writing, it is possible to take a walking tour of this neighborhood with Herron. (Call 510-287-9540.) He has also published *The Dashiell Hammett Tour* for self-guided explorers on foot (see Bibliography).

Between Taylor and Van Ness, Geary Street travels through part of San Francisco's Tenderloin, wherein live many of the city's older "nonaffluent" citizens. The somewhat threadbare general scene is enlivened by several points of interest. The brown apartment house on the northwest corner of Taylor and Geary stands on the site of the little house where dancer and early advocate of free love Isadora Duncan was born in 1877; she died in 1927 when the long scarf she was wearing caught in the axle of her touring car and strangled her. (There is a commemorative Duncan plaque next to the door of 501 Taylor.) At 656 is the wonderfully flamboyant Alcazar Theatre, designed by a Shriner for the Shriners in 1917. Was the architect inspired by the equally flamboyant Alhambra Building at 860 that went up in 1914? Across the street is the Jewell Theatre at 655 Geary. With 32 seats in a 750-square-foot space, it has the unofficial title as the smallest theatre in the Bay Area. On "Geary near Leavenworth" (which side of the street?), Floyd Thursby was done in by Wilmer Cook in *The Maltese Falcon*. Note in passing the Rossmore Apartments, number 765, built in 1916, and at 825, the Castle Apartments, built about 1920; both are interesting period pieces.

On the corner of Van Ness and Geary, the gaudy edifice labeled, inescapably, Tommy's Joynt may consider itself a San Francisco landmark: the distinction is not official. It should not distract you from admiring number 1117 just up the hill, which *is* a designated San Francisco landmark. This is the Goodman Building, one of the oldest utilitarian buildings still in use in the city. Its architects (in 1864) were Rousseau and Son. Remodeled during the years since, it was occupied by artists (grateful for low rents) at the time of the city's big redevelopment project in the 1960s. Targeted for replacement, the building was purchased by the city over the bitter objections of the owner and many of its tenants, and for quite a while its fate hung in the balance. Finally, it was sold back (not to its original owner) and has recently been extensively remodeled into the good-looking building you see today. The low rents, of course, have vanished, and so have the artists.

The First Unitarian Church on the corner of Franklin dates back to 1889: it lost its bell tower, since rebuilt, in the 1906 catastrophe. This fine old building with its beautiful rose window is noted not only for its place in present-day San Francisco—it is used extensively for musical and civic as well as religious purposes—but for having on its grounds the sarcophagus of Thomas Starr King, patriot, champion of freedom, and the city's pioneer Unitarian minister. (His earlier church, built in 1864, stood on the corner of Geary and Stockton and was said to be the most beautiful church in the city: it gave way to the series of buildings that have culminated in Neiman-Marcus.) King was an eloquent orator and fervently antislavery: he is one of those for whom Union Square was named. He is credited with having been highly influential in keeping San Francisco (and so California) in the Union during the Civil War. He died during the last year of that war, when he was not yet 40. South on Franklin near (appropriately enough) Starr King Way, you will find his statue and his cenotaph, a California registered historical landmark. It is worth noting that King is one of only two men who represent California in the national Capitol (the other is Father Junipero Serra) and that one of Yosemite's beautiful peaks, Mount Starr King, immortalizes this early San Franciscan who died much too young. Although he never saw the present Unitarian church, he would doubtless have approved of its place in the community and welcomed as neighbor the ILWU (named for the late Harry R. Bridges, the colorful former leader of the Longshoremen's Union), whose building stands across the street.

Geary Walk 2 — Gough Street to Twenty-sixth Avenue—This is the longest of the Geary walks—3.6 miles—but it can easily be taken in shorter sections.

As you stand on the corner of Geary and Gough, it is easy to see why the street now becomes a boulevard, for here, not overly wide, one-way Geary Street suddenly turns into a broad, two-way thoroughfare with four lanes running in each direction. This opening up of the street gives a good feeling of open space (although it cost the city a park) and this is emphasized by St. Mary's Cathedral and its grounds, which occupy the southwest corner block. This landmark cathedral, which dominates the view here, also dominates the cityscape from many vantage points.

The architecture of St. Mary's has been talked about since the cathedral was built in 1971. Some people describe the four huge (190-foot-high) marble walls, which twist from a cross-shaped top into geometric shapes known as paraboloids, as looking like giant washing machine agitators; others see them as the magnificent sails of great ships. You can decide for yourself: the design is unique, and the play of light and shadow on the high surfaces is always intriguing.

Whatever you think of the exterior of this cathedral you must see the interior to fully appreciate what the architects (Angus McSweeney, Paul A. Ryan, and John Michael Lee, with Pietro Belluchi [of the Massachusetts Institute of Technology] and Pier Luig Nervi [Rome] design consultants) had in mind. A few minutes—or longer—inside is highly recommended. When you enter, your eyes are carried upward by the four narrow vertical stained-glass windows that fit between the walls; the lift is immense, the full 190-foot height of the church. The vast space of the body of the church—255 feet by 255 feet—is powerfully defined. Each window is dominated by its own color representing one of the four primitive elements—fire (flame colored), water (blue), earth (green), and air (gold). Halfway to the apex of the apse, a mobile of slender silvery rods—the baldacchino, or canopy above the massive marble altar—descends like a circular shower of rain. Along the walls are stations of the cross in bronze. If you are fortunate, you may hear the organist at work on the cathedral's beautiful instrument; the music as well as the architecture seems to soar. (The freestanding organ, itself a masterpiece, has 4,842 pipes.)

On your way again, you may want to take a moment to orient yourself before proceeding westward. You are in the city district known as the Western Addition, the subdivision that went on city maps in 1856 when James Van Ness was mayor. You are standing on Cathedral Hill, 206 feet high and one of San Francisco's 43 official hills. (Although some people say that the city, like Rome, has just 7 hills, it actually has 42 rises of 200 feet or more, and 1—Rincon Hill—of 120 feet; its highest point is Mount Davidson at 938 feet.) Between Gough Street and the ocean, Geary Boulevard will travel over 2 more recognized rises before it deadends on Sutro Heights (260 feet); the rise you see to the west of you is Laurel Hill, which tops out at 264 feet.

You are also standing within the boundaries of an ambitious redevelopment project undertaken by the city in 1956. In that year, a 108-acre area delineated by Franklin, Broderick, Post, and Eddy streets was designated not just for improvement but quite literally for redevelopment. Eight years after it was started, the project was enlarged by 277 of the acres that surrounded it.

It was the redevelopment project and not the 1906 fire (which was pretty well contained at Van Ness Avenue) that brought about the paucity of Victorian houses in this part of the city. Many fine old homes once stood here but were doomed because they had fallen into major disrepair; although the city offered them for almost nothing to anyone who would move them and restore them, there were few takers, and most of the old places sadly were destroyed. You will see some of the standardized housing that replaced Victorians along the south side of Geary.

As you walk westward, notice the fitting buildings and aspect of the consulate of the People's Republic of China on the south side of the street. Across from it on the north side of Geary is the Japan Business and Community Center, another part of the redevelopment project, and the heart of the city's small Japantown, which lies roughly between Geary and Sutter. Although without the mellow flavor of

Chinatown—which is so very much more extensive and has been, after all, a part of San Francisco almost from its beginnings—Japantown, or at least Japan Center, is well worth a detour.

The entrance to the center is marked by the giant Peace Pagoda that was "Presented in Friendship by the People of Japan to the People of the United States" on March 28, 1968. North of it is the Peace Plaza, a streetwide space (once Buchanan Street) that runs from Geary to Sutter Street. Clustered around the plaza are the shops, eating places, and night spots that make up the Nihonmachi shopping area. Here you will find an assortment of merchandise—souvenirs, hardware, shoji screens, etc., etc.—imported not just from Japan but from other parts of Asia. Soko Hardware Store is worth a visit, just to marvel at the variety of merchandise. You'll also find that just about every other door opens into a restaurant, many of them sushi bars. You can partake of some excellent exotic food in these Japanese dining places (you could, in fact, eat your way through Japantown—there's even a Denny's!). Many Japanese dishes are displayed in the windows of the restaurants, being artfully (and realistically) contrived in plastic. Flanking the plaza are two shopping malls, with more restaurants!

Back on Geary Boulevard, you'll find that it drops into a slot tunnel designed to speed traffic past the busy Fillmore Street intersection; walkers stay aboveground to take advantage of the sidewalks. On the south side of Geary between Fillmore and Steiner stands the building that was the People's Temple, a reminder of the Reverend Jim Jones and the cult tragedy in Guyana in 1978. The building was part of the complex of the Temple Beth Israel built in 1908 by the oldest and at one time the largest conservative Jewish congregation on the West Coast. It could (and did) seat 1,500 people and was considered one of the finest places of worship in the city.

As you continue westward across Divisadero Street, you'll be close to the onetime home of William Saroyan, who lived only two blocks to the north in 1929. Up Laurel Hill to the south is the Kaiser-Permanente Medical Center, which dominates this part of Geary quite obviously. Again, the middle lanes of Geary go underground, this time through a tunnel. Stay on the north side; from this vantage point, look back for a fine view of the city. (Photographers may want to stop on the east side of Presidio for an interesting perspective down the boulevard all the way to the bay, where a small wedge of the Bay Bridge can be seen.) Note how St. Mary's Cathedral, which you saw at the start of this walk, spreads its paraboloid wings like strange great sails against the downtown skyline.

From Gough Street to Presidio Avenue you have come 1.2 miles; it is another 0.8 mile to Arguello Boulevard, a walk best enjoyed on the north side of the street. In this distance, you'll pass through the easternmost part of the marketplace section of Geary Boulevard, along a wide street with another, more eclectic, array of restaurants. (You may want to cross the street to visit the Nippon Goldfish Company at 3109 Geary—it's the next best thing to an Aquarium with a capital *A*.) (*Note:* On the northwest corner of Parker is Strait's Shanghai Food, a restaurant recommended for its unique, delicious fare.) Looming on the horizon to the south is Lone Mountain, which rises steeply to 448 feet just one block away. What appears to be a medieval monastery on top of it is a university complex. The campus dates back to 1930 and has been used successively by the San Francisco College for Women and Lone Mountain College; since 1978, it has been part of the University of San Francisco. There is a pleasant stairway on Turk Street (two blocks south) leading up Lone Mountain, if you would like a leafy detour for some wonderful (360-degree) views.

Another point of immediate interest is the Neptune Society Columbarium, formerly the San Francisco Memorial Columbarium, whose well-proportioned green dome is surrounded by trees to the southeast and south of the Coronet Theatre. This elegant neoclassic structure was designed by British architect Bernard J. S. Cahill and erected in 1898 for the Independent Order of Odd Fellows as a memorial repository; now it is the last reminder of the order's cemetery, which was founded in 1865 and which took up a good part of Laurel Hill. San Francisco's only columbarium (and the largest on the West Coast), this early American Renaissance building was sturdy enough to ride out the 1906 earthquake without serious damage; more unusually, it also survived the ordinance passed by the city in 1935 outlawing cemeteries within the boundaries of San Francisco. (Only two were allowed to remain, the Mission Dolores cemetery, which dates back to 1776, and the National Cemetery in the Presidio.) The columbarium escaped only because its 3 acres of land had been homesteaded under the Homestead Act before the ordinance was passed. If you make a short detour (south on Stanyan one block, then west just a few steps to number 1 Lorraine Court, you can get a better look at the columbarium and its fine stained-glass

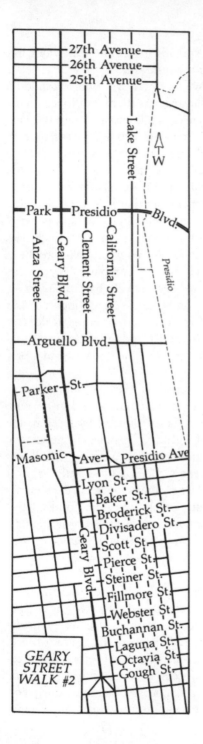

27th Avenue
26th Avenue
25th Avenue

Lake Street

⇧ W

Park — Presidio — Blvd.

Anza Street
Geary Blvd.
Clement Street
California Street

Presidio

Arguello Blvd.

Parker St.

Masonic — Ave. — Presidio Ave.

Lyon St.
Baker St.
Broderick St.
Divisadero St.
Scott St.
Pierce St.
Steiner St.
Fillmore St.
Webster St.
Buchannan St.
Laguna St.
Octavia St.
Gough St.

Geary Blvd.

GEARY STREET WALK #2

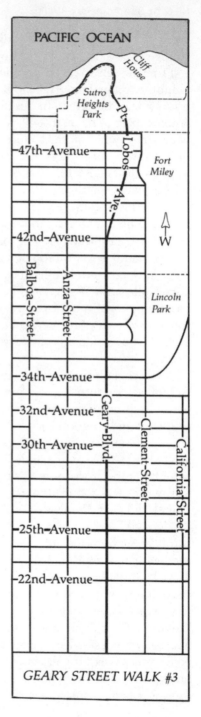

PACIFIC OCEAN

Cliff House

Sutro Heights Park

Pt. Lobos Ave.

47th Avenue

Fort Miley

42nd Avenue

⇧ W

Balboa Street
Anza Street

Lincoln Park

34th Avenue

32nd Avenue

30th Avenue

Geary Blvd.
Clement Street
California Street

25th Avenue

22nd Avenue

GEARY STREET WALK #3

windows, many of which are painted. It is open to the public from
10:00 A.M. until 1:00 P.M. every day. (The columbarium was
acquired by the Neptune Society in 1980 after years of neglect and
disrepair. The Society has done a beautiful job of restoration, and the
building is now an official city historic landmark.)

Arguello Boulevard is another of San Francisco's boundary
streets: running north-south, it defines the eastern limit of the Richmond district, which extends westward to Ocean Beach and is bordered on the north by the Presidio and on the south by Golden Gate
Park. This part of the city was known for many years as the Great
Sand Waste, being little more than a stretch of undulating sand dunes
and blowing sand with here and there a rocky hill sticking up. In
1853, some ambitious folks strung a telegraph wire from Point
Lobos (the northwest tip of the area) to Telegraph Hill downtown,
this to alert the merchants to the arrival of ships and thus a load of
potential customers, but this was Point Lobos's only link to San
Francisco's busily growing downtown until 1863, when its first
building of note, the Cliff House, was completed. The Cliff House
needed a usable access, of course, and a privately owned 4-mile toll
road to it (later Geary Boulevard) was ready to be used in 1864: the
tolls paid for the upkeep. You could take your own horse and buggy
on it to the beach for a picnic—a favorite all-day family outing—or
you could take a horse-drawn omnibus from Portsmouth Square for
50 cents, a sizable sum in those days. A few roadhouses were built
along the way to feed and water travelers. (One is still in use as a
restaurant on the northwest corner of Geary and Thirty-fourth
Avenue.) Italians, Swiss, and Germans settled in on dairy farms in
this rural area next to the city. Those were the days when wild goats
roamed Land's End, vegetable gardens sprouted where now Sea Cliff
stands, and Chinese fishermen not only camped on the little beach
that would one day be named in their honor but grew strawberries
nearby. In the late 1860s, the Outside Lands Committee drew the
boundaries of Golden Gate Park and set a street grid for the area to
its north. Unwittingly, they created a subdivision with some of the
finest views in the world—views that sweep from Point San Pedro in
the south to Point Reyes in the north, with the beautiful hills of
Marin in the foreground, the Farallon Islands studding the horizon
to the west, and the Golden Gate opening the way to the east.

The new district did not get its name until 1889. By then there were
homeowners here and there throughout it; there was a livery stable on

the corner of Eighth Avenue and Geary; there were cemeteries, including a potter's field; there was a horse-racing course off Geary between Twenty-fourth and Twenty-fifth avenues; and Adolph Sutro had become interested in the area (he acquired much of it and sold off lots for income). It was the members of the homeowners' club who chose the name Richmond. There is some disagreement as to how they came to this selection. One version says that the group, after an evening of argument, could reach no decision: then one member said, "Oh, we'll pick a name all right, just like Grant took Richmond." Another, inspired, said, "What's wrong with calling the place Richmond?" Another, more colorful, version says that one homeowner, George T. Marsh, a highly successful dealer in Japanese art (he had a shop in Billy Ralston's Palace Hotel) insisted on calling the area Richmond after his hometown in Australia (which, in turn, was doubtless named for England's Earl of Richmond). Marsh, an influential and hospitable man, is said to have commuted from his home among the sand dunes (he had a fine place on the corner of Clement Street and Twelfth Avenue) to his downtown place of business by horseback; he carried with him every morning a homing pigeon that he would release at 4:00 P.M. to inform his wife of the hour he would arrive home for dinner and of the number of guests that he would be bringing along. The same George T. Marsh was responsible for the Japanese Tea Garden in Golden Gate Park.

(Although the city fathers officially changed the name of the Richmond district to the Park Presidio district in 1917, this to avoid confusion with the town of Richmond in the East Bay, the original name stuck, and today most San Franciscans refer to the district simply as "the Richmond.")

It was not until after the turn of the century and the 1906 quake and fire that the Richmond really came to be settled. Following that disaster, the city erected over 5,000 refugee shacks in 11 city parks, including Golden Gate Park, for some of the tens of thousands of people who had been left homeless. As things got better, the city had to remove the shacks to get back the parks and made the little buildings available for a small sum. Since lots were cheap in the Richmond, many hauled their meager dwellings into this district. According to one local historian, there was a whole parade of shacks hauled on wagons to their new sites. (Some 40-odd of these refugee shacks still stand in San Francisco; you can see 2 restored models—

rescued from their Richmond sites—in the Presidio: see Natural History Museums appendix.)

Other San Franciscans moved westward in the years that followed. Interestingly, there was little uniformity in the houses that they built (the Richmond is noted for its eclectic architectural styles)—but for one feature: since middle-class families were coming to own automobiles in the late teens and twenties, some of the early architectural experiments with designing and building garages took place in this part of the city; virtually every new house had a garage. While a few were located separately on easements, most were integrated into the houses themselves. You will note many narrow garage doors tucked next to the front steps of a wide variety of architecturally different houses. (Between Thirty-fourth and Thirty-fifth avenues on the south side of Geary, you will also note some very narrow and steep driveways that evoke the Model T era.) There are also many houses in the Richmond that recall the bungalow styles of the twenties, and in Sea Cliff and Shoreview Terrace—both Richmond enclaves—there are some quite grand near-mansions. (There are a couple of Willis Polk designs on Sea Cliff Avenue and one Julia Morgan house on the southeast corner of Forty-sixth Avenue and Anza.) Only along the outer avenues of the Richmond will you find examples of the uniform Bauhaus type of building that is more characteristic of another San Francisco "bedroom," the Sunset.

The Richmond is notable not only for its eclectic architecture but for its ethnic diversity. This is probably the most cosmopolitan district in the city, with a kind of United Nations population in which Chinese, Koreans, Russians, Filipinos, Vietnamese, French, Arabs, and deeper-rooted Americans live next to one another. The schools, in fact, count children from more than 20 different countries in their classrooms. There is also a variety of handsome places of worship, including synagogues, Protestant and Roman Catholic churches, and perhaps the finest Russian Orthodox cathedral in the Bay Area. The eating places reflect this wide ethnic mix with a few extra exotic cuisines—such as Thai—thrown in for good measure. In the business sections, there are many individual shops where you can find all sorts of different items—from jeans to jewelry, icons to Irish imports, and futons to florists. Grocers display their fruits and vegetables on the sidewalks; there's one of the city's best used bookstores here (the Green Apple on Clement Street near Sixth Avenue); movie theatres, locksmiths, hardware vendors, florists, stationers, printers, cleaners, antique dealers, computer salesmen (waterbed salesmen, too), bakers, bagel makers—name a product or a service that you want, and chances are good that you'll find it in the Richmond.

From Arguello to Twenty-sixth Avenue, Geary will take you through one of the Richmond's busiest small-business districts. (*Note:* Before you leave Geary and Arguello, notice the exotic Indian consulate at 540 Arguello.) Or here you may, if you choose, detour a block to the north and take Clement Street as far as park Presidio Drive (Fourteenth Avenue). This is another colorful small-business district, and as Clement Street is considerably narrower than Geary, it is more intimate. Virtually every building has one or two stores in it; thus, if you like being closer to the action, this small (0.2-mile) jog in your walk may be a worthwhile option. This section of Geary, however, has its own particular ambience and is recommended for your first foray into this part of the city.

You may hear half a dozen languages as you walk along Geary, and you'll also see evidence of the city's Russian colony—Russian delis, a bookstore, a restaurant, a café—and perhaps an Orthodox priest in his flowing black cassock. Many White Russians settled in this part of the city after World War I and the Revolution. Others came in after World War II when they fled from Singapore and the Communist takeover of China.

You'll pass a recommended Italian restaurant (Café Riggio, number 4112 on the north side of Geary), a recommended Cambodian restaurant (Angkor Wat, number 4217 on the south side of the street), a recommended Thai restaurant (Khan Toke at number 5937), and a recommended Chinese (Shanghai) restaurant, the Hong Kong Flower Lounge (number 5322). You may find it difficult to pass by the wonderful smell of French bread from the bakery at Tenth, or to pass up the wonderful bagel bakery (the House of Bagels) and Jewish deli (Shenson's) just west of Park Presidio Drive. The Star of the Sea (number 4420) and St. Monica's (number 5920) are both lovely churches, and both will welcome your visit. You can enter St. Monica's through the side door, via the schoolyard; Star of the Sea's doors are open for noon and evening Mass or telephone 415-751-0450 to arrange a visit. Note between Twenty-fifth and Twenty-sixth, Paul's Hat Works, the only such store in the city and, indeed, unique anywhere.

Geary Walk 3—Twenty-sixth Avenue to Ocean Beach—Between Twenty-sixth and Twenty-seventh avenues on the north side of Geary stands the Russian Holy Virgin Cathedral of the Church of Exile, described by its architect, Oleg N. Ivanitsky, as "the largest and most beautiful [Russian Orthodox cathedral] on the Pacific Coast." His were not idle words, for this church, built in the first five years of the 1960s, is a most impressive religious structure. Topped with five golden-tiled domes, it dominates the skyline for many blocks and forms a shining spot in the cityscape when viewed from higher grounds. (Should you travel on the bay itself, you'll find it equally a landmark from the water.) The several large icons in bright mosaics add a colorful, if solemn, touch to its exterior facade. The inside of the cathedral is overwhelming, with warm-toned frescoes, beautiful golden fretwork, and dark crimson curtains concealing—or revealing—one or more of the three altars. High above, the figure of God the Father looks down upon the assembled congregation. There are no pews, since worshippers traditionally stand during the service. And this Russian service may involve a good deal of singing and chanting; among the priests in this church there are some fine voices, and when the basso profundo lets his voice out fully, spines shiver although there are no rafters to do so. The Holy Virgin Cathedral is closed except for services, but visitors are welcome when the doors are open (8:00 A.M. to 9:00 A.M. and 6:00 P.M. to 7:00 P.M. most weekdays, and 8:00 A.M. to noon on Sundays) as long as they respect the church's customs; women wearing slacks may not enter. The church bookstore is worth a visit for its unique collection of Russian icons and nesting dolls, as well as books and cards. It's closed Mondays, but open at least part of the day the other days of the week. There is a parish school next to the cathedral where children learn the language and religion of their Russian forebears; the school choir of young voices (very lovely) may be heard at early mass on Sunday. Outdoor processions take place at various church celebrations, and the Holy Virgin Cathedral is noted for its Russian Easter observance.

From here it is about 1½ miles to the beach through one of the Outer Richmond's quieter residential areas. Here's where you will find a good spectrum of the district's eclectic architecture ranging from Victorian (workingmen's) peaked-roof cottages—there are some attractive ones between Thirty-fourth and Thirty-fifth avenues on the south side of Geary—to small set-back shingled beach houses, built when front yards were affordable, to solid-looking Spanish-style apartment buildings dating from the twenties and thirties, to contemporary, too-often-from-the-same mold two-story flats. One of the city's nicer enclaves, Shoreview Terrace, is uphill between Thirty-sixth and Thirty-eighth avenues off Geary.

This is also the part of the Richmond where the views begin to open up in all directions, and the cross streets serve as windows to both the north and south. Walking along the north side of Geary, you continue to see the Marin Headlands, and you will soon recognize Mount Tamalpais, the Indian maiden, lying on the northern horizon.

After passing a last cluster of shops across from a supermarket, you'll note a large complex of buildings crowning the hill between Thirtieth and Thirty-second avenues to the south; this is George Washington High School, topping another of San Francisco's 43 hills, Washington Heights. It was built during the mid-thirties on the site of an old rock quarry, and its architecture is a W.P.A. Moderne or stripped-down classic. If you're interested in the art produced during the thirties, you will find it worthwhile to climb the hill on Thirty-second Avenue; the frieze above the football field was done by Sargent Johnson, a Works Progress Administration artist who also did the Aquatic Park marquee and mosaics; and the murals in the school are by the same artists—Victor Armantoff, Ralph Stackpole, and Gordon Langdon—whose work ornaments Coit Tower. This school, like most in the Richmond, has a diverse and extensive program of second languages.

At Thirty-fourth Avenue, note first the building on the northwest corner, once a roadhouse out in the country. (The refugee shacks now in the Presidio stood behind it until 1985.) Then turn and look back for a nice view (even better at Thirty-sixth) downtown with the Holy Virgin Cathedral's golden domes gleaming against the cityscape; the church dominating the skyline to the southeast is St. Ignatius, built in 1914 for $300,000. Now cross the street for your first open vista to the south. In the next few blocks there will be an increasingly good view to the southwest of the Pacific Ocean with Golden Gate Park in the foreground and the Montara Range as a backdrop.

At Thirty-fourth Avenue, you will also have the option of a possible 1-mile detour. Just a block to the north is Lincoln Park with its city golf course and some of the city's grandest old pine, eucalyptus, and cypress trees. This was once Golden Gate Cemetery, one of the city's early graveyards. Acquired in 1868, it was in use (by among others, the Chinese community and as a potter's field) until 1900, when the city fathers decided that the city could no longer allow interment within its limits. In 1909, this cemetery was turned into a park, and many of the bodies were left where they were—and still are. The Lincoln Park Golf Course above them has still got to be one of the most beautifully located in the world. (Should you stroll through it—not recommended when golfers are present—you may come upon a monument marking a Chinese burial site—the shrine of K'ong Chou Hui Chan—among the stands of trees.) Located at the high point of Lincoln Park, just a half mile from Geary, is the Palace of the Legion of Honor, one of San Francisco's major art museums. (Others are the de Young Museum and the Asian Art Museum in Golden Gate Park and the San Francisco Museum of Modern Art.) The Palace of the Legion of Honor was given to the city by members of the Spreckels family as a memorial to San Franciscans killed in World War I. It is noted for its design (a replica of the French building of the same name), for its Rodin statuary, and for its graphic arts collection, which has been called the finest on the West Coast. The plaza in front of the museum commands a superlative view of the city and Mount Diablo (when it's a clear day), and across the street there are equally superlative views of the Golden Gate Bridge (striking when viewed from the west) and the Marin Headlands. Accenting the city view is one of the museum's outstanding sculptures. Just below the plaza on the golf course is a reminder of those early Victorian days—a memorial to the city's seamen lying in their "last earthly port and resting place"; this was presented to the Ladies' Seamen's Friends by Dr. Henry D. Cogswell, a dentist who was fond of public monuments (see Golden Gate Park). At the northern end of the plaza there is a powerful reminder of some horrors of World War II, George Segal's sculpture *The Holocaust*.

Note: Should you prefer to continue your walk on to Ocean Beach in a natural rather than urban setting, you can pick up the Golden Gate National Recreation Area trail around Land's End at this point. Cross El Camino Del Mar and admire the gift (a handsome stone tablet) of one of San Francisco's many sister cities, Osaka, Japan (celebrating the diplomatic relations between our two countries); then take the road northward and downhill through the golf course to the old railroad grade and there turn westward: this will give you some extra-special views if it's a clear day.

If, instead, you continue west on Geary, you will find that it becomes two two-way boulevards at Fortieth Avenue. At Forty-first Avenue, the northernmost branch then becomes Point Lobos, a remnant of the original east-west toll road, while the southernmost continues as Geary. This unusual division marks the place where the first street grid diverted Geary to accommodate its pattern of blocks. Admire the firehouse on the island between these two wide streets (recently restored): it has been likened to a country church of northern Italy. If you're in a hurry to reach the beach, continue west on Point Lobos and you will dead-end at the Ocean Beach—Land's End complex of the GGNRA with the Cliff House and Seal Rocks. If you follow Geary, you will end up, instead, in the pleasant park that was once Adolph Sutro's lovely gardens. (En route, you may want to walk one block south down Forty-sixth Avenue to Anza to admire the handsome house on the southeast corner, the work of the famous San Francisco architect Julia Morgan.)

Adolph Sutro was one of San Francisco's angels and an extraordinarily versatile and gifted man. A Prussian immigrant, he made his first fortune as an engineer when he designed and constructed a controversial tunnel for the Comstock silver mines in Nevada. He sold his tunnel in 1879 just before the mines closed, and following this coup he made San Francisco his permanent home and its beautification and culturization his vocation. He went extensively into real estate: at one time he owned one-twelfth of the city, including a good part of the Richmond; 1,000 of his acres were around Land's End (21.21 acres now remain as Sutro Heights Park). He helped initiate and then supported the introduction of kindergartens into the city's educational program. A lover of trees, Sutro was responsible for California's first Arbor Day (in 1886), and he planted Sutro Forest (still growing on Mount Sutro) and called his pines and eucalyptus "the children of my old age which will live on long after I am laid to rest." He bought the Cliff House (in 1882) and renovated and improved it, returning it to respectability (it had a shady reputation at the time). When it burned in 1894, he rebuilt it as a fairy-tale Victorian hotel. Sutro designed and built his famous saltwater baths, where you could select the temperature of your plunge. He was elected mayor of San Francisco on the Populist ticket the year the Cliff House burned. This generous man donated 26 acres to the University of California for its medical school, which still thrives on Parnassus Heights at the edge of Sutro Forest. He assembled a famous book collection, known as the finest library in the country: he left it to the public, but most of it burned in 1906 after it had been moved, ironically, from its downtown location for safety. Sutro also assembled a fine collection of Egyptian art, which he displayed at his baths. (This can now be enjoyed at San Francisco State University.) He gained protection (through congressional action) for the sea lions that occupied Seal Rocks by having the rocky islands turned over to the city: in this process, the animals actually became citizens of San Francisco (if only they could vote!). He saw to the building of a "scenic railroad" around Land's End and in 1888 managed to keep the fare on the Geary Park and Ocean Trolley Line at an affordable 5 cents. He developed a fabulous garden in Sutro Heights where he pioneered in discovering sand-holding grasses and where he had a nursery for his beloved trees. Sutro prided himself on his formal gardens with their numerous classical and neoclassical statues, which he imported from Europe for San Franciscans to enjoy. (He paid more for the freight on his statuary than he did for the pieces themselves, which were shipped as ballast.)

Sutro died in 1898, having left an indelible mark on the city he loved so much. In the winter of 1979, a National Park Service ranger discovered an urn in the rockwork of the cliff below Sutro Heights, part of a cliff protection project that had been undertaken by the Works Projects Administration in the 1930s. It had long been assumed that Adolph Sutro's ashes were in the family vault at the columbarium off Geary Boulevard; a check showed that they were missing, removed anonymously in the 1930s (possibly by his daughter, who, ill herself, may have been carrying out her father's last wish to be buried near his beloved coast). Speculation bloomed that the urn contained the missing remains; before this could be ascertained, the urn was claimed by a "Sutro descendant," and where they ultimately repose is unknown.

After the death of Sutro's daughter, Emma Merritt (one of San Francisco's first women doctors), these gardens, famous for their flowers and statuary, went to the city, the generous gift—following Adolph's wish—of the Sutro family. Unfortunately, they subsequently fell into neglect and ruin, and the statues were vandalized and eventually destroyed. The property became a part of the Golden Gate National Recreation Area in 1979, and the National Park Service has a program to restore as much as possible of the original scene. It would like to replicate Sutro's original main gate, flanked by its twin lion guardians, and has already restored one of the early, more famous pieces of sculpture, *Diana and the Stag*. (Sutro's wonderful baths burned in 1966 and are lost forever.) While the present parklands are still informal, they make for a most pleasant place to stroll and to sun, to look down onto the great ocean and its beach, marveling at the stone parapets that Sutro built to mount a grand cannon, facing westward. This used to be a great place to listen to the wonderful raucous conversations of the sea lions, descendants of Sutro's friends; now these charming animals have adopted Pier 39 (south of Fisherman's Wharf) for their home. Perhaps one day they will return.

From Adolph's gardens, you must turn back to Point Lobos Avenue to get down the last hill (Sutro Heights) and so to the Cliff House and Ocean Beach, and the end of your walk out Geary Boulevard.

The GGNRA Waterfront

The Golden Gate National Recreation Area's shoreline trails in San Francisco add up to some 13 miles of spectacular walking. Although they are generally undemanding—especially for a seasoned hiker—it is not recommended that you take them all at one time. Various sections of these pathways offer quite different experiences, and they link all 10 San Francisco units (except Alcatraz) or subparks, of the GGNRA, each of which calls for taking some time to explore. (GGNRA has an extraordinary total of 16 subparks in San Francisco and Marin County, as well as 3 subparks in San Mateo County.)

The four waterfront walks described run from Hyde Street Pier near Fisherman's Wharf in downtown San Francisco to Fort Funston near the southwest limits of the city. The mileage given for each is approximate and the suggested time is arbitrary, but may provide a maximum required for getting the most out of your stroll. Recommendations for detours are, of course, arbitrary as well.

GGNRA Walk 1—Hyde Street Pier (San Francisco Maritime National Historical Park), Fort Mason Center, Marina Green—The easiest way to start this walk is to take the Hyde Street cable car northward, ride it to its last stop, and then walk to the foot of Hyde Street. It is not a good idea to drive to this section of the city and try to park: this particular area is adjacent to the Cannery and just downhill from Ghirardelli Square, both very popular tourist attrac-

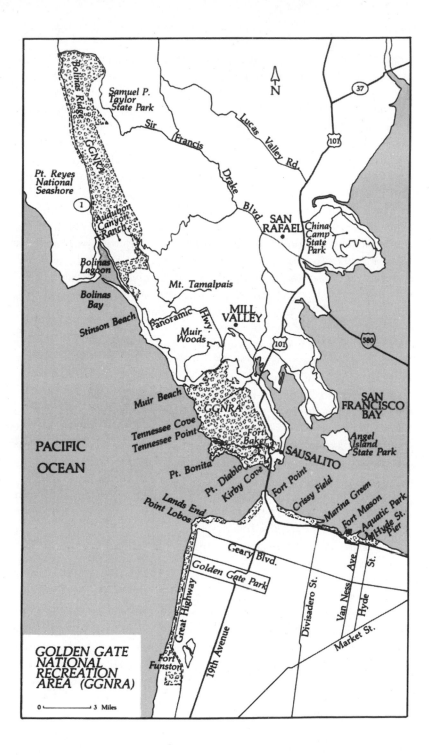

PACIFIC
OCEAN

GOLDEN GATE
NATIONAL
RECREATION
AREA (GGNRA)

0 ———— 3 Miles

tions. If you can get into a local parking facility (even in nearby Fisherman's Wharf), you will find parking very expensive. Metered parking is limited and on an hourly or half-hourly basis.

The Hyde Street Pier is part of the San Francisco Maritime National Historical Park (NHP), which, independent of the GGNRA, includes an important piece of San Francisco's waterfront, a unique museum, and a number of ships that have been part of Bay Area history. You may want to visit a ship or two before starting your 2-mile stroll (modest fee).

The *Eureka,* which did yeoman service for 67 years, was in her time the world's largest ferry. She could, and frequently did, carry 2,300 passengers along with 120 cars on her 20-minute run between the San Francisco Ferry Building and the Oakland Mole, the western terminus of the Southern Pacific Railroad. *Eureka*'s "walking beam" was one of the bay's special sights until the ship went out of commission when San Francisco's ferry service was suspended in the mid-1950s. Now restored, her brass is polished and her walking beam is on display. A dozen or so antique automobiles, including a Model A Ford, a 1915 delivery truck, and a spiffy twin-six 1933 Packard, all in ready-to-go condition, are on view on her lower deck.

A three-masted wooden-hulled schooner, the *C. A. Thayer,* is likewise moored at the Hyde Street Pier. Built in northern California in 1895, this was the last commercial vessel to sail the Pacific Coast. It hauled lumber for more than two decades, then carried salmon from Alaska to San Francisco, and finished its service hauling codfish. The *C. A. Thayer*'s career tells the history of some of the city's commerce well: it is worth a visit. You can also board the ocean-going tug *Hercules,* which has a 1,000-horsepower triple-expansion steam engine and once hauled caissons for the building of the Panama Canal. *Note:* There are monthly (free) chantey sings held in the hold of this venerable ship. Call 415-556-1871 for information and reservations (necessary).

(Some ships at the historical park are meant to be admired and photographed but not boarded. These are the *Eppleton Hall,* a paddle tug built in England in 1914, much like the tugs that towed ships into San Francisco Bay during Gold Rush times, and the last scow schooner still afloat in San Francisco Bay (and the United States), the *Alma.* The *Alma* was noted for her nonstop endurance and once served 16- to 18-hour days six days a week as an oyster-shell dredge; on Sundays, she was hosed down and cleaned up to be ready for work the next morning. The *Alma* traditionally leads the bay's annual Master's Regatta.)

Arguably the greatest attraction among the historical ships is the three-masted ship *Balclutha*. This grand, century-old square-rigger is a relic of more romantic sailing days. She was used in the salmon industry, as a carnival ship, and even in the movie *Mutiny on the Bounty*. Although the *Balclutha* belongs to the National Park Service, she is the special darling of local shipbuilders' unions, whose members have lovingly restored her and continue to care for her.

Walking west from Hyde Street Pier, you pass through Aquatic Park, which includes the small, grassy Victorian Park (good for picnicking—if you get there first—and for kite flying). Continue on to reach the National Maritime Museum. This unique enclave in the San Francisco Maritime Park is a monument to the Great Depression–inspired Works Projects Administration and its noble efforts during the 1930s. The museum building was designed to be a marvelous "people's palace" located shoreside of its own swimming beach, with accommodations for a grandiose 5,000 bathers to change in (and gray wool tank suits and towels to rent). The beach offered not only safe waters to swim and wade in, but a wide strip of sand for sunbathing and bleachers where the crowds could sit and watch the glorious swimming pageants—à la Eleanor Holm—of that period. A father-son architect team—William Mooser II and III—conceived of the streamlined "palace" as resembling a huge grounded ship. Its marquee and mosaics were created by Sargent Johnson. Its tile floors and wall murals by Hilaire Hiler recall that artist's pioneer work with color: he was the first to experiment with the effect that color has on the viewer. The "palace" now houses an unusual cultural amenity, one of a handful in the country, a maritime museum. This one has a fine collection of nautical artifacts and art, including handsome ships' figureheads and scrimshaw. This unique museum is free and is open every day from 10:00 A.M. to 5:00 P.M. (Call 415-556-3002 for further information and regarding tours conducted by the park.) (If you're a truly dedicated ship buff, you may want to visit the historical collection of the Maritime NHP; ask at the museum front desk or call 415-556-9870; the collection is housed in the park's maritime library to be visited in nearby Fort Mason.) A section of the building is also used for a senior citizens' center.

Although the cove of Aquatic Park was the place that Billy Ralston took his last swim that fateful day in 1875, its beach and waters are now considered the safest in San Francisco. This is a good place for children to wade and swim, and the bleachers are great fun to climb on and scramble around. *Note:* The National Museum Association, a private, nonprofit organization that supports the museum, maintains a World War II submarine—with an extraordinary history—which you can visit at Pier 45 (recommended). There is a modest fee.

As you leave the national historical park and pass the Municipal Pier—the long pier serves both fishermen and photographers well—you will take a short, pretty paved pathway that leads uphill and westward to Fort Mason: this is the beginning of the Golden Gateway Promenade (and part of the Bay Trail). Running through the GGNRA, it will take you just below a restored Civil War battery and an American Youth Hostel (formerly a Civil War army barracks) that has got to be one of the most beautifully situated hostels in the world. It is small wonder that it is one of the United States' most popular hostels and is used to capacity. (See Campgrounds and Youth Hostels appendixes.) The Great Meadow beyond it is the site of a giant statue of the late Philip Burton, congressional father of the GGNRA. The GGNRA headquarters and the National Park Service's Western Regional Information Center are also located here, in Building 201.

Fort Mason Center—where 50-odd other compatible organizations are located is below you, near the water. This community center is the park service's answer for what to do with a large, surplus military complex—a historic army installation dating back to the Civil War. Used as a major embarkation center from which 1.5 million troops sailed during World War II, Fort Mason with its three piers was turned over to the park service as part of the GGNRA. Although many of its buildings were in a sorry state—long abandoned and allowed to fall into disrepair—all were protected as historic structures and so could not be demolished. The GGNRA opted to renovate them for occupation by organizations dedicated to compatible pursuits, i.e., educational, environmental, and cultural activities. A separate nonprofit group, the Fort Mason Foundation, was formed to administer the center, screen applicants for space in the center, and help with renovation.

Since the GGNRA came up with this happy solution, ten large buildings and one 60,000-square-foot pier have been put into use. (The pier is used for fairs, exhibits, and even circuses.) And the San

Francisco community and hundreds of thousands of visitors can now enjoy such amenities as theatre performances, numerous interesting classes, museums (including an African and Mexican Museum and a San Francisco Art Museum rental gallery), a thriving community garden (behind park headquarters), Greens Restaurant (wonderful vegetarian food served in a renovated warehouse with a superb bay view), and more. You may want to take a few minutes to explore Fort Mason Center, or if there a special event—a circus, a fair, or even a quilt show—taking place, you may want to join in the fun. *Note:* A calendar of Fort Mason events is available at Fort Mason Center and at GGNRA headquarters; many of the center's events and classes are free. If you can spare a few moments to look around Fort Mason you'll find several wonderful buildings dating back to pre-Civil War days; the information people at GGNRA headquarters can steer you in the right direction.

For those interested in such, the GGNRA's exercise course starts in Upper Fort Mason, next to the youth hostel; it continues at stations around the Great Meadow. It is popular with joggers and other health-minded people, and you can test your own fitness at its exercise stations as you walk—or jog—past Gas House Cove and westward along the Green, which also has an exercise course and a Gamefield Fitness Court as well.

The Marina Green is a memento of the 1915 Panama Pacific International Exposition. Once a marshy stretch of coast, this filled land now provides San Francisco kite flyers, field-game players, and sunbathers with a broad sweep of level grassland. On sunny days when the breeze is right, this is one of the most popular spots in the city; while the green is crowded with people, the sky above it is crowded with kites. Another memento of the 1915 exposition is the Palace of Fine Arts. Designed by Bernard Maybeck, this was planned to be a temporary building, but civic pride and architectural interest prompted the people of San Francisco to raise the funds to reconstruct it and make it permanent. The first fund-raising event was an Artists Ball in 1916, but it took another five decades and a gift of $2 million from a lumber baron in the early 1960s to rescue the handsome structure. This domed, rose-colored building across Marina Boulevard at the western end of the green now houses the Exploratorium, a unique hands-on scientific museum—one of the best in the country—that appeals to grown-ups as well as children and that may be worth a detour from your walk.

Fitted into the Marina Green are the San Francisco Yacht Harbor and the St. Francis Yacht Club. The jetty enclosing the harbor offers photographers some unusual opportunities: you can point your camera northward for a bayscape and Marin landscape shot, or point it southeast for a cityscape with a foreground of picturesque sailboats. (If you have the time, another very worthwhile detour from your walk can be made here—into the Presidio, a national treasure that became a unit of GGNRA in 1994, when the U.S. Army moved out. The Presidio abuts Crissy Field to the south: it is to the west of the Exploratorium. With 1,480 beautiful acres, 510 historic structures, a museum, and miles of interesting trails, this wonderful National Historic Monument actually warrants an all-day visit.)

GGNRA Walk 2—Golden Gate Promenade to Fort Point—From the Marina Green, 2 miles of the Golden Gate Promenade run the length of Crissy Field and lead to Fort Point National Historical Site. You can easily walk this in a crisp one hour, or take a happy morning or afternoon. It has some of the most stunning views you will see in San Francisco and the added attraction of being at water's edge.

Crissy Field dates back to the teens and was San Francisco's first military airstrip. Used by pioneer aviators, it was the terminus of many record-setting flights and was named, in fact, for a pioneer pilot, Major Davis H. Crissy, who died in 1919 in an air race across the country. Crissy Field served during World War II and for several years afterwards. Now it is part of the GGNRA and provides an easy, level, 2-mile walk along a paved trail (wheelchair accessible). This stretch of the bay's shore is notable for both its native flora (in glorious bloom in May) and its close-up views of the Golden Gate Bridge. It's a particularly good place to watch ships sail in and out of the Gate beneath the graceful arch that spans it. It also frequently offers a splendid spectacle of windsurfing, this stretch of the bay being one of the best places in the West—indeed, the world—for this beautiful and challenging sport. Windsurfing off Crissy Field, in fact, calls for extra daring, strength, and expertise since the winds and currents here can be dangerous as well as exhilarating. These very winds, incidentally, can also be very chilly (onshore as well as off), and you'll probably be glad if you've brought along a windbreaker and possibly a sweater to form another layer beneath it. *Note:* You can stay on the Golden Gateway Promenade right into Fort Point, or you can bypass this historical site by taking the Hill Walk at the fort;

this will take you to Lincoln Boulevard and thence to the Coastal
Trail and Baker Beach. Anyone interested in military history—or just
plain history—however, will probably enjoy a visit to this, the only
brick fort ever built west of the Mississippi River. It is, incidentally, a
twin of South Carolina's Fort Sumter.

Where Fort Point is located—at the narrowest point of the Golden
Gate—was once a 100-foot-high cliff. There in 1776, officer Juan
Bautista de Anza planted, and Father Pedro Font blessed, the wind-
whipped Spanish flag. And there in 1794, the Spanish built an adobe
fort to take advantage of the commanding position. When the United
States acquired California, the army moved in and shortly thereafter
demolished the Spanish fort, leveled the cliff to a height of only 10
feet, and between 1853 and 1861 erected Fort Point. Army engineer
Captain Charles de Russy was in charge of the construction and left
as his monument not only a fine, irregular-hexagonal-shaped brick
building but the descendants of roses and lilies that once grew in his
garden up the hill. *Note:* If you do any off-the-trail exploring in this
area, keep a sharp eye out for poison oak.

To recreate the original scene at Fort Point, the rangers wear Civil
War uniforms (Yankee, of course), and a few replicas of the 126 original mighty cannons (their balls weighed as much as 128 pounds
each) still point from their casements, or gun rooms, on the fort's
three levels and from their emplacements on the barbette tier, or
walled roof. (There are particularly interesting views of the city from
the barbette tier.) The fort has several intriguing architectural features, including arched casements and ceilings throughout and circular staircases, the treads of which are miraculously balanced to
support each other.

Fort Point with its clumsy cannon was obsolete only a couple of
decades after it was completed, and it was out of use from 1887 to
1934, when it was pressed into service as a base of operations for the
building of the Golden Gate Bridge. (As you will notice, the bridge
was designed specifically and ingeniously to leave intact this historic
structure.) The army put it to use again during World War II when
100 soldiers were billetted there: they must have been miserably
uncomfortable during the winters for no heating system could make
the old fort toasty. (Originally, heat was supplied only by the coal-
burning fireplaces in the troops' quarters.) It was also during World
War II that the waters of the Golden Gate were mined (with defen-
sive, remotely controlled mines) and a giant antisubmarine net was

strung from the Marina Green to Fort Baker in Sausalito. The West Coast was understandably suffering from serious jitters in those days, and, legend has it, the only for-serious shot that was ever fired from a San Francisco fortification came from Fort Point: a young soldier, doubtless an inlander, mistook the neck of a cormorant for the periscope of a submarine and squeezed his trigger on the poor bird.

Splendid building that it is, Fort Point is located right at water's edge, where it takes the full brunt of the weather; it is almost always windy, drafty, and cold. This makes it an ideal place to visit on one of the few sizzling days you'll encounter in San Francisco—usually in September or possibly October. Otherwise, come prepared for chilly breezes inside the fort as well as outside. Photographers will find many interesting possibilities at Fort Point, including shots of the windsurfers who skim the waves like crowds of big bright butterflies or just plain surfers riding the great swells against the Gate. There's also an opportunity on most days for dramatic close-ups of those swells bursting against the rocks on which the fort stands, or for interesting perspectives of the Golden Gate Bridge soaring directly overhead. And there are those architectural details mentioned above. Geology buffs might want to walk uphill to the west for a closeup view of asbestos-laced serpentine.

From Fort Point it's another short walk (up a path, this time) to the viewing area below the Golden Gate Bridge Toll Plaza and more good opportunities for photographers. Continue your walk by going under the bridge (via tunnel) through a small piece of the army's Presidio to Battery Marcus Miller and thence along a short section of paved road (Lincoln Boulevard) to pick up the Coastal Trail. Total mileage of GGNRA Walk 2 is about 2 miles.

GGNRA Walk 3 — Coastal Trail: Baker Beach to the Cliff House—

This 4-mile section of the GGNRA's shoreside walk will take you past two attractive beaches and through one of the more or less natural parts of the city—Land's End—to one of the city's most historic spots, the Cliff House. Allow at least a half a day if you want to see it all.

You must first find your way along the top of the cliff above Baker Beach and then drop down to this beautifully curving crescent of sand. (There's a steep staircase in sand down to the beach at the north end. Children love it.) Baker Beach is beloved of sunbathers in hot weather and of beachcombers and surf fishermen in all kinds of weather. It is not, however, safe for swimming since the shore drops off precipitously, causing a dangerous encounter between surf and sand. Near the beach (at the north end of the parking lot) is Battery Chamberlain, one of the GGNRA's military attractions. Cast in 1906, this is a 95-thousand-pound cannon that, like many other military installations around the bay, became obsolete not long after it was ready for service. On weekends, park rangers demonstrate this extraordinary disappearing gun, which can be cranked into firing position and then lowered out of sight. (This remarkable bit of military machinery was a gift from the Smithsonian Institution: it was mounted by the GGNRA. There's also a military museum here, open the first weekend of the month, weather permitting.) You will find picnic tables, grills, drinking water, and restroom facilities available at Baker Beach. You will also find great crowds of people, no place to park, and impossible traffic conditions when the weather is warm and sunny—especially on a weekend. The San Francisco Muni serves Baker Beach directly, and this public transportation is recommended should you want to visit this popular beach on wheels. (It is possible, incidentally, during certain minus tides to follow Baker Beach under the Golden Gate Bridge and along the shore, but this is a rare happening.)

It's only a short scramble from the southern end of Baker Beach to Twenty-fifth Avenue North and thence uphill to Sea Cliff Avenue, which will take you west the few blocks to El Camino Del Mar through one of San Francisco's tonier neighborhoods. At this intersection, you can drop down the hill to China Beach, where you can take a dip if the day is benign and the spirit moves you. This small, protected cove, named for the early Chinese fishermen who camped here during the 1860s and 1870s, forms the second best of GGNRA's two San Francisco swimming beaches. Add to its safe waters a bathhouse (dating back to the fifties) with changing rooms and showers, drinking water and restrooms, and a protected sundeck on its roof where you can get out of the wind. Before leaving, admire the elegant Sea Cliff houses above China Beach and imagine how it looked when there were strawberry patches and vegetable gardens among the sand dunes that once were here.

To continue your walk, retrace your steps uphill to El Camino Del Mar and head westward. You will shortly leave behind Sea Cliff's mansions and come to the Land's End turnoff. (It is just east of the Lincoln Park Golf Course and only a short distance downhill from the Palace of the Legion of Honor: see Geary Walk 3.) Be prepared for breathtaking views across the Gate to the Marin Headlands and Mount Tamalpais and back to the Golden Gate Bridge. The Coastal Trail here runs in part along what remains of the bed of the old steam railroad that once delighted travelers. In some places, you'll walk along the edge of high, precipitous cliffs, in others you'll be within detouring distance of water's edge, and in still others you'll have to make your way across wide landslides. The land in this part of the San Francisco peninsula is extremely unstable—which explains why the old railroad didn't last too many years and why no paved road runs around Land's End (although there have been many attempts to build one) and also why the park service must constantly shore up its trail. Hikers should exercise care and good judgment; stay away from exposed areas, especially when the ground is waterlogged. (You'll be comfortable in light hiking boots on this part of your GGNRA walk, although many people get by very well in running shoes. A light windbreaker will also stand you in good stead.)

The Land's End walk is lovely. You pass through stands of wind-sculpted Monterey cypress and pine, both picturesque if exotic, and there are wildflowers and blossoms escaped from nearby gardens along the way. You stand a chance of hearing and seeing many birds, especially during February and March, when songbirds linger in this roadless and houseless part of the city. (I have listened to a great gray owl along this trail on a September evening and found his yellow eyes watching me from the high branch of a tree.) The vistas to the north and out to sea are unequaled. You'll pass Mile Rock, a sentinel sea-mark just offshore; it was once occupied by a lighthouse with a keeper, but it is now only a beacon, automated, and serviced by a helicopter. Between Mile Rock and the shore here many ships have come to grief: you may catch a glimpse of the rusty bones of the *Lyman Stewart,* the *Frank Buck,* the *Coos Bay,* or the *Ohioan* awash in the surf. The *Lyman Stewart* and the *Frank Buck* shared extraordinary fates: each was built in the same foundry in San Francisco Bay; each was forced aground on Land's End's rocky shores. Although born and sunk in different years, the "siblings" now rest beside one another as though in adjacent family graves.

Just before you reach Point Lobos, the westernmost tip of the San Francisco peninsula, you will come to West Fort Miley, named for the Spanish War hero Lieutenant Colonel John David Miley. Miley, who died in Manila (of malaria), designed the plan for arming the

Golden Gate, both north and south. Before walking uphill to Fort Miley's higher ground for more views in more directions and picnic and restroom facilities, take a moment to see the monument on the west side of the parking lot here. This is the bridge of the USS *San Francisco,* which lost 107 members of its crew in the devastating Battle of Guadalcanal in November 1942: these men are memorialized here. It was near here, too, incidentally, that a lookout used to sight incoming ships and telegraph news of their arrival to anxious merchants awaiting business downtown. And on the coast below you, in the white surf creaming against the rocks, two entrepreneurs—Ralph Star in 1909 and Lewis Reece in 1948—tried (independently) to harness the energy of the tides with wave machines. Each of these men raised considerable money for his project, and each scheduled an opening day when his wave machine could be viewed in marvelous action. In perhaps not-so-curious coincidence, neither showed up the day the audience gathered to witness his remarkable invention; and neither man has been heard from since.

Continue on the Coastal Trail—now the western fragment of El Camino Del Mar, the ill-fated street that has washed out so many times—until it dead-ends in Point Lobos Avenue. Here you turn down the hill past Merrie Way and the ruins of Sutro's famous baths to the Cliff House and Seal Rocks. *Note:* It is possible to make a loop hike and return to the Palace of the Legion of Honor should you choose to do so. Turn east on what's left of El Camino Del Mar and you will find a trail leading back to the Palace of the Legion of Honor.

The Cliff House is one of the most popular tourist destinations in San Francisco, and you should be prepared for the crowds that seem always to be milling around it. Nonetheless, it is worth pausing a moment in this historic part of San Francisco that has had a fascination for people since the first Cliff House was built here and opened on October 15, 1863. (There is actually some question as to whether this was the first building on this site, but it's the first for sure with the famous name.) Looking around, it is not hard to see why that early hostelry became a mecca even when it meant a long and sometimes weary ride out (and back) through the sand dunes of the "Outside Lands" to visit it. Where else will you find such dramatic coastal views? You can see north along the Marin coast all the way to Point Reyes on clear days. Westward you can admire the Farallon Islands with a foredrop of the waves bursting into rainbows over Seal Rocks.

To the south, there is the long straight line of the beach outlined in the wet sand and the white cream of the surf. Add to this the song of the sea lions mingling with the cries of gulls and the timeless sound of the sea and you have a magic place indeed.

The Cliff House shares a noteworthy history with the several other Cliff Houses that have stood here. The first Cliff House was perilously close to being destroyed on January 16, 1887, when the schooner *Parallel,* loaded with 2,000 pounds of dynamite, ran aground on the rocks below it and exploded like a huge bomb, sending two night watchmen flying through the night (they landed miraculously still alive) and hurling bits of the ship the length of the Golden Gate Park. The building was reconstructed and put back into service, but on Christmas Day in 1894—some time after Adolph Sutro had acquired it—it was totally consumed by fire. This gave the talented and imaginative Sutro the chance to dream up and build his gorgeous Victorian palace of a hotel. It was in the dining room of this Cliff House that the first ship-to-shore wireless telegraph message in the United States was received—in 1899—sent from the San Francisco lightship lying offshore. But in 1907, this Sutro creation (like his famous baths some six decades later) went up in flames. The present building has survived since 1909 but has been remodeled and closed and reopened several times: it has now been acquired by the GGNRA and is operated by a concessioner.

You may have to fight the crowds to get into the Cliff House proper, but you might enjoy looking at the historic pictures of its predecessors inside, or if you're feeling hungry you might enjoy having a meal in this historic place. Sunday brunch in the Cliff House was a San Francisco custom for many years, and it's still not a bad idea; the food is generally good, if dear.

If you're more interested in the view and a bit of interpretation of the general scene, you can walk down a couple of flights of stairs to viewing areas and to the park service visitor center. The center is worth a stop if only to look through the albums of Sutro photographs or study the exhibit on gray whales, which can sometimes be seen from this spot as they pass on their great migratory travels (they are best seen as they travel northward in March)—or you may just want to get out of the wind, since this is a particularly breezy point. On the same level, you will also find a Musée Méchanique that's fun if you like player pianos and old-time mechanical wonders, some of which are unique; take plenty of quarters to make things work. Nearby, there's also a Camera Obscura and Holograph Gallery, along with telescopes you can train onto the sea lions and seabirds below. The Seal Rocks are a wildlife sanctuary—the first marine sanctuary in the country—and a perpetual trust of the city of San Francisco, thanks to Adolph Sutro. (See Geary Walk 3.)

Before leaving this part of the GGNRA, you may want to spend a few minutes at the ruins of Sutro Baths (just north of the Cliff House) and imagine them with five saltwater pools of different temperatures and one freshwater plunge, plus extensive collections of Egyptian, Polynesian, and Mexican artifacts on public display. And you may want to cross the street uphill and visit Sutro's once-formal gardens, now also a part of GGNRA, and picture them in riotous blossom and open to the public—free. (See Geary Walk 3.)

GGNRA Walk 4—Ocean Beach and Fort Funston—As you walk down the hill toward Ocean Beach, note the fancy artificial rock-work on the cliffs across the street. This facade was rock-lover John McLaren's work. (See San Francisco's Parks.) This is also the place where an urn believed to contain the ashes of Adolph Sutro was found in 1979. (See Geary Walk 3.)

The area south of the Cliff House used to be a grand amusement park known as Playland at the Beach, with a merry-go-round and roller coaster and an enormously fat papier-mâché lady (known as Laughing Sal) who chuckled loudly, uproariously, and continuously in a corner window, delighting (or sometimes terrifying!) young as well as old for decades. She's now housed in the aforementioned Musée Méchanique. In 1972, however, bending to progress, Playland closed and was subsequently replaced by the condominiums you now see.

If you would like to get your feet wet in the Pacific Ocean, feel the sea rainbow-spray on your face, and walk or jog on firm wet sand, you can now head for Ocean Beach, which will offer you all these opportunities. You can follow the line of surf for five gorgeous miles—during the summer months, that is; in winter you may have to leave the beach at higher tides midway through the Sunset district and at Fort Funston as well. At Fort Funston, you will find the Phillip Burton Beach and the cable stairway to the top of the cliff. If walking on the beach for such a long stretch seems like too much of the same thing, you can enjoy what you want of the beach below the Cliff House and continue your walk along the Great Highway:

there's a good path, or you can take the paved sidewalk just below the shoulder and walk along the edge of the Sunset district. There's a potpourri of houses, some dating back to the era of shingled beach cottages, that marches along this 2-mile stretch between Lincoln Way (at the southern end of Golden Gate Park) and Sloat Boulevard. If you want to detour a bit and look for refugee shacks left from 1906, there are several tucked between later houses along the avenues here.

As an alternative, you can stay on the paved esplanade along the northern end of Ocean Beach for close to a mile before taking to the sand at Lincoln Way. If you choose the latter course, you can admire the Beach Chalet and the two windmills in Golden Gate Park across the Great Highway. Both were built as working windmills to pump fresh water from the streams beneath them. The northernmost, known as the Dutch Windmill, was built in 1902, and its sails turned for 20 years before an electric pump was found to be more efficient; it grew more and more forlorn and dilapidated, losing its sails and shingles as well, until it was rebuilt and resailed in the late 1970s by the navy Seabees. A banker named Murphy gave the city the southern mill in 1901, but its working years came to an end, too, decades ago, and no one has gotten around to restoring it.

Whichever route you take through this wide open stretch of San Francisco, keep in mind that the cool westerlies (obviously) pour directly onto this coastal area during the spring and summer months. And if any part of the city is foggy, this beach is almost sure to be likewise. Another caveat: although the ocean waters here may look quite peaceful with their even rhythm of breaking waves, this is a delusion. Ocean Beach is dangerous for swimming, with a powerful undertow adding to the hazards of its strong surf. In places you many find wet-suited surfers, but swimming is not recommended under any circumstances. And there is the aforementioned caveat re high tides to keep in mind; be sure to check a tide table (available at sporting goods stores or park visitor centers) before spending any amount of time on Ocean Beach.

The paved esplanade, with its wind-breaking wall at the northern end of the beach, is part of an ambitious seawall that was built in 1929 and has held up remarkably well under the onslaught of decades of waves. Further south you will see evidence of some other, not-so-attractive, attempts to tame the shore. The sand dunes, which used to erupt in sandstorms and drift across the Great Highway, have been bodily removed, and a monoculture of beach grass has been planted in place of the native flora that once delighted the eye here. This dune amputation was part of the city's recent sewage project. (During winter low tides, look for the wreck of the *King Philip* at the foot of Ortega Street.)

At Sloat Boulevard, you may want to detour to visit a major San Francisco urban nicety, its zoological gardens. San Francisco Zoo is one of the best in the country, with most of the usual attractions and a fine primate exhibit, a white tiger, koala bears, and a splendid penguin colony. You must cross the Great Highway and walk a couple of blocks to the east on Sloat Boulevard to reach the entrance: there is an admission fee. Should you find yourself wearied at this point, you can easily take a Muni bus for your return; there is good service to the zoo.

South of the zoo is another one of San Francisco's special attractions, Lake Merced. Named by the Spanish Laguna de Nuestra Señora de la Merced—"the lake of Our Lady of Mercy"—this large, V-shaped natural lake is fed by freshwater springs along the San Andreas Fault and is dammed from the ocean by the wide dunes of Fort Funston. Its 2.5 billion gallons of water are considered an emergency water supply but are used ordinarily for sprinkling the golf course (part of the Lake Merced Harding City Park) that forms the wedge between its arms. There is a bike path around the lake—very popular with joggers and runners, who also enjoy the ten-station Parcourse at the north end—and birdwatchers may enjoy a stroll at lake's edge. Because of a variety of habitats (there are trees around the golf course), the lake and its sometimes marshy shores attract everything from loons, grebes, herons, ducks, geese, swans, black-shouldered kites, and osprey to rails and several species of gulls and even warblers and meadowlarks. (There's also a windsurfing concession here.) If you walk south along Lake Merced Boulevard, you'll pass one of San Francisco sculptor Benamino Bufano's whimsical works; this one—a large, orange-beaked bird—is entitled *Penguin's Prayer.*

History buffs may want to meet the challenge of finding the spot where Judge David S. Terry killed Senator David B. Broderick in San Francisco's last duel, which took place on September 14, 1859. Nearby it is the place where the Spanish party with Rivera y Moncada camped in 1774. These interesting spots are located at the southeast end of the lake across Lake Merced Boulevard. Look for a state historical site marker pointing to a large sign that says Lake

Merced Hill, Private Club, 1100 Lake Merced Boulevard. Take the road into this development, and close to the tennis court you will find the marker noting the Spaniards' campsite. Persevere and you will come to a chain-link fence with a small park and picnic tables on the other side. Continue east past another marker and you will finally come into the shady glen where stand two markers commemorating the spots where the protagonists stood: the requisite distance apart, the small white monuments still look awfully close together, and it is not hard to see how Broderick fell, mortally wounded by Terry's cruel shot. Incidentally, Broderick died in a house in Fort Mason.

If you take these byways or walk along the Great Highway rather than the beach, you may have to do some fancy street crossing to get to Fort Funston, which begins where the Great Highway dead-ends in Skyline Boulevard. This part of the fort is little more than trailless sand dunes, and it is recommended that you proceed on the east side of Skyline Boulevard the approximate ¾ mile that will bring you to an easier point of entry. If you want to get to the main GGNRA parking lot, you will have to continue up the hill southward another ½ mile.

If you choose, instead, to walk along the ocean the full 5 miles from the Cliff House to Fort Funston, you'll probably have good views of seabirds and shorebirds along the way and, here and there, the human seals riding the waves. After you pass Sloat Boulevard, you may want to start looking for fossil sand dollars. *Anorthoscutum interlineatum* populated the sands of a prehistoric ocean whose waters washed a beach that now lies at the foot of Fort Funston and extends a couple of miles to the south. These beautiful sea creatures flourished for millions of years, and some date back nearly 9 million years; their present-day descendants, *Dendraster excentricus* (named by Johann Friedrich Eschscholtz when he visited San Francisco in the early 1800s; for more on this early botanist, see the Bay Area Wildflowers appendix) now occupy the same wet sands. (Gentle reminder: It is illegal to beachcomb in national parks.) A little over ½ mile past the pier, you'll come to Phillip Burton Beach with its cable-ladder steps up the steep, nearly 200-foot cliff to the viewing area of Fort Funston. Don't forget to check your tide table before you make this walk. *Note:* The park service is committed to protecting the Snowy plover, an endangered species that nests in this area. During nesting season—late winter and early spring—dogs are not allowed on this part of the beach and visitors are asked not to disturb these very special birds.

This is the cliff beloved of Bay Area hang-gliders for its height, its more or less steady onshore breeze between the year's equinoxes (see Geology and Weather)—note the neatly wind-pruned trees close by—and its beauty. On good, breezy days you may see as many as two dozen hang-gliders aloft, soaring like enormous, colorful birds. This may be the second most dangerous sport in the United States— only sky-diving is more so—but it is certainly one of the loveliest to watch. The GGNRA has thoughtfully built a fine place for viewers to sit or stand, perhaps open mouthed, to follow the graceful maneuvers of the hang-gliders in the sky. This viewing platform is also a good place to watch for whales during their northward migration in March. If you find yourself hopelessly attracted to hang-gliding, you'll find the names of local hang-gliding schools and other pertinent hang-gliding information tacked on the back of the big GGNRA sign at the entrance to the viewing platform. (Stay well away from the takeoff and landing areas; hang-gliders are impressively large when seen close up and, if knocked awry, can be dangerous for both glider and earthbound spectator.)

Fort Funston was named for General Frederick Funston after his death in 1917. Although several fortifications have been emplaced here over the years, the fort boasted little in the way of military development other than a few surplus buildings and Battery Davis, a relic of the 1930s, when it became part of the GGNRA. Plans for a military psychiatric hospital here failed, which was probably just as well since this high coastal area, which can be so stunningly beautiful on bright days, can be depressing indeed in lingering fog and wind. It seems fitting that the area be preserved, instead, for everyone to enjoy. (Would that other surplus military properties could enjoy the same fate.)

Fort Funston provides an example of the way the city of San Francisco once looked throughout most of its terrain—sandy and dune shaped, with a few tough trees and sturdy flowers like lupine and poppies brightening the landscape. The park service has an ambitious program going to bring back gardens of native plants here. They have a good nursery and many volunteers (from local high schools as well as San Francisco State University). You will find signs asking your help in the park's landscaping efforts.

The GGNRA has developed a trail system utilizing the paved

roads left here by the army, and this makes it pleasant for walking arm in arm. (It is also wheelchair-accessible.) Although short, only about 1½ miles, this is a view-ful trail with great vistas seaward, north and west and south. There are a ranger station, restrooms, and a telephone at Fort Funston but no direct transportation. The closest Muni stop is across Skyline Boulevard near the junction of John Muir Drive. South of Fort Funston you will find yourself shortly in San Mateo County with more lovely coastline and further adventures awaiting you.

PART IV

North Bay

Introduction

Gentle hills, occasional mountains, wide deep-soiled valleys, warm springs, cool streams and rivers, fine forests, a coast on an ocean and one on a bay, an abundance of wildlife, and a delightful climate: indeed, it would be hard to find a lovelier, more welcoming land than the country north of San Francisco Bay when people first discovered it. The first people were, of course, the Indians, who used and enjoyed the place with enough care and respect to keep it for many millennia much as it was when they arrived. When the first Europeans moved into what we call the North Bay, however, history began to be written—in books, and on the land.

A philosopher once described a "civilized" person as one who could successfully alter his environment to meet his perceived needs; and so it was that first the civilized Spanish, the Russians, and finally the Americans brought their needs and changes to this pleasant area. The Russians had only a few short decades (and not very merry ones) to make their mark; the Spanish had a little more time (and mostly a wonderful one, if records can be believed) to make theirs; and two centuries later, the Americans are still happily and busily rearranging the landscape, planting new vineyards, and expanding their industries, their cities, and communities—and having books written about it all.

As a consequence, an outdoor adventurer may find this naturally idyllic area very interesting, as well as beautiful, to explore. However, should you visit the old adobe buildings that mark the remains of Spain's northernmost colony in the New World, or should you climb Mount Saint Helena, named (it is said) for the patron saint of Princess Helena de Gagarin, wife of the last Russian governor in California, or perhaps pay a visit to restored Fort Ross, or should you taste the good wine in Buena Vista Winery, founded by Agoston Haraszthy over a century ago, or stroll the shady walk to Jack London's grave, or gasp at the view from a mile-high balloon, keep in mind, if you can, how it must have been when young Commandante-Generale Mariano Guadalupe Vallejo located his headquarters north of San Francisco Bay in 1835. Not only were there many Indian people in this part of Alta California at that time, but there were grizzly, black, and cinnamon bears, elk, deer, antelope (the prong-horn antelope were as "numerous as flocks of sheep," according to one early report), panthers, wildcats, wolves, coyotes, weasels, skunks, porcupines, opossums, raccoons, hares, rabbits, squirrels, rats, mice, seals, sea otters, sea lions, and beavers, not to mention condors, in local residence. There were virgin forests of redwoods in the canyons and on the lower ridges of the mountains. The grass was shoulder high in places (even higher inland), and there were wildflowers everywhere.

Mariano Vallejo played a major role in the history of that early California. Born in Monterey in 1807, he was the eighth of the 13 children of Ignacio Vicente Ferrer Vallejo, a Spanish military adventurer, and his wife (who was described as being of "good lineage"). Mariano was made an officer in the Mexican army when still very young, and in 1829 he was sent north to take charge of the presidio in Yerba Buena. He was also instructed to keep the Russians from taking over Alta California, for the Russian presence along the coast north of San Francisco Bay was becoming a threat to Mexico.

The Russians had been interested in Alta California since Rezanof had visited Yerba Buena in 1806 (and it is said stolen the heart of Concepçion Arguello, the beautiful daughter of the presidio's commandante). Three years after Rezanof had reported on his observations around the Bay Area, Alexander Ivan Kuskof arrived, with a party of 40 men, to do some exploring, to kill some 2,000 otters for their fur, and to thoughtfully plant wheat around Bodega Bay. In 1811, Kuskof returned with 95 Russians, 80 Aleuts, and an armada of 40 bidarkas; the next year he located Fort Rossiya, "Little Russia," on a bluff above the ocean north of Bodega Bay (which he called Port Romanzof). By the time Vallejo arrived on the scene, the Russian colony on the coast and another at Slavianka (up the Russian River) had grown to number several hundred people: the Russian soldiers were doubling as farmers and chief hunters; the Aleuts were the fishermen and fur hunters; and many local Indians had been pressed into service for the menial tasks. The Russians had planted the first vineyard north of the San Francisco Bay (in 1823, in the Coleman Valley west of Occidental). They had also built up quite a formidable fortification at Fort Ross—with a proper church—out of redwood taken conveniently from the forests nearby, and built a few ships and accumulated a substantial number of horses, sheep, and cattle. They were ostensibly in the business of growing food for their brothers in Alaska, who had found farming around Sitka an impossibility. But not at all incidentally, the California Russians had also been engaging in what trade they could, and systematically hunting out the area's valuable furbearers—notably the sea otter and fur seal. (It is reported that in the space of just two years, they had seen their annual take drop from 1,500 animals to 500, so rapacious had they been.) They were also gathering thousands of eggs off the Farallon Islands (where camps of Aleuts had been established) and shooting as many as 50,000 "gulls" (for so they called the birds that were probably murres) a year.

In 1833, four years after he reached Yerba Buena, Vallejo rode out to meet a party of Russians from Fort Ross to tell them that the colony must depart. This was an annual affair where everybody was very polite and not terribly impressed: the Russians knew that the Spanish forces in Yerba Buena had been reduced to ragged uniforms, no pay for years, and not much in the way of military equipment. At the same time, the Russians could hardly precipitate a battle when their own country was feeling stretched to the limit in the New World, a situation of which Vallejo was probably aware. (Vallejo undoubtedly traded with the Russians, as did most of his peers.)

In fact, despite their achievements at Fort Ross, things were not all that happy for the Russians by the mid-1830s. They were reaching the end of the lucrative sea mammal supply. (They were still taking sea lions, some 200 animals a year, for subsistence: like their Aleut friends, they used the animals completely—the meat for food, the skins for boats, the bladders for watertight sacks, the blubber for food and oil.) Ranching along the coast was not as easy as it had once been thought to be. Trading was sparse, they were isolated from the world, and it was a long and usually very miserable trip to Sitka and back. Life in the old country must have seemed more and more attractive, and they may have already been thinking fondly of quitting California when they met with Vallejo. As it turned out, however, they did not make the move until 1841. That year, they sold out lock, stock, and barrel to John A. Sutter for all they could get—some $32,000. (It is worth noting that in 1867, Russia sold all of Alaska, which amounted to 375 million acres—or 0.5 million square miles— to the United States for $7.2 million.)

Although it now seems impossible, during the nearly three decades that they were in Alta California, the Russians were able to go their way and the Spanish theirs with singularly few encounters. Vallejo had been charged with colonizing the northern frontier as well as meeting with the Russians in 1833, and he considered himself enough in control of the situation in 1835 to move his headquarters from the miserable flea-ridden presidio in Yerba Buena to the sunny site of what would become the town of Sonoma and its environs (where, alas, there turned out to be fleas, too). Here the twenty-first and last of the missions—Mission San Francisco de Solano (named for the apostle to South America's Indians, a Franciscan friar beloved of the Spanish padres)—had been located by Padre Altamira in 1824 (this good Father is credited with having brought mustard to the North Bay, carrying seeds that he dropped wherever he went). Vallejo was to secularize the mission and take over its plentiful lands (some 350,000 acres) and to replace its "sacred" control with the more practical military. Vallejo of necessity left some troops behind him but brought along about 100 men—La Compañía de San Francisco—to keep the local Indians under control. (In 1844, Vallejo retired from the military and turned his army over to his brother, Salvator, refusing to be part of a political rebellion that was dividing Mexican leaders in Monterey. Salvator, incidentally, owned all of what would later be Telegraph Hill in San Francisco, but he lost everything he had—including his epaulets—at a sheriff's sale in 1853.)

Following a decree from Generale Don José Figuero, Mexican governor of Alta California, Vallejo also laid out a town of generous-size lots with "room for kitchen gardens"; he called it Sonoma, probably for a local tribe of Indians. (The name presumably came from the Wintun word for "nose" and perhaps remembers an Indian chief with a notable proboscis.) There he built the barracks for his men (you can visit these, restored, in present-day Sonoma) and a fine adobe house, known as La Casa Grande, for himself (one wing of this also remains on the Plaza in Sonoma). He then went on to set himself up another extensive (44,000-acre) ranching operation—with fort—not far away (part of which can still be seen in nearby Petaluma). Vallejo also continued about the serious business (which he had started early on) of acquiring vast amounts of land for his family and his friends, as well as for himself; he ended up with about 170,000 acres. (At the time of California's statehood, all of the land north of the bay was considered to be in the "Sonoma District"; after the partitioning into four counties—Marin, Sonoma, Napa, and Solano—in February 1850, it turned out that Vallejo had owned most of Solano County, as well as substantial chunks of Napa and Sonoma counties during his more halcyon days; he had also been responsible for bestowing large grants of land in these three counties.)

Vallejo had been involved in campaigns against the Indians—including the "fierce and warlike" Suisuns, who in one terrible incident immolated themselves rather than submit to capture—when he first arrived in the Bay Area, and he went on to have some 100 further military encounters with them between 1835 and 1844 after he moved to Sonoma. He managed, however, to make friends with even those whom he had defeated. One of them, Sum-Yet-Ho ("The Mighty Arm") was the tall and imposing chief of the tribes living between the Napa and the Sacramento rivers. Through early good missionary work, this man was converted to Catholicism and given the name of the Sonoma mission—Francisco Solano. Chief Solano, as he came to be known, is reported to have received a large grant of land (the Suisun grant) through the offices of Vallejo, who is also reported to have said of his Indian friend, "I know of no one with a finer natural mind." (There is a romantic story that says that Solano and Princess Helena de Gagarin fell in love, but that, of course, nothing was allowed to come of it.) Solano's people were among the thousands of Indians—according to Vallejo, 70,000—who died of *la plaga*, or smallpox, before 1840. Solano County is named to remember this near-legendary Indian leader.

As more and more Americans arrived in the Bay Area during the 1830s and the 1840s, it became clear that they—and their country, which had tried to acquire California land through purchase—would influence the future of this part of the world. This fact did not escape Commandante Generale of the Frontier Vallejo, who knew, perhaps better than most, of the weaknesses of his homeland, Mexico, and of the need for a better-established government. And while he enjoyed the many pleasures of being a landed Mexican Californio, he was not at all unsympathetic to the Yankees. In fact, he made part of his livelihood by trading with them, and he got along well with several non-Spanish neighbors, men such as John Reed (who was probably the first English-speaking person to settle in Sonoma, and who was fated to die young in the terrible explosion of the Bay ferry *Jenny*

Lind) and George C. Yount, who in 1836 built the first log house in the area and planted one of the first non-Russian vineyards. Yount in the early 1840s cut the shingles for the roof of Vallejo's Petaluma adobe, and in payment for this—and other achievements—Vallejo gave him a 12,000-acre land grant in Napa Valley, where the town of Yountville now stands. Then there was William Richardson, one of the first sons-in-law, who had also built the first house in Yerba Buena and had then settled on his land grant around Sausalito. (In his immediate family, Vallejo had many Yankee in-laws, including Jacob Leese—married to a sister—for whom he had no use, but for reasons that had nothing to do with his being a Yankee. [According to a well-known historian, Leese was a "lying, duplicious snake."] He would also see all but three of his ten surviving daughters and sons marry Americans as time went on, and he would send his son Platon to fight on the side of the Union in the Civil War.) This cosmopolitan man was known for his graciousness and for opening his door to any traveler who came his way.

The short decade that Vallejo enjoyed in a Mexican California was evidently idyllic. The Californios were known for their partying, their gambling, their marvelous skill as horsemen (their *rodeos* were social gatherings to show off their skills), and for their wealth and power. Thomas O. Larkin, the first and only American consul to Mexico, who got around perhaps more than any other American in that period, later looked back on that "golden age" with nostalgia and remembered "the times prior to July 1846 and all their honest pleasures and the fleshpots of those days. Halcyon days they were. We shall not see their likes again."

When it appeared that Mexico and America would almost certainly go to war, Vallejo must have had mixed feelings, but he remained steadfast in his friendship to such men as Larkin (who would become a neighbor when he traded his Monterey property for Leese's rancho in Sonoma). And Larkin and other "real" Americans—as opposed to Bear Flag revolutionaries who were egged on by the ambitious Frémont—shuddered when the Bear Flaggers seized and imprisoned their good Californio friend in 1846. The story has it that when the Bear Flag rebels came to get Vallejo that pretty June day—having divested himself of his troops, he was completely defenseless—he invited their leaders in for a glass of wine before going off with them, agreeably enough. Although he was treated badly, as it turned out, he remained a friend of the Americans, so much so that when California was made a state, he donated some 10 acres of his land for a state capital complete with a capitol building. He continued to be highly respected in the new American society and was elected a member of the constitutional convention that drafted the new state constitution—in Spanish as well as English—a state senator in the first state legislature, and, later, mayor of Sonoma. He was also appointed the "sub Indian agent" for northern California by the United States government. He did not entirely forget the Bear Flaggers, however: when, sitting in the meetings in Monterey to discuss the state flag, he suggested a vaquero lassoing a grizzly, and everyone laughed at his "unconscious" jibe at the Bear Flaggers.

But his days as a grandee were over. His capital of Vallejo was barely used (see Solano County), for he found himself without the money to properly set it up. (The town bearing his name at least is still flourishing.) And he suffered great losses of land and property. However, he stayed afloat enough to erect a (prefab) "Carpenter-Victorian" mansion near Sonoma, named Lachryma Montis—"tears of the mountain," for the springs on his hillside—in 1852, and to become one of the county's leading vintners, competing with Agoston Haraszthy, who acquired land nearby. (Two of Vallejo's daughters married two of Haraszthy's sons.) Both men did well in the wine business during the 1860s and 1870s, a time when Sonoma was the state's leading wine-producing county. But the terrible plague of phylloxera ended Vallejo's Lachryma Montis Vineyard and its prize-winning wine. Vallejo lived out his long life in reasonably comfortable, if dwindling, circumstances; he died in 1890 at the age of 82. (His Lachryma Montis home is now a state historical park just outside of the town of Sonoma; inquire at the state park visitor center on the Plaza in Sonoma for directions.)

When county lines were finally drawn in the North Bay in 1850, much of the land in all four counties had been subdivided, into large grants if not into smaller parcels, and it began to change hands with increasing rapidity as this lovely area was discovered during the gold rush. A more or less distinctive pattern of land use emerged in each of the new counties: West Marin remained largely in extensive ranches (soon to belong to the Yankee lawyers who had arrived to "help" the Spanish grantees secure their claims with the new government), while East Marin, readily accessible from San Francisco, became more developed; Sonoma and Napa were planted to agriculture and, increasingly, to vines; and Solano became one of the state's most productive agricultural centers, as well as a stop on the way to and from the capital in Sacramento. And, as time went on, the four counties would, each in its own way, deal with the continuing process of "civilization."

Marin County

Marin was linked to San Francisco early on when John Reed launched the first ferry service in the 1830s. His small boat served the Fathers and their charges who were bound for San Rafael (established in 1823 as something of a hospice for the many Indians whose health was failing in alien San Francisco), and the whalers and other seamen who had put it at Sausalito ("little willow grove"), where Guillermo Richardson had taken advantage of the natural harbor to open his own little port. He was so successful that the place was soon being called El Puerto de los Balleneros—"the harbor of the whalers." (After the American takeover, Richardson lost most of his extensive land grant in southern Marin to a lawyer named Throckmorton: Richardson left his name on the bay that once was his and on a freeway bridge, and Throckmorton left his on one of Mount Tamalpais's great hiking trails and one of Mill Valley's main streets.)

The redwood forests immediately north of San Francisco were not as extensive nor as valuable as those on the hills to the east, but redwoods there were, and those that stood in Marin were among the first to go: hence Mill Valley and Corte Madera ("a place where wood is cut"); hence, also, Dogtown in the Olema Valley, named by the loggers who brought along their four-legged protectors to scare off the local bears.

As more of northern California began to open up to settlement, a railroad was built to link Marin to Sonoma, and East Marin to West Marin. Ferry service was improved, and stage roads were developed. And being exceptionally beautiful (even for the Bay Area) and having a mountain all its own, Marin early on attracted people who liked their recreation outdoors. Its clement weather, especially in its eastern part where Mount Tamalpais formed a "sunshine shadow" in the summer (it forms a rain shadow in the winter, too, it should be noted), attracted fog-bound San Franciscans, and the wealthier built vacation homes and cottages (some grand); those not so blessed took the morning ferry and then the train, enjoyed Mount Tam and its sunny eastern slopes on foot, and then rode the evening ferry back home to foggy San Francisco. Mount Tam was soon established as one of the favored playgrounds of the city to the south.

Before the turn of the century, local capitalists were eyeing Mount Tamalpais for its money-making recreational potential. (At that time, capitalism was considered a profession, more than is venture capitalism today, and there were a number of "capitalists" listed as such in San Francisco's city directory.) Among these ambitious entrepreneurs was Sidney B. Cushing, who became convinced that Willow Camp (now Stinson Beach), where the mountain slopes to the sea, was an ideal setup for a "Coney Island of the Pacific." He and his family camped on the beach in tents (with a Chinese cook along) to get title to some of the sandy strand. Then he initiated what would become the famous Dipsea Race from Mill Valley to the sea and, incidentally, to the Dipsea Inn, which he hoped would become a magnet for dreamed-of crowds. (The tough little 7.3-mile Dipsea Race is still an annual event.) Being no slouch, Cushing entered the first race with his daughter, Dolly. But his grand plans for making Stinson Beach a playland did not succeed. (He would probably have been happy with the jams of cars and people that move into Stinson Beach now on sunny weekends.) The old logging town of Bolinas across the lagoon did become something of a summer resort as a result of Cushing's interest and efforts, but it also failed to make headlines in his time.

Cushing and others did better with building a narrow-gage railroad to the top of Mount Tamalpais, known first as the Mill Valley and Tamalpais Scenic Railroad, later as the Mount Tamalpais and Muir Woods Railway—and throughout as The Crookedest Railroad in the World (it had 281 curves in 8.5 miles). The ascent up the steep southern side of the mountain was achieved via a double bow knot, where the track ran parallel to itself five times to gain altitude, and the descent was via gravity—silent and swift and, if old memories are right, absolutely thrilling. At the top was the quite elegant Tamalpais Inn. (It had been Cushing's thought to run a spur from this railroad to Stinson Beach, and the roadbed was actually laid, only to become a wagon road; now it is part of Panoramic Highway, and Pantoll is the old toll stop.) Fire destroyed the inn and the railroad during the 1920s. Today, the railroad grade is a splendid and view-ful hiking trail.

As it happened, the center of the 1906 earthquake was located in West Marin near the little town of Olema. Geologists differ as to the exact number of feet the Point Reyes Peninsula jerked northward in this monumental event, but some say it was all of 20. Whatever it was, the results were spectacular: you can still explore a few of them at Point Reyes National Seashore (see below). Despite Marin's fault-laced geography, however, thousands of people fled to it after the 1906 debacle in San Francisco, and, as they did in other parts of the Bay Area, many stayed, swelling the population by 60 percent. This was the biggest infusion of population that the county had until the Golden Gate Bridge was opened in 1937. After that, World War II with its major shipbuilding projects and influx of workers brought another crowd, and many remained. Today, people—and more recently, industries—continue to move into this county north of the Golden Gate.

A large percentage of the people who live in Marin do so because of the beautiful natural features of the place—the bay front with its tidelands, the coast with its white surf creaming against the best ocean swimming beach in the Bay Area (Stinson Beach), its rolling hills, its varied wildlife, its extraordinary flora (the late botanist John Thomas Howell, lover of Marin and doyen of its flora, listed 34 species of lupine, 18 of oak, and 18 of ceanothus—or mountain lilac—in the county), and, perhaps most important of all, its mountain. Mount Tamalpais has been called the Sacred Cow of Marin County, and it is quite true that many Marinites will go to almost any extremes to protect it.

Mount Tamalpais State Park

Mount Tam, as it is often referred to locally, is a result of plate tectonic action, geologists believe, having been bulldozed up in long-ago collisions of plates moving in opposing directions. Mount Tam rises some 2,600 feet from the ocean to its highest peak in the east. With a long summit, it offers some of the world's most spectacular views. On a clear, cold day, it is often possible to see—from the mountain's high ridges—a snowy Sierra Nevada shimmering on the eastern hori-

Golden Gate National Recreation Area looking south across the headlands. PHOTO BY RICHARD FREAR.

zon, as well as Mount Diablo, Mount Hamilton, and the coastal mountains to the north and south.

(An Indian legend explains the derivation of Mount Tamalpais much more poetically than do the geologists. It tells the story that the God of the Sun came to earth to be with a lovely Indian maiden. He lingered with her many hours, thus creating the night, and when he was forced to return to the sky, he turned his beloved into a beautiful mountain. She lies on her back, her long hair streaming to the east, forever looking for him, forever open to his caress. Perhaps less romantically, the mountain is also known simply as the Sleeping Lady.)

How Mount Tamalpais got its name is open to conjecture. The Spanish called the southern Coast Miwoks the Tamales—whether for their tamale-making prowess or because the Coast Miwok word for the west was *Tamal* is another unknown. One way or another, the name probably immortalizes the people who first lived at its feet.

Mount Tam has many pleasures to offer the outdoor minded. It has Marin County's one remaining virgin redwood stand—in Muir Woods, which is small and exquisite. Its other forests, though second growth, are lovely in their own right. Wildflowers bloom in the forest shadows and in the high meadows in the spring, and anyone interested in botany will find a wonderful chaparral community to explore. The mountain has an extensive and delightful trail system, and it is possible to enjoy a stroll, a short or long climb, or a scramble or even roped rock climbing on its more resistant rocks (much of it is Franciscan melange). It offers many good bicycle trails as well, and heights beloved of hang-gliders. As noted, the surf at Stinson Beach is swimmable (and life-guarded by the National Park Service during the warmer months of the year) and is good for surfing and kayaking. Windsurfers seem to prefer the more sheltered waters of Seadrift Lagoon, but some do take, thrillingly, to sea. Birders have a field day on and around Mount Tam, finding literally hundreds of different species in its many and varied natural environments.

Marinites helped launch the conservation movement in the Bay Area, and because of their efforts and the efforts of their neighbors to the south, more than 40 percent of this beautiful county is protected in federal, state, county, or community park status. Mount Tamalpais is in the middle of one such protected area, perhaps the grandest metropolitan parkland in the country—the Golden Gate National Recreation Area (GGNRA)–Point Reyes National Seashore complex, which totals some 150,000 acres—shades of the old Spanish land grants! (see West Marin). Note that there are also about 17,500 Marin Municipal Water District acres on and around the mountain—and open to the public. Thus, while communities may lap at its feet to the east and to the north, and one small town may sit between it and its ocean coast on the west, the rest of this wonderful mountain is in parkland or reserved watersheds. In its size, beauty, and diversity, Mount Tamalpais makes a fitting monument to the tremendous and ongoing efforts of the people who have worked to save it for everyone to enjoy.

There are several gateways onto the more than 200 miles of trails on Mount Tamalpais. Many hikers like to start out of Muir Woods, which is, unfortunately, often crowded. (To reach Muir Woods, take Highway 101 north and follow signs; allow a half hour from San Francisco.) Visitation to this small national monument comes to around 2 million people a year, out of which a hefty 10 percent may be hikers. Maps are obtainable in the visitor center, and park rangers can help direct hikers in their explorations. The short walks that can be taken through Muir Woods proper are delightful in themselves, and anyone with limited time can get a feeling for the beauty of the original redwood forests by taking a stroll here. This last of Marin's virgin redwood stands was given to the American people by William Kent, another capitalist, in 1906. Kent had purchased the 295 acres known as Redwood Canyon for $45,000 in 1905, and to protect it from being logged and flooded by the local water barons he deeded it to the federal government in honor of John Muir. Muir accepted the honor with the statement, "This is the best tree-lover's monument that could be found in all the forests of the world." It was the only coast redwood forest in federal parklands until 1968, when Congress finally established a Redwood National Park.

From the west, the ridges of Mount Tam can be reached out of Stinson Beach (the Matt Davis Trail and Steep Ravine), and from several trails that lead from Highway 1 (through Olema Valley) to the top of Bolinas Ridge, all in the GGNRA. From the north, Bolinas Ridge can be reached from Sir Francis Drake Highway, and other trails on the mountain originate in Samuel P. Taylor State Park, 2,882 lovely acres along Papermill Creek. From the more populated eastern side, Mount Tam can be reached via Phoenix Lake (out of Ross), Deer Park (out of Fairfax), and via the Indian Fire Trail out of Larkspur.

It is possible to drive via Panoramic Highway and Ridgecrest Boulevard to the top of Mount Tamalpais (where there are, again, many trailheads) and to take a short loop hike from the parking lot around the eastern nose of the mountain for that great overview of the Bay Area on a clear day. On foggy days, the top of Mount Tam is most often above the clouds, and the view is enhanced thereby. Photographers take note.

There are five large man-made lakes on Mount Tamalpais, which are part of the Marin County Water District—Phoenix, Lagunitas, Alpine, Kent, and Bon Tempe. The first three date back to the early days of the twentieth century, when dams were more or less hand built; the dam at Alpine Lake (off the Bolinas-Fairfax Road), built in 1917, is noteworthy for its architecture, which reminds some people of a Roman amphitheatre. Since the lakes' waters are used for local consumption, swimming and boating are prohibited, but fishing and lakeside sitting are not. The lakes are stocked with bass and trout, there are trails connecting all five of them, there's a lovely picnic area at Lake Lagunitas, and it is possible to drive to all of the lakes except Kent. You may have to pay a fee for your car. A state park map of the mountain, available at park headquarters at Pantoll, will get you on your way to these pleasant places.

Tamalpais Trails

Muir Woods to Mountaintop

People who enjoy gaining the summit of a mountain will find several pleasant opportunities on Mount Tamalpais, which rises from sea level to just under 2,600 feet. If you're an enthusiastic hiker, one of the nicest ways to climb it is from Muir Woods, the lovely little forest of virgin redwoods. There are at least four possible routes—the one described is intended to inspire further exploration—and each is a class 1 (no technical difficulties) walk up. This one adds up to a respectable 10- or 12-mile loop and involves a gain of over 2,200 feet. A day given over to it should provide time to enjoy the trails and to pause for looks at the wonderful views the mountain offers. Tuck a picnic lunch into your knapsack (along with plenty of water and a pair of binoculars) and plan to stop at a streamside or at a view-ful spot along the trail.

Public transportation to Muir Woods has been an on-again, off-again kind of thing, so don't count on it. Best to call Golden Gate Transit (from San Francisco, 415-332-6600; from Marin County, 415-453-2100) to check its current status. (You can walk down via the Dipsea Trail from a bus stop on Panoramic Highway; weekends only.) The woods are easily reached by car, but expect some prime mountain curves as you descend from Panoramic Highway. Take Highway 101 north across the Golden Gate Bridge to the Highway 1 exit and follow the road signs to Muir Woods; they will lead you onto Panoramic Highway—which has splendid views to the populated east as well as to the open-country west—and then down the aforementioned curvy road. Allow a half hour from San Francisco to reach William Kent's great gift to the American people. A weekday is the best time to visit this part of Mount Tam, though even that may find the park—and the parking lot—full of sightseers, especially in the summer. It's a good idea to get an early start if you want to avoid the crowds.

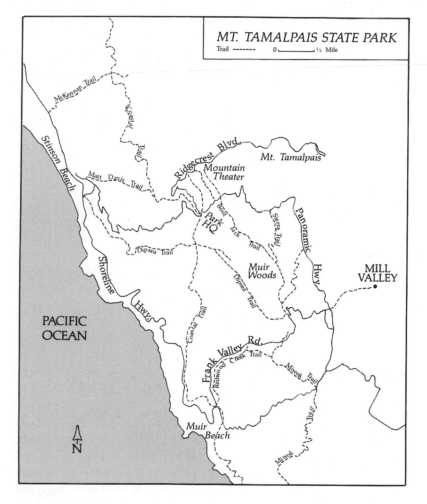

Before you start your walk, you may want to stop in the Muir Woods visitor center and pick up a copy of a park map. Then have a good drink of water at one of the park's fountains, and you're set to take off.

From the Muir Woods entrance, stay on the right bank of Redwood Creek; very soon you will come to the *Ocean View Trail* (which may be signed differently on your map as the *Panoramic Highway Trail*). This will take you uphill through the mixed forest of redwoods and broad-leafed bays and maples. On a bright day, enjoy the lacy pattern of sunlight on the forest floor, or if you decide to climb Mount Tam in the fog (my choice), enjoy the cool feel of the fog and the mysterious shapes of the trees in the mist. Also, enjoy the feel of the forest duff—formed by the forest's efficient built-in composting system—beneath your feet. The ferns that make green fountains along the slopes are sword ferns, so named for the hiltlike shape of their leaves where they join the stem. In winter and early spring, you will soon cross a mossy little waterfall that accentuates the silence of the forest with its music. In less than 2 miles, this trail will bring you finally to its ocean views and Panoramic Highway.

A short walk to the north along the road will lead you to Mountain Home, once a hiker's delight for the snacks and liquid refreshments it served, now an elegant restaurant and hotel. (Its fine—and expensive—dining room is, alas, not for dusty foot travelers, but there is a nice deck.) Just past this establishment, the dirt road leading north to a conspicuous fire station makes a Y; take the way to the right and slightly downhill. You are now on the *Old Railroad Grade* that leads from Corte Madera Avenue in Mill Valley to the mountain's east peak. You are also traveling through one of the chaparral communities that clothe the upper slopes of Mount Tam. The great botanist John Thomas Howell, who especially loved the chaparral, described it as having a "velvety" aspect, but up close you will find that it is more apt to be prickly—a protective device of many plants that live in tough environments. You will also find a lovely variety among the chaparral community—dwarfed oaks, manzanita (a delight when decorated by its little bell blossoms that identify it immediately as a member of the ubiquitous heath family), chamise, deer brush, mountain lilac, etc. A good part of Mount Tam's chaparral burned in a spectacular fire in 1945, and the plants have regenerated wonderfully since then; fire may be a part of the chaparral community's ecosystem, but now every effort is made to either regulate it through controlled burning (which is being practiced by the park people) or prevent it. The wide trails you see streaking up the mountain were put in as firebreaks.

As you follow along the railroad grade, you will have views to the east and to the south. The mansion that you see below you encircled by large grounds is the Ralston L. White Memorial Retreat, designed by Willis Polk in 1913 and dubbed the Garden of Allah. If the day is hot, it won't be hard to imagine what fun it must have been to chug-chug along this pathway, admiring the vistas, as a little steam engine did all the work. If it's a foggy day, you may soon be topping out above a world of streaming white clouds that half conceal the blue of the bay.

Continuing on your way, you will come before long to the famous double bow knot where the Mount Tamalpais and Muir Woods Railway paralleled itself some five times to gain the elevation needed to proceed upward. Keep going about 1 mile to the *Fern Canyon Trail,* where you go uphill on a short, steep, and lovely shortcut to the parking lot below the summit of Mount Tam. There, if you're feeling more like a stroll than a climb, take the ½-mile, virtually level *Verna Dunshee Trail* around the peak. If you're a more dedicated hiker, you'll probably want to make the final "assault" on the mountain— about 150 feet up the well-used trail from the parking lot to the east peak fire lookout (manned during fire-dangerous months). Either way, on bright days you can enjoy a 360-degree panorama of the bay—and beyond to the Sierra Nevada when the air is snapping clear, as it sometimes is in late fall and early winter. You can look for the bay communities spread out at your feet, and then for Mount Saint Helena to the north, Mount Diablo to the east, Mount Hamilton to the south, and the shining Pacific to the west. You'll also be able to see the gently folded hills that roll through the GGNRA to the edge of the Golden Gate with its elegant bridge. San Francisco's skyline with its cluster of skyscrapers and its unmistakable Sutro Tower may add a final fillip.

(Unfortunately, there's no public transportation to Mount Tam's summit—the bus runs only along Panoramic Highway on weekends. If the rest of this walk sounds to you too tiring, plan to do this hike with a shuttle; leave one car in Muir Woods and park the other at the summit—via Panoramic Highway and Ridgecrest Boulevard. Remember, however, that from here on it's all downhill.)

The easiest way to return to Muir Woods is to walk along *Ridgecrest Boulevard* to pick up the *Old Railroad Grade* again. En route, you can savor your last views to the north; you'll be able to see two of the Marin Municipal Water District's lakes—Lagunitas and Phoenix—nestled among the lower ridges of the mountain and Tomales Bay gleaming in the distance. The Old Railroad Grade will take you downhill 2 miles—full of choice views to the south—to West Point Inn. This is the old station that marked the westernmost point of the railroad, and the only building that remains from that early operation. It is now a club known as the West Point Inn Association.

From West Point Inn, take the *Old Stage Road* west to Bootjack Camp. This will give you more fine views to the south, and it will also carry you through a nice stand of Sargent cypress, the index conifer that grows only on or near serpentine rock. Look for the greenish rock and soil that mark this interesting formation, then notice the trees and plants growing on it. Associated with the Sargent cypress, and also flourishing only on serpentine soil, are three other plants: *Ceanothus jepsonia,* with its handsome scalloped and pointed leaves and purple flowers; *Quercus durata,* a small leathery oak; and *Arctostaphylos montana,* the low-growing manzanita ("little apple," once a staple food of the local Indians), with the lovely deep pink blossoms.

At Bootjack, you can cross the road (Panoramic Highway again) and follow the trail through Van Wyck Meadow and on down the mountain directly into Muir Woods. You'll be walking beside a rushing whitewater stream during the winter and early springtime. And in springtime you can look for tawny—and fragrant—azaleas beside your path along the upper valley floor. This route will make your total distance covered a good 10 miles. It will also call for a tolerance for steep downhill, for the trail from Van Wyck Meadow to Muir Woods is vertical enough in places to require steps.

Should you still feel like exploring more of Mount Tam after you've climbed to its tip-top, you can take a little longer to return via the *Rock Springs Trail, Mountain Theatre,* and the *Easy Grade Trail* to Pantoll. At Pantoll, you might enjoy finding the *Old Mine Trail* for a beautiful and gentle walk down through high meadows that grace the rolling hills. The Old Mine Trail ends on Frank Valley Road a little west of Muir Woods, but there is a spur off it—signed— that drops immediately into the Muir Woods parking lot. (Watch out for poison oak alongside this little trail.) The pluses on this walk are the great bay panoramas that open up along the high trail to Mountain Theatre—which is very much a plus on its own—and a chance to see Pantoll, which at one time was the toll stop on the old stage road to Ridgecrest Boulevard. The name came from a contraction of Panoramic Meadow and toll gate. (This highway to West Marin was not paved until the 1930s, and when it was, it signaled the end of the ferry boat *Owl,* which had plied between Bolinas and San Francisco for decades.) Should you find a full moon rising as you walk the Old Mine Trail, you will add a singularly lovely picture to your gallery of memories.

Mountain Theatre was one of the works accomplished by the Civilian Conservation Corps (CCC) in the 1930s. The first play produced in this high mountain dell was called *Abraham and Isaac;* the show went on in 1913 under the auspices of three lovers of Mount Tam, "Dad" O'Rourke (O'Rourke's Bench commands a lovely view a short distance away), John Catlin, and Garnett Holme. Three years later, William Kent gave a 6-acre site to the Mountain Play Association for a theatre to remember his friend and mentor Sidney B. Cushing, the man who taught him that "this mountain [was] too good a thing to be reserved in the hands of a few and that it should not be a place from which the great public [would] be excluded." The Mountain Play has continued to be performed annually (with but one exception in 1924, the year of an alarming hoof and mouth disease epidemic) in the natural setting even after 1930, the year that Emerson Knight, a San Francisco landscape architect, presented his plans—drawn up under the auspices of the Mountain Play Association—for a more formal outdoor theatre. Work on the Cushing Memorial Theatre finally got under way in 1934, but it took five years for the job to be completed. Not only were CCC funds limited, but the construction was exceptionally demanding; Knight's plan called for the placing and partial burying of some 5,000 native stones, each weighing between ⅓ ton and 2 tons, to seat some 6,000 people.

Since its completion, the Mountain Theatre has been one of the most popular of Mount Tam's wonderful and varied features, and the annual Mountain Play (usually performed for several weekends in late spring) has become a cherished Bay Area tradition. (Telephone 415-383-1100 for information.) *Note:* Should you want to attend it, plan to get a very early start if you're even thinking about using the (inadequate) parking lot near the theatre; many local people park lower on the mountain and hike up for the show, or you can take a shuttle bus from Mill Valley. With its remarkable seats, its well-placed stage, and its spacious views of the metropolitan landscape and bayscape, the Mountain Theatre is not only one of a kind, but the match of most amphitheatres worldwide.

Leading from Mountain Theatre to Pantoll (and heavily used when productions are being performed), the *Easy Grade Trail* is just that; it travels unhurriedly beneath a typical Mount Tam community of Douglas firs and tanbark oaks and ends at Panoramic Highway, just across from Pantoll, which is a pleasant, shady place to stop and rest. The Mount Tamalpais State Park headquarters is at Pantoll (telephone 415-388-2070) should you have any questions about routes, flora or fauna, etc. (Notice the pleasant walk-in camping facilities here. This state park also has rustic cabins for rent on the coast; call headquarters for information.) To get on the *Old Mine Trail,* take the road that leads west past the ranger's residence and bear to the south. On your way to Muir Woods, you will parallel a part of the Dipsea Trail. And once back, you can enjoy the pleasant, tired feeling that comes of having traveled more than 12 miles, with virtually none of them level.

West Marin

The Coast Ranges (Mount Tamalpais with its radiating ridges, in particular) more or less neatly divide Marin County into two geographical entities—one on the east, fronting on the bay, the other on the west, fronting on the ocean. East Marin, with its bay front and its generally gentle terrain, is readily accessible from San Francisco and the East Bay; it is the more heavily populated area and has the most history. West Marin, on the other hand, being more rugged country less easily reached, and having less dependable sunshine, has been more lightly touched. It has survived as something of a world of its own. People who live in this part of Marin speak of "going over the hill," somewhat the way Alaskans speak of going "outside" or Hawaiians speak of going to "the mainland." It's less than an hour from the heart of West Marin to the heart of San Rafael—yet it's a journey taken only when necessary; few in number, West Marinites are generally self-sufficient folks who enjoy their relaxed and rural way of life, their distance from the madding crowd, and their closeness to their natural world.

And a remarkably lovely and unspoiled natural world it is. Before the coming of the Europeans, Miwok Indians enjoyed its beauty and its bounty; it was populated by deer and elk, grizzlies and condors, among other creatures, and the richness of its estuaries—now known as Bolinas Lagoon, Limantour Estero, and Tomales Bay—and of its coastal waters provided for pleasant variety in the daily diet. As noted in the history of Marin County, West Marin was divided into large land grants by the Spanish, and much of the land remained in large parcels after the Americans took over. (The Miwoks were effectively evicted.) As a result, although a good part of the area's trees and forests has been cut over (the redwood going into buildings in San Francisco—and frequently up in smoke as the city burned and burned again—the oak going for firewood), and cows have largely supplanted the native grazers and foragers, West Marin has been gently used.

The Spanish land grants of the southern portion of West Marin—the area now known as the Marin Headlands—were early taken over by the U.S. military because of their strategic location along the Golden Gate. But gun emplacements, barracks, a riding stable, and a few other buildings were about all that came out of this development. And while a few entrepreneurs around the turn of the century did try hard to turn the fine bathing beaches of central and northern West Marin into amusement centers for the Bay Area (and, indeed, the West Coast), they did not succeed (see Marin County). The few affluent people who discovered the area's special charms and generally equable weather were content to build summer cottages along the pleasant shores. And the towns of West Marin that grew up—Inverness (named for the hometown of an early Scotch settler—the local country was thought to resemble parts of Scotland, and so it does); Tomales Bay (named for the Tamal Indians); Point Reyes Station (a way stop for the early railroad); Dogtown (population 30); Marshall (named for four Marshall brothers who built a hotel here in 1870); Bolinas (exact origin of this name is unclear); Stinson Beach (originally Willow Camp, the town was renamed in 1871 for the gentleman who acquired it, Nathan II. Stinson)—remained notably few and small. Ranching and cottage industries supported the local economy. (Because of this lack of heavy industry, West Marin has remained smogless. It has also remained the best place in the Bay Area to enjoy the starry spectacle of a clear night sky.)

During the 1950s, when the Bay Area was being carved into subdivisions at a frightening pace, and some developers came up with preposterous proposals (one dreamer wanted to make Bolinas Lagoon a racetrack; another thought it should be a small-boat harbor with restaurants, multiple dwellings, and a 1-acre "wilderness area"), a few far-sighted conservationists—notable among them Edgar Wayburn and Ansel Adams—recognized the grand (and fortunate) park potential of West Marin and initiated the movement to keep the area in open space. When, in the late 1950s and early 1960s, West Marin ranchers were faced with paying prohibitively high property taxes or selling their land for subdivision, the park idea provided a way out: Mount Tamalpais State Park was greatly expanded during the 1950s to include two large ranches. Then, in 1962, Point Reyes National Seashore (the first national park unit in the country to be "bought back" from privately owned property, and the first to provide for the continuation of established uses of that property) came into existence. When, in the 1960s, the proposed development of Marincello—a "model community" to accommodate 20,000 people—threatened some of the most beautiful parts of the West Marin Headlands (adjacent to the army land), there was a veritable groundswell of public opposition. With the support of virtually every segment of the community—and local, state, and congressional representatives as well—another magnificent parkland, the Golden Gate National Recreation Area, was established in 1972, and the headlands remained intact.

Because of its ongoing rural character, and particularly because of its parks, West Marin offers an unparalleled opportunity for outdoor recreation—to the millions of Bay Area people, and to people from all over the world. Following are some suggestions for ways you can enjoy this remarkable resource, which totals nearly 150,000 magnificent acres in two federal parks: *Point Reyes National Seashore*— which occupies much of the Point Reyes Peninsula—and the *Golden Gate National Recreation Area (GGNRA)*, which has six beautiful units in West Marin—the Marin Headlands, Tennessee Valley, Muir Woods, Stinson Beach, and the eastern slopes of Olema Valley and lands to the north across Sir Francis Drake Boulevard. Samuel P. Taylor State Park has nice campgrounds and beautiful second-growth redwoods. The Marin Municipal Water District Watershed (de facto parklands) is continguous to the GGNRA, adding an extra 17,000 acres of lovely public land. *Note:* GGNRA boundaries also embrace Mount Tamalpais State Park as well as Samuel P. Taylor State Park, and Point Reyes National Seashore embraces Tomales Bay State Park; all these parks are still administered by the state.

The Marin Headlands

The Headlands unit of the Golden Gate National Recreation Area rims the Golden Gate from Sausalito all the way to the ocean and extends north to meet Tennessee Valley. It is made up partly of army surplus lands—Forts Baker, Barry, and Cronkhite—and partly of lands that were slated for development but were rescued by a concerned public (see West Marin) with the help of The Nature Conservancy, which held this acreage until it could be included in the park.

The headlands are best reached by car from San Francisco, except on Sundays, when public transportation is available from San Francisco (on a limited schedule: telephone the headlands ranger station at Rodeo Lagoon for information: 415-331-1540). It is also possible to walk across the Golden Gate Bridge and explore the eastern end of this lovely parkland on foot. This makes for a long walk and probably calls for carrying your lunch. To gain the headlands from the bridge, take the dirt road that runs northeast from the north end of the Vista Point parking lot on the Marin side of the bridge (just before the reentry point on Highway 101). Follow it downhill; it will curve around, go under the bridge, and meet a paved road. Follow this uphill to Conzelman Road—the view-ful main road that follows the curvatures of the southern edge of the headlands. You might then plan to take the steep roadway down to Kirby Cove (about ⅓ mile along Conzelman Road), where you'll find picnic tables and fine views of passing ships, the northwest end of San Francisco, and colorful windsurfers in the Golden Gate when the breeze is right. Cars can drive the steep near-mile from Conzelman Road to Kirby Cove only with ranger permission; call 415-331-1540 for information. *Note:* The steep cliffs of the headlands are treacherous; they offer

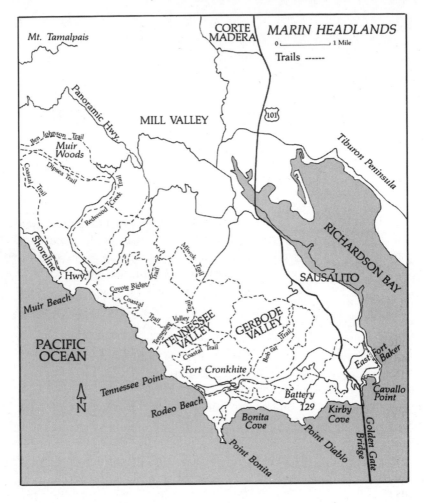

poor footing; people picnicking on them near the water have been washed away by heavy ocean swells. Be careful as you wander through this beautiful but sometimes dangerous countryside; best to stay on the beaten track.

To get to the Marin Headlands from San Francisco by car, take Highway 101 across the Golden Gate Bridge and then exit on Alexander Avenue. Here, turn left immediately, drive under the freeway, bear left, and then immediately turn right onto Conzelman Road in the Golden Gate National Recreation Area. Stay on Conzelman Road until you bear right into Rodeo Valley, then continue until you come to signs for the visitor center, located in the former Fort Barry Chapel. En route, you might be able to visit the Point Bonita Lighthouse, which is on the northwesternmost tip of the Marin Headlands in a spectacularly scenic location. This was the location of the first foghorn in the San Francisco Bay Area (see Foghorns and Lighthouses).

If you are coming from the north on Highway 101 and want to visit the Marin Headlands and/or the Point Bonita Lighthouse, you can turn west directly onto Conzelman Road just short of the Golden Gate Bridge. (Watch for the sign saying GOLDEN GATE NRA NEXT RIGHT.) Then proceed as described above.

Whatever way you enter the headlands, be prepared for stunning views of San Francisco (from Conzelman Road); the best hawk-watching hill in the Bay Area, a Bird Rock just offshore (of Rodeo Beach) that hosts cormorants year round and pelicans in season; a good spot for watchers of wintering wildfowl (Rodeo Lagoon); fine geologic displays, if you're interested in such (the beach at Rodeo Lagoon is composed of pillow basalt pebbles, and there are fine displays of chert along Conzelman Road); two small beaches for wave watching (Rodeo Beach and Tennessee Cove); historic army bunkers and batteries (along Conzelman Road and at Kirby Cove and the hills above Rodeo Lagoon); great shows of wildflowers; the Marine Mammal Center (near Rodeo Lagoon), where sick or injured marine mammals are nursed back to health and returned to the sea (open daily from 10:00 A.M. to 4:00 P.M.; telephone 415-289-7325); a lighthouse that you can visit (inquire at the park's visitor center for how and when); wonderful hills for kite flying (and hang-gliding); and, it goes without saying, superb hiking. You will also find numerous ranger-led walks; telephone 415-331-1540 to find out when they will be held. As an added plus for dog owners, it is possible to walk your dog off leash in specified places in the headlands: ask at the visitor center (located in an erstwhile church) at Rodeo Lagoon for a hiking map that will indicate which trails to take. The same hiking map will be useful even if you don't have a dog but do want to get out on the trails.

(Photographers will almost certainly want to drive Conzelman Road just for the views. There are numerous places where you can park along the way for a unique look at the Golden Gate Bridge with the city as a backdrop. Particularly wonderful times to visit this area are when the late afternoon sun is setting the windows across the bay on fire, or when lingering storm clouds compliment the city's skyline, or when a great full moon is rising in the east.)

Hawk Hill

During the months of September, October, and November, bird-watchers—or anyone who thrills to the sight of hawks in flight—will probably want to head for Battery 129, otherwise known as Hawk Hill. Go 1.8 miles along Conzelman Road from Highway 101, and park along the side of the road just before it becomes one-way. (Battery 129 is not signed, but you will see a fortified tunnel and closed dirt road on the right.) From your car it's a short climb to the top of the hill, where the old bunker offers a flat space for viewers and a place to sit down. (You may find you have quite a bit of company, since hawk watching has become a popular Bay Area sport.) Soaring above you there will likely be one or more red-tailed hawks, Cooper's hawks, sharp-shinned hawks, and kestrels, these being the most commonly seen raptors. (Be sure you have your binoculars!) However, 19 different species of raptors, including the golden eagle, the bald eagle, and the peregrine falcon, have been observed from this spot. The birds come through in extraordinary numbers on their migratory travels to the south; the ornithologist who discovered this spot where they congregate before crossing the Golden Gate chalked up over 4,000 observations in 29 days. Why do the raptors gather here and pause in their migratory journeys? Do they, like we, want to enjoy the fabulous view that can be had from this particular part of West Marin? Although these diurnal travelers have extraordinarily good vision and so might enjoy a vast panorama, indeed, that seems unlikely, particularly since they fear flying over water. Rather, and because they travel by gliding, they need as much height as possible to start a good long glide. They probably come together here to take advantage of the thermals, or updrafts, that form from the heat of the land. (Thermals do not form above water.) Once the raptors are high in the sky, they can get up the nerve to slide through the air across the waters of the Golden Gate, then pick up another thermal over the Presidio and continue on their way safely to the south. Watching these beautiful birds rise skyward, hang motionless for what seems minutes, and then tilt themselves toward their southern destination is one of the great sights in the Bay Area. (There are only two or three such gathering places for raptors known in the United States.)

The National Park Service has a program of events during the raptors' migratory season. These include raptor-banding sessions on Hill 129, slide shows, and hawk talks with docents from the Golden Gate Raptor Observatory. For information, call 415-331-1540. *Note:* The park service operates one of the country's busiest raptor migration observatories here.

┌─── Hiking the Headlands

Gerbode Valley Loop

The Marin Headlands offer the hiker an exceptional chance to get away from it all within sight of one of the world's great cities. Less than a half hour from San Francisco, you can taste the freedom and joy of open rolling hills that provide you with a good chance of seeing such wild creatures as foxes, rabbits, and perhaps a bobcat—and that rise high enough to open up some magnificent views. The headlands are beloved of raptors, as well (see Hawk Hill, above), and I have had the good fortune to find myself watched by a great gray owl one winter afternoon as I passed beneath an old eucalyptus tree in the deepening twilight; a few yards down the trail, I looked back, and the bird called, it seemed, to me. From September through December, you also stand an excellent chance of seeing some of the migrating hawks that pass this way en route to crossing the Golden Gate. And in the springtime, you may see a male lazuli bunting, surely one of the most gorgeously colored of birds, balanced delicately on a lacy branch of fennel, its turquoise feathers glowing like jewels. (The female lazuli bunting, alas, is dull colored and completely unremarkable.) As one final bonus, the headlands are home for myriad wildflowers, and from late March into June, a hiker may revel in slopes blue with lupine or golden with California poppies. Dozens of other species star the grasses along the trails, and a flower aficionado can, quite literally, have a field day.

There are several hikes that start near Rodeo Lagoon; one of my favorites is the Gerbode Valley loop. It's a good idea to stop by the

Marin Headland's attractive visitor center and pick up a trail map before you start on this or any other local stroll. (While there, you may want to confirm the way to return to Highway 101 via Conzelman Road, which has those breathtaking views of San Francisco seen through the Golden Gate Bridge; the turn off of Bunker Road is not well marked.) You can either leave your car at the visitor center and walk (less than a mile) to the Miwok Rodeo Valley trailhead on Bunker Road, or you can park your car at the old warehouse building at the head of Rodeo Lagoon. (When you exit your car be sure not to leave any valuables on view in it, locked or not.) From there you can start on one of the most pleasant of hikes—one that should leave you with memories of a lovely morning or afternoon. This is the Miwok Trail–Bobcat Trail loop that encircles the Gerbode Preserve, gaining about 900 feet and taking a little over 5 miles to make the circuit.

From the warehouse building, head east for about ½ mile until you come to a fork in the old dirt road; choose the way north, and this will put you onto the *Miwok Trail*. This trail remembers the first people who inhabited this part of the world, the Coast Miwok Indians. They were among those who could not tolerate the ways of the Europeans, and most of them had perished by the time this pleasant land became part of a Mexican land grant and subsequently a cattle ranch. It was grazed for many decades but was sold for subdivision after World War II. It was here that part of Marincello, the proposed "Model Community" (see West Marin) would have located 20,000 people in the early 1970s had not local environmentalists fought hard to save the headlands from such a fate. Happily, they succeeded, and this valley became part of the Golden Gate National Recreation Area; it is named for Martha Alexander Gerbode, whose interest and generosity helped preserve it.

The Miwok Trail climbs the eastern face of the gentle hills that provide protection from the cool ocean breezes. You may be toasty as you wind your way around their ridges on the old ranch road, admiring the bright bursts of crimson paintbrush at your feet, but when you top the first rise that opens westward, you'll be glad if you have brought along a jacket. At this point, the Wolf Ridge Trail (remembering animals that once were here) comes in, intersecting the small "pass" that you have reached; do not take this trail unless you want to return to your car via Rodeo Lagoon, along the road.

After climbing a short way, you will come out on a ridge that opens up the country to the north of you. Tennessee Valley lies at your feet; this would have been the gateway to Marincello. Looking to your right, you can see the Tiburon Peninsula and Richardson Bay—once part of the Rancho Saucelito, too. On the horizon sleeps the princess of Indian legend, waiting for the sun to touch her; we call her Mount Tamalpais. Above you is a Federal Aviation Administration device—a Very High Frequency Omni Range and Tactical Air Navigation Aid, known familiarly as VORTAC—which helps commercial aircraft find their way home and lets hikers know they've about reached the top of their climb.

The *Bobcat Trail* now winds onto the hills forming the east slope above the valley. (This section of Bobcat Trail is part of the Bay Area Ridge Trail). In springtime, keep your eyes out for more wildflowers in the damp places along the road. Soon the Rodeo Valley Trail comes in from the south. As an alternative to staying on the Bobcat Trail, photographers may want to take this side trip (the Rodeo Valley Trail leads back into the Bobcat) for a unique view of San Francisco; viewed from one special vantage point, the hills slope to make a perfect V framing the magic city. Staying on the Bobcat Trail will give you lovely views of the ocean, Rodeo Lagoon, and the country at your feet. Either trail will bring you back to the willow-bordered stream, the big old eucalyptus trees marking the site where a ranchhouse once stood, and, finally, to your car.

Tennessee Valley

Tennessee Valley was not named by a homesick easterner, but for a ship whose steel bones still lie just offshore. She was a fine 210-foot steamer, launched in New York the year gold was discovered at Sutter's Mill and pressed into service soon thereafter to ply between Panama and San Francisco. On March 5, 1853, she was traveling offshore in a dense fog, her nearly 600 passengers dressed in their Sunday best as they waited impatiently to step ashore after their long weeks at sea. Her captain had laid over near the Farallones the night before, not wanting to risk a blind entrance into the bay. Now he was feeling his way in the cold gray light filtering through the fog. Suddenly, ahead of him loomed high rocks, and for one glad moment he thought he was passing Mile Rocks; then, aghast, he realized that there was a beach directly in front of his bow. With remarkable presence of mind, he called for full speed ahead and deliberately ran his ship onto the sand to avoid a horrible encounter with the cruel cliffs looming around him. His chief mate leapt from the ship and secured a hawser on the shore, and the crew hauled all the passengers to safety. The only casualty was the beautiful *Tennessee,* which was stuck fast and fated to be battered and broken by the waves. (More than a century later, park service historians and archaeologists are still finding bits and pieces of the wreck.) By coincidence, members of the U.S. Geological Survey were mapping and naming parts of Marin that spring in 1853; they chose to memorialize a shipwreck that could have been far more tragic than it was. So we have Tennessee Valley and Tennessee Cove, where the ship was beached. The names are listed in the National Register of Historic Places.

Tennessee Valley Trails

To Tennessee Cove . . . and on to Muir Beach

If you love to walk within sight and sound of the sea, Tennessee Valley provides a lovely gateway. It also provides the alternative of an easy stroll from the warmth of an inland valley to the coolness of the coast. And, however you enjoy it, it provides for a moment of rejoicing that it is the way it is, well used, but essentially natural; it was one of the principal stakes in a hard-fought battle between developers and conservationists (see West Marin). Anyone who takes pleasure in the unspoiled out-of-doors can be grateful that the conservationists won.

For a pleasant morning's stroll, you can take your car north over the Golden Gate Bridge, turn onto Highway 1, and about ½ mile farther on, proceed west on Tennessee Valley Road. Another mile and you're at the roadhead for the trail to the cove, just short of the Miwok (public) Stables, where, if you are so minded, you can rent a horse. (It is also possible to take Golden Gate Transit to Tamalpais Junction and walk 1½ miles to the trail.) From here, it's an easy 2-mile saunter to the coast through the nearly level valley delineated by Wolf Ridge to the south and Coyote Ridge to the north. No need to walk on the paved road; take a pathway beside it until it runs out. Enjoy the shade of the eucalyptus along the creek. Inland from the coast, you'll find a lagoon formed by damming the stream and probably occupied by waterfowl. Then you come to the aforementioned cliffs and, although you may not see them, the remains of the *Tennessee*. There's no water on the trail, so carry your own. And, as anywhere along the coast, be prepared for wind. You can find a sheltered nook to lie in the sun and contemplate the fate of the *Tennessee* or listen to the conversation of the gulls before you return to your starting point.

If you want a more strenuous—and adventurous—outing, you can plan to take a longer, more scenic jaunt along the coast from Tennessee Valley to Muir Beach and back; this is a 9-mile round trip, versus the 4-mile turn described above. Start at the same spot and bear northward on the **Coastal Trail,** which is well signed here. Soon starts the pleasure of walking to the sound of the surf in a place so remote that you might think you were far more than a mere 2 miles—in a straight line, that is—from the city by the Golden Gate. There are ups and downs, some of them steep, on this trail, but the views are more than worth it. Before you reach Muir Beach, you will be able to see as far north as Point Reyes and as far south as Ocean Beach and beyond. Looking westward, you can marvel at sea stacks that mark the ceaseless work of the waves in rearranging the coast. Even when the weather's hot elsewhere, you can get a cool breath of wind off the ocean; more often there's the exhilarating snap of a lively breeze.

Bear to the left on the Coastal Trail (not so well marked here) if you don't want to loop back into Tennessee Valley (another possibility; consult your GGNRA map). You will descend into Pirates Cove (probably named for some Prohibition bandits), and when you top Coyote Ridge on the other side, the trail will join an old ranch road.

Your last downhill will bring you to Muir Beach, at the foot of Green Gulch Valley, home of the Zen Center's Green Gulch Farm. This is another interesting place you may want to visit in your exploration of West Marin. Ahead of you on the rise to the north is Sea Cape, the only subdivision in this part of the world. Keep going to the beach and cross the bridge. For a perfect rest stop, you can then drop into the Tudor-styled Pelican Inn for refreshment, perhaps a draught of beer or a cup of tea. This should put you in the right frame of mind for a return trip along the coast, but before you go check out the Terwilliger Monarch Butterfly Grove (see Monarch Butterflies appendix) nearby.

Note: Haypress Backpack Camp is an easy half mile from the Tennessee Valley trailhead. If you're introducing children to the joys of backpacking, this might be the place you're looking for. It has minimum facilities—no water—and is open all year. For information and reservations (necessary), phone 415-331-1540.

Muir Beach

This small beach is good for beachcombing, sunbathing, wading, picnicking, or enjoying the meeting of the sea with the shore. Surfers and fishermen find it attractive, too. Here the Golden Gate National Recreation Area maintains picnic tables, grills, water, phone, chemical toilets, and a parking lot. No lifeguard is in attendance, and swimming is not recommended. Muir Beach gets just as crowded as Stinson on warm weekends, but you might enjoy it during the week. Adjacent to it is the Pelican Inn, which is good for a getaway from the urban scene: it has nice food as well as afternoon tea in a publike setting. Look for overwintering monarch butterflies (see Monarch Butterflies appendix) hanging inconspicuously with folded wings dull side out in the trees of the Terwilliger Monarch Butterfly Grove along the road from Muir Beach to the Pelican Inn. A sunny day in spring may awaken flights in the hundreds.

You might also be interested in the 110-acre Green Gulch Farm (part of the San Francisco Zen Center) up the hill from Muir Beach. Its garden, designed by Alan Chadwick, produces the delicious vegetables served in Greens Restaurant in Fort Mason Center. Visitors can enjoy the gardens and hike the Green Gulch Farm's rolling hills. You can also join in Buddhist services and buy baked goods as well as vegetables from the farm. You can reach the farm by car from Highway 1 or take the trail up the valley through the fields from Muir Beach.

To reach Muir Beach, take Highway 1 and follow the signs to Stinson Beach; or you can take the Frank Valley Road from Muir Woods; it's 2½ miles from the woods. Allow 40 minutes from San Francisco either way.

Stinson Beach

Stinson Beach is a 3-mile sweep of white sand that curves across the mouth of Bolinas Bay and Bolinas Lagoon in a lovely new-moon-shaped sandspit. It is the finest ocean front in the Bay Area for playing in the surf, wading, sunbathing, swimming (if you can take the cool Pacific waters, almost never warmer than 60 degrees Fahrenheit, even in the hottest weather). One-third of Stinson Beach is administered by the Golden Gate National Recreation Area; the rest, including the beach tidelands of the exclusive Seadrift community on the spit, is open to the public. (It took a landmark court decision to gain access to the Seadrift section.) The GGNRA has picnic tables (there's also a fast-food stand in summer), lifeguards on duty during the summer, and a large parking lot. Alas, these facilities, which seemed adequate a decade or so ago, have proved to be totally inadequate. On sunny summer weekends, every cranny of the parking lot and roadside space along Highway 1 is occupied by a car; the beach would gladden the heart of Sidney Cushing if he could see it, for it is as crowded as Coney Island at the height of its season. If you must visit Stinson Beach on a sunny Saturday or Sunday, plan to get there early—it's about an hour's drive from San Francisco—and plan to leave early, too, for the traffic problems increase geometrically as the sun goes down and you may have to wait in line for a half hour before you can inch your way along Highway 1 back to the city.

There are two routes that access Stinson Beach: Take Highway 101 north to the signed turnoff onto Highway 1 and follow that highly scenic and highly twisting shorefront highway directly into the town of Stinson Beach and the GGNRA park. (You'll pass Green Gulch Farm and Muir Beach on the way.) Alternatively, take Highway 101 to Highway 1 as above, turn onto Panoramic Highway at the sign to Muir Woods, and stay on Panoramic until it rejoins Highway 1 at Stinson Beach. This is also a highly scenic (grand views of the bay en route and pleasant stretches through cool redwood forests) and highly twisting route. It takes about the same length of time—about 50 minutes from San Francisco if traffic if light—whichever route you choose. (You can also visit Muir Woods on your way—follow the signs: from Muir Woods take Frank Valley Road, which will put you onto Highway 1 just north of Muir Beach.) Golden Gate Transit serves Stinson Beach on weekends; use it if you can and save yourself the headache of driving; telephone 415-923-2000 (San Francisco) or 415-455-2000 (Marin) for information about schedules.

Note: The climate often varies widely between Stinson Beach and San Francisco or San Rafael; call 415-868-1922 for a taped update on weather conditions—and a spiel on park regulations. If you need further information, 415-868-0942 will put you in touch with a live park ranger. There is no camping at this park.

The town of Stinson Beach has a couple of motels, a flower shop, a bookstore, and several restaurants, including the Sand Dollar (on Highway 1), the Stinson Beach Grill (also on Highway 1), and the Parkside (not the Parkside Snack Bar), which you reach by turning west at Calle del Mar (the only stop sign) and left at Arenal. The Parkside has nice, homey food, and, frequently, pleasant informal music. (Its grand piano came around Cape Horn.)

Audubon Canyon Ranch

Two miles north of Stinson Beach on Highway 1, at the edge of Bolinas Lagoon, is Audubon Canyon Ranch, where great blue herons and egrets—both great and snowy—nest in one of the few heronries near a metropolitan area anywhere. Bolinas Lagoon itself is a favorite place of migrating pelicans, shorebirds, and ducks, and as many as 8,000 birds have been sighted in this small estuary at the peak of the migratory season.

No one knows just how long the herons and egrets have been coming in to nest in the redwood treetops that crowd Picher Canyon in Audubon Canyon Ranch, but their presence has been verified back to 1945. However, since 1962, when the ranch was established, the birds have arrived regularly each year at their "apartments" in the tall trees. Heronries are not noted for the stability of their populations, and thus the numbers and the visitations of the various species vary, but there may be as many as 150 nests built and occupied at the height of the season, and half again as many young egrets and herons fledged. Many of the birds feed in the lagoon directly across from the ranch and you can watch them spread their wings—the wingspread of the great blue heron, the largest wading bird in North America, is as much as 6 feet—in breathtaking flight as they travel to and fro.

Nesting activity can be seen from the ranchyard, but the best views are from Henderson Outlook, from which you can look down into the nests and watch the assiduous parents caring for their young, an exciting glimpse of avian life. The ranch kindly provides telescopes, but since you may find them in use, bring your own field glasses if you have them. To reach the overlook, you climb a steep ¼-mile trail, so wear comfortable walking shoes.

There is a very pleasant picnic ground at Audubon Canyon Ranch (and restrooms) and an excellent exhibit hall that, incidentally, has an interesting geological description of the region. (The San Andreas Fault runs generally through the lagoon, perhaps beneath the spot where you see the herons and the egrets feeding.) There is also a bookshop with a good selection for birders and would-be naturalists, posters, binoculars and telescopes, items for children, and even birdhouses.

Audubon Canyon Ranch is open to the public from 10:00 A.M. to 4:00 P.M., Saturdays, Sundays, and holidays during the nesting season—from mid-March to mid-July and by appointment Tuesdays, Wednesdays, and Thursdays, 2:00 P.M. to 4:00 P.M. (telephone 415-868-9244). There is no entrance fee to this Bay Area treasure, but donations are appreciated.

Point Reyes Bird Observatory

Point Reyes Bird Observatory (PRBO) is a unique environmental and ornithological resource. Established in 1965, it was the first bird observatory in the United States. (There are now a handful of others, including the San Francisco Bay Observatory located at the south end of the bay in Alviso.) Working in two principal locations—the Farallon Islands and nearby Palomarin (in Point Reyes National Seashore)—PRBO carries on a multifaceted program that focuses on research, education, and conservation. PRBO's research also takes it to Mono Lake, the High Sierra, and Antarctica. Volunteers play a vital role in all of the PRBO programs.

Visitors are welcome at the Palomarin PRBO station, where there is an attractive nature trail and an interpretive exhibit of local landbirds and their habitats. This is where PRBO conducts frequent classes for a wide variety of groups—from schoolchildren to senior citizens. It is also where the observatory is carrying on its long-term work in the study of landbirds, their life cycles, habits, and ecology. PRBO is perhaps the only ornithological station in the world where, by color-banding individual birds, researchers have followed land-bird families through several generations. Valuable insights into bird behavior have been gained: one of the most interesting is that every bird is an individual with its own unique characteristics—as much as any human being. If you happen on the scene when birds are being banded, you may be able to hold a bird and listen to the race of its heartbeat: children, especially, enjoy this opportunity. The Palomarin banding station is open every day on a more or less informal basis. Banding is most active in the early morning hours. You might want to call ahead (415-868-1221) before you drop by.

PRBO's Palomarin station is on Mesa Road shortly before you reach the Palomarin trailhead of Point Reyes National Seashore. Take Highway 1 for 4½ miles north of the stop sign in Stinson Beach to the north end of Bolinas Lagoon where highway marker 17.00 marks a crossroad. (Along the way you will pass PRBO headquarters in Galloway Canyon, 2990 Shoreline Highway; telephone 415-868-1221.) This turnoff is not signed for the simple reason that the folks in Bolinas don't want it to be. Caltrans has given up on trying to put up road signs—they're always gone the following morning. You turn left here toward Bolinas and keep following the lagoon to your left until you reach a stop sign at Mesa Road about 2 miles further on; this is short of the town. Turn right on Mesa Road and follow it about 4 miles to the banding station. You will pass a large "chateau" on the coast, built for an early visit from Guglielmo Marconi to his wireless station here: another was built on the shores of Tomales Bay to offer the great man his choice of environments. (He stayed here; the Tomales Bay edifice was later sold to Synanon.) You will also pass grazing cows, the network of a Coast Guard installation, and the station itself, an interesting structure built partly underground. The paved road gives way to good old dirt soon after you enter the Point Reyes National Seashore, and shortly after you make a sharp down-and-up hairpin turn, you'll come to the turnoff left to the banding station. (If you continue on for another mile, you'll come to the end of the Mesa Road and the seashore's Palomarin trailhead.)

Point Reyes National Seashore

Point Reyes National Seashore offers an extraordinary variety of park experiences. Only an hour from downtown San Francisco, it provides (classified-by-Congress) wilderness that not only is beautiful but offers the chance to see bobcats, deer, coyotes, and, some people swear, mountain lions. You may also get a glimpse of tule elk that have been reintroduced into what was once their native territory here. With several sandy beaches, the seashore also provides for swimming, beachcombing, and simply communing with the blue Pacific Ocean. It is a favorite place for horseback riders and has one stable where you can rent horses. (Check at park headquarters in Bear Valley or telephone 415-663-1092 for information on rental stables.) The park's system of trails gives hikers (and horseback riders) a choice of everything from a 1-mile loop to an all-day trek over the mountains to the coast and back; there are trails for bicyclists as well. There are four backpackers' camps. (No car camping, alas, but see Campgrounds appendix for nearby camping accommodations.) And, with pristine marshes and a wide range of upland and inland habitats, Point Reyes National Seashore has some of the best birding anywhere around. (More than 430 species have been identified within its boundaries: in annual Christmas bird counts, the seashore consistently ranks among the highest in the United States in number and species.) There are also a self-guided earthquake trail (wheelchair accessible), a nature trail, a restored Coast Miwok Indian village, and a Morgan horse ranch to explore—all within one central location (Bear Valley). And the seashore provides the best whale-watching opportunities along this part of the coast. (See The Pleasures of Watching Gray Whales.) For cream on top, this park has one of the best-designed, comprehensive, and interesting visitor centers in

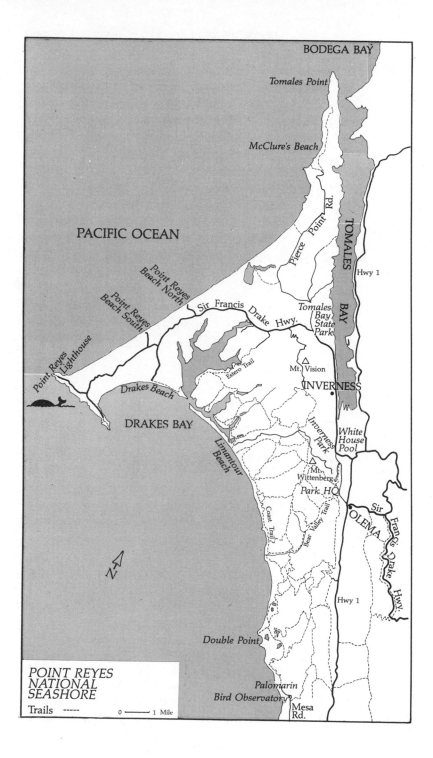

BODEGA BAY

Tomales Point

McClure's Beach

PACIFIC OCEAN

Point Reyes Beach North

Point Reyes Beach South

Pierce Point Rd.

TOMALES BAY

Hwy 1

Sir Francis Drake Hwy.

Tomales Bay State Park

Point Reyes Lighthouse

Estero Trail

△ Mt. Vision

INVERNESS

Drakes Beach

DRAKES BAY

Limantour Beach

Inverness Park

White House Pool

△ Mt. Wittenberg

Park HQ

Coast Trail

Bear Valley Trail

OLEMA

Sir Francis Drake Hwy.

N

Double Point

Hwy 1

Palomarin Bird Observatory

Mesa Rd.

POINT REYES NATIONAL SEASHORE

Trails -----   0 ——— 1 Mile

Point Reyes National Seashore. PHOTO BY REDWOOD EMPIRE ASSOCIATION.

the national park system. And Golden Gate Transit stops at park headquarters on weekends (See Public Transportation appendix), so you can visit Point Reyes National Seashore without a car.

Encompassing a good part of the Point Reyes Peninsula (see Geology and Weather), the seashore has an interesting variety of terrain. Its northern and southern sections are decidedly different in character. Park explorers can find new and interesting country in both directions; hikers need never get bored with "the same old thing." To the north, the great sweep of lupine-covered dunes that culminates in the northwest tip of Point Reyes is as wild and windswept as anything in *Wuthering Heights;* it may be flooded with sunshine, but it is often shrouded in fog, which adds a dimension of mystery and wildness to the land. It should be quickly added, however, that it is a wonderful place to enjoy wildflowers—along with lovely mass plantings of yellow lupine, there are exquisite spring gardens around Chimney Rock, just short of the lighthouse on the tip of the peninsula. This northern part of the park is also a wonderful place to watch for hawks; marsh hawks (now known as northern harriers), in particular, favor this open-to-the-sky moor. It has a long, beautiful, and lonely beach where you can encounter the untamed sea, and sheltered esteros where you can commune more comfortably with the myriad beautiful creatures, avian and marine, that occupy them. (Limantour Estero, in particular, is renowned for its wintering shorebirds, and, at low tide, you may find some of its live sand dollars, moon snails, or gorgeous nudibranchs.) In the park's northern section, you will also find open forests of fragrant bishop pine on higher ground; these picturesque trees are of a scale that does not encompass or dwarf the hiker, and they are unique to this particular terrain. For history buffs, there's a partly restored old-time cattle ranch, and for lovers of the bucolic scene, there are modern cattle ranches in full operation. (These are part of the park; ranchers' lands were acquired with the stipulation that owners could remain on them throughout their lifetimes. *Note:* Please respect the privacy of the people living on these ranches when you travel through the seashore.) The park's best beaches—Drake's Beach, Limantour Beach on Drake's Bay, and Heart's Desire Beach on Tomales Bay (the last still administered by the state)—lie to the north.

The southern stretch of the seashore, on the other hand, rises high and open above the Pacific for many miles, with only a few breaks in the tall coastal cliffs to allow waders, sun worshipers, and beachcombers down to the sand. Old ranch roads wind in and out of the canyons and along the ridges, some following the meadowy coast, others running through the ancient forests of Douglas fir that thickly clothe the higher reaches of Inverness Ridge—the long ridge that forms a backbone the length of the park. These fir forests are magic in the fog. Most of the trees are ancient and of a towering size, and many of them grow in strange and fantastic shapes, sculpted by the wind. When you walk among them in a quiet fog, they stand like insubstantial shadowy giants. If the fog is gusting in, you may hear it sing through the branches as though through the strings of great harps.

It is unstable land here in this part of the Point Reyes Peninsula, land subject to sliding on a massive scale; past slides have pushed up several natural dams that have trapped spring waters to make fresh-water lakes. Several of these lakes lie along the shore, and their waters spill over in pluming waterfalls onto the beach. It is possible to walk along the coast admiring brown pelicans in flight and come suddenly upon a small pond rimmed with a tule marsh—full of red-winged blackbirds.

Note: On October 3, 1995, a spectacular fire erupted near Mount Vision, and driven by 40–50 mph winds, swept through the heart of the seashore. Before it was contained, on October 11, it had burned some 14 percent of the park's wilderness. Remarkably, the burned area regenerated rapidly, and a year later the bird population had actually increased. All in all, although the conflagration caused over $5 million in damage, its long-term effects were beneficial.

Bear Valley

You can enter the park at the northern and southern ends, but the most popular gateway is the central Bear Valley headquarters and visitor center area, where there are parking places for 200 cars. To get there, you take Sir Francis Drake Boulevard (see Access Guide) west to Olema. Turn northward and, almost immediately, turn west on Bear Valley Road and follow the signs to Point Reyes National Seashore; you will soon be at the Bear Valley entrance (allow an hour from San Francisco). An hour or so in the park's highly informative visitor center is well spent, however you plan to use the park. Should you decide to remain in the Bear Valley area, you could happily take a day to see and enjoy the outdoor interpretive exhibits (mentioned above); since each involves a mile or so of walking, you could easily chalk up a 5-mile hike if you visit them all. You might also want to join in one of the free naturalist activities. You can bring a picnic lunch (there are picnic tables here) or pick one up in Olema near the park entrance, where there are two good restaurants and a nice old-fashioned country store.

Bear Valley cuts gently through Inverness Ridge from the ocean to the park headquarters area, gaining and losing less than 300 feet in a distance of about 4 miles. There is a clear, sweet-sounding stream running through the valley; it rises in Divide Meadow and takes off in two directions, eastward and westward (another index of the uneasy arrangement of the earthquake-vulnerable landscape here). The near-level old ranch road, *Bear Valley Trail,* that runs streamside is one of the park's most popular trails. It is wide enough for several people to walk abreast: this makes it a favorite with families with small children. Older couples enjoy its easy grade and good footing. It's good for walk-in picnics: there are picnic tables and chemical toilets at Divide Meadow, about 1½ miles along the way. Alders, laurels, and Douglas firs arch over the trail for virtually its entire 4-mile length like an airy, stretched-out, sun-spattered green tent. In spring and summer, yellow mimulus blooms in the wetter places along the way, and a profusion of blue forget-me-nots—perhaps a momento of earlier times when this area was ranched—mist the fern-draped banks. One nice thing about this trail is that you can enjoy it in both directions as your perspective changes; thus it is possible to take as long or as short a walk along it as you have the time and the inclination to do.

Taking off from the Bear Valley Trail are several upward pathways that lead to Mount Wittenberg (1,407 feet) or to one of its ridges. *Sky Trail* (see Bay Area Wildflowers appendix) and *Meadow Trail* are only 0.6 mile apart at the bottom and 0.4 mile at the top, and each is steep, beautiful, and about 1½ miles in length, through pleasant meadows and forests of laurels, firs, and ferns. A good hiker can make a happy loop excursion on these two trails in about two hours (or less), gaining (and losing) 1,000 feet or so. There is a small, extra pull if you want to gain the summit of Mount Wittenberg, which is the highest point in the seashore and a great place for kite flying. In clear weather, the views from the top of Mount Wittenberg (and even from its ridges) are stunning: photographers will probably want a wide-angle lens—and lots of film. This is a good place to watch the hawks in flight (sometimes attacked by the smaller resident birds) in autumn months.

The Sky Trail or the Meadow Trail will open up other options for grand walks to the ocean, or for easier loop hikes: Bear Valley Trail provides a nice return. Take the Sky Trail to Woodward Valley, for instance, and thence to the coast, where you turn southward for a couple of seaside miles and then pick up the Bear Valley Trail. This hike totals a good 12 miles. Or take the Sky Trail or Meadow Trail to the *Old Pine Trail* and back to Bear Valley for your return; this is a 7-mile loop, and one of my special favorites. (The "old pine" forest through which the trail runs is a particularly grand stand of Douglas firs; there's not a pine tree in sight!) You can draw this hike out by passing the Old Pine Trail and continuing on to *Old Baldy Trail,* which also leads downhill to Bear Valley; this makes a 9-mile loop.

Bear Valley is also a gateway to the park's very popular backpacker camps, Sky Camp (2.5 miles up to the north, with 12 sites), Coast Camp (almost 9 miles to the northwest, with 14 sites), and Glen Camp (4.5 miles to the southwest, with 12 sites). (It also leads southwest to Wildcat Camp, a little over 6 miles away, with 4 group sites and 3 individual sites.) Backpackers need permits, and generally advance reservations (obtained at park headquarters; telephone 415-663-1092), and stays are limited to four nights total; figure a good 15 miles if you want to make the circuit. (This mileage omits Wildcat Camp, which is about 4 miles from Glen Camp.) There is a modest fee. Glen Camp and Sky Camp are both tree-sheltered, being on Inverness Ridge; Coast Camp and Wildcat Camp are closer to the shore and open to the sky; they also access the beach. All the camps have toilets, picnic tables, and water (you'll still want to carry water when you're on the trail). Wood fires are not allowed, except on the beach (permit required), and dogs are forbidden on trails in Point Reyes National Seashore. When planning a backpack outing here, remember that the temperature may vary many degrees between the Bear Valley headquarters and the coast; be prepared for cool fog as well as warm sunshine.

Bear Valley also ties in to an extensive network of trails that lace the park to the north and to the south. However, you may want to enter these opposite ends of the park more directly. To the north, there is easy access via road to *Limantour Spit,* a perfectly lovely seaside area, with the aforementioned estero. When you leave the Bear Valley headquarters area, turn left onto Bear Valley Road, then left again in about 1½ miles on Limantour Road; you'll go over the crest of Inverness Ridge through Douglas fir forests and drop down to the coast; it takes about a half hour to reach the small parking lot at Limantour, where there are also restrooms and water. A limited trail system out of the Limantour roadhead will let you see a little more of the surrounding countryside.

The Northern Seashore

It's a considerably longer drive to the north end of the seashore with its unique landscapes and seascapes; allow an hour for the 21.5 miles to the lighthouse (see The Pleasures of Watching Gray Whales). You take the Bear Valley Road left from the headquarters area and stay on it until you reach Sir Francis Drake Boulevard, which you follow until it dead-ends at the tip of Point Reyes Peninsula. About 10 miles along the way, you'll have the option of driving 1.5 miles up *Mount Vision* (through a stand of bishop pines with salal making vivid green patterns at their feet) to an overlook with excellent views of the northern portion of the park, including the white cliffs above Drake's Beach. You might also see some of the exotic white (fallow) deer that were introduced here during the 1940s, when this was private land. Or you can stay on Sir Francis Drake Boulevard to North Beach (13.5 miles from Bear Valley) or South Beach (16.5 miles from park headquarters). Together, these two beaches make one of the grandest wild stretches of surf-washed shore anywhere. Dogs, on leash, are allowed on these beaches. Alternatively, you can turn off just short of South Beach and continue to *Drake's Beach* for a swim if the weather's good. On the way, you'll pass Johnson's Oyster Farm, where you can sample the succulent locally grown (Japanese, alas) bi-valves. There is a nice, weathered wood visitor center, restrooms, and food service (all wheelchair-accessible) as well as picnic tables at Drake's Beach—another exceptionally beautiful part of the West Marin coast. While there, you can watch for shorebirds while you ponder whether Sir Francis Drake did or didn't make landfall here in the "stynking fogges" of 1579.

If you continue on to the lighthouse, you'll pass three signed ranches, where the Nunes, Spaletta, and Mendoza families run their cattle. The Monterey pines and cypresses that form windbreaks for these ranches are the only trees for miles around and so provide havens for migrating landbirds. If it's migration time and you're interested in adding to your personal bird list, you might want to call the Northern California Bird Box—415-681-7422—which records and plays back callers' messages about rare and unusual bird sightings. The ranchers are tolerant of birdwatchers, so you can park your car on the side of the road and walk among the trees.

Another portion of the park, where hiking is great, splendid wildflower shows occur, there's good birding for wintering ducks and shorebirds, and where you can visit the Pierce Point ranch and look for tule elk, is accessed by Sir Francis Drake Boulevard—through Inverness Park and Inverness (you could get a treat at the Knave of Hearts Bakery or Perry's Delicatessen en route, or an excellent pizza at The Gray Whale on your way home)—and Pierce Point Road, which you pick up just short of 7½ miles from Bear Valley headquarters. (Sir Francis Drake branches left here; you branch right.) You will pass *Heart's Desire Beach,* where there are picnic tables, restrooms, water, and significantly warmer swimming (the beach is on Tomales Bay), a short trail to *Abbott's Lagoon* (where ducks and shorebirds winter), and another to *Kehoe Beach,* before the road dead-ends just above *McClure's Beach,* where there's good tidepooling. A friend of mine makes an annual pilgrimage to this part of Point Reyes every spring to see the wildflowers—poppies, yellow vetch, and lupine that light up the moor like sunshine, even if the fog is heavy. (Strong hikers may enjoy the exceptionally lovely 9.4-mile round-trip hike from the McClure's Beach parking lot out to *Tomales Point.*) Marsh hawks add their aerial dimension to the spectacle.

The Southern Seashore

There are two principal gateways into Point Reyes National Seashore south of Bear Valley: one at Five Brooks and the other at Palomarin. To reach either of these from park headquarters, you turn south on Highway 1 at Olema; Five Brooks is about 3 miles along the way; Palomarin, which is reached via a turn onto the Olema-Bolinas Road at the head of Bolinas Lagoon (see Access Guide), is 15 miles from Bear Valley. This section of Highway 1 is interesting to travel, since the Olema Valley, through which it runs, demarcates the San Andreas Fault. This great fault, of course, marks the uneasy junction of the Pacific Plate with the North American Plate (see Geology and Weather). Notice marshy areas on the west side of the valley, especially toward its southern end; such wet places are formed when complex faulting, caused by immense stresses deep in the earth, fractures the surface. Note, too, the name Five Brooks; this remarks the fact that five streams emerge from the disarranged landscape here. Two of them join to flow northward into Tomales Bay, while the other three merge to travel southward into Bolinas Lagoon; along the way, the two opposite-flowing streams run parallel for quite a distance.

There is excellent hiking out of Palomarin (see Palomarin to Pelican Lake, below) as well as along the two substantial ridges—Inverness Ridge to the west and Bolinas Ridge to the east (both ridges actually trend northwest-southeast)—that cradle the Olema Valley. Thus there are good opportunities to view this intriguing valley from different perspectives and to note the subtle differences in the landscape and the flora of the two different geologic formations. For instance, redwoods thrive on Bolinas Ridge (on the North American Plate); not so across the fault line on Inverness Ridge (the Pacific Plate). A little further to the north, bishop pines flourish on the granitic soil of Point Reyes (Pacific Plate); they do not take to Bolinas Ridge. You may find other interesting variations yourself. It is worth noting that this unique watershed is fortunately almost entirely in parkland: Inverness Ridge is in the Point Reyes National Seashore; Bolinas Ridge is in the Golden Gate National Recreation Area.

Worlds Apart: Hiking Both Sides of the San Andreas Fault

The San Andreas Fault marks the rift in the earth's crust where the Pacific and North American plates grind past each other (see Geology and Weather). The fault is strongly defined in West Marin's Olema Valley, a long rift valley bearing evidence of its origins in its sag ponds and pressure ridges. On the west side of the valley, Five Brooks and Inverness Ridge—on the Pacific Plate—offer a geology and fauna contrasting that of Bolinas Ridge on the east—on the North American Plate (see Southern Seashore, above). The Olema Valley Ridge hikes offer good views and an experience of the different ecological communities on each side of the fault, and the Palomarin hike into Point Reyes Seashore adds marvelous ocean views to its "Pacific Plate" character.

Olema Valley Ridge Hikes

Here are a couple of my favorite hikes out of the Olema Valley. Note that the two parks—Point Reyes National Seashore and the GGNRA—here share the landscape, and indeed a couple of the trails.

You can gain the top of Inverness Ridge most pleasantly from the *Five Brooks* trailhead. From the parking lot, you can make a beautiful two-to-three-hour loop; walk left (or right) around the small pond, which is a relic of an aborted logging show that was brought to an end by the establishment of the seashore in the early 1960s. The pond has become a favored place for such wintering wildfowl as pied-billed grebes, ring-necked ducks, and hooded mergansers; there also seems to be a resident green-backed heron here that you might want to look for. Past the pond, you'll turn left onto the *Bolema Trail.* This will take you uphill to the ridgetop along a generally shaded old ranch road. Notice the exceptionally tall laurels and Douglas firs beside this trail, evidence of some special growing condition. You can pause a couple of times farther along the trail for nice views across the valley toward Black Mountain (see Geology and Weather); this picturesque mountain is also known as Elephant Mountain, for obvious reasons. When you walk through a small stand of digger pines, don't think you've been transported magically to the Sierra foothills, where this species is native; these trees were planted here decades ago.

At the top of the hill, turn right to follow along the ridge. This is an especially lovely mile-long stretch of trail when the fog is creeping in from the ocean and the setting sun backlights it in wide, slanting rays through the grand Douglas fir forests that thrive here on this Pacific Plate soil. After about a mile along the ridge, you'll come to the *Stewart Trail;* take this (it's a turn to the right, downhill) and follow it back to the point where you started.

While you gain enough altitude (about 1,000 feet) on this walk to feel like you've gotten some exercise, your steps will probably still be springy when you complete its 6-plus miles. It's a specially nice hike (or horseback ride—there's a rental stable at the Five Brooks trailhead) for a late summer afternoon or for a winter morning—between storms, that is.

Across the valley, *Bolinas Ridge* rises higher—to over 1,800 feet in places. It offers a nice choice of walks—short or long—and there are several entrances to its 12-mile-long ridgetop trail, which is partly a Marin Municipal Water District service road that is in active use, and thus well kept. (GGNRA lands abut Marin Municipal Water District lands to the east.) This trail system also offers a number of good chances for a shuttle hike (these will be noted), if you're traveling with friends who have another car. It is extremely attractive to bicyclists.

If you want an easy stroll, park your car at the top of the ridge off the Bolinas-Fairfax Road (an old stage road—travelers uphill often had to get out and walk so that the horses could make it); you can take this road out of Fairfax or from the Olema Valley floor at the north end of Bolinas Lagoon (it's the unsigned crossroad at mileage marker 17.00 on Highway 1 that you take in the opposite direction for Bolinas). There's a small parking lot in the redwoods where this road meets Ridgecrest Boulevard, and there's a locked gate (easily bypassed on foot) across the street from it. You start generally north on the ridge through a nice stand of redwoods past the site of an inn that once served the stage passengers coming through. Soon you're out in the open for a couple of miles of gently rolling ridgetop. Here you walk through chaparral and gain some nice views seaward. Then once more you will pass among the redwoods. These are beautiful and good-size second-growth trees here, and you can see how grand their ancestors were by the size of some of the stumps and family circles in the forest. (See Coast Redwoods appendix.) The original forest here was logged in the 1840s and 1850s to supply a burgeoning San Francisco. The fine second-growth forest tempted loggers again in the 1960s, but outraged Marinites halted the operation, and the county subsequently forbade all logging without its permission inside its boundaries.

When you reach the *McCurdy Trail* (3.5 miles), you can turn and retrace your steps (things will look quite different). Or, if you can arrange a shuttle, you can take this old ranch road and drop down to the valley floor at the Dogtown trailhead on Highway 1. (Dogtown was named for the dogs kept by those early loggers to scare away the bears.) Here there is a small parking area where you can leave a car when you start this hike. Incidentally, this is one of the places where trails in the two parks meet one another: on the west side of the Dogtown trailhead, there's a pathway that divides, with one branch leading up to the Inverness Ridge (about 2 miles) and another running along the valley to Five Brooks (about 4 miles).

If you would like a longer walk along Bolinas Ridge, you can take the full 11 miles north from the Bolinas-Fairfax Road parking spot to Sir Francis Drake Boulevard, to the east of Olema. While this is a considerable distance, it's quite easy walking, with few major ups and downs, and it gives you perhaps the best overview of the restless landscape of the Olema Valley and its ridges. You'll look out from redwoods across the valley to the Douglas fir forests on Inverness Ridge, and you can admire the rolling open meadows—especially when they are starred with wildflowers in the spring—on the valley's east slopes that rise to Bolinas Ridge. You can also make a loop hike up to and along the ridgetop from the valley floor: for instance, take the McCurdy Trail to the top of the hill, bear north, and come down the *Randall Trail*—you'll cover about 6 miles on this one with a nice little climb of over 1,600 feet. Or you can take the McCurdy Trail up and continue all the way along the ridgetop to Sir Francis Drake Boulevard, about an 11-mile pull plus that initial climb. These hikes, too, call for a shuttle, but, as noted, the distances are not too great, and it doesn't take much of a drive—or too much time—to get a car to the destination trailhead. Bolinas Ridge is always lovely (cool along the top even on hot days) and especially so in the fog. Dog owners, incidentally, can take their pets along in this section of the GGNRA if they keep them on leash. No dogs are allowed in Point Reyes Seashore on Inverness Ridge.

Palomarin to Pelican Lake

To reach the Palomarin trailhead in Point Reyes National Seashore, follow directions to Point Reyes Bird Observatory from Stinson Beach (see Stinson Beach). You will be parking your car where Mesa Road out of Bolinas dead-ends. Your driving time from San Francisco to this point will be at least an hour, although the distance is only a little over 30 miles. Highway 1, as noted, is famous for its hairpin turns as well as its gorgeous views, and it is a two-lane road—a single lane in each direction—all the way. (It does have a few pull-outs for passing.) On your way to or from this trailhead, you may want to stop at the Point Reyes Bird Observatory (see Point Reyes Bird Observatory). Mornings—when the birds are more active—are the best time to observe a banding operation, when there may be that wonderful opportunity—for children especially—to hear the incredibly rapid heartbeat of a small bird.

The hike to Pelican Lake described here will make for a happy day's outing if you bring your lunch; otherwise it offers a good morning or afternoon on the trail—7 or 8 miles round-trip in all. Should you want more of a workout, you can start on the Coast Trail and add a loop by taking the Lake Ranch Trail to the top of Inverness Ridge, walking north on the ridge, and then following the same ranch road as it returns to the coast. This will give you not only a coast experience but a forest experience as well. It will also increase your elevation gain by some 1,000 feet, and your distance covered by a good 6 miles; you'll want to carry your lunch for this one, for sure. And whatever hike you take in southern Point Reyes, fill your canteen before you leave civilization; the stream water here is not potable, and the park does not provide a drinking fountain at the Palomarin trailhead—for lack of funds.

As you start walking along the *Coast Trail* out of Palomarin, you come almost immediately to the site of a ranch house that stood here for many decades until the seashore was established in 1962. Great old eucalyptus trees mark the location; this will be the last shade you'll get for the 2 miles that the trail winds along high above the blue Pacific and then inland up to the first of the freshwater lakes that you'll come to on this hike. This is a particularly wonderful stretch of trail; there's a grand, exhilarating sense of space and freedom as you walk past wildflowers on the one side and the sea's misty and infinitely distant horizon on the other. Should you see a long line of pelicans undulating against the sky, you may also feel the timelessness of this place; pelicans are the descendants of birds much like them that flew millions of years ago, among the earliest species in the avian line of evolution. As much as a redwood forest, this coast with its brown pelicans links us to our ancient past.

After passing above the sea, the Coast Trail turns inland and uphill past high meadows (colored blue and purple with wild iris in the spring) and rock gardens of flowers along the road cut. As you come out on the level, you go by the site of another ranch house; this was the Lake Ranch, where former owners had their home and, across the road, their barn. This is where the *Lake Ranch Trail* takes off up the hill. Continuing on the Coast Trail for about ½ mile, you will come to *Bass Lake,* a popular destination on warm days, when hikers like to cool off with a swim. Another mile or so will bring you to *Pelican Lake,* the largest and loveliest of the lakes above the sea. You'll find nice spots to stop and rest, admire the scene, and picnic. Then, if it's spring or early summer and you'd like to add the sight of harbor seals to your adventure, walk around the north side of the lake and climb to the top of the hill that helps form the lake's natural dam. (The two hills here are known as *Double Point.*) From here you can look down on a strip of beach that is inaccessible except during one or two minus tides a year. This is where the harbor seals and their newborn pups bask in the sun. (It is not wise at all to try to get to this beach except when one of the aforementioned minus tides lets you approach it along the shore, and then you must pay strict attention to the rhythm of the tides; the beach is off limits even then if it's pupping season.) Leaving Pelican Lake, photographers should look back (if they have any film left, that is); at certain times of the year the sun in the western sky is framed perfectly in the deep V made by the two hills of Double Point.

Unlike some trails that seem boring when you retrace your steps, the Coast Trail from Pelican Lake to Palomarin offers a whole new set of views on a return trip. Perspectives are quite different as you drop down the hill past the rock gardens and approach the coast with its wide sweep of horizon. On clear days, you can see the Farallones off to the west, and if it's a late spring afternoon, you can watch Venus blaze out in a pale apple-green sky. Should you be traveling when the tide is low, you'll look down on the rocks of RCA reef with the surf crocheting lacy white patterns as it churns over them. (This is a good reef for exploring marine life, and local biology classes occasionally visit it, but the trail down from the Palomarin parking lot is a steep scramble.) As you approach Palomarin, you can feel the crunch of eucalyptus buttons beneath your boots, and the memory of their pungent scent will go with you as you climb into your car for your return to the "real" world.

Note: This walk is especially recommended for a time when the full moon can add its magic to your evening walk above the sea.

Point Reyes Field Seminars

Along with weekly naturalist events, Point Reyes National Seashore sponsors seasonal field seminars of unusual interest. These attract people from distant parts of California as well as from out of state. A wide range of subjects are loosely categorized: "Arts and Natural Crafts" may include classes in basketry, watercolor workshops, nature illustration, and pencil sketching of the natural scene. "The Natural History of Point Reyes" focuses on many aspects of human and natural history, such as tide-pooling, identifying wildflowers, and exploring the natural scene after nightfall. Master classes explore technical and aesthetic aspects of photography, with lectures, slide shows, and field sessions at the water's edge. There are classes for senior citizens (in cooperation with the nationwide Elderhostel program) and several classes to be enjoyed by the whole family. The faculty includes distinguished and professional photographers, biologists, and naturalists: many are from the faculties of local colleges and universities. Most of the classes may be taken for credit through Dominican College. Accommodations are not generally provided, except for courses with evening classes, when the Point Reyes/Clem Miller Environmental Education Center or the Point Reyes Hostel (both near Limantour) is used. Local bed and breakfasts, motels, and campgrounds provide attractive facilities. For further, more detailed information and copies of the seminar catalogue, write Seminar Coordinator, Point Reyes Field Seminars, Point Reyes, CA 94956 or call 415-663-1200. The headquarters is located in the white house just to your right as you enter the park off Bear Valley Road.

The Pleasures of Watching Gray Whales

Which of the marine mammals travels over 10,000 miles every year—on one of the longest migratory journeys taken by any animal on earth? The answer is the gray whale, which routinely makes an annual round-trip from the Bering Sea to the waters off Baja California. (Only the humpback whale travels farther.) Leaving the Arctic—generally in late October when the short days are growing shorter and the thick ice is growing thicker—these highly evolved, intelligent creatures make their way southward, hugging the shores of North America to remain in the waters above the continental shelf. (Adapted to relatively shallow water, the species becomes uncomfortable at the 100-fathom—600-foot—depth.) They make the return journey from Mexico in three waves or pulses: the first group (newly pregnant females and adult males) and the second (juveniles of both sexes) leave in February; the third group (new mothers and their calves) departs a month or so later (good sightings have been had in May). Early migrants to the north and late migrants to the south may, in fact, pass one another on the way.

There are several places along the California coast where the edge of the continental shelf crowds the traveling whales close to the shore and it is easy to view their passage: the tip of the Point Reyes Peninsula is one of the best of them. Thrusting westward into the ocean some 15 miles from the mainland, this spur of land all but intersects the pathway of the migrating giants. At the peak of the migratory tide, it is not uncommon for 60 to 80 whales a day to pass this well-placed observatory. The peak often occurs around mid-January for those bound for the southland, but seasoned whalewatchers start looking in December and keep their eyes open throughout the next few months.

What is the best way to see these mighty voyagers? Take yourself to a good observation post—in this case, the Point Reyes Lighthouse is recommended—preferably on a day when there is neither wind nor rain nor, of course, heavy fog. Don't insist on sun; a softly gray day may make your sightings more vivid and memorable. Dress comfortably, preferably using the layering technique to be sure you stay warm, and be prepared to spend as much time as you may find necessary to see a passing whale. Keep in mind that they do not travel on a regular schedule and you may have to wait out their arrival. Sometimes a half dozen whales will swim by in a matter of minutes; other times not one will appear for an hour or more. The viewing platforms at the Point Reyes Lighthouse are not large and quickly fill up with whalewatchers on weekends during the whale-watching season, especially on clear Saturdays and Sundays. You will do better to whale-watch during the week, if you can, or to arrive early—by 9:00 or 10:00 A.M.—on a weekend day. Early hours are better under any circumstance since the sea tends to be calmer before afternoon breezes spring up. *Note:* There are 309 (official national park count) steps down to the best viewing space at the Point Reyes Lighthouse, so if you don't want to descend—and climb—the equivalent height of a 30-story building, you'd best settle for looking from the top, or find yourself another place to whale-watch, perhaps at nearby South or North Beach, or Drake's Beach, or even at Año Nuevo (see San Mateo Coast). People also report good whale-watching from Chimney Rock, just up the way; from San Francisco's Cliff House; and from Fort Funston, especially when the animals are traveling northward and come closer to shore.

What to look for when you whale-watch? The first sign of a gray whale is likely to be a small, roundish fountain that looks like a puff of steam. It is, in fact, a combination of steam that forms when the whale's warm breath encounters cool sea air and of water blown out when the whale exhales through its two 8-foot-long blowholes, or nostrils. This is the whale's blow—as in "thar she blows!"—and it can be seen for great distances on calm, clear days. The sound, a gentle explosion, is audible for up to a half mile. The blow may be repeated in a half minute or so, and you can expect the phenomenon to occur three or four times before your whale goes under in a dive.

(It may stay under only 4 to 7 minutes as a rule or, rarely, as long as 15.) It is best to start your watching without binoculars, letting your eyes scan back and forth across the water a few inches below the horizon. Once you have located a traveler, use your binoculars to get a better close-up view.

If you're lucky, you may see a whale spyhop, that is, rise straight up in the water by thrusting its flukes until its head is as much as 10 feet above the surface: the animal may then pivot slowly, as though surveying the four points of the compass. The 30 seconds that it may spend in this maneuver will probably seem like minutes to you, and you may find yourself yelling "oh!" and "ah!" along with your fellow watchers. Seasoned biologists sometimes refer to spyhopping as "oh and ah" whale behavior, and the same goes for breaching, when the whale launches its body high out of the water, rolls on its side or back, and then plops back into the water with a tremendous burst of spray. Just what the whale is doing by breaching is not well understood: it may be displaying stress, trying to rid its body of parasites (it may have several hundred pounds of barnacles attached to it!), or simply having a good time. When the whale sounds, or dives for an extended period of time, you may also have the chance to see its 12-foot, 300-plus-pound flukes (which are attached at right angles to its body), one of the classic views a whalewatcher can hope for.

The California gray whale is only medium size as whales go, but it may grow to be 50 feet long and weigh as much as 40 tons. (This makes it just a little over half the size of its cousin, the blue whale, which at 89 feet long and 100 tons is the largest animal ever known to live.) A toothless species, the gray whale is equipped with a curtain of baleen—a heavily fringed growth of fingernail-like material— which hangs from its upper jaw. Grazing on the sea's bottom ooze, where it roots out masses of tiny amphipods, or gulping in huge mouthfuls of crustacean-rich water, the gray whale strains out anything inedible or unappetizing through its baleen filter. It is believed that its migratory pattern is triggered by the availability of food or lack thereof. Prior to taking their great journey southward when deep winter locks the Arctic waters into ice, the animals "whale out," gorging themselves until they have laid on a full complement of body fat or blubber. (To fuel themselves for their long trips, they can consume up to a quarter of their body weight in food.) Along the way they may go through the motions of feeding, but it is thought that they take in very little food.

Unlike such species as the killer whale, which mates for life, the gray whale is a promiscuous animal. Male and female may copulate on their way south (and you may see a pair in their courtship play, rolling and splashing in the water), or they may wait until they reach the more hospitable waters of the Mexican lagoons. The gestation period is between 11 and 13 months, and once impregnated, the females usually make a full round-trip from, say, Scammon's Lagoon on the west coast of Mexico to the Bering Sea and back again before giving birth. Occasionally, a calf is born along the way south: its chances for survival are believed to be greatly lessened when this occurs since the cold water and arduous travel may take their toll. A calf weighs in at around three-quarters of a ton at birth and is, on the average, 15 feet long. Fattening on about 50 gallons of its mother's nutritious milk every day (for the first eight months of its life), however, the youngster enlarges rapidly, gaining as much as 70 pounds a day. Its life expectancy will be 30 to 40 years, but some whales have been known to survive for 60.

Calling these great whales gray may be misleading. Their color ranges from light to dark and is distinctive primarily for the mottled white pattern that their resident barnacles produce. These small crustaceans (which more or less cement themselves onto the whale by their heads and feed by waving their feet) move in on newborn calves within a day or so after birth. Along with these uninvited guests, another parasite, the orange-colored whale louse—which can be an inch long—occupies the whale in great numbers, living among the barnacles or nibbling the discarded skin of the whale itself.

It is thought that gray whales travel as much as 100 miles a day on their migratory trips, sleeping only 4 out of the 24 hours. They can swim as fast as 10 knots an hour in short bursts but normally cruise along at from 2 to 4 knots. Although they can dive as deep as 600 feet, they normally descend only 120 feet or so. While in their breeding grounds, they vocalize in very low-register tones to communicate with one another.

The only predators of the gray whales are the killer whales and, of course, people. Although for millennia the whales coexisted with aboriginal hunters, more "civilized" hunters reduced their numbers so drastically in less than a century that in 1947 they were declared an endangered species. Since then, when their population was estimated to be about 2,000, they have made a respectable comeback and are now believed to number around 22,000 plus. No longer con-

sidered endangered, they are still protected as "sustained management stock" by the International Whaling Commission: only 140
may be taken per year, and these go to the Russian government for
use by aboriginals whose culture has evolved around this species.

When you plan your whale-watching outing to the Point Reyes
Lighthouse, it's a good idea to telephone the Point Reyes National
Seashore Lighthouse Information Center (415-669-1534) in advance
to find out weather and parking conditions. The park people accommodate as many whale-watchers as possible at the lighthouse, but
parking space is extremely limited, and when big crowds show up,
cars may have to wait in line. (The park people may ask you to park
at Drake's Beach and take a shuttle bus.) Count on an hour and a
half to two hours' pleasant driving time from San Francisco. If you
want to make a picnic out of your expedition, you can pick up good
eating fare in Olema or in Inverness, which you pass through on the
way to the lighthouse.

A bonus to whale-watching at the Point Reyes Lighthouse is the
lighthouse itself: installed in 1867, it is still in working order
although its function has been taken over by a computerized model.
National park rangers give 15-minute interpretive talks to visitors
about the original mechanism and its history, and they may even let
you crank up the weight that rotates the beautiful Fresnel light. *Note:*
This light may be lit the last Saturday of the month; the park service
people will give you the information. (The foghorn at Point Reyes
Lighthouse is not a bonus. It operates 24 hours a day no matter what
the weather, and while it does set off interesting echoes against any
fogbank that is around, it is loud when you stand near it.)

Whale-watching is one of the most delightful spectator sports.
Enjoy your encounters with these "extraterrestrials" (as John Lilly
called them) and marvel that these remarkable marine creatures are,
like ourselves, true mammals, warm-blooded, air breathing, and
nursers of their young. They have evolved over the millennia to take
their special place in the ocean world. Although some of their species
are protected from overhunting, they face ongoing threats from the
pollution of our seas and from testing (by detonating depth charges)
for underwater oil or for other reasons. As you watch these magnificent animals with whom we share our planet, it is well to remember
that their well-being and survival are, quite simply, in our hands.

Note: Elephant seals, among the most extraordinary and interesting creatures of the sea, have returned to this area of the seashore. The

park people have designated areas of overview where you may see and wonder at these remarkable animals without disturbing them (or endangering yourself!) Call the number above for latest information.

Tips for Photographers

Along with the whales themselves, there are wonderful opportunities around the Point Reyes Lighthouse for photographers, especially for those who are interested in capturing the drama of sea meeting shore. There are apt to be deep ocean swells, and the troubled water, now pale, now deep green, boils around the dark rocks and sea stacks, the waves surging and bursting into white fountains, then leaving waterfalls as they withdraw. The orientation of the point—north, west, and south—offers good options for lighting, and there are many patterns of rocks to choose from. If the fog is low and swirling, it will give added excitement to the scene as it hides and then suddenly reveals the wild beauty of the shore.

For a different subject—and perspective—you might choose the end-on view of the surf that creams ceaselessly against South Beach in a wide white band stretching straight to the horizon. Or you might prefer to photograph the wind-pruned cypresses with their leathery little plumes of ferns on their branches—or the sandstone rocks that are tufted with fuzzy, bittersweet-red algae. Almost all year one or another avian hunter will be around: in January you may find young red-tailed hawks sitting on fence posts right next to the road and watching the cars go by. Or you may catch sight of a kestrel swooping from its perch on a telephone wire, moving with heart-stopping grace as it dives onto its prey. There are vast and sweeping views of Drake's Bay in the distance. Looking over the moors, the softly rolling sand dunes that are covered with green, you may be reminded of Scotland. In late April and May, the landscape, covered with clumps of silvery-leaved, sweet-smelling yellow lupine in bloom, will glow as though flooded with sunlight—no matter how foggy the day. In fact, all year long there is an ever-changing provocative scene, and all year, too, there is a special beauty to this place.

Note: It is also possible to whale-watch from the water, and many oceangoing tours—half-day or daylong—are conducted during the months of whale migration. Contact the Oceanic Society Expeditions for starters. (See Nature Outings appendix for this and other organizations sponsoring whale-watching tours.)

East Marin

China Camp State Park

The extraordinary amount of Marin land set aside or dedicated for parks, open space, or agricultural use has left less than 20 percent available for conventional development. Most of this undedicated land—beautiful and highly desirable—is in East Marin and has been subdivided, and much of it is occupied. It comes as a pleasant surprise, therefore, to find an exceptionally lovely 1,640 acres in one of East Marin's most attractive residential areas set aside as a state parkland (with the enthusiastic help of the local people). This is China Camp State Park, which occupies roughly half of San Pedro Point, a peninsula jutting into the bay east of populous San Rafael. This is a relatively undisturbed and charming sample of the Bay Area's coastal laurel and oak woodland community, with low rolling hills, open meadows, marshy shores, and a small pebbly beach that is suitable for swimming on hot days.

The park commemorates the early Chinese shrimp fishermen who began to ply their traditional trade in San Francisco Bay as early as 1865. When a huge supply of shrimp was discovered in San Pablo Bay, China Camp sprang up as a fishing village not unlike those along the Yangtze River. Picturesque sampans and junks sailed from here to haul in the catch from the handmade 25- to 40-foot-long bag nets that the fishermen staked to the bottom of the bay. On good days, a junk might take 3 tons of the little shrimp, and most weeks the fishermen could count on 8 to 10 tons of the delicacy (a popular food in Asian countries). The shrimps were boiled and then dried on shore and winnowed before most of them were shipped off to China.

Toward the end of the century, the number of hard-working Chinese shrimp fishermen had become substantial enough so that there were at least 29 shrimp-fishing villages dotted around the bay. Threatened by increasing competition in fishing (and in other

trades), local people began to show resentment and inordinate preju-
dice against the Chinese. (San Franciscan Labororator Dennis Kearney was an instigator of the anti-Chinese movement and a fanner of
the flames of anti-Chinese sentiment.) So strong grew the feeling
against these industrious people that they were persecuted legally as
well as socially. Their rights as citizens were denied, and the livelihood of the shrimp fishermen was effectively taken away by the state
fish-and-game regulations and by the shutting down of shrimp
exporting in 1905. China Camp, originally one of the largest and
most thriving of the shrimp-fishing villages, became more and more
a place of refuge. (This was especially true after the 1906 earthquake
and fire disaster, which left many Chinese homeless and with no
place to go.) Gradually its population waned. Although shrimp fishing was revived in the 1920s by the invention of the cone-shaped net
and enjoyed a brief period of success during the 1930s, it never again
became the lucrative business that it once had been. Increasing pollution in San Francisco Bay sounded its death knell as a commercial
endeavor in the decades following World War II. And although the
pollution has been somewhat controlled, the bay (grass) shrimp population has never returned to its former glory.

Only a few people—the Quan family—stayed on at China Camp.
Through a series of lucky coincidences, the land around China
Camp, originally the property of the McNear family, escaped the
bulldozer. In the late sixties and the early seventies the movement
swelled to keep it as it was and to recognize the people who had been
the first settlers of the area, the Chinese shrimp fishermen and their
families. To this end, the state park people have set up a small
museum (open 10:00 A.M. to 5:00 P.M. on weekends) in one of the
village's still-standing wharf buildings, and they have restored some
of the old equipment used for processing the shrimp. By great good
fortune, one member of the Quan family, Frank, lives in the village,
and his cousin Georgette spends much of her time there as well.
Frank still plies the shrimp-fishing trade, and Georgette runs a small
café that is open weekends and holidays. Although most of Frank's
catch goes for bait, if his haul is plentiful enough you may be able to
sample the delicious grass shrimp in a cocktail or, if you're lucky, by
the pound; when available, it is sold in the snack shop.

China Camp State Park is a most pleasant place for hiking. The
park ranger counts 24 pleasant miles for walkers (and bicyclists!)—
or more, if you don't mind retracing a few steps. There are several

loop trails that start in the Back Ranch Meadow Campground just inside the entrance to the park. This makes for a lovely walk in springtime when the shooting stars are in bloom in the meadows. The park is also a good place for fishing (the pier is open on weekends and holidays, and a state fishing license is required), picnicking (there are several roadside picnic sites with tables), sunbathing or swimming, birding (there seem always to be egrets standing along the roadside in the marshes), or for simply enjoying this unique scrap of the native scene. (Artists like this place for its bay views, as well.) The park's capacity is small, however, and limited by lack of available space for parking; level (dry) land is at a premium. A weekday visit may be preferable, for this is a popular place on good weekends. *Note:* Back Ranch Meadow Campground is one of the few public car campgrounds in the Bay Area. There are 30 walk-in sites less than 200 yards from the parking lot, with water, firewood, toilets, and showers available. There are modest charges for parking, camping, firewood, and pets (which must be kept leashed). Telephone 415-456-0766.

To reach China Camp, take Highway 101 north through San Rafael; watch for and follow signs to the park. Allow a half hour from San Francisco. *Note:* Just north of the turnoff for this park is the Marin County Civic Center, one of Frank Lloyd Wright's famous works.

Some Special Places Near Tiburon

There are two special places in Marin County between Highway 101 and Tiburon that might tempt birdwatchers, wildflower lovers, and history-minded people to make a side trip. To reach them, you turn off Highway 101 east onto Tiburon Boulevard (follow the signs to Tiburon). Turn right onto Greenwood Cove Road, which soon becomes Greenwood Beach Road. This leads to the Audubon Society's 911-acre *Richardson Bay Center and Wildlife Sanctuary*—a fine place for birdwatching, especially during the late fall and winter months, when crowds of migrating birds come through. Audubon's Richardson Bay Sanctuary has 11 acres of land and 900 acres of tidal bay water; it is closed to boating October through March. The education center includes a bookstore with displays of local wildlife and the Lyford house, a Victorian gem that was rescued by the society from being wrecked and moved to this location in the 1950s. The house has been put into top Victorian shape; group tours can be arranged. Audubon conducts interpretive walks on weekends, as well as workshops and classes. Telephone 415-388-2524 for information and a schedule of events.

Back on Tiburon Boulevard, you travel east for about 2 miles to reach the turnoff for *Old St. Hilary's Church,* which is marked by a historical landmark sign. (Turn left on Mar West Street—there's a historical marker pointing to the church—and left again on Esperanza for about a mile.) Local people rescued this choice example of "Carpenter Gothic" when it was threatened by development, and it now belongs to the Belvedere-Tiburon Landmarks Society. (It is used for weddings and concerts and other local events.) Not only does it command a splendid view of the Tiburon Peninsula, Belvedere Island, and San Francisco, but it is surrounded by a 4-acre field of exceptional wildflowers. There are nearly 220 different species of plants growing here, including three rare, endangered flowers— Tiburon buckwheat (*Eriogonum caninum*), Tiburon paintbrush (*Castilleja neglecta*), and Marin dwarf flax (*Hesperolinon congestum*)—and the very rare black jewel flower (*Streptanthus niger*), which is found only on this peninsula on serpentine soil. The best time to visit this garden is during the months of April and May, when you're also likely to see a show of other springtime bloomers. The Nature Conservancy's Ring Mountain Preserve provides additional protection for this special spot.

After you have visited these special places, you might want to continue into Tiburon ("Shark"), where you can catch the ferry to Angel Island. Or you might prefer to stop for lunch at one of Tiburon's waterfront restaurants (more wonderful views of the city by the Golden Gate) and then go on to explore the eastern side of Tiburon Peninsula. Stay on the main street, and about 3 miles northeast from downtown Tiburon, you will come to Paradise Beach, a 19-acre county park that has a fishing pier, picnic facilities, and restrooms. It also has a seasonally varying fee for cars and motorcycles (but not for bicycles). In summer, you might have some good views of brown pelicans and Heermann's gulls in this part of the world.

Sonoma and Napa Counties

Early histories of the long lovely valleys of Napa and Sonoma—now often referred to as "the wine country"—picture them as paradisaical, and it is easy to see why—in autumn, winter, and spring, that is. In summer, these inland places north of the bay can become furnacelike under the burning sun; temperatures above 100 degrees Fahrenheit are not all that uncommon. Anyone wanting to explore this part of the North Bay should plan accordingly; if time dictates a summer outing, try to make it early in the morning. Also, be aware that the wine country of Napa and Sonoma is apt to be jammed with sightseers during the summer months; regular tourist outings to visit wineries are very popular and are usually a part of any Bay Area convention; added to these crowds are the thousands of people who converge onto this lovely area in their own cars. Napa is already fighting smog in the summer months; recent figures total over 2 million visitors a year. There are only 30,000 acres (out of Napa's some half million) that are planted to grapes. Since there are also 140-plus Napa wineries, large and small, this means a concentration of use and visitation that may make an excursion not optimum during the tourist season. The same holds true for Sonoma.

Almost any other time of year, this part of the North Bay offers certain special pleasures that you will not find in other parts of the Bay Area. In early spring (late February and March), the vineyards are striped with brilliant mustard blooms, and in early fall, the wineries are heady with the smell of the crush, and the air is sweet with the scent of apples. And there are charming reminders of the Bay Area's past.

Sonoma's Valley of the Moon, so named by Jack London, for example, is full of early California history as well as vineyards and a poignant look at the ill-starred writer's world. The state park people have good interpretive programs in their several historic units here, and it is possible to spend a happy day exploring their well-restored and well-preserved mementos of Sonoma's earlier days. You could start at, say, *Olampali State Historical Park* on Highway 101, 2.5 miles north of Novato, then go on to *Petaluma Adobe State Historical Park* (General Mariano Vallejo's restored historical ranch) near Petaluma on Highway 116 and proceed to Sonoma for lunch and looks at Vallejo's Lachryma Montis and the Sonoma Mission, the Spanish Barracks, and other historical buildings on the Plaza. Lunch at the Sonoma Hotel on the northwest corner of the Plaza is good and reasonable, and most days you can eat in the garden as well as inside. Or, if you want to combine history with some pleasant walking, visit *Jack London State Historic Park* in Glen Ellen. There you can see the ruins of London's Wolf House—the building he designed and into which he poured his royalties and his dreams for years, only to have it all go up in flames just as he was prepared to move in. (Arson was suspected until forensic experts examined the evidence recently and concluded the fire was caused by spontaneous combustion. Workers had left linseed-oil-soaked rags near a fireplace and on the fateful hot August evening, they ignited.) There is also the Jack London Museum in the House of Happy Walls, built by his wife, Charmian; and there's the Pig Palace, the elegant circular piggery designed by London for his pampered porkers (each pig family had its own quarters). And, of course, his grave is here, as he had wished it to be. Along with enjoying mementos of this extraordinary man, you can stroll along several miles of easy and lovely trails in this park. Or, if you're feeling more energetic, you can tackle the 3.3-mile climb to the top of 2,460-foot Mount Sonoma, which starts here. (The parking lot is at about 600 feet.) There are also nice picnic grounds. You can rent horses at the park from April through October; for reservations telephone 707-996-8566.

Two other state parks in the Sonoma Valley beckon the hiker. *Annadel,* a nearly 5,000-acre natural park, has 40 miles of trails, with elevations ranging from 360 to 1,880 feet. There is no camping (but a Sonoma County campground right next door may be able to put you up), no fires, no drinking water, and no backpacking. This park has many of the plant communities found in Sonoma: Douglas fir stands on its north-facing slopes and chaparral on the south sides of its canyons. There are a few redwoods growing alongside moist streambeds (streams do not run year-round), and meadows fringed and tufted with oaks. (Look for coast live oak, Oregon oak, black oak, and blue oak.) If you would like a sampling of Sonoma countryside, you could take a nice day's hike, a 5-mile loop, to Lake Ilsanjo (named for Ilsa and Joe Coney, former owners of this part of the park), where there are picnic tables and fishing (a California fishing license is required). This hike is recommended in April or early May, when the wildflowers are at their height.

Sugarloaf Ridge State Park is smaller—with 2,700 acres and some 21 miles of trails—and has a less varied landscape. But it does have 49 campsites, drinking water, limited toilet facilities, picnic tables, and a creekside nature trail. It is in volcanic hill country, and its stream—Sonoma Creek, which also goes dry at summer's end—was probably used by the Wappo Indians. Most of its trails follow the park's higher ridges, and some lead to the modest peaks inside or near the park boundaries—Brushy Peak (2,243 feet), Bald Mountain (2,729 feet), and Red Mountain (the 2,548-foot peak is just outside the park but is open to hikers). Elevation in the campgrounds is around 1,100 feet.

Adjacent to Sugarloaf Ridge State Park is Sonoma County's **Hood Mountain Regional Park** (close to 1,500 acres), which has a couple of walk-in camps, and a trail to the top of Mount Hood. Although not of great height—it is 2,730 feet high—Mount Hood commands good vistas and is itself visible from such places as Mount Tamalpais in Marin County. The park is only open weekends and holidays and closed altogether during the fire season. There is no running water.

Sonoma County has other lovely parks to draw you northward, including the 750-acre *Armstrong Redwoods State Reserve,* 2 miles north of Guerneville, and the 5,700-acre *Austin Creek State Recreation Area.* The latter is undeveloped but for 24 primitive (and attractively situated) car campsites and several hike-in or horseback-ride-in backcountry camps. The close-in country is open rolling hills, but deeper into the area there are streams and forests providing nice hiking when it's not too hot. The road in is a real backcountry experience; it will not accommodate trailers. Adjoining these parklands to the south, and reached by a more comfortable road, is the *Armstrong Redwood Grove,* which remembers a local developer, Colonel James Armstrong, who, like William Kent, saw to it that at least this small forest would be protected in a reserve. It is a beautiful deep-

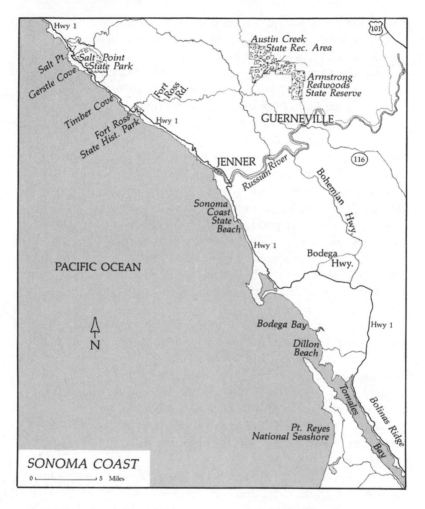

Hwy 1

101

Salt Pt.
Gerstle Cove
Salt Point
State Park

Austin Creek
State Rec. Area

Armstrong
Redwoods
State Reserve

Fort Ross Rd.

Timber Cove

Fort Ross
State Hist. Park

Hwy 1

GUERNEVILLE

JENNER

Russian River

116

Bohemian Hwy

Sonoma
Coast
State
Beach

Hwy 1

Bodega
Hwy.

PACIFIC OCEAN

N

Bodega Bay

Hwy 1

Dillon
Beach

Tomales Bay

Bolinas Ridge

Pt. Reyes
National Seashore

SONOMA COAST

0   5 Miles

shadowed stand that was feared by the local Indians for its mysteri-ous darkness. It offers some pleasant short walks, a picnic area, and the redwood experience in Sonoma County. This sample of the grand trees that once forested long stretches of the mid-California coast makes you wish that there had been more people like Kent and Arm-strong among those earlier movers and shakers—people who cared enough about these invaluable forests to save them instead of cutting them down.

Along the Sonoma coast itself, there are two large, beautifully located state parks with extensive camping facilities. Both of these offer good bases for exploring Sonoma's beaches and shores, but they are a long way from San Francisco and Bay Area action. You can expect them to be cool (and often foggy) during the summer months. They are also very popular. *Salt Point State Park* has nearly 6,000 acres with 109 family campsites and 20 walk-in tent sites. *Sonoma Coast State Park* has 5,000 acres right along the shore and offers camping ½ mile north of Bodega Bay (98 developed campsites) and 6 miles north of Bodega Bay (30 developed campsites, but no showers). There are also 30 more remote walk-in campsites in two campgrounds 10 miles north of Bodega Bay. Both of these state parks have gorgeous ocean views, hiking trails, and places where you can beachcomb or fish, and both have protected underwater areas where you can dive (with a good wetsuit), although you cannot take the shellfish at Salt Point's Gerstle Cove, a marine reserve. *Note:* "Very rough" diving. Reservations for the developed campgrounds can be made through DESTINET (1-800-444-PARK) (see Campgrounds appendix). The walk-in campground, open April–November, is first-come, first-served.

If you choose to adventure along the Sonoma coast, you can explore *Fort Ross State Historic Park,* which is just 12 miles north of Jenner. The park people and volunteers have done extensive restoration (and replication) of the Russian settlement that was located here from 1812 to 1842. (Unfortunately, the original fort burned.) It's a nice job, and you can also picnic and fish here as well; there are 20 undeveloped campsites and a visitor center. The campground is 1 mile south of Fort Ross; it has the amenities of flush toilets and running water.

Sonoma County itself has several county reserves with camping facilities along with those mentioned above. (Two are on the coast at Bodega Bay.) These operate on a first-come basis. For information, telephone 707-527-2041.

An interesting and unusual addition to any of your Sonoma Valley excursions—or an excursion in itself—would be a visit to any of the stops listed on the Sonoma Farm Trails map (available free from visitor centers in the county's larger towns). This map—updated yearly—shows agricultural growers and local crafts outlets. You can buy many fruits and vegetables at the source or pick them yourself, depending on the season.

If you're a birdwatcher, and are willing to hike, the overwintering shorebirds and waterfowl at the San Pablo Bay Wildlife Refuge may

Flowering orchards in Napa County with Mount Saint Helena in the background. PHOTO BY REDWOOD EMPIRE ASSOCIATION.

draw you. Access is from Highway 37. (See Some Remarkable Bay Area Parklands and Preserves.)

Napa Valley has only one state historical park, the small and charming **Bale Grist Mill,** which is just north of Saint Helena. This has no facilities, but the restored water-powered mill offers a glimpse into pioneer life in this part of the world, and there is a little visitor center (a small fee to enter). A stroll to the old mill pond will take you through a meadow with blue oaks and, in the spring, lovely wildflowers.

Less than 2 miles north of the mill is *Bothe-Napa Valley State Park,* which has some lovely car-camping sites with all the niceties, and walk-in camps for bicyclists or hikers—plus a swimming pool (open during the summer months). This 1,917-acre park offers several pleasant short strolls, including the History Trail, which leads through the Pioneer Cemetery and an oak and madrone forest for the 1.5 miles back to the mill. This park is a good place to look for pileated woodpeckers and for trillium and calypso orchids around the third week of April. Reservations for campsites can be made (if space is available) as late as one day before you arrive. For reservations, call DESTINET (see Campgrounds appendix); the park telephone is 707-942-4575 should you want to check out the status of the flowers. There's a swimming pool, and you can rent horses in summer and fall (for reservations telephone 707-996-8566). (San Franciscans—or visitors to Coit Tower on Telegraph Hill—may be intrigued to learn that most of this park was once the estate of the Charles M. Hitchcock family, and their daughter, Lillie, spent a good part of her childhood in their home here, a mansion called Lonely [since burned down]; Lillie Hitchcock Coit was, of course, the lady would-be firefighter who left the money for the tower that bears her name.)

Napa Valley also boasts a 4,343-foot mountain that is easily ascended; since you start from about 2,200 feet, the altitude gain is not overwhelming. This is Mount Saint Helena, named, it is said (but nobody knows for sure), after the patron saint of the princess wife of Alexander Rotchev, last Russian governor in California; the lady was supposed to have been with the party of Russians who scaled the mountain in 1841. Mount Saint Helena is almost, but not entirely, in state park ownership; a gracious pioneer family cooperates in allowing hikers across their lands. The view from its summit, which is actually the highest in the Bay Area, is almost as good as that from Mount Diablo and a lot more intimate, since the only road up is a firebreak not open to the public. This lookout will give you another perspective on the California topography, with closer sights of Mount Lassen and Mount Shasta to the north, a panorama of the wine country with San Francisco in the background, and even a glimpse of the white surf on Point Reyes Seashore's North Beach. There are also sugar pine and ponderosa pine at the north summit. Tours to the top of Mount Saint Helena are allowed by special permit; if you're interested in such, you can inquire in Robert Louis Stevenson State Park headquarters; telephone 707-942-4575.)

Mount Saint Helena is approached from **Robert Louis Stevenson State Park** north of Calistoga, and since it is a nearly two-hour drive from San Francisco, the 5-mile climb (4 miles on the open fire road) to its summit is not recommended unless you are staying north of the city. If you do decide to visit this nearly 3,700-acre undeveloped state park, you can check out the Silverado Mine, where Stevenson honeymooned with his bride, Fanny Osbourne, and wrote "The Silverado Squatters" (delightful reading); it is a 1-mile, generally uphill walk to the mine, which was worked between 1872 and 1874 and supposedly yielded $93,000 in gold and silver. (Accounts differ as to how many thousands of dollars were poured into the mine, and there are even reports that the mine was "salted" with precious metals to interest investors; salting was a not uncommon practice of the time.) For further insights into the Robert Louis Stevenson story, you might want to stop by the excellent Silverado Museum in Saint Helena. There is another interesting museum in Calistoga, the Sharpsteen, which is devoted to local history, and which includes one of Sam Brannan's original resort cottages (see San Francisco History).

The state parks in Napa are located along Highway 29, which is the principal thoroughfare through Napa's wine country. Along this road there is also a parade of the larger wineries, which welcome everyday visitors during their scheduled hours (usually 10:00 A.M. to 4:00 P.M.). It is not necessary to phone ahead to visit one of these. Some of the older ones, such as Charles Krug, Beringer, and Sutter Home, are California state historical landmarks, so long have they been in operation. (See Historic Bay Area Vineyards and Wineries appendix.) You will also find many wineries along the Silverado Trail, which more or less parallels Highway 29. The smaller wineries, which some wine aficionados think are more interesting, do need advance warning if you want to taste their wares; to find out which ones can be visited and when you will be welcome, telephone the Napa Valley Vintner's Association at 707-942-9775.

Note to wildflower lovers: The grassy meadows in Napa's Pope Valley are good places to see shows of spring wildflowers—poppies, lupine, owl's clover, tidy tips, cream cups, and more. Snell Valley offers more individual species of wildflowers, especially those that do well on serpentine soil, but no mass plantings; this is a get-out-of-the-car-and-look-closely area. The time to come looking is mid-April to early May, assuming it's not an offbeat season; you could always call the Bothe-Napa Valley State Park headquarters (telephone 707-942-

4575) to find out what's in bloom. If you are lucky, you might see a roadrunner dashing beside you on the way into Pope Valley.

Note: About 10 percent of Napa County is under the aegis of the federal government; this includes Lake Berryessa, which is the largest manmade lake in California. This was formerly a particularly lovely (and settled) valley that was flooded in the late 1950s when Monticello Dam was completed. Lake Berryessa is the favored place of water skiers and motorboaters and is jam-packed and overused on most warm weekends. It is not recommended for those who love the unspoiled natural scene.

Like other Bay Area counties, Sonoma and Napa have been feeling the press of increasing population. Most of their choice valley and gentle hillside land is now occupied (price per acre for good vineyard sites is astronomical), and there are hydrological and erosion problems when steep hillsides are developed, and environmental problems when water supplies and waste disposal systems are overtaxed. Yet people and industries keep moving in, attracted by the charm and livability of this delightful region. Now both counties are being confronted by the difficult question of how to keep from being loved to death. Napa has launched pioneer zoning ordinances that may (or may not) provide some answers; Sonoma is still in the process of coming up with solutions. You might keep this in mind should you be tempted to stay forever when you adventure in this special part of the world.

California Wine

Being an essential part of the Mass, wine traveled along with the Spanish padres when they entered Alta California. At first, it rode in barrels on the backs of mules, and when a barrel was used up, or when, as it once happened, one fell off the mule, shattered, and lost the precious liquid, "masses were not said," as Father Junípero Serra put it succinctly. When the wine supply was finished, Serra was forced to turn to the government supplies for more, and he was humiliated when he had to pay for it "like an ordinary soldier." To remedy this sorry situation, Serra saw to it early on that vines were imported so that the missions could plant and produce their own wine. (Wheat was planted at the same time to provide the requisite bread for the holy services.)

Historians conjecture that the first vines arrived (probably from Spain via Mexico) on May 16, 1782, on the good ship *San Antonio,* captained by Don José Camacho, and that the first successful press took place at the Capistrano Mission in 1782. Roy Brady comes up with the delightful label that might have been affixed to that first bottling: Mission San Juan Capistrano Mission 1782, estate grown and bottled by Fr. Pablo Mugartequi and Fr. Gregorio Amurrio. From this, it can be seen that California's first wine grape was called the Mission. (California's two species of wild grapes—*Vitis californica* and *Vitis girdiana*—are no good for wine.) A potable sweet wine is still distilled from the Mission grape, but now—as then—it makes an undistinguished dry table wine, described by one wine lover as being "rather flat and dull."

It is believed that the early mission vines were head pruned, a growing method that requires no stakes or trellises, and, in fact, until very recently, so were all California vines. The early winemakers heaped their crop onto cowhides, and "well-washed Indians" were called into service to crush the grapes with their feet.

As it happened, the Los Angeles area became the cradle of California's commercial winemaking. The climate and the soils of the southern California region were well suited to the culture of the grape, particularly to the production of sweet wines. After the secularization of the missions, local ranchers took over the growing of the grapes, and when the gold rush got under way, shrewd businessmen like San Francisco's Charles Köhler and John Fröhling—two Germans who by first profession were musicians (Köhler played the flute, Fröhling the violin)—set up winemaking in the sunny south. In the course of their operations, they established the Anaheim Colony in 1857 and imported fellow Germans to grow the vines for their company, known as the Los Angeles Vineyard Society. So successful were they and their neighboring viticulturists that until 1880 California wine was synonymous with Los Angeles wine. Many pioneer wine growers, however, chose the cooler Bay Area counties for their plantings, introducing new varieties of vines and producing dry table wines as well as sweeter varieties. By 1860, parts of Sonoma, Napa,

Solano, Santa Clara, San Mateo, Alameda, and Contra Costa counties—and even San Francisco itself, though unsuccessfully—had been
tilled and planted to grapes.

Winegrowing came to be an attractive and challenging business
venture, and some of San Francisco's wealthiest and best-known
characters tried their hands at it. Sam Brannan, among the earliest,
had vineyards and a winery in his doomed Calistoga venture (see San
Francisco History) and, probably inadvertently, chose for himself
what later came to be considered by some the finest winegrowing
property in the United States. Senator George Hearst and, later, his
son, William Randolph, dabbled in winegrowing. And, most spectacularly, Leland Stanford—who was, among other things, responsible for achieving a transcontinental railroad linking San Francisco to
the rest of the United States in 1869—bought thousands of acres (he
eventually owned 55,000) in Tehama County for "the largest vineyard in the world." Unfortunately, the soil and climate of Tehama
County proved to be less than ideal for the production of wine, and
the grand venture did not succeed.

It remained for Count Agoston Haraszthy to realize the potential
of wine growing in the Bay Area. With his energy and expertise, he
brought both art and science to winemaking, and, thanks in part to
him, the production of wine had by the early 1860s become established as a lasting part of California's agriculture.

Agoston Haraszthy de Mokesa was born in 1812 in what was then
Hungary. Evidently he was an "operator" from the start. By the time
he was 28, he had become a member of parliament, a silkworm
grower, an officer, a public official, and a vintner. He had also married
a Polish noblewoman and fathered three sons. Haraszthy was not only
extraordinarily energetic and versatile but tough. He lost as many fortunes as he made—and that was several—and he was once tried for
embezzlement (and was later cleared). He had the rare ability, each
time misfortune struck, to pick up the pieces and keep going as though
nothing had happened. He might have left even more of a fabled
legacy to California than he did had he not died when he was 57.

Haraszthy migrated to the United States in 1840, and, after a colorful career in Wisconsin—in his first two years there, he had, with
an English partner, established a brickyard, a steamboat line, a
sawmill, and a gristmill, and, before he left in 1849, he is said to have
introduced hops and sheep to the state—he brought his family to
California, following the lure of gold. By 1850, the year he arrived in

San Diego, he had fathered three more children—girls—and he had with him not only his wife but his father and a young stepmother. He was also broke, his Wisconsin partner having sold him out and taken off with the money. Unfazed, Haraszthy in short order owned a butcher shop, a livery, and an omnibus company, and before long he was farming 160 acres. He soon became a sheriff—the county's first—and before moving on to San Francisco in 1852, he served a term in the state's first legislature.

In his usual fashion, Haraszthy began "stirring the pot" in San Francisco as soon as he got settled. He planted 200 acres in grapes in the city and began raising cattle and growing strawberries and grain. He planted more grapes in San Mateo County (athwart the San Andreas Fault), and he went into the business of smelting gold and silver. His grapes did not flourish, however, in the cool coastal climate, and when he became entangled in litigation over land to which he claimed ownership, and when his operation as smelter for the United States Mint became suspect, he was indicted for embezzlement. His property, which he had offered if he were found guilty, was confiscated and not returned to him until three years later, when he was found innocent of all charges.

From San Francisco, Haraszthy moved to Sonoma—in 1856 or 1857, the date is uncertain—and in the following decade, in the words of historian John N. Hutchison, "he changed the shape and direction of California winemaking and moved its center of gravity to northern California from Los Angeles County, where it had its commercial beginnings." Not only did he establish his own sumptuous Pompeian villa and a stone winery near the town of Sonoma (the remnants of his grand 36,000-acre estate, which he called Buena Vista, can still be seen at the winery that bears this name), but he planted as many as 165 varieties of grapes, which he imported from Europe; he bucked contemporary opinion and employed Chinese at a time when it was all but illegal to do so; and, most important, with his unique gifts as a publicist, he brought the vineyards of northern California to the attention of the world. In addition, he wrote well and prolifically on viticulture, he is credited with innovating the use of redwood in place of oak for cooperage, and in 1861 he traveled Europe extensively for the state of California to report on foreign winegrowing practices. (The same year he produced his report for the legislature—he did a notably thorough job of it—he also published an excellent book on winemaking and grape culture.)

Haraszthy paid for his European excursion and for shipping back 100,000 vines representing 300 varieties as well, expecting the state to reimburse him. Although he presented a bill for only a third of his expenses, he was never paid. During the next few years, his fortunes declined steadily, and in 1864, he left California for Nicaragua. He died there five years later, some said in a flood; others claimed he was eaten by alligators. However he met his end, he will be remembered as the Father of California Wine, and he changed the course of California's history.

Not surprisingly, most of the Bay Area wine grown in early California poured either into—or through—the city of San Francisco. The benign character of its climate made the city an ideal place to store wine, and wine merchants soon built large warehouses. The per capita consumption of wine also kept pace with the Bay Area's population explosion from gold rush days on. By the time of the earthquake and fire in 1906, there were at least 15 million gallons of wine stored in San Francisco that were lost. And this does not count the untold gallons of red wine used by the Italians of North Beach and Telegraph Hill to quench their local fires.

When Prohibition hit the winemaking industry in 1919, there were some 700 producing wineries in California. By December 5, 1933, when Prohibition officially ended, there were scarcely more than 200. Those wineries that managed to stay alive did so largely by producing medicinal and sacramental wine. (Along with the Roman Catholic church, the Jewish, Greek and Roman Orthodox, Episcopalian, and Lutheran religions all consider wine a part of worship.) Some also produced grapes and grape juice for "home consumption." Although it is a little-known fact, winemaking actually increased in the United States during the 14 years Prohibition was in effect—some 90 percent of it being carried on by "vintners" in their homes. The Bay Area undoubtedly contributed a good share to this statistic: the sale of "juice grapes" brought out crowds in San Francisco during the vintage season. Trucks and railroad cars hauled the grapes into the city, and the buyers gathered around. A writer in the *California Journal* reported the happy scene thusly in 1930:

> One of the interesting sights of San Francisco . . . is the grape market on the Drumm Street tracks just off Broadway. Each day during September and October from thirty to forty cars, all practically [*sic*] juice grapes, are opened and hundreds of purchasers are on hand to inspect

the offerings and buy the grapes they need for the manufacture of their year's supply of "non intoxicating" fruit juices. During the height of the season, on Saturday afternoon and Sundays, the tracks are crowded . . . and the handlers of the grapes do a thriving business.

Some vintners were most obliging: they would deliver the "grape juice" already pressed, in a barrel, to the home of the purchaser. Then there were independent servicemen who would follow through a month or two later to help with the job of bottling.

Although the Bay Area was one of the country's major markets for grapes and ready-to-brew grape juice during Prohibition, Bay Area winemakers were stuck with growing principally grapes—such as the Alicante Bouschet—that were suitable for home winemaking. Thus the art of the vintner had to wait out the dry years. And when Prohibition ended on December 5, 1933, the country was still in the throes of the Depression, and there was little demand for fine wines. Furthermore, public taste had changed, and sweet wines had become unexpectedly popular . . . not much of a challenge to greatness. During the next decade or so, however, things gradually improved, and the California winegrowing industry not only came to flourish, it came to produce increasingly good wine. In 1946, more than 100 million gallons of California wine were sold, and during the next two and a half decades, that number tripled: in 1981, a total of 358 million gallons were sold. Moreover, by 1967, the industry was producing five and a half bottles of dry wine for every bottle of sweet. In more recent years, it has begun to turn out fine wines that some experts consider unequaled anywhere for their quality and taste. Small wineries dedicated to producing fine wines have proliferated enormously: in Napa County, for example, their number went from 15 in the 1960s to more than 200 in the 1990s. (*Note:* Several European companies now produce wine here.) In the state as a whole, there are over 700 bonded wineries and wine cellars, with perhaps 90 percent of them actively producing wine. Of the approximately 1 million acres planted to vines in the United States, California claims some 90 percent. And of the hundreds of millions of gallons of wine produced per year, California accounts for over 92 percent. Interestingly, California also has the highest per capita consumption of wine, more than twice that of the national average. California winemakers are producing wine commercially from more than 60 different grape varieties.

The Wineries of Sonoma and Napa

Visiting the wineries of Sonoma and Napa counties to taste their wines is only part of the fun. There are the obvious beauties of the landscape to be savored as well, and parks and forests to be explored. There are restaurants offering fine fare for virtually every purse and palate. And there are the wineries themselves. As oenophile Robert Louis Stevenson wrote in "The Silverado Squatters," "The stirring sunlight and the growing vines and the vats and bottles in the cavern [make] pleasant music for the mind." Each cavern—or winery—is a little different; each has its own character and makes its own particular music. And there are hundreds of wineries to be enjoyed. Along with seeking out particular wines to try, you may want to take into account the ambience of the winery that produces it. There are many good books to give you guidance (see Bibliography), but to start you on your way, here are a few suggestions.

Many California wineries are mellow with history, and, indeed, the state of California has recognized them by naming them state historical landmarks. See Historic Bay Area Vineyards and Wineries appendix for the names and addresses of historic wineries in Sonoma and Napa (and in Alameda and Santa Clara counties as well).

A great many of the wineries in Sonoma and Napa are of recent vintage, and they continue to proliferate. Having neither a colorful past nor an instant identity, these newcomers must depend upon their setting and their architecture, as well as their wine, for their particular image and for the experience they give their visitors.

Once, in a provocative article entitled "Architectural 'Tasting' in the Napa-Sonoma Wine Country," *Sunset* magazine suggested that many of the newer vintners deliberately design their wineries to "imprint their identity." The magazine categorized loosely the archi-

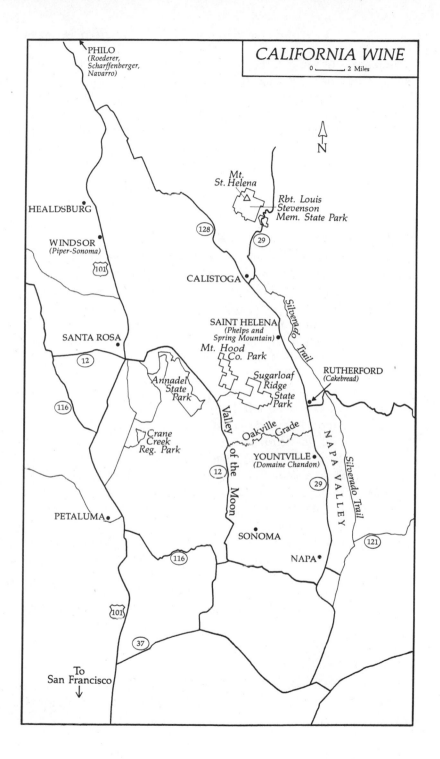

CALIFORNIA WINE

0 ———— 2 Miles

N

PHILO
(Roederer,
Scharffenberger,
Navarro)

Mt.
St. Helena

Rbt. Louis
Stevenson
Mem. State Park

HEALDSBURG

128

29

WINDSOR
(Piper-Sonoma)

101

CALISTOGA

Silverado Trail

SANTA ROSA

SAINT HELENA
(Phelps and
Spring Mountain)

Mt. Hood
Co. Park

12

Annadel
State
Park

Sugarloaf
Ridge
State
Park

RUTHERFORD
(Cakebread)

116

Crane
Creek
Reg. Park

Oakville Grade

Valley

of the

Moon

12

YOUNTVILLE
(Domaine Chandon)

NAPA VALLEY

Silverado Trail

29

PETALUMA

116

SONOMA

NAPA

121

101

37

To
San Francisco

tectural styles of some of the more outstanding results as (1) "barn-like" or traditional buildings that reflect the region's rural character; (2) "manors" that take their inspiration from everything from American colonial to California mission to French provincial; and (3) "modern" buildings that depend on their own merits of contemporary design. If you're architecturally minded, you might plan to sample one new winery from each category—along with the wines from its vineyard. Here are a few for you to choose from; since some of them may require an appointment for a visit, plan to call ahead.

Sonoma County

Chateau Souverain—Designed by architect John Marsh Davis, this chateau with its bluish slate roof received an American Institute of Architecture (AIA) award in 1974. Located just south of Geyserville off Highway 101: take Independence Lane uphill to the winery. A producer of several types of table wines, Chateau Souverain has a restaurant open Friday–Sunday for lunch and dinner. Tasting daily. Address: 400 Souverain Road, Geyserville; telephone 707-433-8281.

Jordan—This tile-roofed, ivy-ornamented, red-shuttered winery conveys a distinct Old World feeling and calls to mind a Bordeaux chateau or manor. It was designed by architects Backen, Arrigoni, and Ross. You'll find it off Highway 101 between Healdsburg and Geyserville. Jordan produces Cabernet Sauvignon and Chardonnay, conducts tours and tastings (by appointment). Open for sales and tours Monday–Saturday. Address: 1474 Alexander Valley Road, Healdsburg; telephone 707-431-5250.

Piper-Sonoma—Roland-Miller Architects of Santa Rosa produced this geometrically designed modern building, with its series of terraces. This producer of sparkling wines is situated west of Highway 101 at 11447 Old Redwood Highway between Windsor and Healdsburg. It is open daily and conducts tours with complimentary tastings. There's a modest charge. Telephone 707-433-8843.

Napa County

Cakebread Cellars—The interior of this large, dormered, barnlike building, the work of architect William Turnbull, is as notable as the exterior; rows of barrels and stainless steel tanks are integrated into its AIA-honor-award-winning design. Cakebread produces a limited amount of Chardonnay, Sauvignon Blanc, and Cabernet Sauvignon. It is at 8300 Saint Helena Highway (west Highway 29) in Rutherford and is open daily from 10:00 A.M. to 4:00 P.M. for tasting. Tours are by appointment. Telephone 707-963-5221.

Clos Pegase—This warm-colored winery—autumn brown and earth tones—was inspired, it is said, by ancient Mediterranean structures. The architect was Michael Graves, who won a design competition initiated by the San Francisco Museum of Modern Art and the winery owner. There is outdoor sculpture—including a grand bronze thumb ("thumbs up!")—to be wandered around and wondered at. There are daily tours of the winery, caves, and art collection. Daily tasting. There's a modest charge. 1060 Dunaweal Lane, Calistoga. Telephone 707-942-4981. If you visit Clos Pegase, you might plan to cross the road to the *Sterling Vineyards* at 1111 Dunaweal Lane. Here you can take their sky tram up the hill to the winery—great views of the valley opening up. Sterling has an excellent self-guided tour, perhaps the best in Napa Valley. The price of the tram ride (modest) covers tasting, too. Telephone 707-942-3300.

Domaine Chandon—This is another modern design that makes use of terracing. The rather dramatic entrance into the winery has been described as "well orchestrated." The San Francisco architectural firm ROMA is responsible. Established in 1973, Domaine Chandon makes fine sparkling wines in the traditional *méthode champenoise* of its French parent company, Moët & Chandon. Domaine Chandon also has a four star restaurant—an elegant one that serves both lunch and dinner. Reservations are recommended; telephone 707-944-2892. The winery is open daily from May through October, and on a limited schedule the rest of the year. There are tours, and wine may be purchased by the glass or bottle. In Yountville, take the California Drive (Veteran's Home) exit off Highway 29 to the west; telephone 707-944-2280.

Joseph Phelps—Sausalito architect John Marsh Davis also designed this large board-and-batten building that is entered beneath a grand wisteria trellis constructed of old bridge timbers. Phelps produces a variety of table and desert wines. It is situated at 200 Taplin Road in

Saint Helena. It is open daily for sales, and you can take a tour and have a tasting by appointment. Telephone 707-963-2745.

Robert Mondavi—The California mission influence is unmistakable in the hefty, creamy white walls and arched gateway of this "manor"; Cliff May was the architect. Robert Mondavi is credited with leading California wine into the international arena. He also innovated a superb cooking class, beloved of gourmets, at his winery. You'll find the Robert Mondavi label on many table wines. Located at 7801 Saint Helena Highway (west Highway 29), the winery is open every day for tours (reservations recommended) and tasting; a first stop on many wine tours, it is apt to be crowded. Reservations required for the winery's specialty tours. Telephone 707-963-9611 for hours, which vary seasonally.

Note: In the Napa area there are some wonderful older buildings, such as those by Captain Hamden McIntyre, a renowned winery architect of the 1880s. He was responsible for the lovely stone building at the *Nieman-Coppola Estate Vineyard and Winery* (1991 Saint Helena Highway, Rutherford; telephone 707-967-3495), the immense three-story wooden building used by *Trefethen Vineyards* (1160 Oak Knoll Avenue, Napa; telephone 707-255-7700), and the *Greystone Restaurant* (2555 Main Street, 100 Saint Helena Highway, Saint Helena; telephone 707-967-1010), which he designed to be the world's largest stone cellars. (The Culinary Institute of America's west coast campus is here as well.)

Beringer, Buena Vista, and *Schramsberg* wineries (see Historic Bay Area Vineyards and Wineries appendix).

Addendum: If you would like to venture a little farther north into less traveled winery country, Highway 128 (west off Highway 101 near Cloverdale) through the Anderson Valley will reward you with some lovely gardens as well as interesting architecture. Architect Jacques Ullman is responsible for the "California Barn" look of *Roederer Estate* (in Philo, at 4501 Highway 128; telephone 707-895-2288): as viewed from the road, the roofline continues the arc of the hill behind it. Ullman also designed the *Scharffenberger Cellars* (also in Philo, at 8501 Highway 128; telephone 707-895-2065), which has a particularly pleasing interior that integrates the various winemaking operations. The beautiful gardens at these two wineries as well as the spectacular show of flowers at the *Navarro Vineyards* (in Philo, at 5601 Highway 128; telephone 707-895-3686) are by local landscape designers Chris and Stephanie Tebbett. (The Gerwurtztraminer wine at Navarro Vineyards is exceptional; tasting is free.)

Ballooning

A little over two centuries ago, two French brothers, Joseph Michel and Jacques Etienne Montgolfier—prosperous proprietors of a paperworks—put together the first balloon to fly. Having watched the way smoke rose in chimneys, they experimented by filling small paper bags with smoke and became convinced that smoke could, indeed, carry a light craft aloft. They designed their fragile balloon of linen—and paper, of course—to be powered by a smoky fire. Sure enough, on September 19, 1783, in Annonay, France, they managed to send aloft their creation. It ascended some 1,500 feet, flew for about a mile and a half, and remained aloft for some eight minutes before the fire went out. (There is no record of how its crew—a sheep, a duck, and a rooster—reacted.) Greatly encouraged, the Montgolfiers went on experimenting, and, the story goes, when one balloon caught on fire, these resourceful designers simply opened a couple of bottles of champagne and doused the flames. Finally, on November 21, after two months of trying, they engineered the first free flight of a manned balloon. That historic day, Monsieur Jean François Pilatre de Rozier, the Marquis François Laurent d'Arlandes, rose 3,000 feet into the air and flew some 5 miles in 20 minutes, thus becoming the first man to fly in a balloon. (It is noteworthy that a hydrogen balloon was developed about the same time, independently, by Jacques Alexandre Cesar Charles, a French physicist. With his friend, Nicolas Louis Robert, he rose 2,000 feet on December 1, 1783, in a balloon of rubberized silk. Upon landing, Monsieur Robert stepped out, at which point Monsieur Charles "rapidly ascended 9,000 feet"; his reaction is not recorded either.)

The Montgolfiers' hot-air balloons, however, for that is what they were finally recognized to be, did not flourish long. A matter of a few years after they were developed, it was found that ordinary heating gas was a better agent for getting a balloon off the ground, and for decades, various other gases were tried and used. It turned out that hydrogen—shades of M. Charles—was perhaps the most efficient. Hydrogen, in fact, could and did lift larger and larger balloons, and it was used extensively and very successfully for many years: one commercial balloon powered by hydrogen made 150 trans-Atlantic crossings. In 1938, however, the Graf Zeppelin *Hindenburg* burst into flames upon landing, with great loss of life among its passengers, and this tragedy caused the use of hydrogen to be banned worldwide. It was not until the early 1960s that hot-air balloons once again got off the ground. At that time, a way was found to package propane gas in neoprene containers, thus making it possible to use it easily and efficiently. The gas fuels a kind of giant blowtorch that the pilot ignites as needed to control the flight. During the past couple of decades, hot-air ballooning has become an ever more popular sport, for people with their own balloons and for commercial operators as well.

Hot-air ballooning in the Bay Area is necessarily an early morning sport, for afternoon breezes, if too strong, can ground all flights. (A 7-knot-per-hour breeze is considered a pleasant maximum.) Thermals also increase during a warm day, and, although beloved of gliders, they can be lethal to balloonists. A morning outing in a hot-air balloon offers a fine chance to see the countryside, and there are several places in the Bay Area where this sport takes place year-round. One of the most popular of them is the Napa Valley.

On a typical Napa balloon outing in February, you need to arrive at, say, Yountville—one of the hot-air balloon centers—at a little before 7:00 A.M. (If you are staying in San Francisco, this means a 5:30 A.M. departure by car; if you're fortunate, you might happen to pick a date when there's a full or three-quarter moon to glow in the west as you drive, with the stars growing dim and a soft mist lingering over the sloughs and the marshes of the bay.) You rendezvous with the balloon people about 7:00 A.M., and, after a cup of coffee and a doughnut, they will let you watch and perhaps help to inflate the balloon that will carry you aloft. An electric blower is used for this job, and, although a "regular" balloon weighs somewhere around 250 pounds and envelopes 105,000 cubic feet of space when inflated, it takes a surprisingly short time to fill one up and set it upright. You then climb into the rather small gondola—it must carry three tanks of gas along with five people, including the pilot, a total of as much as 2,200 pounds—and with the help of the ground crew you are kept earthbound (somewhat) as you bob along to a good launching spot.

The pilot gives the blowtorch a few blasts—which sound like the panting of a dragon—to get you aloft (a good blowtorch can deliver 21 million BTUs of heat). Once airborne, you will be partly at the mercy of the prevailing winds, if winds there are. Balloons cannot be steered per se, although they can be raised and lowered by controlling the input of hot air. However, your knowledgeable pilot—who must be licensed, and have his or her balloon approved by the Federal Aviation Administration—will use air currents, sliding along their edges, to control the direction of flight. Your pilot may also ask you, at times, to shift your weight in the gondola. You stand and hold on to the riggings during the flight, and although there's not much space, nobody seems to mind.

Balloon flight offers a unique experience: it combines the up-down flexibility and hoverability of a helicopter without the helicopter noise; it mimics avian flight by slipping easily through the air; and it provides you with wonderful, lingering views. You may find yourself low above the vineyards, which are laid out in patterns of perfect alignment. (In late February, they are usually striped with brilliant yellow mustard, which glows against the soft green hills.) Or you may find the world rapidly dropping away from beneath you until you are a mile high in the sky above a countryside of toy houses and toy automobiles, with San Francisco in the faint distance and Mount Saint Helena low on your horizon. You may skim the dark green Napa River, passing so close you can all but reach out and touch a tree along its bank. And then you may land in the middle of a vineyard or in a downtown Napa parking lot. (If the latter is the case, you will probably stop early morning traffic as curious drivers try to see what on earth is going on.) In whatever circumstance, a four-wheel-drive truck will be following your balloon to help you land and pick you up: the driver keeps in radio contact with your pilot throughout your flight.

Photographers should be warned: ballooning is one of the most picturesque of sports, and you are apt to go slightly berserk trying to decide which of the many pictures that are constantly composing themselves should be taken first. The balloons themselves are gorgeously colorful: each is custom made, and the multicolors reflect the taste of the owner. Sunlit, aloft, they glow like rainbows. Looking up into one, especially when the blowtorch is exhaling visible dragon-smoke, is a wonderful sight. Near you there are other balloons hanging in the air like giant flowers against the sky. And below you is a patterned panorama that you will never see again so easily. Bring plenty of film!

Once on the ground, you will retire to your meeting place for brunch complete with champagne, which, history tells us, is after all the handiest bottle to have around a balloon. You'll also have a pleasant chance to get acquainted with your fellow flyers. Then, if you want to make a day out of your adventure, you can visit nearby wineries or take a pleasant hike ending up with a gourmet dinner in one of the many fine restaurants in Yountville, Napa, or Saint Helena. (The Spring Street—on Spring Street, of course, in downtown Saint Helena—is charming, reasonable, and has good food.)

Ballooning is not inexpensive recreation. Except to pay nearly $200 for 45 to 60 minutes. (The time will depend upon air conditions and your pilot.) It has also become unpopular, alas, with many of the local people, who, understandably, feel that they may be put on view and that they may have a balloon suddenly "drop in on them." If possible, discuss with your pilot ahead of time the desirability of having that mile-high view—which takes you up-up-and-away from the neighbors' homes. Hopefully, your pilot will bring your balloon down in an acceptable place; most good ones manage to do so.

You will find many commercial balloon outfits—in several Bay Area counties—listed in the Yellow Pages of the San Francisco telephone book. A call ahead is, of course, essential.

Solano County

San Francisco has been center stage in the Bay Area so long that it is easy to overlook the fact that this was not always the case. In the early days, the settlement was passed over several times in favor of nearby communities elsewhere on the bay—Vallejo and Benicia, for instance, north and east of San Francisco, in Solano County—for important developments. It was also the founding of one of these towns during the turbulent weeks of the late 1840s that, some historians say, caused little Yerba Buena to change its name.

Behind the early successes of the Solano County communities—indeed, behind the establishment of Solano County itself, was the remarkable General Mariano Guadalupe Vallejo, the man who played such a major role in the history of the Bay Area and California (see Sonoma and Napa Counties). It was Vallejo who gave the land for two out of the first three state capitals, Vallejo (pronounced *Va-lay'-oh*) and Benicia. The latter was named for the general's wife, Francesca, and therein lies the tale of why Yerba Buena changed its name. Among the Bear Flag renegades who "captured" Vallejo in June 1846 was Robert Semple, a Kentucky dentist and an ambitious man. (He is described as having been inordinately tall with such long legs that when he stopped his burro, the animal could walk out from under him: those long legs, it is reported, caused him to wear his spurs on his calves.) As the party bore Vallejo to Fort Sutter for his two months' imprisonment, Semple remarked the attractiveness of the land along the Carquinez Straits and noted what a good spot it would be for a seaport. The land was part of Vallejo's grand holdings, and he offered to present a sizable piece of it to Semple for a community, provided he would name the place for Francesca (so the story goes). When Yerba Buena heard the news, it quickly took the name of San Francisco (something it had evidently been thinking about doing for a long time) to forestall a rival use of the magic moniker. Although Semple (with the help of the ubiquitous Thomas O.

Larkin) had lost no time in establishing the new town, he—and Vallejo—had to settle for calling it Benicia, which was Francesca's middle name.

It was when statehood was achieved a couple of years later that Vallejo proceeded to donate several choice acres for a state capital. Being land poor and hard up for cash, however, he nearly impoverished himself building a proper statehouse. This evidently extraordinary structure, constructed from hand-hewn timber from Hawaii, had three floors; the top was for the senate, the ground floor for the assembly, and the basement for a ten-pin alley and saloon, known as the Third House. (Unfortunately, like so many early Bay Area buildings, it went up in flames, in this case less than two decades after it was erected.) As was only fitting, this, the first "permanent" state capital, was named for the beneficent general. However, alas, the capital did not stay put very long: the legislature was convened before there was suitable housing for the lawmakers, who were thus obliged to live aboard the steamer *Empire*, which was neither comfortable nor clean. After the legislature met for a miserable week in January 1852, the capital was moved forthwith to Sacramento. But when that settlement was flooded in May, back it came to Vallejo.

Benicia, meantime, had persuaded the capital choosers (or movers) that it had more to offer, and it became the capital in February 1853. (The Benicia statehouse, happily, has survived the various holocausts—including two major earthquakes—of the ensuing years and is still standing and is a pleasure to visit.) The movers and shakers, however, were still dissatisfied, and in 1854 the capital moved once more, and finally, to Sacramento.

Although Vallejo and Benicia lost out on their bids for state capitalhood, both communities benefited from their fame, evanescent though it was. In 1852, Congress made Mare Island (named by Vallejo La Isla de la Yegua when he found a lost and cherished horse in that place), virtually adjacent to Vallejo—it was bridged directly to the city during World War I—the U.S. Navy's Pacific outpost: with both ship repair and shipbuilding facilities, it was for decades second only to New York's Navy Yard in size and importance. Commander (later Admiral) David G. Farragut, of Mobile Bay fame, presided over the Mare Island Naval Yard for several years, and by 1859 the installation had turned out the first United States warship built in the Pacific. It distinguished itself further by building and launching a destroyer in 17½ days in 1918; by 1966 it had produced a dozen nuclear submarines. (During World War II, the Mare Island Naval Yard was merged with Hunter's Point Naval Yard to become the San Francisco Bay Naval Shipyard.)

(Since the close of World War II, Suisun Bay between Benicia and Vallejo has been the home base of the National Defense Reserve Fleet, more commonly known as the "Mothball Fleet." At one time, more than 400 vessels were lined up here—mostly merchant marine ships, with a few troop transport and attack cargo ships—but there remain only 70. Although usually thought of as belonging to the U.S. Navy, the Mothball Fleet—headquartered on a floating barge—is actually the property of the U.S. Department of Transportation's Maritime Administration, which took it over from the Department of Commerce.)

About the same time that Vallejo was picked by the navy, Benicia was chosen by the army as the site for its Pacific Arsenal and Barracks. The army's scout, General Percifer F. Smith, had turned down San Francisco for the honor, declaring that it would never do because it was "too far from the mainland," had a dreadful climate, and was vulnerable to enemy attacks along its 4-mile beach. Established in 1851, the Benicia Arsenal counted Ulysses S. Grant (then Lieutenant Sam Grant and renowned for his boozing) and William Tecumseh Sherman among its famous (temporary) occupants, and for nearly three decades (1857 to 1886), it enjoyed a lively and social command under Colonel Julian McAllister, brother of Ward McAllister (of the New York "400") and Hall McAllister (a prominent San Francisco lawyer whose statue stands at City Hall on the street named for him). In 1912, the arsenal's original four-story fort on Suisun Bay was blown up in what has been described modestly as a "spectacular explosion": the building caught fire, and the burning timbers ignited a storehouse full of ammunition, which sprayed bullets in all directions, miraculously injuring no one. Rebuilt as a two-story structure, known as the Clock Tower, this is one of the many historic buildings that remain in the arsenal, which is now an industrial park. Colonel McAllister's handsome mansion, built in 1860 (across the street from the Clock Tower), now houses a restaurant.

Among other historical gems in Benicia are the camel barns, undoubtedly the only army structures of their kind extant. In 1855, in a somewhat bizarre experiment, the secretary of war purchased 77 camels—both the two-hump and one-hump varieties—from the Near East for use in transport in the arid Southwest. Alas, the poor "ships of the desert" were not royally received, since they proved to be mean and to stink, besides, and eight years later it was decided to round up their remaining numbers—which had shrunk to only 34 beasts—and to auction them off. Two Benicia Arsenal warehouses were converted into camel barns to house the animals, which were soon led to the block and sold to the highest bidder. Bidding was singularly unenthusiastic, and the army realized less than $1,500 from the sale. The end of the army camels came in 1934 when the lone survivor died in Los Angeles's Griffith Park Zoo. There is a small museum in one of the camel barns that history buffs may enjoy.

Along with beating out San Francisco for the important army arsenal, Benicia attracted the Pacific Mail Steamship Company. This was the outfit that sailed such ships as the ill-fated USS *Tennessee* (see Tennessee Valley) back and forth between Panama and San Francisco. Until the completion of the transcontinental railroad in 1869, this company provided perhaps the chief means of transportation from the Bay Area to the East Coast. When Pacific Mail located in Benicia in 1851, building its shops and foundry there, the town became the seat of the first major industrial activity in the state. (A few Pacific Mail buildings still stand in Benicia at 7th and H streets, near the old arsenal.) Soon after Pacific Mail went out of business, one Matthew Turner located his shipyard in Benicia: this was in 1883, and during the next two decades, Turner produced 165 vessels.

In 1942, Travis Air Force Base, through which all air force flights, men, and material were funneled into the Pacific Theatre during World War II, was also located in Solano County, some 4 miles from the county seat, Fairfield. Thus Solano County has enjoyed military support, both literally and figuratively, since almost its beginnings.

It has also enjoyed being one of the most productive agricultural counties in the state. Early visitors described its lush grasses, so tall that a man on horseback could reach to his right and left and tie the grass together over his head. The grasses gave way to wheat (and other grains), and by 1872 Vallejo was the leading wheat export port in the United States, with 110 wheat-bearing clipper ships setting sail to England alone from its harbor. John R. Wolfskill, the first American settler in Solano—he arrived in 1842—pioneered in developing the growing of apricots, olives, oranges, nuts, figs, and vines, and he produced the first dates grown commercially in the country. A generous man, he shared his agricultural expertise and his cuttings with his neighbors. (In 1934, his daughter perpetuated the family tradition by giving 107 acres—now a state historical landmark—to the University of California to be used for agricultural experiments.) Thus fruit trees also grew early where grasses once stood, and by 1888 Solano produced half of the state's deciduous fruits: in 1925 it exhibited 321 varieties at the state fair.

Solano County has established records on other scores as well. It was, early on, an educational center, with Benicia being known as the Athens of the Bay Area. Benicia's First Presbyterian Church, built in 1849, was the state's first Protestant church. St. Paul's Episcopal Church, erected ten years later, remains as one of the Bay Area's oldest and most beautiful. Solano produced the country's first great prizefighter, John C. Heenan, the Benicia Boy, who took on England's Tom Sayers in a famous engagement in 1860. In 1874, Solano integrated its schools, eliminating a separate educational system for "colored" children. In 1879, the Southern Pacific Railroad initiated transport of its cars across Carquinez Straits from Benicia to Oakland on the "largest ferry in the world," the *Solano*. In the aftermath of the 1906 earthquake, which largely spared it, the county welcomed and took care of an estimated 30,000 people, many of them injured. In Rio Vista it developed the Bay Area's first gas-producing wells.

Throughout most of Solano's past, the county has been largely oriented toward agriculture or other farming activity (including the production of turkey eggs for breeding)—and toward Sacramento, what with early ties to the state government and the links to the capital of its waterways and roads. In more recent years, however, the pressures of urban growth from the Bay Area have begun to be felt in what has been a lightly populated area. More and more people have been moving into the county's seven distinctively different cities, and how to handle metropolitan expansion into traditional—and treasured—agricultural open space has become a major issue. Solano residents have taken a first step toward solving this problem by enacting unique legislation to control the disposition of county land, and they are seeking further solutions.

Its boosters like to call Solano County the Seven Corners, since Bay Area land and water traffic passes through it en route to the northeast. They also say that their county has something for everybody. Certainly anyone interested in California's early history and architecture will enjoy strolling the streets of Benicia and visiting the old arsenal. And while outdoor adventurers may not travel to Solano

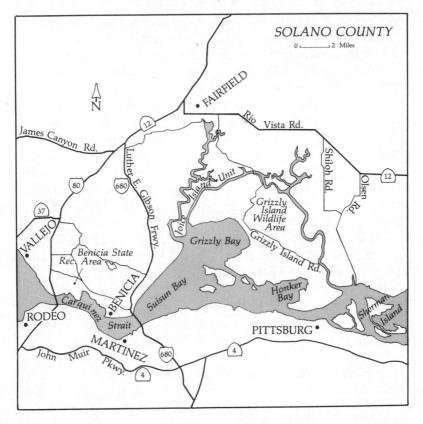

for hiking trails, they will find some of the state's—indeed, the country's—finest estuarine marshes in Southampton and Suisun bays. Both are accessible by car, and Southampton Bay has the added plus of the **Benicia State Recreation Area,** a preserve on Dillon Point that offers opportunities for easy jogging, strolling, birdwatching, observing the changing tides (this is the narrowest channel through which bay waters travel), or simply enjoying the waterfront view, with Mount Diablo in the background. An automated entrance gate requires dollar bills.

Here are some of the other areas that can be reached by car for bird and wetland watching:

Joice Island Wildlife Area—near Suisun City. Part of the Suisun Marsh, this 2,137-acre wildlife reserve offers hiking along its levees and fishing (and hunting, in season) as well as photography. It is open mid-May through August for those uses, but closed the rest of the year, except during the waterfowl season for limited hunting. To reach it, take the Rio Vista Road from Suisun City to Grizzly Island Road; follow Grizzly Island Road about 4 miles to the signs for Joice Island. The reserve is administered by the California Department of Fish and Game. For information, telephone 707-425-3828.

Grizzly Island Wildlife Area—Near Suisun City. A larger—8,600-acre—wildlife reserve; about 150,000 waterfowl winter here (1.5 million ducks and geese have been counted in the whole Suisun Marsh). It is open sunrise to sunset from mid-January to August; closed to all uses except hunting the rest of the year. To reach it, follow Grizzly Island Road 9 miles past the Joice Island Wildlife Area to its end. This reserve is also administered by the California Department of Fish and Game, which has an office in the reserve where you can obtain maps; open weekdays 8:00 A.M. to 4:30 P.M. For information, telephone 707-425-3828.

Brannan Island State Recreation Area—3 miles south of Rio Vista on Highway 160 (actually in Sacramento County, but it can be reached via Rio Vista, which is about 20 miles east of Suisun City). It has over 100 developed campsites, a visitor center, and accommodations for small boats. You can picnic here, or, if you don't want to go that far, try one of the grassy areas along the city of Vallejo's Shoreline Promenade. You can also get good views of the Mare Island Strait from Vallejo's waterfront.

Jepson Prairie—This Nature Conservancy Preserve has some of the area's only native grassland left as well as vernal pools (pools full of water only after the rainy season, and thus unique) and wonderful wildflowers. If you are interested, you can get a brochure by writing The Nature Conservancy, California Field Office, 201 Mission Street, Fourth Floor, San Francisco, CA 94105; telephone 415-777-0487.

People exploring Solano County might want to find some of the backcountry roads and take a bicycle along. There's a good-size parking lot at Solano County Community College off Suisun Valley Road where you can leave your car, for example, and proceed north on your bike into Napa County; you then take Wooden Valley Cross Road to Gordon Valley Road; turn south and then west at Manka's

Corner to return to Suisun Valley Road and your car. This would be close to a 20-mile ride; it's one favored by the locals. You will find vegetable and fruit stands full of wonderful fresh local produce along the way. The Fairfield Chamber of Commerce can give you other leads. (See Chambers of Commerce appendix.)

Note: The Bay Area's famous westerly winds streak across the bay through the narrows of the Carquinez Straits and on into parts of Solano County. (Suisun is supposed to be an Indian word meaning "west wind.") It is said that navy pilots have been trained at Travis Field for landing on aircraft carriers because the high winds simulate conditions they might find on a stormy sea. It can be too windy to picnic in the Benicia State Recreation Area during August, for instance. Spring and fall are the best times to go exploring in Solano, and September brings the ripening of many luscious local fruits and vegetables.

In Benicia, there's an excellent place to have lunch, Mabel's Café, at 2034 Columbus Parkway; it's closed, alas, on Sunday and Monday.

The popular Marine World Africa USA is located in Vallejo, and children might enjoy an outing there to feed the sea lions and harbor seals; there's fish for sale for this purpose. (Telephone 707-643-6722 for information.) Being one of the oldest settlements in California, Vallejo has its special history, too: there's a Vallejo Naval and Historical Museum (in what was once the City Hall) and a Vallejo Architectural Heritage District. Best to visit Vallejo early in the week, if possible, since crowds are at their greatest on weekends and many restaurants are closed on Sundays. The Blue and Gold Ferries serve Vallejo from San Francisco; telephone 415-705-5555.

PART V

East Bay

Alameda and Contra Costa Counties

For a while during the turbulent 1850s and 1860s, it seemed quite possible that the East Bay would become the center of Bay Area life and development (see also Solano County). After all, it was the terminus for people traveling west by land (and, most important, after 1869, by train); there were good harbors along its shores, and, unquestionably, the climate was better than that across the bay. But something there was about the city by the Golden Gate, and though the East Bay communities grew and prospered, and one became the seat of the state's first university, people happily took the ferry to San Francisco to work, to visit, to admire the scenery, and to savor the city's zesty spirit, the same spirit that prompted Mark Twain to describe San Franciscans as "fairly [reveling] in gold, whiskey, fights and fandangoes, and [being] unspeakably happy." Early on, Oakland became known as the bedroom of San Francisco, a soubriquet that has never been entirely fair; Berkeley remained a town-and-gown community in the minds of many San Franciscans; and the communities to the north and east were places to be passed through en route to other destinations. East Bay residents, however, have always known they had a very good thing, and none but the most die-hard chambers-of-commerce people would even bother now to challenge San Francisco's front-and-center Bay Area role.

The East Bay, like the rest of the Bay Area, was first subdivided into large ranchos, foremost among them being that of Luis María Peralta, who in 1820 was rewarded for his "meritorious service" at the Presidio by a grant from Spain of 5 leagues of land. Luis Peralta fathered 17 children, and 5 daughters and 4 sons survived into adulthood. In 1842, his eighty-fourth year (he lived to be 92), he divided his estate among his sons: to Hermenegildo Ignacio (1791–1874) went nearly 9,500 acres; to José Vicente (1812–1871) and Domingo (1795–1865) went nearly 19,000 acres; and to Antonio María (1801–1879) went the remaining 15,200. Although his will spelled out this division and the United States courts eventually confirmed it after statehood, the land was occupied by squatters, its redwoods were invaded by loggers, and communities were emerging on Peralta land long before the Peralta sons were able to establish their ownership; they ended up with almost nothing. Today, the cities of Albany, El Cerrito, Emeryville, Berkeley, Piedmont, Oakland, and part of San Leandro occupy the original Peralta grant.

The two East Bay counties started out as one. Contra Costa ("the coast across" or "the opposite coast") was one of the state's original 27 counties, established in 1850. In 1853, however, the county of Alameda was split off it, largely at the instigation of one Horace W. Carpentier, who in an era of manipulative operators was surely the most manipulative of all. Carpentier was the founder of Oakland, but that was just the beginning: he played a major part not only in the history of that city but in the history of the entire East Bay as well. A New Yorker and graduate in law from Columbia University, he came onto the scene in 1849 when he was 26 years old. He was out to make his fortune, but not necessarily in the gold fields: it was far easier to get a couple of partners (Edson Adams and Andrew J. Moon) to join him in leasing land from Vicente Peralta—and then selling it off in lots. And it proved not difficult at all to have the resulting subdivision quietly named Oakland and to have it incorporated by the state legislature on May 4, 1852, with a provision in the incorporating act that provided "for the construction of wharves thereat." (Carpentier was a friend of Broderick, who was then a state senator, and he had managed to get himself appointed the senate's enrolling clerk.) The plus-or-minus 100 people who were living within the area that Carpentier had chosen were greatly surprised to hear of the new town and are said to have asked, "Where is this place called Oakland?" (Shades of things to come, notably Gertrude Stein's famous comment on Oakland, "There is no there there.")

Carpentier's next step was to have the town deed its entire waterfront to him, some 10,000 acres, "in fee simple forever," in return for which he paid $5 and agreed to construct three wharves—"at least twenty feet wide by fifteen feet long"—and a schoolhouse. As sole owner of the new port, he collected wharfage and dockage at rates he set himself. (This created a civic mess that disadvantaged the city for nearly 60 years before it was finally cleared up.) Wanting to enlarge his sphere of influence, the ambitious Carpentier went on to get himself elected to the state legislature, by 519 votes, he claimed, although a very recent census had counted only 150 eligible voters in the township. It was his goal to make Oakland the seat of a new county, but although he got the county—Alameda—he didn't get the courthouse. (It was two decades before Oakland, at last, became the county seat, but by then Carpentier had left the Bay Area behind him.) He did see to it that Alameda got its share of the magnificent redwoods that then still crowned the East Bay hills: the county line was drawn through the middle of the forest, dividing it evenly between Contra Costa and Alameda.

In the ensuing years, Carpentier became Oakland's mayor (using his earlier method of padding the voting rolls) and continued to consolidate his empire by, among other things, starting (and keeping a monopoly on) the lucrative transbay ferry business—always skirting within the letter of the law, though this might mean conveniently misplacing documents, etc., etc.—and it was he who got the Central Pacific Railroad to locate its West Coast terminal in Oakland in 1869, thus setting the course for growth in all of the East Bay for many decades. To do this, he managed to share his rights to the Oakland waterfront with the Central Pacific (later the Southern Pacific) Railroad in return for a seat on its board of directors. At the same time, he made himself the president (with controlling interest) of a brand-new Oakland Waterfront Company, still with no obligation to the city. (It was not until 1911, under the aegis of Mayor Frank K. Mott, that Oakland finally got back its waterfront.) For reasons unknown, Carpentier left Oakland before the November 1869 day when the Central Pacific's "Great Iron Horse" came thundering into the city: he died in New York City in 1918 and left most of his $20 million fortune to educational institutions in the East. (Mel Scott, a well-known Bay Area city planner, once commented, "Oakland was conceived in iniquity and nurtured on corruption." Considering the era during which it came into being, it is probably entitled to call itself, as it does, an All American City; so says one historian.)

It was the aforementioned redwoods that brought the first real influx of American settlers to the East Bay and provided the principal base for the pioneer economy (along with hunting to supply game for San Francisco's tables—and the selling of pilfered land, of course!). Looking at the Berkeley and Oakland hills today, it is hard to imagine that they were once covered with one of the finest stands of coast redwoods (*Sequoia sempervirens*) that grew in California: there were trees, history tells us, more than 32 feet in diameter and over 300 feet high, far larger than any we have managed to save. In 1826, the English Navy Captain F. Beechey noted in his ship's log, "In order to miss treacherous Blossom Rock [off Alcatraz Island] . . . one should line the northern tip of Yerba Buena Island with two trees . . . over San Antonio too conspicuous to be overlooked." Beechey's two navigational redwoods were 16 miles from his sighting point.

The first loggers moved in with the gold rush, and the gracious Peraltas, who traditionally used little wood in their buildings, tried to accommodate this new use of their trees. Before long, they were over-whelmed by the squatters, and the tall trees fell ever more rapidly. (It is noteworthy that the first Protestant service in the East Bay was per-formed by a Methodist minister—who was also a logger—in front of "a giant redwood tree" on October 21, 1849.) By hook or by crook, the redwoods were completely cut out in Contra Costa County by 1857, and in Alameda they had become a sea of stumps by 1860. Some people ended up with fortunes—one tree alone could produce 15,000 shingles; the San Francisco rascal Meiggs is said to have made at least a half million dollars out of the East Bay forests, but, as Sher-wood D. Burgess put it, "In tune with the unsentimental economy of the day, not a single original redwood was saved for posterity." (Even the Blossom Rock giants were felled. All that remains are giant stumps, which you can see near the Madrone picnic area in Roberts Regional Recreation Area. They've earned historic landmark status from the state.)

Soon to follow the redwoods were the oaks and other trees that gave their pleasant shade in the East Bay woodlands (and a name to its largest city): they were all cut down for firewood. It is worth not-ing that logging operations were largely responsible for the road sys-tem that eventually evolved in the East Bay; many of the early roads were paved with shells from Indian middens. (Later, tennis courts were, too.)

With the trees exhausted, it was natural—and profitable—to turn to agriculture, and both Alameda and Contra Costa proved to be suitable for all sorts of crops—grains, vegetables, and fruits. (Some

East Bay vineyards and wineries dating back over a hundred years are still in production, and open to the public. See Historic Bay Area Vineyards and Wineries appendix.) Canneries followed, and then, since land was reasonable and there seemed to be plenty of it, more and more industries moved in. Coal was discovered early on (in 1848, in fact, although Thomas O. Larkin had noted in 1846 that the roofs of some houses, perhaps Spanish haciendas, were covered with "a bituminous pitch"), and from the 1850s until well into the 1880s, coal mining and, later, sand mining in Contra Costa boomed, and so did the shipping industry. (As a footnote to this particular bit of history, William Tecumseh Sherman surveyed and laid out a town in Contra Costa known as New York of the Pacific to handle anticipated coal shipments: for his labors, he received $500. The town, alas, never quite made it.) A popular unit of the East Bay regional parks is the Black Diamond Coal Mine, which dates back to those halcyon days: naturalist programs and exhibits at the park's visitor center celebrate the history and culture of the original mining communities.

In 1853, Oakland's first public school moved out of the fandango house where it had started and into a proper brand-new schoolhouse: Mayor Carpentier had honored his contract. Soon, however, this and other public schools that followed became overcrowded, and a number of private schools were started. (At that time, public schools were not expected to prepare their students for higher education, and private schools filled a real need.) Like several other Bay Area cities, Oakland declared itself the Athens of the Pacific, and, as it turned out, it had a better claim than most to that distinction: the distinguished Mills College for Women was chartered in Oakland in 1885, and the University of California grew, albeit circuitously, out of an Oakland private school, one established in 1853 by the Reverend Henry Durant (launched in yet another fandango house). Durant's College School engendered a private College of California, which donated its 160 acres of land for and became the nucleus of the state's first university, authorized by the legislature in 1868. The 160 acres proved to be outside of Oakland, and thus Berkeley— named for George Berkeley, Bishop of Cloyne (of "Westward the course of empire takes its way" fame, a man of "so much understanding, so much knowledge, so much innocence" according to one of his contemporaries)—came to be. Frederick Law Olmsted laid out the grounds, and the first all-university commencement took place on July 16, 1873, the same year the first baseball team was formed. The university football team waited until 1882 and the track team until 1885. The Greek Theatre, which is still enjoyed by Bay Area residents, was opened in 1903 with a production of Aristophanes' *The Birds*—in the original Greek. And there, less than a month after the 1906 earthquake, Sarah Bernhardt performed in Racine's *Phedre.* For years, many Berkeley students rode a ferry and a horsecar to get to the campus; and no liquor was allowed within a mile of this "sanctuary of mind and spirit." (Little did anyone dream that this would be the heart of the 1960s student rebellions.) The university's prominent bell tower, or campanile, is one of the East Bay's prominent landmarks.

By the 1870s, East Bay communities were beginning to burgeon as commuter towns: between 1873 and 1877 alone, ferry volume increased from 2,655,671 passengers to 5,570,555. Berkeley and Oakland both annexed neighboring communities and swelled their populations thereby. And during the next decades, these and other East Bay cities continued to attract industry: at first, items such as canned goods, leather, ink, and beer were produced, but then came chemicals, explosives (the town of Hercules was named for the Hercules Powder Company, and the blue gum eucalyptus trees at Point Pinole Regional Shoreline were originally planted to shield the bunkers where explosives were manufactured), machinery, motors, engines, cement, and other heavier products. In 1910, three railroads were serving the East Bay—Western Pacific; Central Pacific (later Southern Pacific); and the Atchison, Topeka, and Santa Fe—and many travelers had their first good look at the city by the Golden Gate from the deck of the San Francisco–bound ferry out of the Oakland Mole. By then, Berkeley had 84 industrial plants; during the next two decades it nearly tripled that number.

Early in 1896, the first refinery (Union Oil) on San Francisco Bay opened at Oleum—the name of the town being the last five letters of the word *petroleum.* Richmond got its first refinery in 1903, and other Contra Costa communities followed soon after. During the next decades, many of the country's major oil companies—such as Shell, Texaco, Richfield, and Standard—also sited refineries in the East Bay. Gas from the nearby Kettleman hills added to the supply being carried in by pipeline. In 1901, Contra Costa County was oiling its roads, and two years later, Alameda was doing likewise: once the automobile was established, truck service followed. Oceangoing tankers to carry products of the refineries followed, too. Shipbuilding, long an important part of the economic base, continued to expand and prosper. In 1921, Henry J. Kaiser made Oakland his headquarters, and the Kaiser Center became a dominant feature of the city. In 1925, the Central National Bank erected a skyscraper, too, and soon Oakland's skyline was vying with that of the city across the bay. Charles Lindbergh said of Oakland's airport, completed in 1927, simply, "It's the best field I have ever seen." That same year, Ford Motor Company located an assembly plant in Richmond; Chevrolet chose Oakland. The East Bay had become, and remains today, the center of heavy industry in the Bay Area. (Contra Costa County has paid for this distinction by being first among California counties in the generating of toxic waste; it is also pioneering in efforts to control this problem.)

Following the 1906 quake and fire, the East Bay opened its arms to refugees from the stricken San Francisco. Merchants donated their stocks of food and blankets; businesses offered their buildings for shelters. Tents and refugee shacks, not unlike those that went up across the bay, went up in vacant lots and city parks. When the smoke finally cleared, many people decided to stay and live in the pleasant place that had made them welcome. (Oakland's population went from 67,000 in 1900 to 150,000 in 1910.) Many of the thousands of workers who poured into the East Bay during the two world wars also elected to remain. (Kaiser's Bay Area shipyards alone built a third of all the war-produced merchant ships during World War II; and the city of Richmond attracted 55 major war industries with its workforce ballooning from 15,000 in 1941 to 130,000 by war's end.) Thus the population of the East Bay boomed, and with it that of the Bay Area. By 1910, Berkeley had grown to be California's fifth-largest city; a half century later, Oakland was the state's fourth largest. By the mid-1980s, Alameda County had nearly 1.2 million residents and Contra Costa another 717,000, and citizens' efforts to control growth were well under way.

Water has been the limiting factor for many growing settlements, and the East Bay communities had to wrestle with this problem from nearly the beginning. Before the arrival of the Spanish, there were many free-flowing, year-round streams, at least 21 according to some historians. (These streams had trout, salmon, steelhead, and even freshwater clams.) After the Yankees arrived, several water companies evolved to take advantage of this handy supply; they acquired

the various local watersheds and soon began engaging in what became ongoing water wars. Primary among the water developers was
Anthony Chabot, known as the Father of Hydraulic Mining in the
Sierra. In 1868, Chabot built the East Bay's first dam, on Temescal
Creek in what is now the heart of Oakland, thereby creating Lake
Temescal. His dam-building methods were unique: he hauled down
his enormous hydraulic equipment from the mining country and
trained his hoses on the stream banks to wash down the dirt for his
fill, then he piled up the damp earth and raced wild horses back and
forth across it until it was compacted into cementlike hardness. His
first dam was so successful that he went on to build a second, larger
one, using the same methods; the lake formed by this one was named
for him, Lake Chabot. (Both of Chabot's lakes have happily ended
up within the East Bay Regional Park District.)

Many of the park district's eucalyptus trees date back to the first
days of dam building, too: there was large-scale planting of blue
gums by East Bay water companies in 1910. (A few years later, water
company officials distinguished themselves for some very original
thinking: during the drought year of 1918, they brought in sea lions
to clean out the trash fish that were clogging the water of their lakes;
the animals promptly humped themselves up and over the hills back
down to the bay.) It was Frank Havens, founder of the Mahogany
Eucalyptus and Land Company, however, who contributed even
more of the blue gum forests you see today in the East Bay hills: he
considered the eucalyptus "the most valuable tree on the face of the
globe." From 1910 to 1913, he employed hundreds of men to set out
eucalyptus trees, which he imported from Australia, along a 14-mile
swath of the hills and, incidentally, sold countless shares in his company, promising fortunes out of what he claimed—and perhaps
believed—would be an instant forest with trees of "glorious hardness." Alas, after all his endeavors, he discovered that he had chosen
the wrong species of eucalyptus: his empire collapsed, leaving his
nine nurseries, his arboretum, Skyline Boulevard—which he built as
a scenic access to his vast holdings—and literally millions of rapidly
growing, and worthless, little eucalyptus trees behind. (Introduced
eucalyptus have proven to be problem trees in the entire Bay Area:
not only do they stifle the growth of native flora, but they are highly
and dangerously flammable.)

After all the local streams had been tapped, it became clear that
water would have to be imported. In 1923, the East Bay Municipal

Utility District (most frequently spoken of as East Bay MUD, and here referred to as EBMUD) was formed to acquire and consolidate most of the lands of the early water companies. EBMUD built up a land bank of tens of thousands of acres that would later "fund" both its own operations and the East Bay Regional Park District. Twenty-seven thousand acres of its near-rural East Bay lands have been made increasingly available for public use (for a modest fee), providing a unique out-of-doors resource. (The Marin Municipal Water District and EBMUD have been pioneers in providing for recreational use of their lands: the San Francisco Water District has to date kept most of its lovely San Mateo County lands locked up.) EBMUD has gone slow on "developed" recreation, and it is to be hoped that this policy will persist, allowing the natural character of its lands to remain relatively undisturbed; among its holdings are rare geological and botanical areas that should be preserved as is.

The same Oakland mayor, John L. Davie (mayor for six terms, who resigned when he noted that the "shadows of life were no longer falling toward the west"), presided over the formation of EBMUD and—along with many far-sighted citizens in the East Bay—the beginning of the East Bay Regional Park District. The push for parks had gotten under way when EBMUD proposed to sell off "surplus" (and beautiful) land for private development and strongly resisted going into the business of managing parks. The East Bay park-loving community responded by finding the funds for a major study of the region's recreational needs. Then, in the midst of the Great Depression, it managed to get the state legislature to pass enabling legislation for a regional park district and in 1934, they voted two to one for the establishment of the district—and an increase in their taxes to fund it. So began what was to become one of the country's unique park resources; it would grow from no land at all (its first acquisition was actually 60 acres of private land in Redwood Canyon: the Depression price was $35 dollars an acre) to nearly 82,000 acres in Alameda and Contra Costa counties in the mid-1990s. (It is worth noting that—in an equally overwhelming majority—East Bay voters approved a $225 million bond to buy new lands in 1988.)

Today the transbay ferry serves only Alameda and Oakland's Jack London Square, but there is good public transportation via BART to the East Bay, and, of course, the area is easily accessible by car. Once there, you will find that the East Bay regional parks offer remarkable opportunities for outdoor recreation. And you can enjoy 55 miles of trails through the EBMUD land as well. The terrain is wonderfully varied and will give you a chance to sample everything from a bay beach to the top of a historic mountain where you can look down on golden eagles soaring below you. Add to these the pleasures of smaller city and county parks and the special wonders of Mount Diablo (especially in the spring) with its state park, and you will understand one very good reason why East Bay people continue to rejoice in the very good thing they have—few urban dwellers in the world have such remarkable recreational resources at their very back doors.

East Bay Regional Parks

Starting with Frederick Law Olmsted in 1866, many people with vision have been aware of the extraordinary potential for sizable park systems in the East Bay area. Olmsted, Sr., made a rather general recommendation that "scenic lanes" be established in the Contra Costa hills. Soon after the turn of the century, city planners Charles Mulford Robinson (in 1906) and Walter Hegemann (in 1915) enlarged on this concept, Hegemann going so far as to propose that Berkeley and Oakland join in establishing parks along the bay shore as well as in their cities and the hills above them. Then, in 1930, a number of conservation organizations led by the East Bay Metropolitan Park Association (and including the Oakland Park League, the Contra Costa Hills Club, and the Sierra Club) commissioned the Olmsted brothers (sons of Frederick Law, Sr.) and Ansel Hall, a National Park Service planner, to survey the recreational needs of the East Bay communities. In their 41-page watershed report, Hall and the Olmsteds took the grand view and recommended a circle of parks around the entire bay, to be started in the East Bay. (Although much of the Hall-Olmsted Report proved to be too far ahead of its time to be immediately implemented, Bay Area park planners many decades later are following its recommendations where they still can.) It also spelled out the need for a new approach—a regional approach—to gain such parklands, and it stiffened citizen opposition to EBMUD's antipark position and determination to sell its "surplus" lands for nonpark development. The end result—and it was a major one—of the Hall-Olmsted study was the establishment of the East Bay Regional Park District (EBRPD) in 1934. (It should be noted that EBMUD was persuaded to sell EBRPD its first major unit, which totaled 2,166 acres and included Wildcat Canyon, now Tilden Regional Park; Round Top, now Sibley Volcanic Regional Preserve; and Lake Temescal. The sales tag was $656,544, or a little over $300 an acre. And there would be many further purchases made from EBMUD in the following years.) As constituted, the new regional park district would be steered by an elected board of directors who represented a spectrum of community interests; Charles Lee Tilden, for whom one of EBRPD's prize parks is named, was the first board president; the board's choice of Elbert Vail as the first general manager proved to be a wise one. Vail took the job without pay to start with but then managed to achieve the munificent monthly salary of $300—about the price of an EBMUD acre.

Vail was a resourceful man. With a 1936 operating budget of less than $195,000, he turned for funds and manpower to the public services provided by the New Deal during those lean years of the Depression. Soon, he had the Civilian Conservation Corps (CCC), the Public Works Administration (PWA), and the Works Projects Administration (WPA) working with federal and state park people to help launch the new park district. The CCC workers built trails for hikers and horseback riders and, with WPA workers, cleared the ground for picnic areas and playfields; they built tables and ovens—and even hostels for overnighters—landscaped archery ranges, and constructed a redwood amphitheatre. The beautiful stonework that was a hallmark of CCC work remains in Lake Temescal's administration building as a reminder of those times gone by. The WPA workers put Skyline Boulevard into shape for the park's most scenic drive and built other park roads as well. Bay Area landscape architect Arthur Cobbledick, with the help of CCC assistants, enlarged the Hall-Olmsted Report to include trails and historical sites, such as Indian camps, adobe homes, and old lumber mills.

Vail was also ingenious: in 1937, he put to use an old military tractor to build a championship golf course. From the 1939 World's Fair on Treasure Island, he rescued the Brazil Building (with the cooperation of the Brazilian government), and the WPA finished its exterior with more beautiful stonework. (The Brazil Building, as it has come to be known, is a much-used and well-loved Tilden landmark.)

Land acquisition did not languish, either, despite those hard times. By 1940, the district had come close to doubling its original acreage; it had, in Vail's words, "a great variety of hill, valley, forest and plains, and the easy accessibility to all parts of the suburban area." It was already drawing crowds of people, over a million visitors a year.

The policies—and philosophy—of EBRPD's early leaders set a standard for the district that would guide its development during most of the years that followed—despite a necessary slow-down during World War II and an era of somewhat cautious expansion during the fifties. During the sixties, under the aggressive and visionary leadership of the late William Penn Mott (who went on to become director of the National Park Service), EBRPD took what has been described as a "quantum leap forward." Known as a man "with an idea a minute," Mott managed to achieve increased tax support, the involvement of Contra Costa as well as Alameda County, and a broad expansion of parklands and park activities. Decades later, the district was still acquiring land by the thousands of acres and launching new park programs to enrich the experience of park users, which numbered many millions a year.

The East Bay Regional Park District has not only provided wonderful outdoor recreation opportunities for the East Bay (and Bay Area) people, it has had far-reaching influence on the overall development of the East Bay: many of the large areas of land that it has acquired were prime candidates for subdivision; it has put to imaginative use such relics as abandoned quarries—which it has turned into great swimming pool parks—and old garbage dumps, which it has "put to sleep," converted into gently hilly shoreside parkland, and tapped for methane gas. The park district has also involved local communities in its endeavors, helping to gain such treasures as the Walnut Creek Open Space unit and the Hayward Shoreline Park for immediate community benefit as well as countywide use.

The remarkable spectrum of outdoor recreational activities EBRPD offers in its 50 units has made it a model for urban park developers nationwide. Consider the following, and you will perhaps better understand why: the district has around 1,000 miles of in-park trails; just as impressively, these trails are linked together by more than 150 miles of trails outside the parks—on easements granted by citizens, communities, and other public agencies. There are highly developed units: you'll find well-equipped children's playgrounds (there's a fine 1920s merry-go-round), golf courses, trailer hookups, a waterslide, numerous swimming areas, marinas with boat rentals, horseback riding accommodations (including rental horses), bicycle trails, senior citizens' centers, a native plant garden, archery ranges, a little farm with domestic animals for children to pet, a miniature steam railroad, a pavilion that can be rented for festive occasions, a shooting range, Parcourses, horseshoe pits, restored historical treasures—and more. There are fine places to picnic, to car camp, to walk-in camp, to backpack, to kite fly, to play volleyball or softball, or to just enjoy the views. There are excellent fishing spots (lakes and streams are planted by the state fish and game people). You can visit an Indian shell mound or learn about an old coal-mining community; you can take self-guided nature tours, or you can pick up a kit to help you identify wildflowers; you can birdwatch—with or without a park-supplied bird list or a naturalist; and there are numerous interpretive programs, including classes in various aspects of local natural history. (The EBRPD employs around 170 rangers and naturalists.) Add to all of this several large wilderness reserves, which are undeveloped but for trails and backpacking facilities. Each major park unit has a folder available that gives its particulars and lists park rules and regulations. (Dog owners will find EBRPD parklands among the few in the Bay Area where you can let your dog run as long as it is under control.) Many of the parks, including those with swimming facilities, are wheelchair-accessible. Many also have food concessions.

The EBRPD prides itself on being ready and willing to grow and change with the times. And, with an eye to the future, it works constantly to add to its land bank: in recent years, for instance, it has acquired almost 22,000 precious acres of land. And while being responsive to people's recreational demands, EBRPD is also very aware of its role as steward of its increasingly valuable and important lands: when recreational demands threaten the parks—as with certain off-road vehicle sports, for example—the parks will be protected.

As you plan your adventure into the East Bay parklands, do not, of course, expect a "pure" wilderness experience. As chronicled briefly above, the lands and waters in this part of California have been put to more or less intensive human use (for ranching, if for nothing else) for upwards of a century and a half. Although bits and pieces of the original landscape remain—as in the small park gem Huckleberry Preserve and in a few clumps of native bunchgrass still growing here and there—the grand, tall grasses that all but drowned early travelers—closing above their heads—are gone, inadvertently replaced by the short, European annuals favored by cattle and carried in by these animals themselves when the Spanish brought them along. Virtually all of the trees are exotics or descendants of those earlier cut down. The bears and wolves and condors that were once common here are long gone, of course, and the elk and antelope have been superseded by the ubiquitous cows. Most of the streams are dammed, and the lakes are all manmade.

But this landscape has its very special charms: it has adapted itself well, and even beautifully in many cases, to the human use it has been subject to. This is especially true where it has been left relatively alone or preserved, as in EBRPD and EBMUD lands. The manmade lakes lie blue and limpid along the feet of the hills; along the lakeshores rest, or nest, countless water-loving birds, and as you walk by on a soft spring evening, you may have a chorus of frogs to cheer you on. Inland, the oaks shade the sunny southern slopes with their dark, glossy leaves; the more intimate forests of the canyons are thriving, and the bay-laurels are fragrant even on the hottest, driest summer day. The creeks, although often seasonal, add their music to the canyons. The trees have a parklike aspect, their branches having been pruned neatly and evenly at cow level; the cows themselves can be picturesque silhouetted against the warm blue sky, or in a field of golden grasses. Along the East Bay hills on the cool foggy northern slopes, the redwoods are reaching high again, slowly reassuming the magnificent growth that is their birthright. There are foxes to come upon, both red and gray, hawks—and even eagles—to feast your eyes on, and the soft clear calls of owls and the spine-tingling cries of coyotes to be heard, if you are lucky. There are many native deer to watch, as they watch you, or as they spring away in leaps that outgrace even Baryshnikov. The views from the summits are awesome, and in the spring, the wildflowers are even more so, the lupine making pools of color bluer than the lakes, the poppies glowing like sunshine incarnate. The spaciousness here and the gentle feel of the country are invaluable tonics when the world presses in too closely. These are lovely parklands to travel through.

You may wonder at the frequent presence of the Black Angus and the white-faced, ruddy-brown Hereford cattle—neither breed is dangerous—that you will almost certainly encounter in the EBMUD lands and will probably come upon even in the so-called regional wilderness parklands. Cattle have not only contributed in a major way to the creation of the present East Bay landscape, they are still a major ecological force. By clipping the meadows closely, they encourage the grasses their ancestors brought in, keeping down the brush (that waits patiently to invade) and preventing a buildup of incendiary plant material that might cause devastating wildfires. (In 1991 the Oakland hills were devastated by wildfires feeding primarily on eucalyptus trees.) Both EBMUD and EBRPD consider cattle to constitute a kind of biological fire control. (In this context, it is worth noting that both districts utilize a biological pest control—a herd of goats, with their goat herder—to reduce the fire hazard and to eradicate poison oak and other noxious brush.) Cattle are also part of the rural economy as well as the rural scene, and by leasing their lands for pasture, both EBMUD and EBRPD generate small incomes.

Public transportation to EBRPD is excellent: there is AC Transit bus-to-park service to most of the urban park units year-round, and during the summer, this service is extended to some of the more remote units. These buses tie in with BART; telephone AC Transit (510-817-1717) for schedules and details. The parks are generally open during daylight hours, but camping and backpacking units remain open during the night as well. There are modest fees for some of the park uses, including parking your car. For general information about EBRPD, call 510-635-0135 or 510-562-PARK; headquarters are at 2950 Peralta Oaks Court, Oakland, CA 94605. Many of the parks have naturalist programs and special events, all listed in "Regional in Nature," the district's quarterly newsletter. Call the public affairs department at one of the numbers above to get on the mailing list.

As you visit these parks, keep in mind that none of them would have been possible without citizens' interest, involvement, and concerted action. Along with many other parklands in the Bay Area, those of the EBRPD constitute a grand monument to the local people—from every walk of life—who had dreams and the commitment to make them come true; many worked long and hard (some for a lifetime)—and most labored for love rather than money—to gain these urban treasures for everyone to enjoy. This kind of all-American effort should be recognized, too.

East Bay Parklands

Here is a list of the East Bay regional parklands. It is necessarily limited, for it is manifestly impossible to describe each park in detail in a book of this size. However, the following will hopefully give the reader some idea of the variety of the parks and their individual characteristics. Hopefully, too, it will prompt a bit of independent exploring as well.

All 50 East Bay regional park units offer opportunities for hiking, birdwatching, picnicking, and nature study; all except the Huckleberry Botanic Preserve and the two island parklands—Brooks Island and Browns Island—offer running and jogging, too. There is horseback riding in most of the parks but not the shoreline and island units and, again, Huckleberry Preserve. The other activities each park provides are noted below.

Note: Dogs under (voice) control are allowed in the East Bay regional parklands away from parking lots and crowded areas, where they must be leashed. Dogs are not allowed at any swimming pool, bathing beach, nature area, or posted area.

There is a useful brochure available from the East Bay Regional Parks District (EBRPD) that will give you up-to-date information on special features of the parks and tell you how to get to them. You can get this brochure from EBRPD, 2950 Peralta Oaks Court, Oakland, CA 94605; telephone 510-635-0135 or 510-562-PARK. There are also individual folders for major park units that have trail maps and other helpful details. You can write for one of these, if you know which park you want to visit, or plan to pick one up at the park entrance.

The East Bay Municipal Utility District (EBMUD) also puts out an attractive folder titled *All About EBMUD* that should answer most questions: this can be obtained, free, by calling 510-287-0150. At present, three (out of five) reservoirs are open for recreational use: *Lake Chabot,* administered by EBRPD (see below); *San Pablo Reser-*

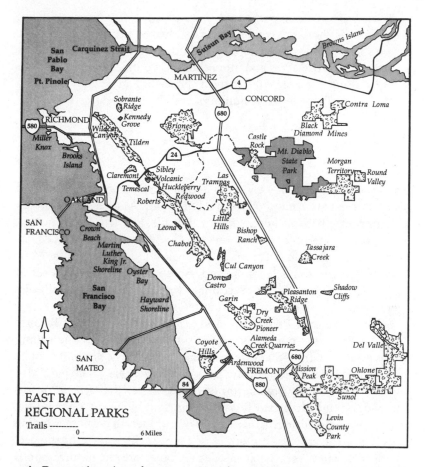

EAST BAY
REGIONAL PARKS
Trails ----------
0   6 Miles

voir Recreation Area between Orinda and El Sobrante, with developed facilities, including boat and canoe rentals, a launching ramp
for sailboats and canoes, fishing, bicycling and hiking trails, a snack
bar—and resident great blue herons; and *Lafayette Reservoir* off
Mount Diablo Boulevard, with the same facilities as San Pablo
(minus the snack bar and great blues) and the advantage of being
close to public transportation via BART (telephone 510-464-6000).
A permit (issued for a year for a very reasonable sum) is necessary if
you want to hike or bicycle the 55 often lovely miles of EBMUD
watershed trails. You can get your permit at San Pablo or Lafayette,
or at the EBMUD business office, 375 11th Street, Oakland, CA
94607; telephone 510-835-3000, or write EBMUD, Box 24055,
Oakland, CA 94623. Dogs are not allowed.

Please respect these parks and open spaces while you use them: don't litter or shortcut switchbacks. (As always, keep a wary eye out for poison oak—there's plenty of it.) And rejoice that there are over 100,000 wonderful acres and more than 1,200 miles of trails for you to enjoy along and above the eastern shores of San Francisco Bay.

Note: East Bay telephone numbers are all area code 510.

Parks

. . . Spacious places with outstanding natural features

Briones Regional Park—Close to 6,000 acres of picturesque land near Lafayette, Orinda, Pleasant Hill, and Martinez. Enjoy an archery range, backpacking, equestrian trails, kite flying, self-guided nature trails, interpretive programs (coordinated through Black Diamond Mines Regional Preserve; see below). Includes John Muir Nature Area, two small lakes, and sweeping vistas of the central Contra Costa area. Park trails connect via Lafayette Ridge with district interpark trail system. (Parking fee.)

Briones Regional Park has a modest mountain known as Briones Peak (1,483 feet)—not really a peak but the highest of the rolling hills within the park—that offers a pleasant and easy climb. (It can be approached from all four of the park's staging areas.) The park also has an extraordinary population of common newts (*Taricha torosa*) and rough-skinned newts (*T. granulosa*). Following the onset of the rainy season, the little creatures come out of their dry-weather hiding places in great crowds, hundreds of them seeking their birthplace, where they will breed. Their ancestral homes are the natural ponds and streams, Sindicich and Miricich lagoons, which lie within a nature area (no dogs allowed) and which can be seen from the Briones Crest Trail en route to the summit of the mountain. "Newt Crossing" signs were erected one year near the park to prevent wholesale destruction of the newts thronging across the roads. The signs, alas, were almost immediately "collected." If you would like to combine a nice outing with a viewing of these interesting amphibians, you can call ahead to find out if they're on the move; telephone 510-229-3020. (See Bay Area Amphibians and Reptiles appendix.)

Access: To reach Bear Creek Road entrance, take I-80 to San Pablo: exit on San Pablo Dam Road and continue to Bear Creek Road; turn left and stay on Bear Creek Road to park entrance.

Mount Diablo seen from Briones Regional Park. PHOTO BY EAST BAY REGIONAL PARK DISTRICT.

Chabot Regional Park—Almost 5,000 acres east of Oakland–San Leandro. Equestrian Center with horses for rent (escorted) and access to equestrian trails. Marksmanship range (fee), backpacking access to East Bay Skyline National Trail (part of the Bay Area Ridge Trail system.) Chabot Family Camp—75 trailer, tent, and hike-in sites overlooking Lake Chabot, showers, self-guiding nature trail and hiking-fishing access to Lake Chabot (camping fee). Eighteen-hole Willow Park Public Golf Course, driving range (fee), and restaurant. Marina—315-acre stocked lake with rental boats—no private boating, year-round fishing (permit fee), year-round coffee shop, boat tours, fishing piers (including one with access for the disabled), large turfed play areas, horseshoe pits, bicycling. (Parking fee.)

This park offers nice facilities for camping in a shady eucalyptus grove. It is also a good trailhead for the East Bay Skyline National Trail. Lake Chabot itself, the work of dam-builder Anthony Chabot, is part of EBMUD (the regional park district administers the recreational facilities for them).

Access: From Hayward, north on I-580, or from Oakland, south on I-580 to Fairmont Avenue exit; east on Fairmont to Lake Chabot Road; right on Lake Chabot Road to park entrance.

Contra Loma Regional Park—776 acres 1 mile south of Antioch. In-season swimming (off-season swimming at your own risk), year-round sandy beach, fishing (permit fee), kite flying, private boating (launching fee), turfed area. Solar area information display at solar-heated bathhouse and office complex, interpretive programs. Bicycling, birdwatching, equestrian trails, food concession. Some trails connect to Black Diamond Regional Preserve. (Seasonal parking fee.)

This is a popular swimming place in warm weather; once the parking fee is paid, swimming is free. The solar-heated bathhouse has changing rooms. Windsurfing is also permitted here.

Access: Take I-80 north to Highway 4; east on Highway 4 to Antioch; exit on Lone Tree Way, turn right on Golf Course Road and right on Frederickson Lane to park entrance.

Coyote Hills Regional Park—Almost 1,000 acres in Fremont. Bicycling, trails, birdwatching, radio-controlled model-glider flying, visitor center, boardwalk view areas in freshwater marsh, self-guided nature trail. Dogs on leash on designated trails. Interesting interpretive programs and guided tours of 2,300-year-old protected Indian shell mounds in the reconstructed Indian village. Access to Alameda Creek Regional Trail and San Francisco Bay National Wildlife Refuge. (Parking fee.)

Coyote Hills is one of the gems of the East Bay. Not only does it have a rich cultural background (movies on the California Indians are shown on request in the visitor center; naturalist-conducted visits to the shell mounds and archeological excavation take place on scheduled weekend days), pleasant walking, and interesting bayfront features, the park is lovely to look at from many points around the bay. Should you be on the southwest side of the bay around sunset, be sure and look eastward to see these beautiful landforms suffused with the evening light.

Access: Take Highway 101 south from San Francisco to Dumbar-

Windsurfing on Del Valle Lake. PHOTO BY EAST BAY REGIONAL PARK DISTRICT.

ton Bridge; cross the bridge and follow signs to the park, which is just to the north.

Del Valle Regional Park—Close to 4,000 acres, 10 miles south of Livermore; includes a 750-acre lake planted with fish. In-season swimming from two sandy beaches when lifeguards are on duty (off-season swimming at your own risk), visitor center, self-guided nature trail, interpretive programs. Four-lane boat ramp (launching fee), sailboating, motorboats (maximum 10 mph), rental boats, tour boat, fishing, equestrian trails. Trail access to Ohlone Regional Wilderness and the Ohlone Wilderness Trail (see below). (Parking fee.) Del Valle Campground offers family camping year-round. Reservations through the park district; telephone 510-562-CAMP. Campers under 18 must be accompanied by an adult family member. (Camping fee.)

This is another very popular campground and swimming and boating area. The park district puts on extensive programs here, including campfire talks, naturalist-led hikes into the adjacent Ohlone Regional Wilderness (wonderful views make this uphill walk well worthwhile), canoe instruction (you can rent your canoe), bicycle tours, slide shows, group singing, and more. A great place for a family outing. *Dog owners, note:* While dogs must be on leash in the campground, they can be off leash in undeveloped areas as long as they are under control.

You can also windsurf at Del Valle. Lessons and rental equipment are available, and there is a modest launching fee.

Access: From Oakland–San Leandro–Hayward, east on I-580 (toward Stockton) to Vasco Road exit; south on Vasco to Tesla Road; right on Tesla; then left on Mines Road to Del Valle Road, the park entrance. Park is 10 miles south of city of Livermore.

Diablo Foothills Regional Park—627 acres in Contra Costa County on the western slopes of Mount Diablo. Access via Briones (see above) to Mount Diablo Regional Trail, which leads up the mountain over Shell Ridge in the Walnut Creek Open Space. Hikers, horseback riders, and joggers must stay on trail. Provides valuable open country and protection for Mount Diablo.

Dry Creek Pioneer Regional Park—1,563 acres (1,163 additional acres have been acquired in the hills above Union City, which will be open to the public once access problems are solved) in hills east of Hayward and Union City, adjacent to Garin Regional Park. Equestrian trails, kite flying, interpretive programs. Enter via Garin Regional Park.

East Shore State Park—The state of California is acquiring the undeveloped tidelands and wetlands between Point Isabel and the Bay Bridge for a new shoreline park that will be operated by the EBRPD. A trail will be developed that will be part of the Bay Trail. Recreational facilities are planned once hazardous and toxic materials are removed. Call EBRPD (510-635-0135 or 510-562-PARK) for information.

Garin Regional Park—1,520 acres in Hayward hills with spectacular vistas of south bay and beautiful, generally year-round creek. Fishing at Jordan Pond, equestrian trails, kite flying, innovative interpretive programs at visitor center barn (farming-oriented), historic farm equipment, turfed play areas. Both fishing and birding are good here and the programs are popular with children. (Parking fee.)

Access: From I-880 in Hayward, take the Industrial Parkway exit east to Mission Boulevard; right on Mission to Garin Avenue; left on Garin to park entrance.

Leona Heights Regional Open Space—A 271-acre pristine wooded canyon near Merritt College in Oakland. Hiking and riding trails; no developed facilities.

Access: Take I-580 south from Oakland to Keller Avenue; then east to staging area on Campus Drive. Or continue north on Campus Drive to Merritt College and park in lot E (the college parking lot is closed weekends).

Pleasanton Ridge Regional Park—3,201 acres of oak-covered ridges that overlook Pleasanton and the Livermore Valley from the west. The park is one of the district's more recent acquisitions and the core of a Ridgelands Regional Park to be acquired over many years. There are wonderful views to the north, east, and south from 25 miles of hiking, riding, and equestrian trails on Pleasanton and Sunol ridges, which descend into the heavily wooded canyons between them. The grasslands support an abundance of wildflowers from spring until fall. Magnificent old sycamores grow near springs on the eastern face of Pleasanton Ridge. This is a good place for birdwatching; hawks and eagles are frequently spotted.

Access: Follow I-580 south to Foothill Road exit (near Dublin); south on Foothill Road to park entrance.

Redwood Regional Park—1,840 acres in Oakland and Contra Costa County. Picnicking, equestrian trails, hiking, jogging and running trails, playfields, children's play area, amphitheatre fire circle, reservable group picnicking, and youth group camping areas. Accessible to backpackers and horseback riders via East Bay Skyline National Trail/Ridge Trail. (Seasonal parking fee.)

Being adjacent to a well-populated area, this is a greatly used—and enjoyed—park. The forests are, of course, the descendants of the great redwood groves that proved so irresistible to the pioneer loggers, and they make for pleasantly shady walking in warm weather. As in most of the more urban district parks, there is an extensive trail system in Redwood. (See under Skyline National Recreation Trail.)

Access: Take Highway 13 to Redwood Road; thence east to park.

Tassajara Creek Regional Park—425 acres north of Pleasanton. At present undeveloped, except for picnic tables. A future link in the regional trail system.

Access: Take I-580 east to Tassajara Road, left to park entrance.

Tilden Regional Park—2,079 acres in Berkeley with something for everybody. At Lake Anza—in-season swimming, sandy beach, bathhouse complex (swim fee), large turfed area, year-round fishing. At Environmental Education Center and Nature Area—more innovative interpretive programs, exhibits, Little Farm, Jewel Lake, all-weather nature trails. At Tilden Public Golf Course—18-hole course, driving range, pro shop. In other park areas—merry-go-round, children's playground, children's pony rides, Redwood Valley Railroad and Golden Gate Live Steamers (scale-model steam locomotives), playfields, horseshoe pits. A treasure of a native plant botanic garden (with representative flora from around the state of California), and a visitor center. (Fees for special activities.) Inspiration Point, hilltop vistas. Brazil Building available for social events and meetings; fee schedule. Hiking, bicycling, equestrian, and jogging trails. Backpacking access via East Bay Skyline National Recreation Trail, part of the Bay Area Ridge Trail.

This was the first of the EBRPD's parks, and it is still one of the loveliest—and especially beloved by the people living around it. The Environmental Education Center has an impressive schedule of events for park lovers of all ages—with everything from a walk at dawn on the summer solstice (you bring fruit and bread to share) to a class on backpacking equipment for women and their friends.

Access: Take Highway 24 east through the Caldecott Tunnel to Claremont Avenue (Fish Ranch Road); west on Claremont Avenue to Grizzly Peak Boulevard; right on Grizzly Peak Boulevard to South Park Drive; right into park to Wildcat Canyon Road (Botanic Garden location).

Note: South Park Drive is closed from October to March to protect migrating newts. During that time, continue on Grizzly Peak Boulevard to Golf Course Road.

Wildcat Canyon Regional Park—Almost 2,500 practically undisturbed acres in the hills east of Richmond and north of Tilden Regional Park. Access from Alvarado Park, or Tilden Nature Area (see above) and via Clark-Boas Trail. (Also northern entrance to East Bay Skyline National Recreation Trail; the Bay Area Ridge Trail joins the Skyline Trail at San Pablo Reservoir; the trail marker is a light blue dot.) Offers bicycling, equestrian trails, kite flying, blanket picnicking, and interpretive programs. Adjacent 90-acre *Alvarado Park,* a historic and prehistoric treasure, was recently transferred to the district by the city of Richmond.

Access: Take I-80 north in Richmond to Amador/Solano Avenue exit; drive north on Amador to McBride; right on McBride; soon after, branch left onto Wildcat Canyon Parkway to park entrance.

Bishop Ranch Regional Open Space—372 acres near San Ramon off Bollinger Canyon Road, with trails for hiking, jogging, and horseback riding. No facilities except for trails and staging area.

Access: Take I-580 south from Oakland to I-680 (past Dublin); north on I-680 to Bollinger Canyon Road; west on Bollinger Canyon Road to Morgan Drive and staging area.

Preserves

> ... *Protecting parklands with natural or historical significance*

Ardenwood Historic Farm—208 acres in Fremont, including the former Patterson House and an 1850–1920 working farm. You can help plant, tend, and harvest organic crops during hands-on weekend programs. There are summer and fall harvest festivals, an old-fashioned Fourth of July celebration, and other special events. Wheelchair-accessible. This is a fun place to bring children for a look at the way things were down on the farm a century ago. There are farm wagon rides, carriage rides (for four), and even a horse-drawn railroad (operated by the Society for the Preservation of Carter Railroad Resources). There's also a working blacksmith shop (with hand-crafted items for sale) and the Patterson House (restored by volunteer community endeavor) is open for tours several days a week during the season (telephone: 510-791-4196). You can bring your lunch for a picnic here or pick up your food at the food concession. The Patterson House is closed from mid-November to April (except for a special Christmas program), as are the other concessions. However, the grounds at Ardenwood are open year-round (Tuesday through Sunday) for picnicking and viewing the farm animals. The weekend naturalist programs are year-round as well; some require reservations (telephone 510-635-0135).

Access: Take Highway 101 to Dumbarton Bridge (Highway 84);

follow Highway 84 to Ardenwood Boulevard. The entrance is at the junction of Ardenwood and Newark boulevards, just north of Highway 84.

Black Diamond Mines Regional Preserve—3,905 historical acres on Mount Diablo, south of Pittsburg and Antioch. Century-old Rose Hill cemetery (going back to Spanish days), eighteenth-century coal and twentieth-century silica sand mining sites; vestiges of Somersville, Stewartville, and Nortonville mining areas. Backpacking, interpretive programs, and the visitor center has mining exhibits. (Seasonal parking fee.)

This makes for a quite different park experience and is recommended for anyone interested in history. If you're in this part of the world and want to take a hike instead of exploring the past, the countryside consists of rolling hills and is perfectly lovely in the springtime, being famous for its wildflower displays (see Mount Diablo).

Access: Take I-80 north to Highway 4, thence west to Sommersville Road, which you follow south to the park.

Claremont Canyon Regional Preserve—236 acres just west of the University of California's Clark Kerr Campus in Berkeley, providing a hiker's and horseback rider's pathway from the Berkeley flatlands to hill lands. (Claremont Canyon is adjacent to and east of the university's ecological reserve in Strawberry Canyon.) Magnificent views along the way.

Access: There are two staging areas: one at the east end of Dwight Way, the other Stonewall Road, off Claremont Avenue.

Huckleberry Botanic Regional Preserve—236 acres in Contra Costa County hills near Oakland. Entrance off Skyline Boulevard. Self-guided nature trail. Rare and beautiful native plants. No horses or dogs are allowed except on the East Bay Skyline National Trail/Ridge Trail (see View-ful Hikes in the East Bay).

The preserve protects an unusually interesting plant community and offers anyone interested in botany a nice chance to explore the plants at leisure. No other use of this park is permitted—jogging or running are even discouraged; this ecological jewel is just for walking and enjoying.

Access: Take Highway 24 east through the Caldecott Tunnel to

Claremont Avenue (Fish Ranch Road); west on Claremont Avenue to
Grizzly Peak Boulevard; west to preserve entrance. (Entrance is on
left about ½ mile south of where Grizzly Peak Boulevard joins Skyline Boulevard.)

Mission Peak Regional Preserve—Virtually 3,000 acres atop Mission Peak and adjoining Monument Peak in Fremont. A clear day
offers great and sweeping views. Bicycling, trails, kite flying, interpretive programs. On Mission Peak are mysterious rock walls constructed at an undetermined (highly controversial) date; their use is
also undetermined. Look, too, for good views of the Hayward fault,
visible from Highway 17 and I-580 and Mission Boulevard.

This preserve provides a critical link in the Ohlone Wilderness
Trail, extending to Del Valle Regional Park. The Bay Area Ridge
Trail also passes through the preserve and connects it with Ed Levin
County Park in Santa Clara County. The countryside is probably
much as it was at the time California became a part of the United
States—high and open, hot in summertime, but lovely on clear win-
ter days and after the rainy season brings on the wildflower show.

Access: Take I-880 south from east side of Dumbarton Bridge
(Highway 84); turn left onto Mission Boulevard to Stanford Avenue,
where you turn east to staging area. You might want to visit the Mission San Jose, which is north on Mission.

Morgan Territory Regional Preserve—Some 4,000 acres southeast of
Clayton and north of Livermore. Beautiful open space with miles of
hiking and riding trails, intriguing geological formations, picturesque
ponds, views of Mount Diablo. Kite flying, blanket picnicking, or
just enjoying the scene.

Access: Take Highway 24 and I-680 east (to Concord); take Willow Pass Road exit to Clayton Road (east); thence right to Clayton
and Marsh Creek Road; turn south to Morgan Territory Road and
south again to the preserve.

Sibley Volcanic Regional Preserve—660 acres in the Oakland hills in
Contra Costa County. Self-guided geology trail. Connects with East
Bay Skyline National Trail/Ridge Trail; bicycle trails.

This park offers the surprise of being volcanic in origin. The relics
of the crater that crowns it caused it to be nicknamed Round Top
long ago. With newer understanding of Bay Area geology, this evi-

dence of past vulcanism is perhaps better understood than it formerly was. Along with being an interesting place for its geologic features, this preserve is a pleasant place for a short walk or stroll. There's a self-guiding trail map and a self-guiding visitor center, as well as restrooms.

Access: Follow directions to Huckleberry Preserve (see above); Sibley is immediately to its north. (You will pass Sibley on the way to Huckleberry.)

Sobrante Ridge Regional Reserve—277 acres in Richmond. A unique ridgetop parkland with forested and open areas, a streamside community along Castro Creek, and a 20-acre stand of the endangered Alameda manzanita (*Arctostaphylos andersoni* var. *pallida*). Very pleasant for hiking and botanizing.

Access: Take I-80 north to San Pablo; east on San Pablo Dam Road; east on Castro Ranch Road to Conestoga Way; north to Carriage Drive; west to Coach Drive; north again to staging area at end of Coach Drive.

Recreation Areas

. . . Offering a variety of outdoor recreation experiences of regional significance

Alameda Creek Quarries Regional Recreation Area—530 acres in the Niles area of Fremont, with only a small portion of the park being open to the public. That part is good for model remote-control boats and fishing. Connects with Alameda Creek Regional Trail. Wheelchair-accessible.

Access: From Niles area of Fremont, enter Niles Community Park at the foot of H Street. Hike along the Alameda Creek Trail to Shinn Pond. Parking available at Niles Community Park.

Castle Rock Recreation Area—230 acres used for group and organizational picnics and recreation. Lovely creek. Walnut Creek area near Mount Diablo State Park. This is one of three park district facilities (the other two are Little Hills Ranch and Ardenwood Farm) operated by a concessioner. Fees vary with size of group. Available by reservation; closed in winter. Call EBRPD (510-635-0135 or 510-562-PARK) for information.

Cull Canyon Regional Recreation Area—360 acres in Castro Valley. In-season swimming (a large shallow lagoon makes it good for children), turfed play area, bathhouse. (Swim fee.) Year-round fishing for catfish, bass, and sunfish; equestrian trails.

Access: Take I-580 to Castro Valley exit (Castro Valley Boulevard); east on Castro Valley Boulevard to Redwood Road; left on Redwood Road to Heyer Avenue; right on Heyer to Cull Canyon Road; left on Cull Canyon to park entrance.

Don Castro Regional Recreation Area—100 acres between Castro Valley and Hayward. In-season swimming in lagoon, bathhouse, sand beach. Year-round lake fishing for bass, bluegill, catfish, sunfish, and trout; limited horseback riding; turfed areas. (Seasonal entrance fee.)

Access: Go east on I-580 to Center Street exit (Castro Valley); right on Center to Kelly Street; left on Kelly to Woodroe (at top of hill) to park entrance.

Kennedy Grove Regional Recreation Area—95 acres near El Sobrante. Turfed play area, horseshoe pits, children's play area, volleyball courts, senior center. Wheelchair-accessible. (Seasonal parking fee.)

Access: I-80 north to San Pablo Dam Road; thence east to park entrance road.

Little Hills Ranch Regional Recreation Area—25 acres in Bollinger Canyon west of Danville and San Ramon. Swimming pool, large table and covered area, two pavilions, children's play area, turfed playfield, barbecue and picnic facilities, horseshoe pits. Available only to groups by reservation. (See Castle Rock Recreation Area.)

Access: See Las Trampas Regional Wilderness, below.

Roberts Regional Recreation Area and Redwoods Bowl—82 acres in Oakland at western boundary of Redwood Regional Park. In-season swimming (Tuesday through Sunday); heated outdoor pool—disabled-accessible with special hoist for wheelchair users; bathhouse. (Swim fee.) Family picnic areas, playfields, volleyball court, hiking, biking, and riding trails, children's play area, wading pool, field and target archery range.

Access: See directions for Redwood Regional Park, above.

Shadow Cliffs Regional Recreation Area—296 acres in Pleasanton. Year-round swimming (lifeguard only in summer months), bathhouse, four-flume waterslide (open daily in summer, weekends only in spring and fall; fee). Year-round fishing for black bass, bluegill, catfish, and trout; volleyball courts, horseshoe pits, rental boats, boat launch (size limit 17 ft., electric motors only), windsurfing (lessons and rentals). Connects with Alameda County bicycle trail. Wheelchair-accessible. (Parking fee; no additional charge for swimming.)

Access: East on I-580 following signs for Stockton to the Santa Rita Road exit; south on Santa Rita Road to Valley Avenue; left on Valley Avenue to Stanley Boulevard; thence left to park entrance.

Temescal Regional Recreation Area—48 acres in Oakland. In-season swimming (swim fee), bathhouse, large turfed play areas, children's play areas, bicycling, year-round fishing.

This small park is right in the middle of a highly developed area and almost completely surrounded by freeways. Still, it manages to be a restful and charming oasis, offering the pleasant sight of people fishing in what is almost downtown. With its popular sand beach, it is apt to be crowded on a warm day. It's nice for strolling, though, at any time. (Lake Temescal was created by Anthony Chabot more than a century ago; see Alameda and Contra Costa Counties.)

Access: Take Highway 24 east to the Broadway/Highway 13 exit. Left onto access road for Highway 13 to Temescal entrance and parking area.

Shorelines

. . . The special lands along rivers, estuaries, or bays

Antioch Regional Shoreline—7 acres on Bridgehead Road, Antioch. Year-round fishing from 500-foot pier. Picnicking.

Access: Take I-80 north to Highway 4; thence east to Wilbur Avenue and Antioch; go left on Bridgehead Road to fishing area.

Brooks Island Regional Shoreline—373-acre island off the Richmond Inner Harbor. Indian shell mounds 2,500 years old. Accessible only by boat. Tours available by reservation. Call EBRPD (510-635-0135 or 510-562-PARK) for information.

Browns Island Regional Shoreline—595-acre island in the Sacramento delta region north of Pittsburg. Site for six rare and endangered plant species; plant list available, boating, fishing, birdwatching. Contact EBRPD (510-635-0135 or 510-562-PARK) for access information.

Carquinez Strait Regional Shoreline—1,305 acres of bluffs and shoreline near Crockett; there are two units, one adjacent to Martinez Regional Shoreline, the other near Port Costa. Wonderful views, open rolling grasslands, wooded ravines, eucalyptus-shaded meadows, river shoreline, and remnants of old brickworks, grain wharf, and resort. Good tugboat watching.

Access: There are two major access points, both on Carquinez Scenic Drive. Take I-80 north to Carquinez Scenic Drive (near Crockett); go east to Bull Valley Staging Area, just west of Port Costa. The Nejedly Staging Area is west of Martinez (see Martinez Regional Shoreline).

Crown Memorial Beach—383 acres in Alameda; 2.5-mile beach, estuary, and reserve. Turfed play areas, wading, sunbathing, swimming (bathhouse), windsurfing (including concession, open summer weekends), fishing, annual sand castle and sand sculpture contest in June, beach hiking, horseshoe pits, volleyball courts, kite flying. Varied and interesting interpretive programs at Crab Cove visitor center.

The spectrum of programs for children and adults includes such things as movies on the bay (and its life expectancy), exploring the tidelands, learning all about (and making) sushi, joining in on sea chanties—you can take your choice. The visitor center itself has interesting displays on marine and tidal life. And, of course, Crown Beach offers a rare chance to swim in the bay itself, if you care to take it. (See more complete description of Crown Beach under A Stroll on Crown Beach.)

Access: Take I-880 south; west on Webster Street through Oakland-Alameda Tube to Central Avenue; left on Central to Eighth Street; right on Eighth Street to park entrance across from Otis Drive on Westline Drive, Alameda.

Hayward Regional Shoreline—1,800 acres in Hayward, one of the largest and most successful marsh restoration projects on the West Coast. It is hard to believe that this was once a garbage dump. Excellent birdwatching. Interpretive programs coordinated through

Coyote Hills Regional Park and Hayward Interpretive Center (see below). Access to the eight-mile-long San Lorenzo Shoreline Trail (part of the Bay Trail), which connects Hayward and Oyster Bay regional shoreline parks.

Access: Take I-80 to I-580 and go south to Highway 238; west on Highway 238 to I-880 (San Lorenzo); where you go south again. There are three staging areas for the shoreline, all off I-880. To reach its northern end, take the Washington exit and go south to Grant Avenue where you turn right. To reach the middle section (and park office), take the West Winton Avenue exit and follow that street to its end. Or turn left on Clawiter Road off west Winton and then right on Breakwater to reach the southern end of the shoreline (where the city of Hayward has an interpretive center).

Martinez Regional Shoreline—343 acres in Martinez; access across from Amtrak station. A highly developed recreational area. Offers Joe DiMaggio baseball diamond, marina and restaurant, boating and launching ramp, bocce ball courts, fishing, horse arena, kite flying, saltwater marsh, bicycling, interpretive programs.

Access: Take I-80 north to Highway 4, thence east to Alhambra Valley Road; there, turn left to waterfront.

Note: About a half block on your way north on Alhambra Valley Road you will come to the charming *John Muir National Historical Site* in Martinez. The Muir home has been restored, and there are walks in the orchards, slide shows, and a good bookstore.

Martin Luther King, Jr., Regional Shoreline—1,219 acres in Oakland with superb bird-watching, boating, fishing, kite flying. Off Doolittle Drive—sunning beach, large turfed play area, two-lane boat-launching ramp, fishing, café. Off Swan Way—boardwalk into Arrowhead Marsh, fishing pier. Trail along San Leandro Creek Channel connects with Hegenberger Road. Off Edgewater Drive— Garretson Point, all-weather trails, Parcourse, children's play area, fishing. Interpretive programs coordinated out of Crab Cove visitor center. Trail to Damon Marsh. Wheelchair-accessible.

Access: Take I-880 to Hegenberger Road west; this gives you three choices of staging areas: (1) Take Doolittle Drive north to signed parking areas at Doolittle Recreation Area. (2) Go north on Pardee to Swan Way to signed entrance of Arrowhead Marsh area. (3) Go north on Edgewater Drive beyond end of paved road to Garretson Point area.

Miller/Knox Regional Shoreline—Almost 300 hill-and-shoreline acres at Point Richmond. Sunbathing and swimming, fishing, kite flying, bicycling. Spectacular views for those who hike the hills.

Access: Take I-80 north toward Richmond; then I-580 toward San Rafael Bridge to West Cutting Boulevard exit; west on West Cutting to Garrard Avenue; left on Garrard through tunnel to park.

Oyster Bay Regional Shoreline—194 acres. Trails (Bay Trail), meadows, picnicking, fishing.

Access: Take I-880 to Marina Boulevard; thence west to Neptune; right on Neptune to parking area.

Point Isabel Regional Shoreline—21 acres on the bay at the foot of Central Avenue, Richmond. Fishing, trails, kite flying, views of the Golden Gate and Marin County. (Can be quite windy.) *Dog owners, note:* Dogs are allowed to run free here. Please pick up after them with provided scoopers.

Access: Take I-80 north to Richmond; take Central Avenue west to Point Isabel, adjacent to the U.S. Postal Service Bulk Mail Center.

Point Pinole Regional Shoreline—2,434 acres of land and water on the Richmond shoreline of San Pablo Bay with meadows, eucalyptus stands, rugged beaches, thriving marshes, and spectacular bay views. (Bay Trail.) Daily shuttle service (fee) from parking lot to 1,250-foot fishing pier at the point. Four miles of shoreline to explore; bicycling, hiking, equestrian, jogging, and running trails; horseshoe pit. State fishing license required only when fishing from shore. (Parking fee, weekends and holidays.)

This very special park is another reclamation miracle: it was once part of an ammunitions manufacturing operation.

Access: Take I-80 north to Hilltop exit (Richmond); west on Hilltop to San Pablo Avenue; right on San Pablo to Atlas Road; left on Atlas Road to parking area for Point Pinole.

Wildernesses

> *. . . Dominantly natural areas for enjoyment isolated from the urban scene*

Las Trampas Regional Wilderness—3,638 acres in hills immediately west of Danville and Alamo. Wilderness area, nature study trails. Las

Trampas Stable offers guided trail rides and horse rental. Permit trails through EBMUD lands connect with Redwood and Chabot regional parks (see above). Picnic sites near entrance, or choose a spot along the trail.

Access: Take Highway 24 east to Walnut Creek; there take I-680 south and turn right on Crow Canyon Road; then right again on Bollinger Canyon Road to the park.

Ohlone Regional Wilderness—9,156 acres in southeastern Alameda County between Sunol Regional Wilderness and Del Valle Regional Park. Ponds, waterfalls, nature trails, backpacking, and horseback riding. Trail permit required. Access via Ohlone Regional Wilderness Trail (see Trails, below).

Sunol Regional Wilderness—6,858 acres south of Pleasanton-Livermore. Interpretive programs, nature center, family camping—limited number of sites (fee), backpack loop available by reservation (fee), trails. Trail access to Ohlone Regional Wilderness Trail. (Parking fee.)

Camp Ohlone—240 acres 7 miles east of Sunol Regional Wilderness. Remote area, for youth groups on a reservation basis only. Telephone 510-635-0135.

Trails

> ... *Linear parkland for walking, jogging, bicycling, and horseback riding. A wonderful 1,000 miles of trails are within EBRPD parks, plus the miles that connect the parks. Since these trails offer numerous options for access, telephone EBRPD at 510-635-0135 or 510-562-PARK for directions or maps.*

Alameda Creek Regional Trail—Parallel 12-mile-long trails follow along the north and south banks of the Alameda Creek Flood Control Channel from the mouth of Niles Canyon through Union City, Newark, and Fremont to San Francisco Bay. There are several staging areas. The paved trail on the south bank connects with a 3.5-mile loop in Coyote Hills Regional Park, making the round-trip qualify for marathon distance and practice, while affording a place for bicycling, hiking, and jogging uninterrupted by motor vehicle traffic. The trail on the north bank is mostly unpaved and is popular with equestrians. Interpretive programs coordinated with Coyote Hills visitor center. Adjacent to Alameda Creek Quarries Regional Recreation Area and Coyote Hills Regional Park.

Briones to Las Trampas Regional Trail—1.5-mile trail link with the Lafayette Ridge staging area on Pleasant Hill Road makes it possible to hike from Briones through downtown Lafayette (something different!) and connect with the Lafayette/Moraga Trail.

Briones to Mount Diablo Regional Trail—A 12-mile trail connects Briones Regional Park with Mount Diablo State Park, affording hikers, bicyclists, and horseback riders scenic and interesting territory in between.

Contra Costa Canal Regional Trail—A 14-mile paved trail linking Concord, Walnut Creek, and Pleasant Hill for bicycling, hiking, and riding.

Chabot to Garin Regional Trail—The first portion of this trail has been completed, from the Chabot Staging Area to Cull Canyon Regional Recreation Area. A segment of the Bay Area Ridge Trail (EBMUD permit). Length is 6 miles.

East Bay Skyline National Recreation Trail—31-mile regional trail, suitable for hiking, backpacking, and horseback riding full length and for bicycling in part; connects six regional parks. Beginning at Wildcat Canyon in Richmond, it goes through Wildcat, Tilden, Sibley, Huckleberry Botanic, Redwood, and Chabot parks. EBMUD permit required between Tilden Park and Sibley Preserve. Connects with entrance road to Chabot Family Camp (fee) near southern end of the trail north of Castro Valley. (This is part of the Bay Area Ridge Trail.)

This national trail is one of the interesting achievements of outdoor enthusiasts, who worked to gain a continuous ridgetop pathway. Although it's too long to take in a single day (unless you're really into hiking—it has been done), its numerous staging areas make it easy to take in sections. Walking this trail offers a nice opportunity to sample six of the EBRPD's parks. (See more complete trail description under View-ful Hikes in the East Bay.)

Lafayette/Moraga Regional Trail—This 7.5-mile trail through the towns of Lafayette and Moraga includes a Parcourse and offers bicycling and equestrian use.

Las Trampas/Mount Diablo—5-mile link to Mount Diablo State Park (see Mount Diablo). The staging area is at La Gonda Way in Danville, just east of I-680. It will ultimately be extended to Las Trampas Regional Park. For hiking, riding, or jogging.

Ohlone Wilderness Trail—Another triumph for outdoor enthusiasts, this 29-mile riding, hiking, and backpacking trail provides for a sampling of the countryside from west to east, from Mission Peak in southern Alameda County east to Del Valle. An EBRPD permit is required; telephone 510-635-0135 or 510-562-PARK. This offers a rare chance (for strong hikers) to enjoy the springtime wildflowers that blossom in profusion in this part of the world. Water must be carried. This trail is not recommended during the warm, dry months of the year.

Old Moraga Ranch Trail—5 miles of trail near Moraga. Access for hiking and horseback via EBMUD Valle Vista staging area on Canyon Road. (EBMUD permit required; telephone 510-835-3000.)

San Lorenzo Shoreline Regional Trail—8-mile trail connects Hayward and Oyster Bay regional shorelines, via San Lorenzo and San Leandro Park and Marina. This segment of the Bay Trail (under several governmental jurisdictions), is one of the bayshore treasures that allows for jogging, hiking, and especially birdwatching along the rim of the bay.

Park Facts

Bicycling. Warning bells are required on bicycles. Narrow footpaths are off-limits, fines are $180 to $270 for offenders.

Fishing. Age 16 or above requires a state license and stamps at Alameda Creek Trail (Shinn Pond), Antioch, Crown Beach, Garin, Martin Luther King Shoreline, Miller/Knox, Point Isabel, Point Pinole, and Tilden (Lake Anza). In addition to state license and stamps, a daily fishing access permit is required at Contra Loma, Cull Canyon, Del Valle, Don Castro, Lake Chabot, Shadow Cliffs, and Temescal. No permit is required when fishing from Point Pinole pier in San Pablo Bay and pier at Martinez shoreline. Access permits are available for day at park concession; for further information, call 510-635-0135 or 510-562-PARK.

Interpretive Services

There are year-round Saturday and Sunday programs at each of the visitor centers. "Regional in Nature," a quarterly newsletter detailing naturalist programs is available at EBRPD headquarters, 2950 Peralta Oaks Court, Oakland, CA 94605; telephone 510-635-0135 or 510-562-PARK.

Reservations

Black Diamond Mine Tours	510-757-2620
Camping	510-562-CAMP
Del Valle Campground	510-636-1684
Little Hills Ranch Reservations	510-462-1400
Ohlone Wilderness Trail	510-636-1684
Sunol Backpack Loop	510-636-1684

Naturalist Services

Ardenwood	510-796-0663
Black Diamond Mine Regional Preserve	510-757-2620
Coyote Hills Visitor Center	510-795-9385
Crab Cove Visitor Center	510-521-6887
Del Valle Visitor Center	510-862-2244
Garin Barn	510-795-9385
Sunol Nature Center	510-862-2244
Tilden Nature Area	510-525-2233

Golf Reservations

Tilden	510-848-7373
Willow Park (Chabot)	510-537-2521

Equestrian Stables

Chabot	510-638-0610
Las Trampas	510-838-7546

Other Numbers

Marksmanship range (Chabot)	510-569-0213
Merry-go-round (Tilden)	510-524-6773
Pony ride (Tilden)	510-527-0421
Train ride (Tilden)	510-548-6100
Waterslide (Shadow Cliffs)	510-846-4900
Emergency	911

AC Transit buses serve several urban EBRPD parks year-round. Unfortunately, bus-to-park service to more remote parks is very limited. Write or telephone for a transit map (1600 Franklin Street, Oakland, CA 94612; 510-817-1717). AC Transit lines connect with BART (telephone 510-465-2278).

Access information for drivers is given from San Francisco. There may be more than one entrance to the larger parks; check your park map, obtainable from EBRPD headquarters (2950 Peralta Oaks Court, Oakland, CA 94605), by mail or in person.

Note: The city of Berkeley has a 131-acre marina, 62 acres of which are land (at Marina Boulevard and University Avenue). This includes a mile-long walkway, a fishing pier, Caesar Chavez Park, and a Shorebird Park that offers good birdwatching. The city sponsors a popular "marina experience" summer program at the Shorebird Nature Center where children and teenagers can learn to boat, fish, waterski, and sail on the bay. There are also classes in marine biology, an annual shoreline cleanup, and a year-round supervised "Adventure" playground. The center is open weekends and holidays during the school year, seven days a week during the summer (telephone 510-644-8623). This marina is a great favorite with windsurfers. Sailboat and sailboard rentals and lessons are available here and at the city's 35-acre Berkeley Aquatic Park, located at the foot of Addison Street. Other cities with bay frontage have points of access for birdwatching and fishing. Contact the San Francisco Bay Trail Project for information; telephone 510-464-7900. (See also Maps appendix.)

Oakland

Oakland has a lovely green backdrop of two spacious regional parks, *Redwood* and *Chabot,* and it shares *Sibley* with Berkeley. It also has three city parks of over 100 acres: 122-acre *Lakeside Park* encircles Lake Merritt and is an especially attractive urban amenity, offering birdwatching, boating, a children's fairyland, and a 2½-mile shore-side run right in the middle of downtown; 453-acre *Knowland Park and Zoo* is primarily a children's petting zoo where the animals run free (located off I-580 at Ninety-eighth Avenue); 513-acre *Joaquin Miller Park,* which remembers the eccentric poet (who lived here), is almost a part of Redwood Park and is large enough and beautiful enough to rate regional status itself. (Born Cincinnatus Hiner, Miller took the forename—and the dress and the swagger—of the western bandit Joaquin Murietta; Miller's house, the Abbey, is near the park entrance, and many of the trees he loved and planted still stand in the forests here.) You can get directly to all of these Oakland parks on AC Transit; telephone 510-817-1717 for information.

Oakland also has the 5-acre Davie Tennis Stadium (in Piedmont) and six swim centers, which AC Transit serves, but not as directly: Diamond Lions Pool, 3860 Hanley Road; deFremery Pool (1269 Eighteenth Street); Fremont Pool (4550 Foothill Boulevard); Live Oak Pool (1055 MacArthur Boulevard); McClymonds Pool (2607 Myrtle); and Temescal Pool (371 Forty-fifth Street). Telephone 510-444-5663 for tennis reservations.

In recent years, Oakland has launched a concerted—and effective—community effort to renovate and preserve some of its beautiful old buildings, thus offering history and architecture buffs some rewarding strolls. Try the Bret Harte Boardwalk starting at 567 Fifth Street, with its row of 1870s Italianate houses-turned-shops. (Although Harte once lived in this neighborhood, it was actually across the street in his uncle's house, now gone.) Or explore Preservation Park, which is bordered by Grove, Castro, Eleventh, and

Fourteenth streets; here you will find the 1868 Pardee Mansion, the 1890 First Unitarian Church with its heavy bell tower and beautiful stained glass windows, the 1880 Remillard House, and the 1900 Greene Library. There's also a "Victorian row" house, which you'll find at Ninth and Washington, and the 1868 deFremery House in the park of the same name at Eighteenth and Adeline. The Antonio María Peralta adobe at Thirty-fourth and Paxton is one of the few mementos of the Spanish family that first settled in the East Bay, and the 1876 Cameron-Stanford House above Lake Merritt recalls the days when a family's broad front lawn sloped all the way to the lakeshore. (Oakland once planned to locate all its civic buildings around this pleasant lake, which, incidentally, was the first official wildlife refuge in the United States, having been so designated by the California state legislature in 1870.)

A particularly successful renovation has taken place along a section of Oakland's waterfront at the foot of Broadway. Known as Jack London Square, this development—somewhat à la San Francisco's Ghirardelli Square—features numerous shops, Jack London's 1890 log cabin rescued from the Yukon and certified by Canada as being genuine, the 1900 First and Last Chance Saloon, and numerous eating places.

Oakland also boasts the Chabot Observatory and Science Center at 4917 Mountain Boulevard (telephone 510-530-5225), the wonderful Oakland Museum (with its excellent exhibit of California's biotic zones) at Tenth and Oak streets near Lake Merritt (see Natural History Museums appendix), and Mills College on MacArthur Boulevard and Seminary; the college has one building dating back to 1871, a good sampling of Spanish colonial architecture, and a campanile designed by Julia Morgan in 1904. And if old graveyards intrigue you, you'll find quite a special one at 5000 Piedmont Avenue, the Mountain View Cemetery; it was designed by Frederick Law Olmsted in 1863 (it is said that he was never paid the full $1,000 promised him for the job) and has many graves dating back to before the turn of the century, including one dated May 8, 1868, which marks the resting place of a "Chinaman, death by hanging."

Berkeley

Should you find yourself with time on your hands and the desire to get some exercise while in Berkeley, you will have several choices. You can:

Take a hike in one of the nearby regional parks—*Tilden, Claremont Canyon Preserve,* or *Sibley Regional Volcanic Preserve.* All are served—more or less—by AC Transit, which runs within two blocks of Tilden and a mile of Sibley. (On weekends, one bus runs through Tilden.)

Take a plunge in one of the four swimming pools: Berkeley High School Swim Center (Milvia and Durant); Martin Luther King, Jr., Swim Center (Hopkins and Colusa); West Campus Swim Center (Browning and Addison); or the Willard Swim Center (Telegraph and Derby). AC Transit serves these.

Go jogging in Aquatic Park (Second and Addison) or in Shorebird Park at the Berkeley Marina. Or run the Parcourse in Ohlone Park (Hearst and Sacramento). AC Transit will get you close to all of these.

Explore the University of California campus, which has many interesting buildings dating from the Victorian era to the present; some of the more historic are listed in the National Registry of Historic Sites. It also has the renowned Bancroft Library, a landmark campanile (patterned after that of St. Mark's in Venice) with tremendous views, and a fine botanical garden (up the hill from its equally renowned stadium). Take AC Transit to the entrance gate on University Avenue where you can get information. *Note:* There are several university museums: among the most outstanding are the Lawrence Hall of Science on Centennial Drive, featuring science exhibits, astronomy (it has a planetarium), and computer games (telephone 510-642-5132), the University Art Museum at 2626 Bancroft (telephone 510-642-0808), and the Hearst Museum of Anthropology in Kroeber Hall on Bancroft Way and College Avenue.

Visit the Rose Garden (recently renovated) across from Codornices Park (Euclid and Eunice); there are at least 3,000 varieties of this flower in this 1930s WPA project. There are also splendid views of the Golden Gate from this vantage point. AC Transit will take you there.

Go climb a rock in Mortar Rock/Indian Rock parks on Indian Rock Avenue above the traffic circle at Marin and Sutter. While you're there, admire the Indian mortar holes, as well.

AC Transit information: 510-817-1717.

Mount Diablo

To the Indians, the big mountain that filled up the eastern horizon was the center of the universe, home of Eagle and Coyote, a magical place. To the Spanish, it was a useful, easily ascended peak that opened up a good view of the Bay Area and provided orientation for the early explorers; both Fages and Crespi climbed it in 1772. To the first—and later—American surveyors, it was a key landmark; starting with Leander Ransom in 1851, it was used as the base meridian point in laying out the townships in two-thirds of the state of California and parts of Nevada and Oregon. To geologists, the mountain is a big mass of Franciscan rock that was squeezed up by the slow collision of two tectonic plates; because it was thrust up through 6 miles of marine sediments, it has a variety of rocks as well as fossils. (Rock climbers also appreciate some of those rocks.) To park proponents, Diablo is a state park that started too small (with only 600 acres in 1931) and one that, despite its enlargement to 15,000 acres during the past several decades, still must be cherished and cared for. To history buffs, Mount Diablo is a state historical landmark and a national natural landmark, and it also played an important part in early East Bay history. (The mountain was mined for coal, quicksilver, and—overoptimistically—for silver and gold; Clayton, on its north flank, was founded in 1857 and was a stage stop and Saturday-night center for local miners.)

To people living in the East Bay, this splendid mountain is a special plus, a lovely place to hike, to see wildflowers, admire waterfalls (in season), and to look for bobcats, golden eagles, California newts, and the rare Alameda striped racer snake. To an outdoor-minded Bay Area visitor, Mount Diablo offers the same pleasures; it is a wonderful mountain to explore. Rising from 300 to nearly 4,000 feet and sitting in solitary splendor as it does—it is sometimes referred to as an island mountain—Mount Diablo also offers one of the most extensive 360-degree views in the world (only 19,000-foot Mount Kilimanjaro in East Africa commands a vaster territory): from the top of Mount Diablo you can look out over literally thousands of miles—40,000 square miles, in fact. If you visit the summit on a clear, cold winter's day just after a storm, you may be able to see: to the west, all of San Francisco Bay, its bridges, the city itself, and the Pacific Ocean beyond the Farallon Islands; to the northwest, Mount Tamalpais (2,600 feet) and San Pablo Bay; to the north, the winding waterways of the delta, the Coast Ranges culminating in Mount Saint Helena (4,350 feet), and against the horizon, the Cascades topped off by Mount Lassen (10,500 feet—and 185 miles away), and if the conditions are right, a refracted image of Mount Shasta (over 14,000 feet—and 200 miles distant); at your feet, you will also be able to see the proliferation of subdivisions in the pleasant countryside of Contra Costa County. (This view gives some insight into why park proponents still might want to enlarge Diablo State Park.) Looking to the east, you may see the white-crested Sierra Nevada, floating above the lush Central Valley, and with binoculars, you may be able to identify Half Dome. Turning to the southeast, you may admire the Livermore-Pleasanton valleys and Mount Hamilton (4,200 feet) with Lick Observatory glinting on its summit; and to the south, the Santa Cruz Mountains with Mount Loma Prieta topping out at 3,800 feet. In all, you may look into parts of at least 35 of California's 58 counties.

The best way to reach Mount Diablo is by car. There are two main entrances, the North Gate (reached via Walnut Creek) and the South Gate (reached via Danville); there is a modest entrance fee. Note that dogs on leash are allowed in the park—but not on the trails—and they, too, are charged an entrance fee.

Depending on the clarity of the day, you may want to drive to the summit for its fabulous views before you start your explorations. On the way up, you will pass the ranger station (Mount Diablo State

Park headquarters) at the 2,200-foot level. The Summit Interpretive Center occupies part of the wonderful old observation tower, which was constructed out of the mountain's own fossil-bearing sandstone by the Civilian Conservation Corps. Once you have admired the surrounding California countryside from the mountain's top, closing your eyes, if you can, to the ugly communications towers that mar the sky, it is highly recommended that, rather than continuing your explorations by car, you now take a hike. Mount Diablo offers much more than great views alone, and the best way to enjoy the mountain is on foot. You may want to drive all or part of the way downhill to reach a trailhead of your choice. Park roads, by the way, are narrow and winding; you should allow an hour and a half for a leisurely trip to the summit and back to a point of departure for your explorations.

Mount Diablo has some choice coast mountain wilderness tucked into its folds and canyons. Because of its variety of rocks, it has a wonderful variety of plant communities and rare native flowers that will delight flower aficionados (over 400 species of plants grow on its slopes). It also has over 160 species of birds visiting or inhabiting it: you can pick up a checklist at park headquarters or on the summit. (There is an unusually good guide to Diablo's trees available, too.)

The *Trail Map of Mount Diablo State Park* provides a good topographic overview of the terrain (it uses 40-foot contour intervals) as well as clearly marked trails for hikers and riders; it also gives good, brief descriptions of 12 recommended hikes, telling the level of difficulty and the average time required for each of them. And it notes the tie-in of regional park trails with those in the state park. It is worth studying this map before choosing your particular outing. (Notice that some of the trails are reached from outside the park.)

If you prefer walking with a knowledgeable leader and a congenial group of people, you will find many opportunities of doing so on Mount Diablo. *Sunset* magazine once listed 22 April hikes on this mountain that were being offered by local environmental groups. A good place to start your inquiries into such an outing is the Sierra Club San Francisco Bay Chapter office in Berkeley (see Environmental Organizations appendix). State park rangers lead hikes and interpretive events throughout the year; telephone 510-837-2525 for information.

Mount Diablo is at its best during the first five months of the year, and at its peak in April. The second-best time to enjoy it is during

October (when the hills are golden) through December (when you might find snow on the summit). Summer months on the mountain are not highly recommended; although some of the canyons may still be lovely, it is apt to be too hot for pleasure, and fire danger may restrict recreational use. However, if you're looking for car camping, the state park does have three family campgrounds, with tables and barbecues—at Live Oak (the shadiest), Juniper (which has the best view), and Junction—which might be available without reservations from June through September. These campgrounds also can be reserved through DESTINET; telephone 1-800-444-PARK for further information about these units. There is a modest fee for camping. You will also find more than 100 family picnic sites in the park located here and there along the road. For an especially fine April picnic, find one of these with a good view, framed, perhaps, by one of the mountain's lovely long-needle (digger) pines.

In all activities on Mount Diablo, try to avoid the poison oak and, in warm weather, a possible encounter with a rattlesnake. Bring your own water and other drinks. The park is open every day from 8:00 A.M. to sunset, when both of its entrance gates are closed. It is completely surrounded by privately owned land (and has a couple of big private inholdings as well), and the rights of the property owners should be respected. The Diablo Ranch on North Gate Road welcomes visitors when it gives demonstrations: these are great fun for children. Information about these and state park activities can be obtained by telephoning the park people at 510-837-2525.

It is not surprising that Mount Diablo has inspired certain of the local people to work with diligence and dedication to protect it and its unique natural features. The effort to keep Diablo from destructive and disfiguring uses has been Herculean, and is ongoing. As more and more people move into the lovely country around Diablo, land becomes increasingly dear, and it is increasingly difficult to preserve it from development. But people pressures are only part of the problem; the very things that make Diablo extra special—its height and its situation—make it an increasingly desirable relay site for various types of communication. The present numerous towers on the North Peak threaten to be only a beginning.

View-ful Hikes in the East Bay

Skyline National Recreation Trail

A good way to get acquainted with the East Bay regional parks is to walk the Skyline Trail (properly the East Bay Skyline National Recreation Trail)—in sections, it should be added hastily, since this trail adds up to 31 miles in all. This was the first trail that Secretary of the Interior Walter J. Hickel—a man who favored parks in metropolitan areas, i.e., "parks for the people"—chose for the National Trails System, set up in 1970. The National Trails System was to identify and include trails close to cities, in public ownership, with "scenic value," and with enough amplitude to accommodate more than one use. Thus horseback riders, nature students, hikers, and—in places—bicyclists use the Skyline Trail. Happily, it is closed to all motorized vehicles. Mr. Hickel chose well.

The Skyline Trail passes through, and ties together, six of the most popular East Bay regional parks, and you can pick it up in any one of them. Although it runs generally along the high ridges of the Berkeley-Oakland hills, it encompasses a good cross section of East Bay landscape. From its northern entrance (in Wildcat Canyon out of Richmond) to its southern terminus (at Lake Chabot in Castro Valley), the trail runs through parkland that ranges from open rolling grassland to deep-shadowed redwood forests and bay-fragrant streamsides with chaparral and stands of oaks in between, and—almost too often—eucalyptus woodlands. Some of it is paved, and these sections are well used by bicyclists. Parts of it go through areas where dogs are not allowed, whereas there are other parts where dogs can run as much as they want. Be guided accordingly if you like to hike with your pet. In general, the parks along the Skyline Trail have restrooms, water, and picnic facilities. Chabot also has a family campground. Backpacking is not recommended along this trail unless you enjoy the company of lots of people along the way.

To identify the Skyline Trail, look for a post with a red, white, and blue dot on it and a triangular sign reading EAST BAY SKYLINE TRAIL, USA, NATIONAL RECREATION TRAIL. The descriptions of the East Bay regional parklands should give some idea of the parks—and the countryside—joined by the Skyline Trail—and the access to them. Contact EBRPD (510-635-0135 or 510-562-PARK) for a good map of the Skyline Trail.

Wildcat Canyon to *Inspiration Point* and *Tilden Park*. Distance, 7.14 miles; elevation gain, 800 easy feet. This regional parkland was formerly East Bay Municipal Utility District (EBMUD) land, sold in 1952 to private investors who were interested in its oil potential. However, Standard Oil had poor luck in exploratory drilling here in 1966, and the following year the East Bay Regional Park District (EBRPD) began acquisition of the land for a park. In the following decade, enough acreage was acquired to make it official, and Wildcat Canyon Regional Park came into being in 1976—and is still being expanded (see East Bay Parklands). The terrain is generally open country with rolling hills cleft by tree-lined creeks (one is Wildcat Creek, along which Pedro Fages and Father Juan Crespi camped in 1772 and there held commerce with the local Indians—"peaceful heathen," the good Father called them). There are pleasant stands of madrone, California bay, and live oak, and several species of pines (introduced). Enjoy the sweeping views of pasture (grazed by cattle) and the panorama of the hills to the east. The southern 4.5 miles of this trail are wide, paved, named for Admiral Chester Nimitz, World War II hero, and popular with bicyclists. Nimitz Way borders EBMUD lands, which make for lovely scenery around San Pablo Reservoir. (This is also where the Bay Area Ridge Trail joins the Skyline Trail and follows it for its distance. The Ridge Trail marker is a light blue dot.) This segment of the Skyline Trail stops at Inspiration Point, where you may want to stop, too, and admire the vista, including San Pablo and Briones reservoirs, both surrounded by EBMUD lands. This is a lovely 7-mile walk to take in the spring when wild-flowers are in bloom, if you don't mind walking on pavement, that is. (The road was built after World War II to access a Nike site, which has since been demolished. Nimitz planted wildflowers along its sides.) The Nimitz Way is, of course, great for bikers. A shuttle between Wildcat Canyon Parkway, Richmond, and the Inspiration Point parking lot off Wildcat Canyon Road is easily arranged, if you have a friend with a car.

Tilden Park to *Sibley (Round Top) Volcanic Regional Preserve.* Distance, 6.4 miles (the EBRPD describes this trail in two 3-mile sections, the first of which is in Tilden Park, the second of which skirts through EBMUD land and back into regional parkland at Sibley [see East Bay Parklands for both]—at midpoint is Vollmer Peak, at 1,913 feet the high point of these hills); elevation change, 860-foot climb, 600-foot drop, 300-foot climb. The high ridge terrain rises to its greatest elevation in this section of the Skyline Trail, and there are spectacular views along the way. There is also a chance for a short extra climb up Vollmer for an exceptionally grand view that sweeps from Mount Diablo to Mount Saint Helena to Mount Tam and the magic city by the Golden Gate, the Golden Gate itself, and beyond it the shining sea. There are open pine forests along the trail, courtesy of the early water companies, and stands of eucalyptus, courtesy of Frank Havens, who planned to make a fortune here out of eucalyptus "hardwood" in the early twentieth century. You'll have a chance to see Lomas Contadas, the home of Tilden Park's steam trains, and on weekends (and summer weekdays) you may hear the happy whistle of the little locomotive. You'll pass through coyote brush, have views to the east as well as to the west, walk over the Caldecott Tunnel, pass volcanic flows, see a eucalyptus forest regenerating after a major freeze (1972), and end up at the old 1,761-foot volcano known as Round Top. This is a favorite spot for geologists; Round Top is said to have come to life over 10 million years ago when it lay beneath a lake; since then, it has spewed out lava at least 11 times and blown its top at least twice. If you have a geological turn of mind, you'll probably want to look around for some of the earth's history recorded in this place.

A shuttle can be easily arranged from Inspiration Point to the parking lot at Sibley Regional Preserve—again, if you have a friend with a car.

Sibley to *Huckleberry Preserve* to *Redwood Park.* Distance, 3.5 miles; elevation change, drops 480 feet, climbs 200 feet. Switchbacks accommodate this section of the Skyline Trail for some necessary down and up, but they're nothing major. This shortest section of the Skyline Trail is more notable for its natural scene than for the vistas it commands. It offers nature students some nice opportunities to birdwatch and, especially, to botanize. Huckleberry Botanic Regional Preserve (see East Bay Parklands) lies along the way, although the Skyline Trail is routed deliberately to avoid passing through the most delicate part of this native ecosystem (requiring intensive research and management). No bicycles are allowed in the preserve and horses and dogs are restricted to the Skyline Trail. The 236-acre preserve contains one of the few unaltered pieces of native California biota extant; it also contains several rare plant species. Among these are two manzanitas (*Arctostaphylos andersoni* var. *pallida,* which may be unique to parts of the East Bay, and *A. crustacea*), silktassel (*Garrya elliptica*), and western leatherwood (*Dirca occidentalis*), which grows only in a few places in the East Bay. You'll also find chinquapin trees here, with their curved and pointed leaves that always remind me of small pagodas and their cones that look like tiny rust-colored mice upon the ground. The area has a fine supply of the plants for which it is named; don't plan on sampling the fruit thereof, however—the locals will undoubtedly have gotten there before you.

To some, Huckleberry Preserve suggests a dwarf forest, and so it may be characterized. Its unique flora is, in fact, dictated by the composition of its soil and its unique location on an eastern slope just outside the fog belt. Its biological clock seems to be set about two months ahead of the other plant communities around it, and anyone who gets tired of winter can often find manzanita and leatherwood in bloom in Huckleberry long before spring has moved into the rest of the Bay Area. Writer Malcolm Margolin, who captures the essence of the East Bay parks most eloquently in his book *The East Bay Out,* finds "something bracing and energizing about these gnarled, strong bushes, the hardness of their branches, the distinctness and crispness of everything, the unconquered history of the area." If you want to explore this exceptional piece of the Bay Area landscape, you can take the self-guided nature trail that winds about 1.7 miles through it; brochures may be available at the entrance to the preserve, but if you want to be sure to get one, best to pick it up at EBRPD headquarters (2950 Peralta Oaks Court, Oakland, CA 94605; telephone 510-635-0135 or 510-562-PARK). (Although the Skyline Trail parallels the trail through Huckleberry Preserve, it actually converges with the nature trail for about ½ mile.)

Redwood Regional Park. For 5.5 miles, the Skyline Trail goes through Redwood Regional Park. In fact, it splits into two routes so that you have a choice of taking a fairly level view-ful route or walking among the redwoods. You also have a choice of entering Redwood Regional Park at its north Skyline Gate (off Skyline Boulevard at Pinehurst Road), its middle Redwood Gate (off Redwood Road), or its south McDonald Gate (off Redwood Road 2 miles east of its intersection with Skyline Boulevard). And you have several choices if you want to make a loop hike from any one of these entrances. (See also Redwood Regional Park information under East Bay Parklands.)

If you take the West Ridge Trail from Skyline Gate, you will have an easy 200-foot uphill pull and a 900-foot descent. You will also have relatively level walking for most of the way, and you will undoubtedly pass joggers along the trail. The West Ridge Trail will take you past the archery range, the popular Redwood Bowl (people like to picnic or get married here), and the short side trail that leads to the top of the tree-covered Redwood Peak—at 1,619 feet this park's highest point. You walk through fairly open brushland for a while and enjoy views toward the sentinel Mount Diablo, the hills of Chabot Park, and the baylands to the west. Follow the red, white, and blue dots and they will take you downhill at the south end of the park and across the Redwood Road to McDonald Gate in Chabot Regional Park (see East Bay Parklands).

Alternatively, you can start off on the West Ridge Trail and in about ½ mile take the French Trail to your left. This leads you through the forest, up, down, and around the canyons, past small streams that burst and bubble into waterfalls in the wet season, and gives you a 400-foot drop followed by a 200-foot climb and a final 600-foot drop. This is a quieter, more intimate forest trail, with the springy forest floor to keep you tripping lightly. (You can pick up this trail off of the West Ridge Trail via Tres Cendes Trail or Orchard Trail as well, which gives you the option of looping back to the north end or continuing on to the south.)

Redwood Regional Park is what remains of the grand redwood forest that towered here before the gold rush. It was logged bare during the 1850s and logged again of its second growth after the great fire of 1906. In between, even the big old stumps were hacked apart for firewood; it is estimated that their wood supplied half the East Bay needs for two decades. The trees you see today are less than 100 years old. Notice how many of them grow in family circles marking the site and size of the original mother tree. Four of the ten East Bay mills that sprang up during the hey-days of logging were located here in what is now parkland, and each of the mills had a shantytown around it to house its hundred or more workers. They were tough pioneers, those loggers, buckers, jack-screwers, and bullwhackers. Imagine bringing down a 20- to 30-foot-diameter tree with a two-man saw, rolling the huge log to a landing, and skidding it to the mill.

Margolin points out that Redwood Park not only has a redwood forest these days, but a big stand of eucalyptus, oak-bay-madrone woods, and "ancient" Monterey pine trees planted decades ago. There are also old orchards in the park, relics of the farmers and ranchers who followed the loggers here. If you decide to do more than take the Skyline Trail, you'll find a varied scene—this park even has a heated pool in the Roberts Recreation Area—and possibly a few luscious plums to refresh you. (The stone buildings along Stream Trail were built by the Civilian Conservation Corps during the 1930s and are now used for group camping.)

Chabot Regional Park. The final 10 miles of the Skyline Trail are located within the 5,000-acre Chabot Regional Park (see East Bay Parklands). This park is more notable for its lake and lakeside trails, its golf course, and its campground than it is for its varied scenery or its backcountry trails. However, if you want to complete the Skyline Trail, you can take a day and make your way up and down the McDonald and Brandon trails to Proctor Gate. The elevation change is 500 feet up, 300 feet down, 320 feet up and, finally, 600 feet down to trail's end.

The terrain is likely to be dusty most of the year, and it is brush covered in places (coyote brush, *Baccharis pilularis consanguinea*), tufted generously with eucalyptus trees and, in places, with poison oak, open in too few stretches to good views (you'll get to see the hill once given over to motorcyclists—they wore it down to bedrock—and now in the process of being rehabilitated) and generally not as interesting as the other East Bay regional parks. There's a rifle range within hearing distance along the way, and if it's in use, you'll get some background music that you could probably do without.

On the plus side, Chabot has one of the largest (75 units) and nicest family camps in the Bay Area, Chabot Family Camp. There are walk-in campsites as well as tent sites, hot showers, and other camping amenities, such as picnic grills. The campgrounds are up the hill from the lake in a (guess what) eucalyptus grove, and it's a pleasant hike down for boating or walking at lakeside and enjoying the bird life around the water. There's an excursion boat that makes stops around the lake, and it can carry you to the marina, where you can rent a canoe, a rowboat, or a small motorboat if you want to venture out on your own or do some fishing. There are 8½ miles of hiking and 14½ miles of biking trails around this large (315-acre) lake, about five miles of which follow its shoreline. (EBMUD still owns the lake and considers it an "emergency water supply," and swimming, of course, is a decided no-no.) You might inquire from EBRPD (call 510-635-0135 or 510-562-PARK) about the possibility of renting a horse at Chabot; it has been suggested by more than one hiker that riding a horse on at least part of this lap of the Skyline Trail might be the better part of valor.

Lake Chabot, by the way, is the body of water that inspired early water company officials to import sea lions to eat up a heavy over-population of fish. Imagine, if you can, the big animals jouncing and jostling their way out of the lake and over the hills to return to the salt water of the bay. The fish are not quite that plentiful now, but the supply of trout and bass is said to be generous here.

This 10-mile lap does also offer your best opportunity for back-packing if you can arrange a shuttle. Plan to leave a car at the Willow Park Golf Course and spend the night at Chabot Family Camp before you pick it up. Reservations are suggested, and camping rates are modest, particularly during the off-season months of November, December, and January.

A Stroll on Crown Beach

With so much of the bay shoreline given over to nonrecreational uses, it is especially nice to find a sand beach stretching along more than 2 miles of the Alameda coast. Granted, the sand must be hauled in and put into place, but it seems only right that modern techniques be used to restore (as much as possible) rather than alter a public treasure like a beach.

Crown Beach has actually had its goodly share of being altered in days gone by. From the 1870s to the 1930s, what started out as a fine broad natural beach with great swimming offshore was the site of amusement parks. There were fancy swimming pools built near it (and gaslit for starlight swims) and resort hotels with elegant restaurants and bars. In 1916, even more ambitious entrepreneurs took over the area and created Neptune Beach, complete with a dance pavilion, illuminated boardwalk, 8,000-seat stadium (Edwin Booth performed here, and "Gentleman Jim" Corbett and Bob Fitzsimmons both sparred in it), a skating rink, two swimming pools, a merry-go-round, amusement park rides, a roller coaster, you name it. As a finishing touch, Neptune Beach had a 100-foot entrance gate in the shape of a Moorish tower. It was sometimes called the Coney Island of the West (everybody, it seemed, wanted to have a Coney Island at hand), and it was enormously popular for a couple of decades. One of its specialties was sponsoring the 14-mile Around the Island swim (Alameda Island, that is); every swimmer had a boat alongside, complete with Boy Scout aboard to send wigwag signals in Morse code. But in the late thirties, however, Neptune Beach fell victim to changing times and went bankrupt. Now it is only a memory.

During World War II, the military took over the beach and turned it into a maritime training center. The long green building now used for the Crab Cove visitor center and naturalists' programs and displays was a military hospital, and the brown two-story boat-shaped structure that is now the maintenance center was the erstwhile training center—called the Glory of the Sea. The beach became a state park in 1959, and the East Bay Regional Park District took over its management in 1967. Long known as Alameda Beach, it was renamed the Robert W. Crown Memorial Beach in honor of the late state legislator who helped gain its protection.

Unfortunately, while buildings can be demolished or pressed into appropriate service, the mechanism of a complex body of water like the bay, once disrupted, can not so easily be put back together again. The great fills that have occurred around the bay have been responsible for major alteration of tidal flows; and what was once a broad sandy beach has been reduced to the narrow strip of (imported) sand that you see today. (And what was once an island to be swum around is now all but smothered with pumped-up sand and development.)

Crown Beach, however, is still special. It is to be savored for the somewhat wistful memories it evokes, as well as for its natural features (it is used extensively by park naturalists for its tidepool exhibits, and Crab Cove is a designated marine reserve), its stunning views, and the opportunities it offers for being close to the wind, the sky, and the bay itself. *Note:* A wheelchair ramp allows disabled access to the tidepools.

The best time to walk on Crown Beach is early in the morning or when it's a little overcast—if you want to be alone. (Sunsets can be breathtaking, too.) This is a very popular park, especially in warm weather. People come to sunbathe, fly kites, shell hunt, build sand castles (there's an annual sand castle contest held in June), windsurf, and to look for birds (you'll probably find good birding for seabirds during high tides in the fall and winter, and good birding for shorebirds when the tides are low; there are freshwater lagoons near the visitor center, and the marshes at the southern end of the beach—the Elsie Roemer Bird Sanctuary—too). There are 2½ miles of bayside that you can find your way along. The sight of San Francisco across the water can be gorgeous, especially when there's a hint of fog in the air; and there are few places where you can better feel the primeval tidal rhythms of the bay. You may want to pick up a tide table at a sporting goods store before you visit Crown Beach, or consult your daily paper. It's apt to be breezy here, so dress accordingly.

While people also swim off Crown Beach, and there's a bathhouse for changing, you may want to think twice about taking a dip in these bay waters; there are no lifeguards. Dogs are allowed only on the lawn areas and paved pathways along the shore—on leash—and there's a fee for them. The Crab Cove visitor center is well worth a visit, especially if you're with children.

To reach Crown Beach and Crab Cove by car, from Oakland, go west on Webster Street through the Oakland-Alameda tunnel and stay on Webster to Central Avenue; there turn right one block to McKay, then left on McKay to the parking area at the visitor center. There's a modest parking fee on weekends and holidays. For alternative access, see Crown Memorial Beach, under East Bay Parklands. *Note for bicyclists:* An 8-mile, generally level shorefront ride is possible through Crown Beach park and around San Leandro Bay; telephone the Bay Trail people (510-464-7935) for a map if you're interested.

PART VI

South Bay

San Mateo and Santa Clara Counties

Being, as it were, an extension of San Francisco itself, San Mateo County has always been a close relative of the city by the Golden Gate. After all, San Francisco shares the San Andreas Fault with it, and the bay's waters wash the contiguous shorelines of the two counties. As a matter of fact, San Francisco and San Mateo were once one and the same county, and even now, San Francisco's cemeteries, its major water supply, and its international airport are inside the boundaries of the county to its south. Santa Clara, on the other hand, has always been closely linked with the county to its north, Alameda; the Mission San Jose is inside the boundaries of that county, and Luis María Peralta, who was granted the land that became the cities of the East Bay, preferred to live out his long life in his hometown, San Jose, founded in 1777, the first civil settlement in California. (His small adobe, built in 1797, still stands there, the only survivor of the Spanish houses built in that city.) Still, the two counties south of San Francisco are usually referred to together as "the Peninsula," and "down the Peninsula" is a familiar phrase in the lexicon of San Franciscans. Linked though it may be to other parts of the bay, however, the Peninsula has a distinct character of its own.

Geologically, San Mateo has that same interesting formation that distinguishes West Marin; the edge of the Pacific Plate is inexorably pressing an alien chunk of land—rafted from hundreds of miles away to the south—against and along the continent here, creating a major zone of grinding contact, the San Andreas Fault. In San Mateo County, the chunk of "foreign" land is a great deal larger than is

Marin's Point Reyes "island." Looking at a map, you can see a clear delineation of the fault running through San Andreas Lake (San Francisco's Crystal Springs Reservoir) and more or less dividing the northern part of the county in half. Standing at the Midpeninsula Regional Open Space District's Los Trancos Preserve, you can look north and south along the San Andreas Fault and see quite clearly how it shapes the landscape. (Interestingly, the fault proves to be dexterous and even climbs the mountains here.) Santa Clara County, on the other hand, lies inland in the valley between the coast mountains and those associated with that other major fault, the Hayward. It is restless country, all of the Peninsula, with a long history of earthquakes. Santa Clara also has its problems with a vulnerable groundwater supply.

Until the coming of the Spanish in the late eighteenth century, the Peninsula knew no map-drawn boundaries, for the people occupying it thought differently of the land. Ohlone Indians, descendants of the first immigrants who arrived unknown millennia ago, shared the bounty of the land and its coasts. They built their dwelling places and their boats from the supple reeds that grew in the marshes; for their utensils, they wove fine grasses so tightly that their baskets could hold water. (Unfortunately, almost none of these extraordinary baskets have survived, but one can be seen at the Los Altos Library in Santa Clara County.) They subsisted on acorns from the plenitude of oaks that dotted the hillsides, on deer and small game, and on the riches of the tidal flats and the bay. Like their cousins to the north, the Ohlones were helpless before the Spanish when the latter arrived in the late eighteenth century. As a contemporary report noted succinctly, "[They] . . . yielded their savage liberty to the service of their Creator under the direction of the missionaries." Within a few decades, their culture was destroyed, and most of them, too—victims of alien ways and diseases. One place name, Mount Umunhum (to the south in Santa Clara County), recalls these people poignantly: *umunhum* is believed to mean "the resting place of the hummingbird," and to the Ohlones, the hummingbird—along with the eagle and the coyote—was a creator of the world. (Mount Umunhum was one of the four mountains considered sacred by the Bay Area Indians; the other three were Mount Hamilton, Mount Diablo, and Mount Tamalpais.) Shell mounds and fragments of a remembered past are virtually all else that remain.

The Spanish actually arrived on the scene one late October day in

1769. Led by Gaspar de Portolá, they were earnestly looking for Monterey, and they had beat their way along the coast and through the mountains for the length of what would become San Mateo County. A hunting party from the group inadvertently discovered the great bay to the north and east of them, but it was not what Portolá was after, so they turned around and left. (Fortunately, the site from which Portolá and his men first viewed the bay is preserved in the Golden Gate National Recreation Area; see Sweeney Ridge). Ill and exhausted, members of the party were evidently much more impressed by the fleas (they called one of their camps, a deserted Indian village on Purisima Creek, Rancheria de las Pulgas, as Father Crespi noted in his diary) and by the tall redwoods (as in Palo Alto, named for the towering redwood under which the party camped; the tree stood until the early 1980s) than by anything else. But those who followed them made up for that.

As in other parts of the bay, the establishment of a mission was the first order of business when the Spanish returned and settled, less than ten years later. Mission de Santa Clara de Asis was founded by Father Tomás de la Peña in early January 1777. (Mission San Jose, now in Alameda County, was dedicated 20 years later.) Along with the missions would come the presidios and the pueblos, or villages. Pueblo de San José de Guadalupe, now San Jose—and actually the first European settlement in California—was brought into being and named by José Joaquin Moraga in late November 1777, in accordance with the orders of his governor, Felipe de Neve.

Such civilized development required land, of course, and along with the souls of the Indians, the Spanish Fathers appropriated enormous pieces of Indian territory—sometimes hundreds of thousands of acres in size—for their ranchos. The Spanish military leaders who founded the towns and meted out the civil lands generally contented themselves—and their faithful soldiers, who didn't get much else— with (relatively) smaller acreages. The mission ranchos were used to run the cattle, which ended up as hide and tallow—and which, incidentally, introduced the Old World grasses that displaced the tall-growing bunchgrasses native to the Peninsula.

When Mexico took over California and decreed the secularization of the missions, those in charge used the mission land for more grants to more faithful soldiers—and to friends and family members, including non-Spanish sons-in-law. There were a number of such grants made throughout the Peninsula, and handsome ones they

were, though none equaled in size those amassed by General Vallejo
in the North Bay or the grand piece of land that was divvied among
the Peraltas in the East Bay. One grant, claimed by the Arguello family, did come to 35,250 acres; it, like Portolá's camp, was named in
honor of the ubiquitous little insects—Rancho de las Pulgas.
Another, bestowed on the Alviso brothers, totaled 17,783 acres. And
still another, Rancho Buri Buri, given to José Antonio Sanchez in
1836, consisted of some 15,000 acres. Sanchez gathered his family
and friends together to help him survey this one, and it took two men
all morning to measure the extent of the perimeter—25 miles. (The
men used lariats—or cordels—that were 50 Castillian *varas* long,
and while one man sat still on his horse holding an end of the lariat,
the other rode ahead the distance of its length; the process was then
reversed.) A Sanchez adobe still stands. Jacob Leese, married to one
of General Vallejo's sisters and the father of the first white child born
in San Francisco, got himself a 9,500-acre grant south of the city.
Son-in-law John Coppinger, a deserter from the British navy, and
James Pease, who jumped a Hudson's Bay Company ship, were each
granted significant pieces of Peninsula land. Señor Candelario Miramontes was given two ranchos to take care of his "long" (*tan larga*)
family of 13 children, and his friend Tiburcio Vasquez (cousin of the
famous bandit of the same name), with almost as large a family, got
a good-size grant right next to Miramontes' along the Pacific coast.
There were even two "Christian Indians"—sturdy survivors—who
received a "league of land" between them.

And so it went. And so, too, did it go when the Americans seized
California. There were countless Yankee squatters who simply took
what they thought should be theirs. There was endless litigation over
the legitimacy of Mexican and Spanish claims, and over boundaries,
as well. And most of the original grantees ended up all but landless—
and broke from paying lawyers. One family, notably, fared well; the
Leonetto Ciprianis (titled Italians) had the good fortune to engage a
clever lawyer, S. M. Mezes, who took care of them—and, incidentally, of himself.

When California became an official state of the Union, it set about
dividing itself into counties. Santa Clara County was among the first
established, being named on January 18, 1850. San Francisco
County (out of which San Mateo County would be carved some six
years later) was created a week later. The lands of the new counties
were in a hodgepodge of what can best be described as fluid owner-

ships, but this in no way deterred those pioneer American settlers who liked what they found down the Peninsula. If they could not get away with "squatting," they demanded "free governmental land" and then took it, by hook or by crook.

What drew many of them southward from San Francisco was the presence of the *Sequoia sempervirens*. The great trees crowded the canyons and stood on the ridges of the mountains closest to the sea, gathering the moisture carried to them by the fog. Condensing on their feathery fronds, the fog drops kept them cool and watered even in the hottest weather. (Redwoods to the north in Humboldt County are known to add as much as 30 inches to the annual rainfall in fog drip.) There were extensive forests of redwoods on the Peninsula that had thrived throughout the millennia—how many millions of years we do not know—but the days of most of them became numbered when the energetic axmen got to work. As in the East Bay, fortunes were made from those virgin forests, and many of the Peninsula place names—Redwood City (a squatters' town there changed the original name of Mezesville—named for the wily lawyer), Page Mill Road, Woodside (the center of the sawmills), for example—bear testimony to this flourishing early industry. Fortunately, the Peninsula forests were not totally cut out as were those of the East Bay, but enough were cleared—and enough oaks were cut for firewood—that by 1860, more and more of those early pioneers were turning from logging to farming, dairying, tanning (there was an ample supply of tanbark oak), salt drying, and winemaking.

By then, San Mateo had become a county as a result of political shenanigans in San Francisco. In 1856, the city of San Francisco was in the hands—and the pocket—of one Billy Mulligan, who had brought the techniques of Tammany Hall to the city by the Golden Gate. The debt of the young city topped $3.5 million, and the good citizens rose up in protest. Because Mulligan's machine was using the county of San Francisco—so large and remote that it was hard to keep tags on it—for its own ends (a city of San Francisco crook could be tried in San Francisco County by one of Mulligan's judges, pardoned, and so escape justice), a solution to some of the problems seemed to be to make the city and the county smaller, more manageable, and one and the same. The state legislature did so, and what was left of the original San Francisco County became a new county of its own, named San Mateo (Saint Matthew) in deference to its Spanish heritage. Mulligan did, however, get in a final bit of finagling: he managed to have the border drawn a mile north of the one originally proposed so as to keep one of his cronies in the new county, which he intended to take over. He then managed to stuff the ballot boxes of the first San Mateo election but was soon afterward run out of town, and his cronies with him.

Until 1864, the principal overland route from San Francisco to the Peninsula was the road that had started out as a mission trail grooved by the footsteps of the padres, gone on to become a county road, and ended up as El Camino Real—"the royal highway"—which is still in use. (The name goes back to the days of the Roman Empire, when all roads were, literally, royal roads, and all roads, in fact, led to Rome.) El Camino Real was a lovely road in those days, bordered on each side by towering eucalyptus and elms. The waters of the bay added sparkle to the view eastward, while the "Sierra Morena Mountains [the Coast Ranges] lent their beauty and grandeur" to the westward vista. (Eucalyptus trees were set out in large groves in the 1860s in the belief that they had an "anti-bilious quality," "absorbed malaria," and that their "roots act as a sponge, pumping water and draining ground and emitting odorous antiseptic emanations from [their] leaves." Because people were convinced that each tree "absorbed from the soil ten times its weight in water every twenty-four hours," the trees were felt to be especially suited for planting—and thus drying up—the Peninsula's marshes.)

Initiated during the early 1850s, there was regular stagecoach service to the south for years: from Woodside to San Francisco, the ride took nine hours and cost $32. There was marine service, too: (horse-drawn) carloads of slaughtered wildfowl—geese, ducks, curlews, and snipe were shot in immense numbers—were loaded onto schooners out of Redwood City bound for San Francisco, and redwood logs and lumber went the same way. (One notable load shipped out in 1859 was 70,000 redwood shingles hauled out of the "top of the mountain" by one William Weaver.) Ferries also plied between many of the South Bay ports. It was the ferry *Jenny Lind,* a trim little side-wheeler, bound from Alviso to San Francisco, that exploded when its boiler burst one day in 1853; the accident took the lives of 31 people—a lot of souls at a time of a scanty population—including those of San Jose's first postmaster and first city clerk and that of the industrious San Francisco son-in-law John Reed, who had married a Sanchez daughter.

During those days of relative isolation, small villages grew up around the few centers of commerce. Along with Woodside, Redwood City, San Jose, and Alviso, there were the settlements along the coast, Purisima, Pescadero, and Half Moon Bay. (Known for decades as Spanishtown, the latter was, until 1866, more populous than Redwood City.) Although the halcyon days of the Spanish grandees were gone, life moved at a pleasant pace. People lived closely with their land, and their land was both beautiful and bountiful. (Along with everything else, fishing was fabulous: in three hours of one February day in 1861, E. K. Howes caught 130 "fine mountain trout" out of San Mateo Creek—a waterway that was subsequently impounded to make the Crystal Springs Reservoir.)

Looking back, it might seem that those early times were idyllic, but they had their dangers, too. Earthquakes were frequent and sometimes devastating: one in 1868 totally destroyed the courthouse in Redwood City. Grizzly bears were a constant menace, and so were mountain lions. (A man almost lost his life in 1863 when he got between a lioness and her cub.) Travel by horse, and by horse-drawn vehicle, was almost as dangerous as travel by automobile would be later. People were thrown from their mounts frequently. Horses hauling wagons could bolt or shy and fling out their cargo—human and otherwise—often with dire results: one poor man was tossed headfirst into the mud and that was the end of him. Farmers fell into their threshing machines. Fires raged unchecked through communities and forests: "Another hotel burned to the ground last night," wrote a newspaper reporter in early 1864, "and a woman sprang from her window into a tree"; it did not hold her and she perished. Murder was not at all uncommon: in 1863, Tiburcio Vasquez was killed while he sat drinking his wine in a Half Moon Bay saloon; the motive was not recorded, but the slaying was described as "deliberate." There were shipwrecks along the coast, often at Año Nuevo. (A later one at Pescadero washed ashore a cargo of white paint, and for years all the buildings in the town were white.)

With a small talent pool, versatile people were at a premium, and an energetic soul could go far: one San Mateo man was a justice of the peace, a notary public, an agent for the state telegraph service, postmaster, secretary of the San Mateo and Half Moon Bay Turnpike Road Company, a magistrate, town clerk, conservator of the public peace, a clerk of St. Matthew's Church, and the agent of all the insurance companies in the county; when a railroad finally went into operation down the Peninsula, he became a clerk for it, too.

It was also a time of great good humor: a surprising number of prisoners "fell out" of jail and escaped when they leaned against the jail door and it "suddenly opened." One Mrs. Yates walloped a maligner with a black snake and was fined $12; "It was dog cheap, wasn't it?" was her comment. The first hearse in San Mateo County was greeted with the straight-faced remark that it "met a long-felt need."

When the first railroad linked San Francisco to San Jose, it ushered in a new era. (Named straightforwardly enough the San Francisco–San Jose Railroad, the line was later acquired by Southern Pacific.) The time was 1864, and wealthy San Franciscans were already beginning to build their "country homes" down the Peninsula (merchant William D. M. Howard was the first, in the 1850s; his was one of the earliest prefab houses in California, being freighted "bodily" by ship from New England), and the men had been traveling back and forth to their businesses by horse-drawn vehicles. (Billy Ralston was one of them, and when the railroad started running, he took great pleasure in beating it by racing his horses—in relays—to literally nose out the train.) Now the commute would be more comfortable and, for all but Ralston, quicker, and guests could be accommodated in a special car when a big party was being thrown. With easier access, more and more wealthy San Franciscans bought estates in the lovely countryside to the south.

The names of many of those country squires down the Peninsula became legendary. There was the aforementioned Ralston: he built his "palatial residence" (still standing) in Belmont and in 1870 entertained Civil War generals Sherman and Scofield—transported by "special train" from San Francisco—at a party that was described as "the greatest affair ever given by any private citizen in the United States." Ralston thought nothing of employing 70 whites and 80 Chinese to build a 100-million-gallon reservoir. (When Ralston died in 1875, the locals were "struck into gloom.") There was Ralston's "friend," William Sharon, who took over Ralston's estate after his death, and later married off his daughter to Sir Thomas Hespeth in a "society wedding" there that was front-page news. There was Darius Ogden Mills, millionaire banker (and, incidentally, owner of the largest dairy in the state), who built a mansion that was pronounced "a castle"—with one master bedroom finished entirely in mother-of-pearl and another in ebony—at Millbrae, a community named for himself and later described as being "as attractive and beautiful as anywhere in the world." (Mills also headed the Crystal Springs

Water Company that supplied Peninsulans with piped water in 1870.) Mills Field, among other things, remembers this tycoon. There was ex-bartender James Flood of railroad fame, who poured the better part of $18 million into his "Linden Towers," labeled by one neighbor "Flood's wedding cake," and by another, a "beautiful atrocity." (The plumbing fixtures were sterling silver.) There was Alvinza Hayward, whose wife was said to have once taken in washing; his estate had its own racetrack, a fenced-in park containing deer and elk, and a lake for swans and ducks. The harnesses for his horses were mounted in silver. (It was not uncommon for a horse to be bought—or sold—for over $5,000.) There was Leland Stanford (despite the railroad, a stage robber was captured on the Stanford estate—later Stanford University—in 1882), who had a cemetery for his horses with a statue of each on its grave. And there were Faxon D. Atherton, Anson Burlingame (the ambassador to China, who, it is said, was persuaded by Ralston to buy—although he never built—in return for having a town named for him), Charles Lux, James Phelan (whose Villa Montalvo happily endures), James Lick (his home also still stands), J. A. Folger, August Schilling, and W. B. Bourn (whose Woodside estate, Filoli, designed by Willis Polk, is still a showpiece)—the list reads like a Who's Who of nineteenth- and early twentieth-century capitalists. Elegant communities for the elite, who were only slightly less well endowed, also became notable: Hillsborough, for example, was one; it was designed without sidewalks because its homeowners never walked along the streets.

The presence of so much wealth was a mainstay of the local economy; the building, improvement, and maintenance of the grand estates kept a great many people gainfully employed. Agriculture, however, early became a booming industry down the Peninsula, and it remained so for many decades. Bayard Taylor described the "huge stacks of sheaves in immense wheatfields, flashing like perfect gold; the grain cleaner, purer, more brilliant in color than any we had ever seen . . . and the most superb orchards and vineyards springing up everywhere." Not surprisingly, the Southern Pacific boasted, soon after it began serving San Jose, that it hauled more fresh fruits and berries than any other railroad in the United States. The Santa Clara Valley became renowned for its magnificent fruit orchards—prunes, cherries, apricots; in the spring, San Franciscans journeyed by the hundreds to enjoy the blossoms that filled the valley with clouds of soft colors and subtly perfumed the lambent air.

As soon as the orchardists started laying out the rows of fruit trees in the Santa Clara Valley, they began to worry about water. Average annual rainfall—always critical in the Bay Area weather—became a crucial concern. It was soon evident that they would have to look underground for the water the clouds did not deliver. (Morgan Hill, in southern Santa Clara County, was so desperate for rain in 1924 that it paid a rainmaker $1,000, and promised him $4,000 more, to produce 5 inches in four weeks; he disappeared.) By 1892, the fruit-growers had sunk 100 wells for irrigation; in 1920, there were 1,700 wells in use. Between 1912 and 1920, the percentage of lands being irrigated jumped from 29 percent to 90 percent. As a consequence, the groundwater level began to drop alarmingly; it fell 64.5 feet between 1915 and 1930. The ground began to drop, too; between 1912 and 1936, San Jose sank 5 feet. Dam building and diversion of small streams were tried, but the demand for water kept growing. And, although increasingly sophisticated methods have been employed to rectify the situation, the problem of subsidence continues. And the vulnerable soil—and the annual average rainfall—remain very much the same.

Along with fruit, walnuts proved to be another lucrative crop. And then there were the vines. The good Spanish Fathers had started raising grapes at the Santa Clara Mission as one of their first endeavors, and one wine lover later said that they produced a "fine red wine." And one of the earliest settlers, Antonio Mario Suñol, was selling wine he produced at San Jose as early as 1823. Pierre Sansevain started his vineyard at San Jose in 1845 and by 1865 was turning out champagne. Many others set out grapes in the Santa Clara Valley— and then moved to the ridges for more suitable soil and a cooler climate. (Montebello Ridge had eight wineries going strong on it in the 1890s.) By 1880, Santa Clara County growers were turning out 2.5 million gallons of wine annually. It took Prohibition to slow down the Peninsula's wine industry, but after the 1930s it made a good comeback. (Today, there are many small wineries—and a few large ones— producing excellent wines. The Cabernet Sauvignon, Pinot Noir, and Chardonnay grapes do especially well here. A visit to this wine country—and perhaps to one of its lovely parks—can make for a most pleasant outing. See Los Trancos Earthquake Trail for details.)

In an age when mining was a magic word, prospectors were out exploring early on. Every once in a while, one would announce a trace of gold in a quartz vein, but it turned out that gold was not one of the local treasures. Quicksilver was. Discovered by the Spanish as early as 1824, a rich lode of cinnabar lay in the hills to the south of San Jose. Most of it proved to be within the rancho of José de los Reyes Berryessa (who was killed by Kit Carson in the Bear Republic Revolt), but Andres Castillero filed a mining claim on it—the first in California—and it then passed into the hands of an English company that named it New Almaden, after the Almaden Mine in Spain. The New Almaden Mine proved to be the most productive quicksilver operation on the continent, and it was worked until 1913. (From 1870 to 1892, one James B. Randol presided over it and established a singularly successful company town.)

Being the oldest community in California, it was not surprising that San Jose was chosen as the first (really the first?) state capital (see Solano County), but it lost that distinction in 1851 after only two sessions of the legislature were held there. This did not stop the little city from prospering, however, especially after it became the terminus of the railroad. Being the center of one of California's most productive agricultural areas, it had lots going on, and it naturally attracted the "agricultural industry"—canning. Del Monte, Libby, and Pict Sweet all set up businesses nearby. And as time went on, other major industries moved into the South Bay—DuPont, General Motors, Lockheed, Kaiser, Ford, General Electric, Westinghouse, and Leslie Salt (which acquired a large chunk of the South Bay itself), to name a few.

The mission settlement of Santa Clara was the site of the first two centers of higher education down the Peninsula: Santa Clara College was founded there by the Reverend John Nobili, S.J., in 1851 (it is now Santa Clara University); and California Wesleyan University was established there in 1852 (it ended up the University of the Pacific, located in Stockton). But it was Palo Alto—largely in Santa Clara County, but still claimed by San Mateo—that got the educational plum when Leland Stanford established a university there in 1891 in memory of his only son, who died at the age of 17. (Because of a clause in Stanford's bequest, the city of Palo Alto did not sell alcoholic beverages for over 70 years.) Stanford University, known by its students as the farm (it is close to 10,000 acres in size and has many marvelous things going on—including the linear accelerator), was to become one of the top campuses in the country, and it was also to play a seminal role in the growth of the Peninsula.

Other towns around the South Bay prospered over the years. Redwood City had the tanneries (which shut down in the 1950s, after the supply of tanbark oaks dwindled) and the breweries, and Colma got the lucrative trade of the cemetery business. (San Mateo provides the land, and San Francisco pays the taxes.) San Mateo became the county seat. Millbrae got the international airport (opened as Mills Field in 1927; it was an embarrassment in 1929 when Lindbergh's plane got stuck in the mud there). The coastal towns, however, being more isolated (they did not get a road across the mountains for decades), grew more slowly. (There is still, happily, a pioneer quality to places like Pescadero, San Gregorio, and Half Moon Bay.)

Like other parts of the Bay Area, the Peninsula opened its arms to victims of the 1906 quake, and many people "discovered" the lovely country south of San Francisco—and remained. Daly City came into being when San Franciscans quartered in refugee shacks were ordered out of the city's parks: many paid $20 for the shack, and another $20 to move it onto friendly John Daly's farm, where lots were going cheap. Daly City (storied by folksinger Malvina Reynolds) could be a good place to look for these "little boxes." Like other parts of the Bay Area, too, the Peninsula was "discovered" again during World War II and was inundated by more people—and more heavy industries—in the postwar years. It was the coming of the electronics age, however, that brought the area its greatest influx of people and business—and headaches. Because Stanford University was a major center of early electronic development, it was natural enough that the original companies moved in nearby: IBM was the first, in the late forties. By 1955, 36 electronic firms were doing business near Stanford; in 1962, there were 152, 78 of which were in Palo Alto. (A local historian noted that "every town had at least one.") Everyone rejoiced, for the electronic industry—unlike many of the others nearby—was thought to be "clean."

But this was only the beginning; electronic production, and with it, population, skyrocketed not only around Stanford but in the beautiful Santa Clara Valley. As a result, orchardists were faced with paying ever higher taxes or selling out to avid subdividers. Slowly—at first—the orchards began to fall. Still, in 1966, Santa Clara County was producing almost a third of California's fruits, and a twelfth of the country's canned, dried, and frozen fruits. But the tempo quickened, and today it is hard to find an orchard among the pleasant ranch-style houses that cover the land. The once blossom-filled Santa Clara Valley has become computer chip–filled Silicon

Valley, instead. And, compounding the usual problems of such a pro-found change—social, economic, and environmental—there is the further problem of what to do with the toxic wastes produced by the electronic industry, which turned out to be less "clean" than had been thought. It is particularly disturbing to consider the implications of poisoning the delicate groundwater supply.

The Peninsula counties, however, are trying hard to hang on to the naturally beautiful environment that still remains—and a wonderful amount still does because of the efforts of local environmentalists. Both Santa Clara and San Mateo have set aside thousands of acres in county parks. Many of the Peninsula cities have established sizable parks, as well: Mountain View, for example, has nearly 700 acres of bay frontage, which it has reclaimed from a garbage dump and trans-formed into a charming waterfront park. Palo Alto has more than 1,200 protected acres on the bay and an environmental center staffed with a fine naturalist. (It is now possible to walk along the bay front here for several miles on publicly owned trails, and efforts are ongo-ing to create an unbroken trail around the southern end of the bay.) Add to this the wonderful state parks down the Peninsula and the lands of the Midpeninsula Regional Open Space District (MROSD) (voted into existence in 1972 under the same act that made possible the establishment of the East Bay Regional Parks almost four decades earlier), which come to more than 41,000 acres and are still increas-ing. Furthermore, there's icing on the cake: sparked by local conser-vationists, the two Peninsula counties, several of their cities, and the MROSD—along with the state—have worked together to establish protected and extensive trail systems that not only run through the parks but frequently link them, at times via easements. (Some Penin-sula communities require that trail easements be included in all sub-divisions within their boundaries.) Thus, long and lovely pathways provide unusual opportunities to explore the countrysides, the forests, the mountains, and the streamsides of many parts of the Peninsula—on foot, on horseback, or on bicycles. The grand total is a marvelous outdoor resource. And while this resource is a particu-lar pleasure for the people living nearby, it also offers fine outdoor experiences to others who visit the area. The following section on Peninsula Parklands should give an idea of the pleasures in store.

Note: The Midpeninsula Open Space Trust (MOST) has played a major role in gaining new parklands on the Peninsula, and continues to do so.

Peninsula Parklands

The Peninsula parklands are especially attractive on clear winter days, in the springtime, and in the autumn. Summer in the inland valleys can bring fiercely hot days. Then you might choose to enjoy a coastal park, or a shady streamside walk, or a stroll among the redwoods. Expect gently rolling hills as well as steep banked canyons and, in places, especially interesting geological formations. Expect, also, breathtaking wildflower shows in the spring. *Note:* Directions are given from San Francisco.

The Parks of San Mateo County

Coyote Point County Recreation Area—This is a large (727-acre) developed recreation area on San Francisco Bay. There's fishing, picnicking, swimming, sailboarding, children's playgrounds, a boat-launching ramp and marina, an animal center, and the usual facilities of water and restrooms plus a restaurant. There are facilities for the disabled. This is also where the Coyote Point Museum—which has an outstanding environmental exhibit on the bay ecosystems—is located. Along with all its other niceties, this park also has fine views across the bay, and the usual (albeit graceful) grove of eucalyptus.

Access: Take Highway 101 south from San Francisco, and about 5 miles past the airport, watch for signs to the recreation area. Coming from the north, you must follow a circuitous route, but persevere, it's worth it. (Approaching from the south, it's a straight shot.)

Edgewood County Park and Preserve—Located about 45 minutes south of San Francisco on the Junipero Serra Freeway (I-280)—the "most beautiful freeway in the United States"—Edgewood Park is an island of grassland, oak woodland, and chaparral communities in the middle of expanding urban development. Before its acquisition by the county and the Midpeninsula Regional Open Space District, this

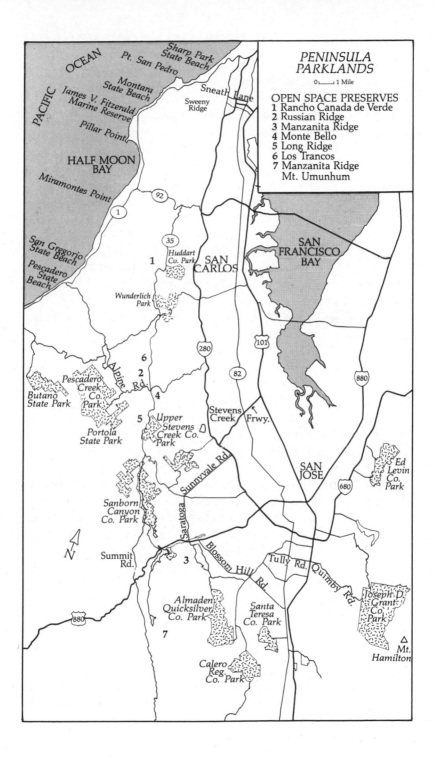

PENINSULA
PARKLANDS

0 ⊢——⊣ 1 Mile

OPEN SPACE PRESERVES
1 Rancho Canada de Verde
2 Russian Ridge
3 Manzanita Ridge
4 Monte Bello
5 Long Ridge
6 Los Trancos
7 Manzanita Ridge
Mt. Umunhum

PACIFIC OCEAN

Sharp Park
State Beach
Pt. San Pedro
Montara
State Beach
Sneath Lane
James V. Fitzgerald
Marine Reserve
Sweeny
Ridge
Pillar Point
HALF MOON
BAY
Miramontes Point
San Gregorio
State Beach
Pescadero
State
Beach

92
1
35
Huddart
Co. Park
1
SAN
CARLOS
SAN
FRANCISCO
BAY

Wunderlich
Park

6
Alpine Rd.
2
4
280
101
82
880

Pescadero
Creek
Co.
Park
Butano
State Park

5
Upper
Stevens
Creek Co.
Park
Stevens
Creek
Frwy.

Portola
State Park

Sunnyvale Rd.

SAN
JOSE
680

Ed
Levin
Co.
Park

Sanborn
Canyon
Co. Park

Saratoga

N

Summit
Rd.
3
Blossom Hill Rd.
Tully Rd.
Quimby Rd.

Joseph D.
Grant
Co.
Park

880
7
Almaden
Quicksilver
Co. Park
Santa
Teresa
Co. Park
Mt.
Hamilton

Calero
Reg.
Co. Park

467 acres of serpentine soil was a playground for motorbikers; now it has been "redesigned" into a gem of a wildlife and wildflower sanctuary. The park shows off a succession of wildflower displays starting in late March and running into the summer (see Bay Area Wildflowers appendix). The serpentine grassland hosts many rare plant species and at least one rare butterfly. There are lovely trails— with breathtaking views—and a day camp.

Access: Take I-280 south to Edgewood Road; thence east to the park's northeast entrance and parking area.

Flood Park—A 21-acre piece of James Flood's $18-million estate (his house here, which burned, alas, was called a "beautiful atrocity"), the park has facilities for outdoor sports, including tennis. It is also known for its lovely old oak and laurel trees. There are picnicking facilities and a playground.

Access: Take Highway 101 south to Marsh Road; west to Bay Road and then south to the park.

Heritage Grove—A 38-acre natural area with old-growth redwoods and a network of trails. This park ties in with the Sam McDonald– Pescadero Creek–Portola State Park complex.

Access: Take I-280 south to Highway 84; follow Highway 84 south to La Honda; turn east on Pescadero Road and east again on Alpine Road to the grove.

Huddart Park—A large (974 acres) hillside park with facilities for hiking, horseback riding, and picnicking. It is notable for its handsome second-growth redwoods and Douglas firs, its oaks, madrones, and laurels, streams, and cool canyons. A nice place for short hikes. Its trail system ties into the Crystal Springs Riding and Hiking Trail to the north and into the Skyline Trail/Bay Area Ridge Trail to Wunderlich Park on the south.

Access: Follow Highway 84 to Kings Mountain Road in Woodside. Huddart Park is 2.2 miles to the west. (You can visit the historical Woodside Store on the way.)

James V. Fitzgerald County Marine Reserve—A 50-acre treasure of tidelands and beach. Its reefs are home to 49 species of intertidal animals and plants. There's a small interpretive center, a restroom, a picnic area, and parking area.

Access: Take Highway 1 south to Moss Beach and go west on California Street, which dead-ends in the reserve.

Junipero Serra County Park—A 108-acre foothill park that has hiking and nature trails, youth day-camping, playgrounds, picnic facilities, and fine views of San Francisco Bay (and the airport).
Access: Take I-280 south to Crystal Springs Road; turn east to the park, which is adjacent to San Bruno and Millbrae.

Memorial County Park—The oldest San Mateo County park, this one has campsites, picnic facilities, a visitor center, a swimming hole, campfire and naturalist programs, a camp store, and virgin redwoods. Its trail system links its 499 acres to nearby Pescadero Creek Park, Portola State Park, and Sam McDonald Park. Families might like to camp here on a visit to the San Mateo redwoods. Has wheelchair-accessible nature trail.
Access: Take Highway 1 south to Pescadero Road (which leads eastward to the park) if you want to combine a visit to the coast as well. Otherwise, take Highway 84 south to Pescadero Road, and thence to the west and the park entrance.

Pescadero Creek County Park—This is a grand, nearly 7,400-acre park that embraces the upper watershed of Pescadero Creek, a major steelhead spawning stream that flows year-round. There are hike-in camps and hiking and horseback-riding trails. The Pomponio Trail and the Old Haul Road Trail run through this park to link Portola State Park (on the east) to Memorial County Park (on the west).
Access: Take I-280 south to Highway 84; follow Highway 84 south to Alpine Road; thence to park entrance.

Sam McDonald County Park—Rolling grasslands, old-growth redwoods, and Douglas firs, along with views of the ocean, make this a popular park. It has youth camps, a horsemen's camp, and a Sierra Club hiker's hut, which involves about 1½ miles of walking. (Call the Loma Prieta Chapter at 650-390-8411 for reservations; there is a small fee.) Sam McDonald's trail system ties its 1,000 acres into the trails of Pescadero Creek Park, Portola State Park, and Memorial County Park.
Access: Take I-280 south to Highway 84; follow Highway 84 to La Honda; take Pescadero Road south 6 miles to reach the park

entrance. Or take Highway 1 south to Pescadero Road and proceed eastward past Memorial County Park to park entrance.

San Bruno Mountain County Park—Early Spanish explorers climbed San Bruno Mountain, and it was probably named for the patron saint of one of them, Captain Bruno Hecate, who mapped the bay and the lands around it. The first settlers found it ideal for grazing, and when Jacob Leese was granted it in 1836 as part of his Rancho Cañada de Guadalupe, Visitacion y Rodeo Viejo, he ran his cattle on it too. In fact, it was used primarily for grazing through World War II, although a large holding on it—some 3,800 acres—had been sold in the 1870s and sold again in the 1880s to H. W. Crocker. When the population began soaring in the Bay Area in the 1950s and 1960s, San Bruno Mountain became the center of contention: what to do with it? Various interests argued bitterly over the answer. One ambitious scheme called for dismantling it and using its rock for fill. Another proposed its massive subdivision into a residential, commercial, and industrial complex (this would have located 20,000 people on it). And still another plea was to simply leave it alone, for it is unique in the Bay Area not only for its geography but—despite the decades of grazing—for its flora, which includes 14 species of rare or endangered plants, and its fauna, which includes 3 species of rare butterflies, 2 of them endangered. It was also already a precious island of open space. While the fight went on, the mountain became the favored recreation area for motorcycles and off-road vehicles.

It was the endangered butterflies that finally won the park: it was decreed that their environment must be preserved. One developer noted, a little sourly, that, surely, Congress had not had butterflies in mind when it wrote the Endangered Species Act. But the act was law, and the butterflies gained at least a modicum of protection. So San Bruno Mountain is now a 2,267-acre state and county park, and it offers many pleasures to people who enjoy the out-of-doors. (The developers got part of it, too, it should be noted; they also donated 500 acres to the park.) Geologists may be interested in this fault block composed largely of graywacke (a mixture of sandstone and shale); it is considered an outlying part of the Santa Cruz Mountains. Hikers will find at least eight nice hikes—they can enjoy a 3-plus-mile summit loop, which gains 725 feet, or a ½-mile turn around a bog, and strolls that are in between. Botanizers and entomologists will, of course, have a field day. Spring comes to the mountain early, often in

February when the iris begin to mist the slopes with blue and purple; the gold of poppies may follow or the soft creamy hue of wallflowers and the glowing red of coast rock cress. (Elizabeth McClintock and Walter Knight in their definitive work *A Flora of the San Bruno Mountains* have counted 384 species—see Bibliography.) One 150-acre slope (above April Brook, not far from Radio Road, which leads to the summit), which has the most varied mix of annuals, is known simply as the Flower Garden. It puts on a succession of shows from early March through May. The three species of rare and/or endangered butterflies are the callippe fritillary (*Speyeria callippe callippe*), the mission blue (*Icaricia icarioides missionensis*), and the San Bruno elfin (*Incisalia mossii bayensis*). The latter two are on the Endangered Species list. Herpetologists will also want to keep an eye out for the endangered San Francisco garter snake. (See Bay Area Amphibians and Reptiles appendix.) Situated as it is in relative isolation, 1,314-foot-high San Bruno Mountain is subject to the whims of the weather. It is frequently swept by fogs and winds. Visitors to the park should be prepared for same. *Note:* The road running to the summit, which is a private inholding, is paved and you can drive or bicycle to the parking lot there. The views are spectacular.

Access: Take Highway 101 south to the Brisbane–Cow Palace exit; continue south about 1¾ miles to Guadalupe Canyon Parkway, and there turn west for 2 miles to the park entrance. The park has picnic sites, restrooms, and a day camp.

San Mateo County Fishing Pier is located in Foster City just off Beach Park Boulevard. This 3-acre park was once part of the old San Mateo Bridge Trailhead for the Bay Trail.

Access: Take Highway 101 to East Hillside Boulevard and drive eastward to Beach Park Boulevard.

San Pedro Valley County Park encompasses the middle and south forks of San Pedro Creek, which are both steelhead spawning streams. The park is more than 1,000 acres of coastal chaparral with trails, picnic facilities, and a visitor center.

Access: Take Highway 1 to Linda Mar; go east on Linda Mar, which dead-ends at the park.

Sawyer Camp Trail, once a pioneer wagon road, is now a beautiful, surfaced 6.2-mile trail (29 acres) for hikers, joggers, horseback riders, and bicyclists. It runs through San Francisco's water district land between the west end of Hillcrest Boulevard in Millbrae and the west end of Crystal Springs Road in San Mateo. *Note:* This trail ties in with the county's 2.9-mile *San Andreas Trail,* which runs along the eastern boundary of the San Francisco watershed; nice views, but noisy from nearby traffic.

Access: Take Highway I-280 south to Black Mountain Road; west to Skyline Boulevard (Highway 35); south to South Gate.

Wunderlich Park is another nearly 1,000-acre hillside area, which has second-growth redwoods, stands of oak and madrone, and lovely open meadows (good for wildflowers in the spring). This was once Folger's Woodside estate and was later given to San Mateo County by Martin Wunderlich. The park has a beautiful 25-mile trail system with nice opportunities for hikers and horseback riders. (Wunderlich Park trails link the Skyline Trail/Ridge Trail north to Huddart Park and south to Skylonda.)

Access: Take I-280 south to Highway 84; follow Highway 84 for 2 miles through Woodside to park entrance.

Note: Sweeney Ridge is a unit of the Golden Gate National Recreation Area. It has the wonderful 360-degree panoramic view of the ocean to the bay that greeted Portolá when he and his weary men topped it one clear November day in 1769. (See Historic Hikes in the South Bay.) Milagra Ridge is a former county park that has been added to GGNRA.

San Mateo County is also home to the San Francisco Bay National Wildlife Refuge. (See Remarkable Bay Area Parklands and Preserves.)

For further information on San Mateo parks, contact the San Mateo Parks and Recreation Division, 590 Hamilton Street, Redwood City, CA 94063; telephone 650-363-4020.

The Parks of Santa Clara County

Almaden Quicksilver County Park—It was once the largest quicksilver (mercury) mine in the United States, and it stayed in production until 1926—the New Almaden Mine, it was called, and it was not only a profitable business venture, it attracted attention, and visitors, from all over the world. Even the emperor of China purchased its ware and was so pleased with the transaction that he presented the mine with a pagoda. (The pillars from it are on view at the New Almaden Quicksilver Mining Museum.) So busy was the mining operation that two "company towns" were established: one was an English town for miners from Cornwall, and the other was a Spanish town for Mexican workers. There was even separate housing for the mine's operating staff along Los Alamitos Creek. There was also a grand 27-room building called La Casa Grande, which was erected in the 1850s as a hotel, but which became the manager's (palatial) residence instead. And there were dozens of shafts, monster ore-reduction smelters, and miles of tunnels.

It had all gone ghost by the 1930s, and the Civilian Conservation Corps (CCC) was set to work demolishing the furnaces, the towns, and even their churches. Many of the shafts were covered over and the tunnels sealed off. All that remained was the New Almaden community along Los Alamitos Creek, La Casa Grande (now a restaurant)—and memories. The United States government thought enough of the place to list the mine as a historic district in the National Register of Historic Sites, and the community is within a county historic zoning district. And, in 1974, Santa Clara County purchased almost 3,600 acres of the mine property for a park. In the years since, the park has received increasing attention and has inspired the formation of a New Almaden Quicksilver County Park Association to help in its development.

Today, the Almaden Quicksilver Park is a popular parkland for hikers, riders, bicyclists, and runners. (The park's terrain has proved suitable for such events as the triathlon.) Twenty-nine miles of the old mining roads have been converted into hiking trails, and you can take an easy stroll along them, or do a strenuous ten-mile stint and tot up a 1,300-foot-elevation gain. Twenty-three miles of trails are open to equestrians; dogs, on leash, are welcome on eleven miles of trails. There is also the New Almaden Quicksilver Mining Museum (21570 Almaden Road) to visit Saturdays (12 P.M.–4 P.M. or by appointment; telephone: 408-268-3883). There's a modest fee.

Access: Take the Almaden Expressway until it becomes Almaden Road (at McKean), then continue 1½ miles to the park entrance.

Almaden Reservoir, adjacent to the old mine, is one of 11 man-made ("water conservation") lakes that are managed as county parks for their recreational use. Several of them have been developed for fishing and boating, canoeing, waterskiing, and sailboarding. (Contact the Santa Clara County Parks Department for current information on reservoir uses.) Most of these reservoirs, including Almaden, are modest in acreage, but a couple are sizable. Unfortunately, all of them are subject to drawdown, which in summer months may make of them large, muddy puddles instead of pretty lakes.

Access: See Almaden Quicksilver County Park, above.

Calero County Park—Calero Reservoir is one of the county's larger, developed "lakes" (347 acres). It has launching ramps for power boats, waterskiing, an area for water sports, and you can picnic around it. You can also hike or horseback ride along the nearly 15 miles of trail that wind through its largely unspoiled 2,074-acre watershed. The trail system often utilizes old ranch roads and riding paths that lead you beside streams and ponds, over rolling hills, and up to ridgetops that command views of the surrounding countryside. In springtime, you can walk through wildflower gardens, including some glorious ones on serpentine soil. Several hikes—ranging from easy strolls to daylong jaunts—are possible. The Calero Stables (whose headquarters occupy an 1865-vintage house) are a ½-mile drive inside the park and supply rental horses for those who choose the role of equestrian.

Access: Take Highway 101 or I-280 south to Monterey Road in San Jose; Monterey south to Bailey Avenue; Bailey west to McKean Road; thence south for ½ mile to the park's entrance.

Coyote Creek, the longest of Santa Clara's streams, rises in the Diablo Range and flows generally northwest to empty eventually into San Francisco Bay. Although its waters are impounded in Coyote Lake (south and east of Morgan Hill) and in Anderson Reservoir (with 1,200 acres, the largest of the county's "lakes"), it is free flowing year-round. Some two-thirds of Coyote Creek's 60-mile streamside is in public ownership, but trails rim only about a third of the watercourse at present. A pathway along the length of the stream from Anderson Dam to the bay, however, is "on the books."

Coyote Creek endows San Jose by flowing right through this busy metropolis, and the city has returned the compliment by protecting its streamside in three city parks—Kelley, Watson, and William Street. Should you be in this part of the world with time to spare on a hot day, you might take a refreshing saunter along Coyote Creek through *Kelley City Park,* enjoying the Japanese Friendship Garden with its ponds, its charming bridges, and its teahouse. If you're with children, you might choose a visit to the Baby Zoo and small-size railroad in the park.

Santa Clara County has completed 15 consecutive miles of paved (and unpaved) trails along Coyote Creek, from its 223-acre Coyote-Hellyer County Park to Anderson Lake County Park. This makes some special Peninsula streamside pleasures available to hikers, bicyclists, and horseback riders as well (the equestrian staging area at Burnett Avenue in Anderson Lake County Park provides access to 8 miles of horse trail, parallel to the paved trail). Parts of the paved trail are wheelchair-accessible. Coyote Creek is a charming waterway, shaded in places by sycamores and cottonwoods, and by some wonderful old oaks. It runs through a variety of countrysides, including farmland, subdivisions, and an area of percolation ponds that form the county's largest freshwater marsh. The trail through the marsh is on a levee, and it offers excellent birding, especially during periods of migration when waterfowl are present. It's also a good place to look for hawks.

Coyote-Hellyer County Park itself offers fishing (for bluegill and trout), boating, and volleyball, and it has a visitor center and an olympic-sized outdoor bicycle track. You'll also find picnic tables and barbecues, in case you want to cook out. The park and its streamside trail follow Coyote Creek for over 2 miles, and then the trail continues another 13 miles to Anderson Lake Park, close enough (and sometimes too close) to a main highway to be accessed at several points. This makes for an easy shuttle should you want to explore only a section of Coyote Creek. Fishing is permitted year-round in Cottonwood Lake and in Coyote Creek during the fishing season.

Access: The principal Coyote-Hellyer County Park entrance is at the park's northern end: stay on Highway 101 south of San Jose about 4 miles to the Hellyer Avenue exit; there turn west ½ mile to the park. There's a parking area near Cottonwood Lake at the southern end of the park. There are three access points for the Coyote Creek Trail: two off Highway 101 at the Blossom Hill Road or Bernal Hill Road exits, and the third near the intersection of Monterey Highway and Metcalf Road.

Note: A 459-acre *Motorcycle County Park* and a 99-acre *Field*

Sports Park (with ranges for pistol, rifle, skeet, and trap shooting) lie just east of the Coyote Creek Trail. *Coyote Lake County Park,* another recreation-oriented reservoir, which offers power boating, waterskiing, camping, fishing, picnicking, sailing, swimming—and and two 1-mile-long hiking trails—is a considerable distance farther south, between Morgan Hill and Gilroy.

Ed R. Levin County Park—This is an interesting parkland on several counts. It came into being in 1967 largely because of the efforts of Ed Levin, a dynamic and indefatigable county supervisor and planning commissioner; a dozen years later it was added onto for a total area of 1,544 acres. It rises from a secluded valley to a mountain top— about a 2,000-foot lift. It has a developed, accessible, and highly popular section where there's a golf course, fishing (for bluegill, bass, and crappie), boating in two lakes, and most pleasant picnicking. It is well watered by its own water system of springs and streams. Part of it is still used for a working ranch and is much as it was a hundred years ago or more. It's a favorite park of hang-gliders and horseback riders. And it has pleasant trails for easy hikes and a climb of a 2,594-foot mountain whose peak lies just inside Alameda County in the East Bay Regional Parks District's Mission Peak Preserve. (You gain the park's approximately 2,000-foot elevation difference on this hike.) Like many former Peninsula ranches, Ed Levin Park also has meadows and beautiful wildflowers in the spring.

Access: Take Highway 101 south to the bottom of the bay; turn east on Highway 237 to Calaveras Road; continue 4 miles on Calaveras Road to the park entrance.

Joseph D. Grant County Park—A former 9,522-acre cattle ranch that survived intact until 1975, when it was purchased by the county, this large parkland lies on the rolling slopes of Mount Hamilton in the Diablo Range due east of San Jose. (Parts of the park are still leased for cattle grazing.) This remarkable county resource has some 40 miles of trails that offer a variety of outings, from short strolls through valley land to longer hikes to higher ground (elevation in the park stretches from 1,350 feet to nearly 3,000 feet). Most of the trails are ranch roads, which allow for walking side by side, and they are popular with horseback riders as well as hikers. The grand old Grant ranch house has been converted into park headquarters and a visitor center that has historical as well as wildlife displays. There are a nature study program and occasional nature walks; the park rangers have the help of docents trained by the Friends of the Grant Ranch. A marshy area around 40-acre Grant Lake has been set aside for environmental protection and study, and the lake itself is stocked for fishing. (Other smaller lakes are stocked as well.) The park offers pleasant, shaded camping for families (35 sites). Tree lovers will enjoy the huge valley oaks near park headquarters and the buckeyes and sycamores along the streams. Bird lovers can keep their eyes out for golden eagles along the higher trails. And in the flower-blooming months of the year—from late February through May—flower lovers will be in for a treat; Grant Park offers some of the finest shows in the Bay Area for those who travel its trails. *Note:* This is also a favorite place for stargazing and is not too far from the Lick Observatory itself.

Access: Take Highway 101 south to Alum Rock Avenue (Highway 130); east on Alum Rock about 2 miles to Mount Hamilton Road; follow Mount Hamilton Road 8 miles to the parking lot near the park headquarters.

Lexington Reservoir County Park—This 844-acre county park (450 acres of which are water, in the rainy season, that is) offers fishing, windsurfing, rowing—collegiate rowing teams practice and hold regattas here, and sailboating, but no swimming.

Access: Take Highway 101 or I-280 south to Highway 17; south on Highway 17 to about 2½ miles south of Los Gatos; take Alma Bridge east to the dam to escape the traffic.

Los Gatos Creek Park and Trail—This is part of another of the Peninsula's attractive streamside parkways that offer paved trails for hikers, joggers (the city of Campbell has a Parcourse en route), bicyclists, and sometimes roller skaters. The 80-acre park itself embraces not only Los Gatos Creek but percolation ponds that are frequently decorated with the brightly colored sails of windsurfers and the model boats of vicarious sailors. It is also good for fishing and bird-watching.

Los Gatos Creek flows out of Lexington Reservoir in a generally northeast direction, runs through Los Gatos and Vasona Lake (where there's *Vasona Lake County Park,* a good—highly popular—place to rent a rowboat or sailboat, have a picnic, or bird-watch), and on through Campbell into the city of San Jose, where it joins the

Guadalupe River. Along with Santa Clara County, the cities of Campbell and Los Gatos and the state have established parks and trails alongside this attractive stream. You can take a creekside stroll—or wheeled ride—or a more strenuous run along Los Gatos Creek for 14 consecutive miles. If you start in Campbell and head upstream, for example, you'll be able to stay by the stream for nearly 5 miles before you reach Vasona Lake County Park. You can also end this walk in Los Gatos Creek Park, which is about halfway along the way. This stretch of creekside pathway also includes the above-mentioned Parcourse, which starts in Campbell Park. A shorter streamside walk is possible from Lexington Dam downstream about 2 miles through a narrow canyon to the Forbes Mill (historic) Museum in Los Gatos. (This is a loop trail, so you can make your way back on the other side of the stream.) The trail along Los Gatos Creek is at times unfortunately close to Highway 17, and it runs through subdivisions and business areas as well as past bird-occupied and windsurfer-decorated ponds.

Access: Take Highway 101 or I-280 south to Highway 17; follow Highway 17 south past Campbell to Los Gatos Creek Park, Vasona Lake Park, and Lexington Dam.

Penitentia Creek Park—This small—83-acre—creekside park borders the lovely stream that flows through San Jose's historic Alum Rock Park into Coyote Creek and thence into the bay. With recent county acquisition of the banks of this section of the creek, it is now possible to enjoy some 4 miles of streamside travel downstream from the 700-acre city park that, famous for its supposedly health-giving hot springs, was a popular spa around the turn of the century. (*Note:* There's an unmarked section at Capitol Avenue where you jog south to pick up the trail.) (*Alum Rock City Park* is not only interesting historically, it, too, offers pleasant hiking.) The paved county creekside trail will take you through suburban countryside and past the familiar percolation ponds that mark Santa Clara's efforts to alleviate its groundwater problems. (Formal links—still missing—between Alum Rock's Creek Trail and the Penitentia Creek Trail are planned for the near future, but it's possible to walk along the road the short intervening distance.)

Access: Take Highway 101 south past the end of the bay to Highway 237; Highway 237 east to I-680; I-680 south to Maybury Road exit; west on Maybury Road. There is parking for this park at the intersection of Maybury Road and Jackson Avenue (the southern end, where there are also some picnic tables), at Noble Avenue (its northern boundary), and in Alum Rock City Park.

Note: The *Overfelt Gardens,* which remember a pioneer San Jose family, are only a short distance from the park, at McKee Road and Education Park Drive. Given to the city by Miss Mildred Overfelt to ensure an ongoing place of serenity in this once serene area, the 33 acres of gardens are a delight to stroll through any day; they are open from 10:00 A.M. to sunset.

Rancho San Antonio—See Midpeninsula Regional Open Space District; this 761-acre county park–district preserve is described therein.

Sanborn-Skyline County Park—Running along Skyline Boulevard and the county line (Santa Clara County's wonderful 3,700-acre *Castle Rock State Park* abuts part of it), this park embraces 3,600 hillside acres of the Coast Ranges that have been happily set aside for hiking, horseback riding (on Skyline Trail/Ridge Trail only), camping (33 walk-in and 15 RV sites), picnicking, fishing, hosteling, and protecting the native scene—albeit in somewhat altered condition. Second-growth redwoods and Douglas firs mark the sites of earlier virgin groves that were logged off before the turn of the century, and most of the original oaks went for firewood or tanning; a good part of the area was cleared for farms and family vineyards, as well. (The area was frequented by the Ohlone Indians long before white settlers arrived, but they left far fewer traces.) Today, much of this pleasant park is heavily wooded once again, and it helps preserve the integrity of the backdrop of dark hills that is so important to the visual beauty of the Peninsula. It also contains a section of the Skyline Trail/Ridge Trail, and at its northern end at Saratoga Gap, it ties into the 37-mile Skyline-to-the-Sea pathway that goes through Castle Rock Park, follows Highway 9 (on an easement), and then drops through *Big Basin State Park* to reach the shore at Waddell Creek. (There are eight backpack camps en route; if you're interested in this unique hiking experience, telephone Big Basin State Park at 408-338-8860 for further information.) Sanborn-Skyline's own trail system is far less pretentious, but it offers chances for steep climbs as well as leisurely saunters. There's ranger-led nature walks (on request; telephone 408-867-9959), a headquarters building (formerly a handsome home), Youth Science Institute displays, the Lake Ranch Reservoir (directly on the San Andreas Fault), and an American Youth Hostel (see Youth Hostels appendix). Known as Welch Hurst, this is the former hunting lodge of Santa Clara County Superior Court Judge James Welch and is listed in the National Registry of Historic Sites; telephone 408-741-0166.

Access: Take I-280 south to Highway 35; Highway 35 south to Highway 9; Highway 9 east to Sanborn Road, thence right for 1 mile to the park entrance and park headquarters.

Santa Teresa County Park—Once a 466-acre truck garden, then a jail farm, this park, now 1,670 acres, was established in 1958. (Before all that, it was part of the 9,646-acre Santa Teresa Ranch, granted to Joaquin Bernal in 1834 when the gentleman was 94 years old: of sturdy stock, Bernal had a total of 77 children and grandchildren.) The park presently has an 18-hole golf course, a driving range, a clubhouse, picnic areas, an archery range, an equestrian assembly area, and trails for hikers and horseback riders through its rolling hills. It is possible to make an easy climb to its highest point, 1,155-foot Coyote Peak, for pleasant views.

Access: Take I-280 south to San Jose; take Monterey Highway (Highway 82) south to Bernal Road and follow it for about 1½ miles to its end.

Stevens Creek County Park—This 1,095-acre parkland was acquired by Santa Clara in 1927 as its first county park. It includes 93-acre Stevens Creek Reservoir, a popular recreational lake. This is also a pleasant park for picnicking and hiking; its trails tie into trails in the Fremont Older Open Space Preserve (which borders it on the east) and in the Picchetti Ranch (which borders it to the west), as well as into the Mount Eden Riding and Hiking Trail (see Midpeninsula Regional Open Space District). A visit to the Sunrise Winery (see Los Trancos Earthquake Trail) might top off a good hike from the Picchetti Ranch into this attractive creek and canyon country; you pass Stevens Creek Reservoir on your way into the ranch. Stevens Creek is one of the Peninsula's principal streams, draining the coastal mountains and flowing into San Francisco Bay where it borders Mountain View's Shoreline Park. The park's visitor center (not always open) is at its northern end off Stevens Canyon Road. Trail maps are available from the Santa Clara County Parks Department.

Access: Take I-280 south past Los Altos to Stevens Canyon

Road—an extension of Foothill Boulevard; continue on Stevens Canyon Road to park entrance.

Sunnyvale Baylands Park—Two hundred years ago, San Francisco Bay was a superbly functioning estuary with clear freshwater streams in great number meandering into the wide salt marshes around its eastern and southern shores. More than 300 square miles of rich wetlands rimmed the shallow waters then, with the extraordinarily productive salt marsh plants—cordgrass prime among them—adding their nourishment to the bay and its wildlife. Fish and shellfish were abundant, and the bay served, too, as nursery for many other ocean-going species of marine life. The wings of tens of thousands of birds darkened the skies as the aerial travelers found the bay marshes for resting on their migratory flights. Thousands more birds were residents among the grasses.

Today, less than 60 square miles of bay wetlands remain "alive"—unfilled and undiked. And, at long last, the value of these special landforms is coming to be recognized. Bay edge communities that once turned a profit from filling their "useless" waterfront with waste are now turning their old garbage dumps into parklands—and sometimes selling the methane from them to boot. Birders and people who enjoy the special beauties of the tidelands, too, are attempting to rescue pathways around the rim of the bay. To date, nearly 200 miles of such trails are in existence (see Bay Trail) and more are planned. And while it may never be possible to walk around the southern end of the bay, you can travel on foot for several miles alongside it, enjoying the slow, stealthy rise of the tide (there is a 5-foot mean tidal range), the sight of egrets and great blue herons as they stalk their prey with elegant grace, and the view of the soft hills delineating the sky to the north above the blue bay waters. Along with Palo Alto, Mountain View, and the Midpeninsula Regional Open Space District, Santa Clara County and Sunnyvale are joining the effort to protect and open to walkers several hundred acres of their wetlands. The county has acquired some 177 acres, 105 acres of which are protected seasonal wetlands. (Seventy-two acres, operated by the city of Sunnyvale, are developed. There are picnic tables, a children's playground, and pathways among native grasses.) And the city of Sunnyvale has established a nearly 4-mile loop trail on the levees around the aeration ponds of its water treatment plant. Here you can see fragments of healthy marshland along with the oxidation ponds, and there are seven benches to rest upon, each with an informational plaque. Birders will find this Sunnyvale Baylands walk particularly rewarding; waterbirds sport in the bay waters, and shorebirds flash bright and then dark against the sky as they settle into the marsh.

Access: Take Highway 101 south to Highway 237; Highway 237 east to the Lawrence Expressway; north on Lawrence Expressway, which runs into Caribbean Avenue; take a right on Borregas Avenue and almost immediately turn left on Carl Drive. There is public parking at the water treatment plant. (The Sunnyvale Baylands are east of Moffett Field, and a short distance north and west of Marriott's Great America, in case you're traveling with children.)

Upper Stevens Creek County Park—1,200 acres of undeveloped "wilderness," this parkland lies upstream from Stevens Reservoir, embracing the headwaters of Stevens Creek. Part of it fronts on Skyline Boulevard. The Bay Area Ridge Trail passes through the park.

Access: Take I-280 south to Highway 92; west on Highway 92 to Skyline Boulevard (Highway 35); south on Skyline Boulevard past Monte Bello Open Space Preserve. There is a parking area 3 miles south of Page Mill Road and 3.2 miles north of Highway 9. You can also hike, bicycle, or ride a horse from Stevens Creek County Park along Stevens Canyon Road (there is no parking on Stevens Canyon Road, so you can't access Upper Stevens Creek by car from the east side of the preserve).

Villa Montalvo County Arboretum—Once the estate of Senator James Phelan, this 178 acres of gardens and natural forests is administered by Santa Clara County Parks Department. There are 2 acres of formal gardens and 3 pleasant miles of trail.

Access: Take I-280 south to Saratoga Avenue; south on Saratoga to Highway 9; east on Highway 9 to Montalvo Road; thence to park entrance.

Note: Two Santa Clara County parks lie in the southern part of the county beyond comfortable driving distance from San Francisco. Should you be near either of them, you will find them of interest. *Uvas Canyon County Park* is over 1,200 acres of more or less steep hillside notable for its waterfalls and its proximity to Sveadal, a Swedish retirement community and retreat. There is first-come, first-served family camping for a reasonable fee. You can also enjoy a stimulating 1,800-foot climb to the park's high point should the spirit move you. Uvas Canyon Park is off Croy Road just east of the Santa Cruz County line. (Take Highway 101 or I-280 south to Monterey Highway in San Jose; Monterey south to Bailey Avenue; Bailey west to McKean Road; south on McKean, which becomes Uvas Road; Uvas Road south to Croy Road and then west to park entrance.) *Mount Madonna County Park,* 3,311 of the 1 million acres once owned by the cattle baron Henry Miller, lies to the southeast directly on the county line and is readily accessible by Highway 152 from either the west (via Highway 1) or the east (via Highway 101). This park has more than 100 campsites, a fishing pond for children, some magnificent madrones, redwoods, lovely spring wildflowers, and some pleasant (mostly up-and-down) hiking country. The park's centerpiece, 1,897-foot Mount Madonna, is the southernmost peak of the Santa Cruz Mountains.

For further information on Santa Clara parks, contact the Santa Clara County Parks Department, 298 Garden Hill Drive, Los Gatos, CA 95030; telephone 408-358-3741.

Henry Coe State Park, with nearly 80,000 acres, is the second-largest of California's state parks. (Only Anza-Borrego Desert State Park in southern California—which has a whopping 600,000 acres—is larger.) It, too, is remote enough to require a long drive from the bay. It is also a remarkable Bay Area resource, since it has pretty much a full spectrum of local animal and plant communities (except for good coastal environments, including redwood groves) one place or another within its boundaries. It is particularly notable for its oak grassland and its many old and colorful oaks—blue, black, valley, and live—its giant manzanitas, its ponderosa and digger pines, its golden eagles and mountain lions, its absolutely fearless raccoons, and its magnificent wildflower shows. It also has a good display of Diablo Range geology (see Mount Diablo), including some of the state's most immense blocks of blueschist, and it commands spectacular views to as far away as the Sierra from its higher points (over 3,600 feet).

This vast and pleasantly undeveloped parkland offers perhaps the best backpacking opportunities in the Bay Area (in spring and fall, that is; as in all inland areas around the bay, summer days can be intolerably hot, and here, the winter days can be not only miserably wet, but snowy and freezing cold). There are 60 backcountry back-pack camps spread out in the park, so you can plan an extensive trip of several days should you want to get away from civilization with-out traveling too far to do it. These camps are small, for one to eight people, and they all are near a source of water, but you'll have to get a permit (available at the visitor center) and carry a stove, for no fires are allowed in the park. There are also 20 drive-in campsites near park headquarters; these have water and picnic facilities, too.

The heart of this grand park was the remarkably generous 13,000-acre gift of Henry W. Coe's granddaughter, Sada Coe Robin-son. She presented her Pine Ridge Ranch to Santa Clara County in 1953 to honor the memory of California's pioneers and to keep this lovely part of the earth from subdivision and other development. The state subsequently acquired the ranch and has been able to enlarge it to its present splendid size. Sada Coe also made gracious gifts to the park's fine Pine Ridge (historical) Museum, which should not be missed when you visit the park. (There's also a neat collection of old wagons.)

There's fishing and a nature trail in Henry W. Coe Park, and there are modest fees for day-use parking as well as the various kinds of camping. The telephone number is 408-779-2728, and it's a good idea to check with the park people for up-to-date information; they lead wildflower walks (mostly in the spring, with the help of docent members of the Pine Ridge Association) and put on interesting Sat-urday evening programs in season. You can also find out the hours—and the days—when the museum will be open.

Access: Take Highway 101 south to Morgan Hill; east on East Dunne Avenue for about 13 miles to park entrance. On the way, you'll pass the *Anderson Lake County Park;* this reservoir is used to recharge groundwater, but is also very popular for recreation.

Note: Big Basin Redwoods State Park, 20 miles north of Santa Cruz, and more than an hour's drive from San Francisco, has 18,000 wonderful acres, including some of the finest redwood groves in the state. (This was the first of California's state parks.) There are devel-oped campsites, tent cabins, a visitor center, and 80 miles of trails. Telephone 408-338-6132 for full information; call DESTINET at 800-444-PARK (7275) for camping reservations.

The Midpeninsula Regional Open Space District

The North Bay has its complex of state parks, county parks, and national parks. The East Bay has its regional park district. San Francisco has its Golden Gate Park and the Golden Gate National Recreation Area. The South Bay counties have their state parks and their own parks; they also have a notable open-space district—one of only three in the state. (The other two are in Marin County and Monterey County; Marin County Open Space is administered by the county parks and recreation department.) Interestingly, the enabling legislation for these open-space districts was the same that established the East Bay Regional Park District in 1936. The Midpeninsula Regional Open Space District plays a key role in preserving the beautiful Peninsula lands and making them available for outdoor recreation. Presently, it has over 41,000 acres under its jurisdiction. The hillsides you enjoy looking at from almost any vantage point in the Peninsula—the scenic backgrounds that make I-280 such a beautiful freeway, for instance—are in large part under the aegis of the district. The district also plays a major role in acquiring key areas to protect them, and in joining already established parks to one another, thus preserving large areas of contiguous parklands.

The Midpeninsula Regional Open Space District was established in 1972 when the people in northwestern Santa Clara County voted to assign a share of their property tax (about 1 cent out of each $100) for acquisition and maintenance of open space. Southern San Mateo County joined the district four years later, and in 1992, the district annexed a small part of Santa Cruz County, making it the only tri-county open space or park district in the state. Now the district's boundaries stretch from Los Gatos to San Carlos, and from west of Skyline Boulevard to San Francisco Bay; 16 cities lie within the district. A board of seven directors—elected from seven different "wards"—is the governing body, and citizen input is a major factor in the decisions that are reached. Most land acquisitions are from willing sellers, although the MROSD has the right of eminent domain. Goals include the establishment of a greenbelt of open space extending the length of the district, with an overall regional trail system, including acquisitions and easements to extend the Bay Area Ridge Trail. The Bay Trail also crosses district lands. The district has used its monies primarily for land acquisition as critical land use decisions continue to be made. It has built an interpretive center with informative programs, but developed recreation—such as ballfields, golf courses, or tennis courts—is not on the books—the goal is to preserve the natural environment in an unspoiled state. The district provides excellent information; there are brochures for many of the units. *Dog owners, note:* Dogs are allowed only in a few specified preserves and must at all time be on leash; telephone the district for specific information if you want to take your pet along.

Presently the district preserves provide some of the best outdoor experiences "down the Peninsula."

Coal Creek Open Space Preserve—Close to 500 acres of rolling open grasslands and the wooded headwaters of two creeks between Alpine Road and Skyline Boulevard. Nice for short hikes and especially nice for picnics.

Access: Take I-280 south to Page Mill Road; turn west to Skyline Boulevard (Highway 35); go north on Highway 35 to preserve entrance.

El Corte De Madera Creek Open Space Preserve—Off Skyline Boulevard and Kings Mountain Road, this 2,788-acre preserve is notable for its handsome second-growth redwoods as well as prime old-growth stands; it also has fascinating sandstone formations. It is near beautiful Purisima Creek Redwoods; there are 20 miles of hiking, biking, and equestrian trails on steep, heavily forested terrain.

Access: Take I-280 south to Highway 92; west on Highway 92 to Skyline Boulevard (Highway 35); then south past Purisima Creek Redwoods Open Space Preserve. There is limited parking at Skeggs Vista Point and off Skyline Boulevard.

El Sereno Open Space Preserve—Named for 2,500-foot Mount El Sereno south of Saratoga and Los Gatos, this 1,112-acre ridgetop preserve offers hikers, bikers, and horseback riders panoramic views of the surrounding countryside and the South Bay from trails through its chaparral.

Access: Take Highway 101 or I-280 south to Highway 17; south on Highway 17; west on Montevina Road about 3 miles to its end. Parking is limited, and a site map is helpful; contact MROSD for same.

Foothills Open Space Preserve—A 211-acre preserve with grassy ridgetop and oak-madrone woodlands. It has a very steep trail to Hidden Villa Ranch. A 1,500-acre easement gives added protection to this preserve. *Dog owners, note:* Dogs on leash are allowed in this preserve.

Access: Take I-280 to Page Mill Road; then southwest 3½ miles to preserve. Small parking area.

Fremont Older Open Space Preserve—Although MROSD does not seek out buildings, occasionally they come with the property that is being acquired. Such is the case here, where the very charming home of a well-known early century San Francisco editor was part of the 739-acre preserve that is being protected for its open-space values. The house has been restored (it is listed on the National Registry of Historic Sites) and is rented to a private party. Notable for its flat roof—unusual in the period during which it was built—and its many pergolas, it is open to the public during annual docent tours. The rest of the preserve has a variety of scenery, including open hayfields, 900-foot-high Hunter's Point—which commands grand views of the Santa Clara Valley—and Seven Springs Canyon, which is known for its abundant wildlife. There are several miles of hiking, bicycling, and horseback riding trails in this preserve, including the Seven Springs loop. *Dog owners, note:* Dogs on leash are allowed in designated areas of the preserve.

Access: Take I-280 south to Highway 85; thence south to Prospect Road; west on Prospect to its end, 1½ miles past its intersection with Stelling Road. There is ample parking.

La Honda Creek Open Space Preserve—This 2,043-acre preserve of open grassy hilltops and redwood–Douglas fir forest is somewhat remote, and its undisturbed plant communities are rich in wildlife. Visitation is by permit from MROSD, which will also supply a map.

Long Ridge Open Space Preserve—The more than 1,500 acres of this preserve command exceptionally fine views of Big Basin State Park in Santa Cruz County, Butano Ridge, and Devils Canyon. Its rolling grasslands are interrupted by stands of oaks, madrones, and Douglas firs; they are starred with wildflowers in the spring. The trails in this preserve tie into Skyline County Park trails, part of the Ridge Trail, and those of the Saratoga Gap Open Space Preserve.

    Access: Long Ridge runs alongside Skyline Boulevard (Highway 35) on the west. Take I-280 south to Page Mill Road; thence west to Highway 35; south on Highway 35 to preserve. Parking is available at the Skyline County Park–Grizzly Flat parking area. There are brochures available on-site.

Los Trancos Preserve—This lovely 274-acre parkland is described at some length in Historic Hikes in the South Bay. It is especially noteworthy for its earthquake exhibit. Monthly docent-led walks along the 1.5-mile earthquake trail; also wildflower walks in the spring. Contact MROSD for times. No reservations are necessary. Located about 6 miles south of Highway 280—and 1 mile north of Skyline Boulevard—on Page Mill Road.

Monte Bello Open Space Preserve—Page Mill Area—With almost 2,800 acres, this is one of the largest of MROSD's preserves, and it has some of the loveliest lands on the Peninsula. Embracing the entire upper watershed of Stevens Creek, it rises from the luxuriant mixed forests of Stevens Canyon to the summit of Black Mountain (at 2,800 feet, a respectable peak). It is also contiguous to other public lands, providing a wonderful sweep of open space from valley floor to ridges on both sides. (Both permits and reservations are required for the backpack camp on Black Mountain.) It has some fascinating geological features, being cleft by the San Andreas Fault. Monte Bello has some 13 miles of trails, including a 3-mile self-guided nature trail that you take from the roomy parking lot on Page Mill Road, directly across from Los Trancos. Monte Bello trails also tie into trail systems in Skyline County Park, Los Trancos, and Hidden Villa Ranch (where there is a youth hostel). Brochures are available at the parking lot.

    Access: See Los Trancos Earthquake Trail.

Monte Bello Open Space Preserve—Picchetti Ranch Area—This charming turn-of-the-century ranch and winery (described under Los Trancos Earthquake Trail) is another preserve that includes historic buildings, along with orchards and a vineyard. Trails also lead through its 308 acres of rolling chaparral and oak-ornamented lands. There are tastings at the winery—now leased to Ronald and Rolayne Stortz's Sunrise Winery—from 11:00 A.M. to 3:00 P.M. Friday, Saturday, and Sunday. Parking is available. You can pick up an informative brochure at the parking lot trailhead.

Access: Take I-280 south to Foothill Boulevard; south on Foothill to Stevens Canyon Road; south to Montebello Road; ½ mile northwest on Montebello to parking area.

Pulgas Ridge Open Space Preserve—This 293-acre preserve immediately across from Edgewood County Park is notable for its views of the San Francisco watershed and the open backdrop that it provides for Edgewood. There are pleasant trails; leashed dogs are permitted.

Access: Take I-280 south to Edgewood Road; go east to Crestview Drive; then north to Edmonds Road and the preserve.

Purisima Creek Redwoods Open Space Preserve—The third-largest of MROSD's preserves, Purisima Creek Redwoods with its 2,633 acres not only is special for its forests, ferns, and wildflowers but is located on the western slopes of the Santa Cruz Mountains above Half Moon Bay, thus making possible a trail from ridgetop to the sea. Purisima's grand old forests once fed seven sawmills that were situated along the creek. Despite its history of logging, this preserve has some of the loveliest readily accessible redwoods near San Francisco. There's a wheelchair-accessible trail (placed with care and a fine feel for the great trees) as well as a system of trails on the old logging roads. There's a 20-car parking lot for Purisima on Skyline Boulevard 4½ miles south of Highway 92, and another 5-car turnout on Skyline Boulevard 6½ miles south of Highway 92. To access the preserve from its western boundary, take Highway 1 about 1 mile south of Half Moon Bay to the intersection of Higgins-Purisima Road; there's parking space for 10 or so vehicles. Brochures are available in the parking lot.

Rancho San Antonio Open Space Preserve—This is the most popular of the MROSD preserves, and it is easy to see why. Readily accessible—it is just west of I-280 in the Los Altos foothills—its 1,235 acres include shady streamsides, grassy meadows, 23 miles of trails—including several possible loops—and a working farm that is run by the city of Mountain View as an environmental education center. The farm is a great favorite with children and is open every day except Mondays; the preserve is open every day. You'll find joggers, horseback riders, and hikers on the trails—and lots of nice places for picnics. The main entrance is in Rancho San Antonio County Park, where there are restrooms and water; the northwest lot is the preserve trailhead, and you will find brochures there.

Access: Take I-280 south to Foothill Boulevard; immediately turn right onto Cristo Rey Drive, which you follow for 1 mile to the preserve.

Rancho San Antonio (Duveneck Windmill Pasture Area)—Most of this beautiful 900-acre preserve was given by Frank and Josephine Duveneck to MROSD, and it adjoins the rest of the Duveneck Foundation's Hidden Villa Ranch, making for a sizable protected area. Among this preserve's special attractions is a lovely secluded meadow above the valley floor; this is ideal for a picnic in the springtime.

Access: Take I-280 south to El Monte Road; turn right on El Monte to Moody Road just past Foothill College; proceed 0.5 mile and turn left on Rhus Ridge Road for 0.2 mile to the parking lot, where you can get a brochure.

Ravenswood Open Space Preserve—Part of the public baylands that extend south to Stevens Creek, this 373-acre area includes rich tidelands and marshes, and a 1-mile trail with observation decks (wheelchair-accessible). It is planned to form a link in the emerging Bay Trail. Contact the MROSD if you're interested in more information about it.

Access: Take Highway 101 south to the University Avenue exit; hence east to Bay Road; then southeast to the nearby preserve.

Russian Ridge Open Space Preserve—This 1,580-acre preserve is the grassy ridge you see just west of Skyline Boulevard near its intersection with Alpine Road. It includes the 2,572-foot summit of Mount Boreal—with gorgeous views that sweep from San Francisco to Monterey Bay and the Berkeley-Oakland hills: a good spot for a camera with a wide-angle lens. There are also lovely views closer by, thanks to the scenic protection that has been gained for this part of the Peninsula. Beautiful expanses of wildflowers explode into color in the spring—one of the best, if not the best, shows in the MROSD. There are several miles of trails, including the Bay Area Ridge Trail, that wander through the preserve from Skyline Boulevard down to Mindego Creek, whose headwaters rise off Russian Ridge, and beyond.

Access: Take I-280 south to Skyline Boulevard (Highway 35). It is possible to access this preserve from two places on Skyline Boulevard: park near the intersection of Alpine Road, where you'll find an ample parking lot (and brochures) and a hiking stile; or park at the Caltrans Vista Point 1 mile northwest of this intersection. (From here you'll need to cross Skyline Boulevard to enter the preserve.)

St. Joseph's Hill Open Space Preserve—This 173-acre preserve offers pleasant hiking and riding opportunities, along with some panoramic views. The grassy meadows that now grow colorful wildflowers were once vineyards managed by the novitiate. Dogs on leash are permitted in designated areas.

Access: Take Highway 17 south of Los Gatos to Alma Bridge Road and the Lexington Reservoir parking lot, where you pick up the trail.

Saratoga Gap Open Space Preserve—This 701-acre preserve is lovely country itself—with stands of Douglas firs, grassy hills, oaks, and madrones and intriguing lichen-covered rocks and outcroppings—and it also provides key tie-ins for several popular trails, including the Ridge Trail.

Access: Take I-280 south to Highway 9 (Saratoga Avenue); the preserve is at the junction of Highway 9 and Skyline Boulevard. Brochures are available at the parking lot.

Sierra Azul–Kennedy-Limekiln Area—Rugged and steep sloped, with chaparral and thickly wooded canyons, this 5,236-acre preserve is a somewhat remote mountainous piece of terrain. Fifteen miles of hiking, bicycling, and equestrian trails have been developed, including ones climbing a 2,000-foot ridge and the 1,762-foot Priest Rock. Both will reward you with spectacular views of the Santa Clara Valley.

Access: Take I-280 or Highway 101 to Highway 85; go south on Highway 85 to Highway 17; south again to Saratoga/Los Gatos

Road where you turn left. Turn left again almost immediately on Los Gatos Boulevard and right on Kennedy Road where you'll find limited parking.

Sierra Azul Open Space Preserve—Mount Umunhum Area—A grand 6,843-acre unit that marks the southern extent of MROSD. Much of the area is still privately owned, so public access is limited. Two trails have been developed through steep chaparral-covered slopes and dense stands of California bay laurel. Views of Santa Clara Valley and Monterey Bay, but no public access as yet to the top of Mount Umunhum. Call the district before visiting.

Access: Take I-280 south to Highway 85; south on Highway 85 to Camden Avenue. South again to Hicks Road, which you follow to Loma Almaden Road; thence left to the very limited roadside parking area (space for two cars).

Note: Sierra Azul–Cathedral Oaks Area is 600 acres of rugged country east of Lexington Reservoir.

Skyline Ridge Open Space Preserve—At the heart of a grand complex of Peninsula parklands—including Los Trancos, Duveneck Windmill Pasture, and Monte Bello preserves and Portola State Park—lies this former ranch that has an unusually varied landscape with expansive meadows, a pond, and a quiet lake frequented by migrating birds. Its 1,612 acres are ideal for picnicking, hiking, or for just contemplating the beautiful views from its ridgetops. You can often watch hawks, as well. The Daniels Nature Center is open Sundays from spring to fall.

Access: Skyline Ridge is located near the intersection of Alpine Road and Skyline Boulevard (Highway 35); turn west on Alpine to parking lot, where brochures are available. The preserve can also be accessed from Russian Ridge Open Space Preserve (see above).

Stevens Creek Shoreline Nature Study Area—This is perhaps the best of MROSD's preserves for dedicated birdwatchers since its bayfront property includes prime avian habitat. It is 55 strategically located acres that abut Stevens Creek and Mountain View's Shoreline Park. The entrance to the preserve is through Shoreline Park via the bicycle-pedestrian path that rims its north-to-south boundary. The walking bridge linking the two parklands makes it possible to travel

The view from Skyline Ridge. PHOTO BY CAROLYN CADDES, MIDPENINSULA REGIONAL OPEN SPACE DISTRICT.

from the Palo Alto Baylands to this preserve, thus forging another link in the Bay Trail.

Access: Take Highway 101 south to Shoreline Boulevard exit; follow this road into the Mountain View Shoreline Park.

Note: **Mountain View Shoreline Park** is over 500 acres of reclaimed bay frontage that has been developed into a golf course, marina, and (more or less) restored marshland. It is an outstanding metropolitan park. The **Palo Alto Baylands** is a 1,500-acre treasure owned by the city of Palo Alto—and, unlike the city's inland park, open to the public. It was set aside in the 1960s to preserve its nat-

Miraculously some of San Francisco Bay has survived in its natural state. Stevens Creek Shoreline Nature Study Area. PHOTO BY CAROLYN CADDES, MIDPENINSULA REGIONAL OPEN SPACE DISTRICT.

ural values. There is an excellent interpretive center, the Lucy Evans Baylands Nature Interpretive Center, staffed by a fine naturalist; it has interesting displays, and a good program of films and lectures. There are also boardwalks that let you get right out into the marsh and close to the mud flats, which, in winter, may teem with migratory birds. This is one of the few sizable South Bay frontage areas that is both undeveloped and protected: it's a good place to look for the endangered clapper rail (and the red-bellied harvest mouse, also endangered) as well as short-eared owls and the northern harrier. You'll also get a good view of the Leslie Salt works from the observation platform here. To reach this special parkland, take Highway 101 south to Embarcadero Road; proceed east on Embarcadero, which ends at the yacht harbor and the baylands. Telephone 650-329-2506 to find out schedules of programs; this is a great place to take children.

Thornewood Open Space Preserve—This 140-acre preserve is a memento of the 1920s era of gracious "summer estates" and includes 3½ acres of landscaped lawns and gardens that surround a handsome house, presently privately leased. (The house and its grounds are open to the public once a year.) Most pleasant if you'd like a stroll to an attractive lake, and if you'd like to indulge in a little nostalgia for a bygone age and admire some superb views of the surrounding countryside.

Access: Take I-280 south to Highway 84 (Woodside Road); located on the south side of Highway 84, 1.2 miles south of its intersection with Portola Road in Woodside.

Windy Hill Open Space Preserve—This 1,132-acre preserve is named for its open-to-the-sky, 1,900-foot hilltop, which is often shrouded in fog (and wind). On clear days, it commands sweeping views from the coast to the bay, and it makes a wonderful place for a picnic. It has a three-table picnic facility at its Skyline parking area, or you can find a shady trailside spot. Along with its high grassy ridges—ideal for kite-flying—this preserve has several small streams that flow year round. It has over 12 miles of trails, including the Bay Area Ridge Trail, and it is possible to make a five-hour loop that will take you into other parts of the countryside. *Dog owners, note:* Dogs on leash are allowed in designated areas of this preserve. Special regulations regarding pets are included in the Windy Hill brochure that you'll find at the parking area. (Windy Hill also has several roadside turnouts along its boundary.)

Access: Take I-280 south to Skyline Boulevard (Highway 35); south on Skyline. Located along Skyline Boulevard and extending to Alpine Road, the preserve has its principal entrance 2 miles south of La Honda Road.

For further information on any of the MROSD's preserves, contact the Midpeninsula Regional Open Space District, 330 Distel Circle, Los Altos, CA 94002-1404; telephone 650-691-1200.

Note: The Peninsula Open Space Trust (POST) plays a unique part in gaining protection for open space and parklands on the San Francisco Peninsula. It is a private, nonprofit organization that is dedicated to acquiring and conserving land as permanently protected open space in San Mateo and Santa Clara counties. During the past two decades, it has gained protection for over 35,000 acres of land:

although the land is turned over to public agencies (frequently MROSD) for administration, POST also builds trails, restores damaged lands, and helps improve the viability of agricultural lands. It also donates money for public facilities, such as visitor centers. POST is located at 3000 Sand Hill Road (Building 4; Suite 135) in Menlo Park, CA 94025; telephone 650-854-7696.

┌──── The San Mateo Coast

Highway 1 south of San Francisco is surely one of the most beautiful roads anywhere. Once it reaches the coast, it travels beside it, in places rimming the surf-swept shore, in others running high above it, in still others, doubling back and forth to gain a rise in the terrain. Along with the view of the blue Pacific Ocean, and of the interesting formations of the landscape, there are other pluses: there are evenly plowed farmlands, some seeming to stretch to the horizon; picturesque old towns—small ones, once you are south of Pacifica; a harbor full of fishing boats; and, in October, fields full of pumpkins glowing in the autumn sunlight, hundreds and hundreds of them, round and orange as just-risen full moons, radiant against the rich brown earth. And in spring, there are gardens of mustard as though an artist had spattered the ground with delicate shades of green and yellow paint. There are also the beaches, many of them pocket-size, but some of them invitingly long and clean looking, and all of them full of the drama of the changing patterns of the surf. At the southern tip of San Mateo County, there is also Año Nuevo, which offers unique opportunities for animal lovers and photographers and people who simply enjoy being on the edge of a continent. And should you want to combine a hike in the redwoods with your special encounter with the sea, the San Mateo coast is the place to do it. To make it even more enticing, there are fine places to picnic and to camp along this lovely coast and in the nearby redwood forests, as well, and there are two hostels en route to give you a choice of lodgings.

California State Beaches

Highway 1 takes off from I-280 south of San Francisco near Colma, goes past Sharp Park (where there's a San Francisco Park Golf Course and a stretch of public beach), past Pacifica (gateway to Sweeney Ridge), across the infamous Devil's Slide that has stymied highway builders for decades (and caused major controversy over routing of the highway) to reach *Gray Whale Cove State Beach,* a small (⅓ acre) state preserve operated by a concessioner. Continue another mile and you'll come to Montara Point with its lighthouse and its outstanding hostel. Here, you can take a hike in the state's 680-acre *Montara State Beach* (the elevation rises from 0 to 1,920 feet in the adjacent McNee Ranch addition, which has several hiking, biking, and riding trails in its rugged coastal hills as well), go fishing, or simply enjoy the superb location. (The hostel has a hot tub.) It's another 8 miles to *Half Moon Bay State Beach,* which is ½ mile off Highway 1 on Kelly Avenue. This is a 170-acre developed park with 55 campsites, facilities for trailers and campers, a hike and bike-in area, a horseback riding trail, and (brrrr) cold outdoor showers. It is wheelchair-accessible. Telephone 650-726-8819 for park information. (Half Moon Bay has a colorful harbor, several seafood restaurants, windsurfing, and kayaking. It's approximately 15 miles along the way on Highway 1.)

South of the city of Half Moon Bay is the 1,300-acre *Cowell Ranch* with a 2-mile-long stretch of coast that is now *Cowell State Beach,* thanks to the Peninsula Open Space Trust (POST). A parking area on Highway 1 provides access to bluff top and beach access trails. The remainder of the ranch is used for agriculture, but future plans call for a link to the Purisima Creek Redwoods trail to connect Skyline Boulevard with the Pacific Ocean. Three miles south of Half Moon Bay and 5 miles inland (off Higgins-Purisima Road), you'll find *Burleigh Murray Ranch State Park.* Three miles of horseback riding and hiking trails make this 1,325-acre preserve popular with local equestrians.

Ten and a half lovely miles south of Half Moon Bay on Highway 1 will bring you to *San Gregorio State Beach,* 172 coastal acres large, which has picnic facilities and food service. Fishermen might choose this park to stop and try their luck. If it's a hot day and this beach is crowded, you can drive another 1½ miles to *Pomponio State Beach,* which is a little over twice as large, and which also has picnic tables and good fishing. Or continue on 2½ miles more and you'll come to 638-acre *Pescadero State Beach,* which is another good place to sunbathe or fish, and which has guided tours of Pescadero Marsh Natural Preserve on weekends. (The preserve, one of the largest coastal marshes in the state, has several trails; bird-watching is best in fall and early spring.) *Bean Hollow State Beach* (which used to be called Arroyo Frijole) is 3 more miles along your way—17½ miles in all from Half Moon Bay. Although this is not a large park, it has a nature trail and picnic facilities and, again, is recommended for fishermen.

Stay on Highway 1 to the south along a particularly picturesque stretch of road for 9½ miles and you will come to *Año Nuevo State Reserve.* With its spare and lonely lighthouse on its offshore island, its ragged sea stacks and surging surf, it is somehow evocative of New England. It was a Spaniard, Sebastián Vizcaíno, however, who found and named this rugged headland when he came upon it in January of 1603. The lighthouse signaled danger to passing ships from 1890 to 1948, when it was abandoned. Its message was not always received; there were many shipwrecks here along this treacherous, and frequently foggy, coast.

Año Nuevo Island is famous as the breeding site of that extraordinary mammal, the elephant seal. (It is also occupied at one time or another by several other pinnipeds, such as California and Steller's sea lions and harbor seals.) Almost extinct until the 1920s, when they received protection after decades of being hunted, the elephant seals chose Año Nuevo Island for their mating rites some time during the 1950s. Here, the males—enormous animals with the long probosces that give them their name—come together early in December through February to do battle and thus establish rank. The winners gather together their harems when pregnant females (which have better-looking noses) arrive, produce the pups they have carried for a year, and mate again about a month later. The poor vanquished males slink away to the mainland to what is known as Loser's Beach. (This was the annual ritual until 1983, when a major storm devastated the island and caused enormous losses in the elephant seal population. Since then, the animals have been using the shore as well as the island for their courtship and pupping.) In March, most of the older seals leave Año Nuevo for life in the ocean, and the pups follow them in April.

So many crowds have come to witness this interesting spectacle that the state park people have set up a schedule for visiting the reserve throughout the mating season—December 15 through March. During this period, you must have a reservation—obtained through DESTINET (telephone 800-444-PARK [7275])—which will entitle you to an officially guided tour (it involves about 3 miles of walking and takes around two and a half hours) and a look at the visitor center, which is open daily these four months of the year (and as staffing permits the rest of the year). Student docents from the University of California at Santa Cruz are the guides, and they offer a highly rewarding experience. (You might also see a passing whale if you visit here in, say, January.) There are usually some seals to be seen at Año Nuevo year-round. If you visit during other months of the year, you walk to the beach on your own. Docents are there to answer questions. You can also picnic at Año Nuevo, wander through its dunes, admire its setting, or beachcomb its strand. This reserve of 4,000 hard-won acres is the southernmost state park on the San Mateo County coast.

Note: Just north of Año Nuevo is Pigeon Point, with another outstanding hostel (see Youth Hostels appendix). The *Gazos Creek* beach access area, operated by Año Nuevo, is just south of Pigeon Point. There's parking and chemical toilets. The 4,000-plus acre *Cascade Ranch,* across Highway 1 from the reserve, is also now protected. The only trails, as of this writing, are dirt roads left over from farming days, but they provide spectacular views.

Swimming along the San Mateo coast, incidentally, is only for the brave, strong, and experienced—and for lovers of cold water or owners of good wetsuits. It is not recommended—unless the day's a real scorcher; the state does not staff most of these beaches with a lifeguard, so you're really on your own.

What is recommended on an outing to this exceptional coast is a side trip to the redwoods. Such an excursion will fit easily into a day's visit if you don't linger too long on a sunny beach. Or you might plan to spend the night in a shady campground. Either way, you will add a new dimension to your experience and enrich your memories thereby.

The 3,200-acre *Butano State Park* is only 7 miles from Highway 1; you turn inland on Pescadero Road for 2½ miles, then take Cloverdale Road 4½ miles to the park road. En route, enjoy the Victorian-Portuguese ambience of the town of Pescadero, which holds an Artichoke Festival every Labor Day as well as a Festival of the

Holy Ghost every sixth Sunday after Easter. If you're a bird-watcher, you'll also want to have your glasses out when you pass Pescadero Marsh. Should you visit Butano on your return from Año Nuevo, you can shortcut the journey through Pescadero by taking the Gazos Creek Road to Cloverdale Road and proceeding thence to the north.

The Butano redwoods were rescued from logging in the 1950s in another struggle where conservationists happily prevailed. The steep and densely clothed slopes and fern-bedecked canyons make for lovely if somewhat strenuous hiking, if you enjoy same. You can also find most pleasant and less challenging walks that will acquaint you with the fragrant, deep-shadowed forest of redwoods and Douglas firs. Rangers lead nature walks on weekends. There are 21 family campsites and 19 developed walk-in sites obtainable through DES-TINET (telephone 800-444-PARK [7275]). There is a modest fee for camping.

Other possible campsites among the redwood are at *Portola Redwoods State Park* (a 21-mile trip from Highway 1 following Pescadero Road to Alpine Road, thence south for 3 miles to Portola State Park Road into the park), which has 53 family campsites, 7 walk-in sites, a backpack camp, the amenity of hot showers, a nature trail, summer naturalist programs, a magnificent grove of old-growth redwoods, and particularly venerable giant called the Old Tree, estimated at 1,500 years. From May through December you must make reservations through DESTINET (telephone 800-444-PARK [7275]) for the family or walk-in campsites. Call the park to reserve the backpack camp (408-948-9098). Or you might consider San Mateo's *Memorial County Park,* which is at 9500 Pescadero Road. This park has fine redwoods, swimming, hiking, summer naturalist programs, and 154 campsites that do not require reservations. You can call the park at 650-879-0212 to find out if space will likely be available. A modest fee is charged. (See Parks of San Mateo County.)

Jasper Ridge
Biological Preserve

Jasper Ridge Biological Preserve is a remarkable 1,200-acre natural treasure, which is owned by Stanford University and operated as a research facility for scientists. Guided tours, however, can be arranged (October–May) and they offer anyone interested in the flora of the Peninsula a unique opportunity to see how the wild gardens of this lovely area once grew. (All of the plant communities of the Santa Cruz Mountains are represented here.) Geologists—and would-be geologists, too—will have a chance to view the San Andreas Fault here, as well as four distinct formations. In this one small area are well-defined samples of Eocene sandstone, exposed serpentine, and the Franciscan and Santa Clara formations: these account, of course, for the rich diversity of flora, for each formation supports a different variety of species. You will have a chance to see mixed evergreen forests (including six stands of second-growth redwoods, which have survived on fog drip), rare native grasses along with the beautiful flora that grows on serpentine, and other wildflowers that color this protected area as they once did the whole landscape in springtime. As bonus, you may also have some lovely distant views of San Francisco to the north.

Jasper Ridge Biological Preserve is located in the Stanford foothill property, touching on the communities of Woodside and Portola Valley (about an hour south of San Francisco). Detailed access directions are given when arrangements are made for a tour. Telephone 650-327-2277—the Jasper Ridge Tour Service (staffed by docents)—for information or an appointment to visit this wonderfully preserved piece of Bay Area land. There is a modest fee for the tours, and participants must be 14 years or older.

Historic Hikes in the South Bay

Los Trancos Earthquake Trail and Picchetti Ranch

If you'd like to sample some of the Peninsula's lovely country along with its geology, its history and, incidentally, its wine, you can spend a most pleasant day doing so, especially in the wildflower season when you can look for such lovelies as poppies, blue-eyed grass, buttercups, lupine, and Indian paintbrush. You can start at the Los Trancos Open Space Preserve and end up on Monte Bello Ridge at the Picchetti Ranch. You might want to bring a picnic lunch. Take I-280 to Page Mill Road, turn west and climb about 6 miles to the parking lot at the preserve; or you can take Skyline Boulevard to Page Mill Road and turn east for about a mile. (Should this parking lot be full—unlikely except on Sundays at 2:00 P.M. when docents lead monthly walks along the earthquake trail—the ample lot for the Monte Bello Preserve is just across the road.)

The San Andreas Fault, here high on the hillside, runs through Los Trancos Preserve and offers an intriguing opportunity to see the effects of the 1906 earthquake. There is a short, signed, self-guided earthquake trail that is easy to follow using the informative brochure provided by the Midpeninsula Regional Open Space District at the trailhead. Look for sag ponds, offset fences, pressure ridges, marshy areas, benches, landslides, and more. You can easily spend an hour on this trail if you're interested. Perhaps the most striking part of it is the high point above the parking lot; here you get unique views along the fault line north to San Francisco, and at your feet are boulders that match those on Loma Prieta Mountain, which you can see some 25 miles to the south. (You can also see Mount Diablo to the east.)

Then to enjoy a little more of this pleasant hillside, start on the Franciscan Loop Trail outlined on your earthquake brochure. This will take you downhill past Fault Marker 2 into the grand bay and oak forest and past a little stream (dry in summer and fall) and a spring; this is the headwaters of Los Trancos Stream, a watercourse that follows a linear break in the rocks caused by fault movements. Keep to the left at each of the two trail junctions you come to and you will be on the Lost Creek Loop Trail. You wind through small open meadows and shadowy fern-ornamented forests where, in the spring, you may find trillium and other shade-loving flowers. When you come to Page Mill Trail, turn to your left again and continue on to the grassy meadows that open up a wonderful view of the bay and the country around you. This is the northernmost boundary of the preserve, and it offers a choice of settings for your picnic lunch. Choose a shady spot beneath an oak or a madrone tree, or stretch yourself out beneath the brilliant sky. Wildflowers may star the grasses, while hawks hang-glide above you, and you may have birdsong for your music.

The first part of your return is a doubling back on Page Mill Trail, but when you reach the Lost Creek Loop Trail, turn to the left instead of retracing your earlier steps. This will lead you into the Franciscan Loop Trail past not-so-old evidence of fault activity, shows of spring wildflowers (starting in February with the brilliant blues and purples of iris), the remnants of an old vineyard, and, lastly, a high meadow that adjoins the parking lot. In all, you will have walked close to 4½ miles.

Before going on to the Picchetti Ranch, you may want to cross the road for a look at the Monte Bello Preserve, whose 2,634 acres embrace all of the upper watershed of Stevens Creek and adjoin Santa Clara County's Upper Stevens Creek Park. This is one of the choicer, wilder areas of open space protected on the Peninsula, and it has some lovely trails as well as wonderful wildflowers. You might want to look at the MROSD brochure that you can pick up here to get an idea—or inspiration—for future hikes.

To reach the Picchetti Ranch, return to I-280, turn right and continue on this freeway to Stevens Canyon Road (about 6 miles), where you turn to the right again. A little over 3 miles on Stevens Canyon Road brings you to a reservoir. Continue past it and keep straight onto Monte Bello Road; you will be at the ranch almost immediately. There's a place to park your car, and, on Fridays, Saturdays, and Sundays, the winery is open between 11:00 A.M. and 3:00 P.M. Visitors are welcome to look around and take a taste or two.

Vincenso and Secondo Picchetti were pioneer Italians who acquired this ranch land in the 1880s. Here they planted grapes and orchards and built their barn, their large ranch house, and lastly their brick winery. The Picchettis kept the property in the family for over a hundred years, and until 1963 the winery produced wine under the Picchetti Brothers label. The volume, however, decreased steadily, and now only 5 acres of the original vineyard remain in grapes. Happily, the Midpeninsula Regional Open Space District was able to acquire the Picchetti Ranch in 1976. Now, another family is living there and is restoring the buildings and carrying on the Picchetti tradition of producing good wines, but under their own Sunrise Winery label. The brick winery is worth a visit for a look at its great old timbers and hand-carved vats alone. The wine itself is well worth a tasting, too. Although the charming Victorian home is off-limits, it can be admired from a short distance away. You can also picnic here. Should you want to stroll a little farther, there's a pleasant trail winding past the buildings and the orchards and through oak woodland and on into this 372-acre preserve. If you're a serious oenophile, and it's a Saturday, you can also visit the Ridge Vineyards about 4 miles farther along Monte Bello Road; tastings are held between 11:00 A.M. and 3:00 P.M. on Saturdays and Sundays.

Allow an hour and a quarter plus for driving back to San Francisco via the Junipero Serra Freeway (I-280). On your way back, note the Stanford University linear accelerator (just past Alpine Road) and the somewhat controversial statue of Father Serra that looms up on a hill to your right.

A Walk Up Sweeney Ridge

A notable unit of the Golden Gate National Recreation Area is in San Mateo County; it is a historical treasure, sometimes called the Plymouth Rock of the West. This is the 1,200-foot-high hilltop where Gaspar de Portolá and his men looked out over San Francisco on a brisk, bright November day in 1769. Although he could see the land from Mount Tamalpais to the north, Mount Diablo to the east, Montara Mountain to the south and, to the west, the sweep of the Pacific Ocean from Pedro Point to Mussel Rock—and at his feet, the shimmer of the South Bay—Portolá was not impressed, and stumped off to the south in pursuit of the elusive Monterey Bay. Anyone positioned where he stood, however, will be dazzled by the view on a clear day, and history buffs can have the added adventure of more or less retracing Portolá's steps to this vantage point. By an accident of fate, this is not known as Portolá's Point, or the Spaniards' Summit, but as Sweeney Ridge. It memorializes a shadowy figure who once ran his cattle here, but little else remains of Mr. Sweeney's claim to fame.

Sweeney Ridge's 1,047-acre parkland can be approached from either the east or the west. From the east, take Sneath Lane off Highway 101 to its end, where you can leave your car, and continue on foot up the mile-long paved road to the top. There's a Portolá monument that supposedly marks the spot the Spanish explorer stood. From the west, you can enjoy a longer walk, and you'll be approaching the summit from the direction in which the Spanish explorers came. (Telephone 650-239-2366 for information on scheduled hikes, perhaps one by moonlight—a reservation is required.) You can also enjoy a somewhat steep ascent from the eastern section of parking lot number 2 of Skyline College in San Bruno; from there, a short road leads to the north end of the park's 3-mile trail up the hill. Or, you can take an easier, shorter (1-mile) route from the Shelldance Nursery at 2000 Cabrillo Highway in Pacifica.

The hike up Sweeney Ridge is especially lovely during the spring wildflower season. Then the meadows glow as though painted with blues and golds and reds. The grasses are fresh and green, and the world seems to be renewing itself. And as you gain the heights, the views begin to open up around you, adding their soft pastels and patterns to the scene. The area at the top is a nice place for a picnic if the day isn't too breezy (which it very well may be, so dress accordingly), or you can drop down the western slope a short distance to a grove of eucalyptus trees to find a sheltered place. Kite flyers find the high ridge a great place to practice their craft. The months of September and October, too, are good months to visit Portolá's monument, for there's less apt to be fog and wind, the proximity to the ocean usually makes for a pleasant coolness on the western slopes, and even then, there are likely to be lingering blooms. Of course, if you're a stickler for reliving historic moments, you can try to take this hike on the fateful date of November 4. *Note:* The city of Pacifica worked hard to have Sweeney Ridge made a park, and is justly proud to have it in its own backyard.

Note: If you would like to explore further south on the Peninsula, the 66NRA unit, the Phleger Estate, adjoins Huddart County Park and, singly or together, they can offer hours of lovely walking. The Phleger Estate is reached via Huddart County Park, in the town of Woodside. From Highway 280, exit at Highway 84 (Woodside Road) and proceed west through Woodside for 1.7 miles, then bear right on Kings Mountain Road for 1.5 miles. The Huddart Park entrance is on the right. Park at the first parking lot, immediately past the entrance station. Huddart Park charges an entrance fee.

Just east of the parking lot is a signed trailhead. Descend on the Crystal Springs Trail to Richards Road Trail. The entry point to the Phleger Estate and Woodside trails is just north of McGarvey Gulch. Telephone 650-239-2366 for further information.

Appendixes

Natural History

Tips for Rock Watchers

People who are interested in geology come from long distances to see the fascinating geological displays that abound in the Bay Area. These are an added plus for any outdoor adventurer, for they mark the ancient actions of the earth that have resulted in this lovely landscape. As you travel through this part of California, keep your eyes open for these natural exhibits: many are very easy to see and to enjoy. For instance, you might like to walk along one of the earth's most famous transform faults, the San Andreas; this is easily done at Point Reyes National Seashore in Marin County, where there is an excellent earthquake walk with signs and exhibits. Or you can drive right along this fault on Highway 1 in the Olema Valley, again in Marin. There is another good perspective of the San Andreas to be had at the Los Trancos unit of the Midpeninsula Regional Open Space District in San Mateo County. You reach this spot by car, and then take a short, signed earthquake walk, using a small, free interpretive brochure that points out the clearly visible fault slicing through the Coast Ranges to the north, and which also identifies some interesting earthquake side effects in the immediate landscape. Alternatively, you can stand on land that was rafted to the Bay Area from hundreds of miles away—the Point Reyes Peninsula. Or walk on the Great Valley land that lies to the east of the Hayward fault in the Berkeley-Oakland hills. Should you be a rock hound, you can look for the many interesting, often lovely, rocks that mark the Bay Area as a scene of turbulent geological action. (*Note:* Rocks may not be collected in parks.) Here are a few that may be easy to find:

Ribbon Chert. This beautiful sedimentary rock forms on the floors of oceans as the tiny skeletons of radiolarians (one-celled animals), diatoms (one-celled plants), and dust particles (often reddish, from their oxidized-iron content) drift down in incredible numbers to be compacted together in bands that are sandwiched with fine layers of shale to form a somewhat uniform ribboned—and quite spectacular—pattern. (Geologists do not know why this even banding occurs; it is not an indicator of discrete geologic processes as is the banding found in some other sedimentary rocks.) There are readily seen displays of ribbon chert in the road cuts of Conzelman Road in the Marin Headlands. Once you have identified ribbon chert, you will recognize it in many other places; it is ubiquitous in the Bay Area.

Graywacke. This is dark sandstone that may occur with dark gray claystone and shale; as it weathers, it becomes lighter, tannish in color, readily broken, and more obviously sandy looking. It, too, is a ubiquitous Bay Area rock. Shale is another dark gray rock, sedimentary, and formed of clay; it breaks into flat-surfaced slices. There's a good display of sandstone on the east-facing cliff of Telegraph Hill in San Francisco (Sansome Street near the Embarcadero).

Pillow Basalt (Greenstone). This is formed when lava is freshly extruded from the midocean spreading zones. Uplifted, it looks something like a stack of dark pillows cemented together; it is quite easy to recognize in its unweathered state, when it is dark green/black in color. When exposed to weather, it turns orange brown or red brown and breaks into curved pieces with very dark surfaces. There is a classic exhibit of unweathered pillow basalt in a road cut of the Petaluma–Point Reyes Road just west of Nicasio Reservoir in Marin County. In fact, Black Mountain (of which this outcropping is a part) is one big heap of this interesting rock.

Serpentine. This highly mineralized rock comes from the earth's upper mantle, which has been metamorphosed and forced up and out during the process of plate subduction. Serpentine comes in shades of green—from light gray-green and bluish green to dark green-black. In some forms it has a surface as smooth as glass and is called slickenside; slickenside is thought to facilitate or lubricate earth movements along fault lines. San Francisco's New Mint Building at Market and Church streets sits on top of a fine outcropping of serpentine; there is a fine exhibit of asbestos-laced serpentine uphill from Fort Point (see GGNRA Walk 2); and there are many exhibits of serpentine on road cuts and in outcroppings on Mount Tamalpais. This is California's official state rock.

It is worth noting that serpentine soil supports a unique plant community that includes the Sargent cypress and a low-growing manzanita with deep pink blossoms and dark green leaves. This community can be found on the Nature Conservancy's Ring Mountain preserve in Tiburon, above and east of Bootjack Camp on Mount Tamalpais, and in the Kent Lake region of Marin County's Municipal Water District off the Bolinas-Fairfax Road; it is worth looking for in late spring (April).

Schist. This metamorphic rock can be formed from sandstone, basalt, chert, shale, or serpentine—given the right conditions of heat and pressure. It splits easily into sheetlike fragments: the word *schistose* is used to describe other rocks that do likewise.

Schist is particularly interesting in its beautiful blueschist form, which can be produced only under precise, demanding conditions: it requires the kind of fierce pressure that occurs deep underground in a region that is normally quite hot, but it also requires a low temperature (between 100 and 300 degrees Celsius) and must be ejected to the surface before that temperature gets higher. The environment most likely to meet these unusual rock-forming requirements, the theory goes, is an active subduction zone. If this is correct, blueschist provides a neat index to the occurrence of subduction. One of the best places to see blueschist is on Angel Island, where it is exposed at Perle's Beach and at Camp Reynolds; it is also found on Ring Mountain.

Mélange. Rocks pulverized in the collision of tectonic plates can end up looking like they had been ground up in a gigantic Cuisinart machine: only the most resistant emerge in any kind of shape. The end product, according to one geologist, is like a vast pudding, studded here and there with a raisin or a piece of walnut. You will notice random outcroppings of more or less large, resistant rocks in homogenous soil throughout the Bay Area; they mark the Franciscan mélange. You can see a display of this quite easily at San Francisco's Baker Beach.

Note: An excellent geological guide for a car-less walker in the Bay Area is the late Clyde Wahrhaftig's *A Streetcar to Subduction* (see Bibliography). This book contains a lucid, somewhat detailed explanation of plate tectonics and descriptions of various Bay Area geological displays; the lay reader must read it carefully, but it is extremely helpful, once understood. The book is highly recommended for (would-be) geologists who enjoy traveling on streetcars, buses, or BART trains.

Bay Area Wildflowers

The best way to see wildflowers is, of course, on foot. There are opportunities—mentioned in this book—in all the nine Bay Area counties. If you're a wildflower aficionado, you might enjoy my favorite wildflower walk—up Mount Wittenberg in Point Reyes National Seashore sometime around the first of April. (You can check with the park people to find out when the show of wildflowers is at its height.) This short, steep climb will take you through lovely old forests, through meadows that may still be starred with wild iris (the first flower to greet the spring), and to an open summit that may stop your heart with its color—when the lupine is at its height, it drenches this hillside with deep, deep blue. West of the summit, the slopes of the mountain glow with lupine, poppies, and tidy tips: well-traveled people agree that this show equals the best anywhere in the world. If you're lucky, you may see a kestrel hovering above this gorgeous display of blossoms, or—as I did one memorable time—a lazuli bunting, showing off its dazzle of colors in contrast.

If you prefer to view your wildflowers from a comfortable car seat, you will also have many opportunities to see outstanding springtime shows in the Bay Area. You can, for example, drive to the top of Twin Peaks in San Francisco, or take Highway 12 in Sonoma County past the Bouverie Wildflower Preserve near Glen Ellen. I-280 down the Peninsula skirts Edgewood Park and other stands of spring bloomers. Mount Hamilton is famous for its wildflower displays, as is Mount Diablo in the East Bay. In fact, the highway cuts along many of the Bay Area freeways are often blue with native lupines in the spring months, and even the meadows where grazing continues may be splashed with the sun-colors of poppies welcoming the warmer days.

On a conservative estimate, there are over 2,000 species of plants to be found in the San Francisco Bay Area. There are also very good illustrated lists of the local flora to be found in Bay Area and national park bookstores. Since it would stretch the seams of this small volume to try to integrate and duplicate such lists, it seemed preferable to take a look at the history of how and where some of the familiar Bay Area flora came to be identified and named.

In October of 1816, Lieutenant Otto von Kotzebue, of the Russian Imperial Navy, sailed the two-masted, square-rigged brig *Rurik* into San Francisco Bay. This small (70- or 80-foot-long) ship was ostensibly exploring the western shores of the New World but was undoubtedly also surveying the condition of Spain's New World empire on behalf of the ambitious Russian crown. The *Rurik*'s crew numbered 31, which included 4 scientists, notable for their youth. Von Kotzebue was only 28; Adelbert von Chamisso, the ship's naturalist and chief scientist—a versatile man who served as interpreter as well—was 34. The ship's doctor, Johann Friedrich Eschscholtz, was 22; the expedition's artist, Login Choris, was 20. These men reflected the cosmopolitan nature of the Russian navy: only one of the group, Eschscholtz, was a native Russian. Von Kotzebue and Choris were both of German extraction, and Chamisso (christened Louis Charles Adelaide de Chamisso) was a French-born German who wrote in both languages and was also fluent in English and Spanish. The volunteer naturalist of the *Rurik*, Martin Wormskjold, who was left behind in Kamchatka, was Danish.

After visiting Brazil and Chile and looking over the Bering Strait in Oonalashka (later Alaska), the *Rurik* headed for Hawaii via San Francisco Bay. Landing on the afternoon of October 2 at four o'clock, the *Rurik* party found the Spanish in a sorry situation, seemingly abandoned and forgotten, and without even a single boat to send in welcome "in this glorious water-basin"; so noted Chamisso in his diary. He went on to write of the members of the Spanish military garrison: "The misery in which they languished, forgotten and deserted for six or seven years . . . did not permit them to be hosts." (The soldiers had received no pay in seven years.) Don Luis de Arguello was the commandant, and he received the Russian party "in an exceptionally friendly manner," undoubtedly delighted to have some new and distinguished company to break up the boredom of his impoverished days. "We ate on shore, in our tent," Chamisso reported, "and our friends from the Presidio were always promptly on hand."

The *Rurik* stayed a month in San Francisco Bay, and although "the country exhibits in autumn only the prospect of bare scorched tracts, alternating with poor stunted bushes, and . . . dazzling wastes of drift sands," the ship's scientists were excited at the prospect of exploring the flora. (They found even this to be "poor.") Archibald Menzies and George W. Langsdorff were the only botanists who had been there before them, and they had catalogued a few of the "well-known North American species—*Ceanothus, Mimulus, Oenothera, Solidago, Aster, Rhamnus, Salix,* etc.," but their work was far from comprehensive or complete. Both Chamisso and Eschscholtz (who was interested in fauna as well as flora) went to work collecting and describing as yet undiscovered specimens. (Chamisso called his pressed specimens "hay.") Their exploration was directed to the "hills and downs" of the Presidio. As it happened, Eschscholtz returned to the same place eight years later (on a different ship, but with the same von Kotzebue, by then a captain in the navy), at which time he added to his collection. In the first expedition, Chamisso and Eschscholtz collected and named 69 species, of which 33—including two genera among them—were new. On his second visit, Eschscholtz added another 13 species, 10 of which were undescribed. In all, the two *Rurik* botanists (and later colleagues) were responsible for naming 82 Bay Area species.

More than 150 years later, botanist and artist Ida Geary, who taught plant identification at Fort Point for San Francisco Community College (and to whom I am indebted for the information presented here), started a search for these plants. She was unaware that Alice Eastwood, doyenne of San Francisco botanists, had written in the 1940s that "very few" of the species remained, most having "been killed by the dense forest of cypress, pine, and eucalyptus planted years ago, and more recently by the *Mesembryanthemum.*" Eastwood would doubtless have been delighted to be proved wrong, and so she was. Geary located 54 (nearly two-thirds) of the species collected by Chamisso and Eschscholtz—all of them in the Presidio. Here is the list, with the plants still surviving in the Presidio identified by an asterisk; virtually all of these plants still grow in other parts of the Bay Area.

Chamisso's List (1816)

Family	Scientific Name	Common Name
Arrow-grass	*†Triglochin maritima	Arrow-grass
Bayberry	*Myrica californica	California wax-myrtle
Borage	Allocarya chorisiana	Forget-me-not

Buckwheat	*_Polygonum paronychia_	Sand jointweed
	†_P. punctatum_	Water smartweed
	*†_Rumex salicifolius_	Willow-leafed dock
Dogwood	*†_Cornus californica_	Creek dogwood
Figwort	*†_Castilleja latifolia_	Indian paintbrush
	*†_Diplacus aurantiacus_	Sticky monkeyflower
	Scrophularia californica	California bee plant
	*†_Veronica americana_	Speedwell
Frankenia	_Frankenia grandifolia_	Frankenia
Hazel	†_Corylus californica_	Hazelnut
Hornwort	_Ceratophyllum demersum_	Hornwort
Mint	*_Satureja chamissonis_	Yerba buena
	Stachys ajugoides	Hedge-nettle
	S. chamissonis	Chamisso's hedge-nettle
Mustard	*_Erysimum franciscanum_	Wallflower
Najas	†_Najas guadalupenis_	Water-plant
Oak	*†_Quercus agrifolia_	Coast live oak
Orobanche	*_Orobanche californica_	California broom-rape
Parsley	†_Hydrocotyle ranunculoides_	Marsh pennywort
Pea	†_Astragalus gambellianus_	Locoweed
	†_Lotus eriophorus_	Lotus
	*†_L. scoparius_	Deerweed
	*†_Trifolium wormskjoldii_	Cow clover
	*†_Vicia gigantea_	Giant vetch
Pink	†_Silene verecunda_	Silene
Plantain	*†_Plantago maritima_	Seaside plantain
Pondweed	_Potamogeton americanus_	Pondweed
Poppy	*_Eschscholzia californica_	California poppy
Rose	*_Fragaria californica_	Wood strawberry
	*†_F. chiloensis_	Beach strawberry
	*†_Photinia arbutifolia_	Toyon
	Potentilla californica	Silverweed
	*†_P. pacifica_	Silverweed
	Rosa californica	California rose
	*_Rubus ursinus_	California blackberry
	*_R. vitifolius_	Grape-leaf blackberry
St. John's Wort	_Hypericum anagalloides_	Marsh–St. John's wort

Sunflower	*†*Achillea borealis*	Yarrow
	Agoseris apargioides	California dandelion
	Ambrosia chamissonis	Chamisso's beachbur
	*†*Anaphalis margaritacea*	Pearly everlasting
	Artemisia californica	California sagebrush
	A. pycnocephala	Dune sagebrush
	†*Baccharis douglasii*	Saltmarsh coyote brush
	*†*B. pilularis*	Coyote brush
	Erigeron glaucus	Seaside daisy
	Eriophyllum artemisiaefolium	Lizard-leaf
	†*Gnaphalium californicum*	Cudweed
	*†*G. chilense*	Cudweed (hybrid)
	†*G. palustre*	Cudweed
	*†*Grindelia maritima*	Seaside gumplant
	Haplopappus ericoides	Mock-heather
	Helenium puberulum	Sneezeweed
	Jaumea carnosa	Jaumea
	Lessingia germanorum	Lessingia
	†*Solidago californica*	California goldenrod
	†*S. elongata*	Goldenrod
	*†*S. occidentalis*	Goldenrod
	*†*S. spathulata*	Goldenrod
	Tanacetum camphoratum	Dune tansy
	*†*Wyethia angustifolia*	Wythia
Violet	*†*Viola adunca*	Blue violet
Waterleaf	*Phacelia californica*	California phacelia
	P. malvaefolia	Mallow-leafed phacelia
Water-Milfoil	†*Myriophyllum exalbescens*	Myriophyllum

* Flowers still extant in the Presidio.
† Species previously described.

Eschscholtz's List (1824)

Family	Scientific Name	Common Name
Buckthorn	*Ceanothus thyrsiflorus*	California lilac
	Rhamnus californica	California coffeeberry
Buckwheat	*†*Eriogonum latifolium*	Buckwheat

Four o'clock	*Abronia latifolia	Yellow sand verbena
Frankenia	†Frankenia grandifolia	Frankenia
Honeysuckle	*Lonicera ledebourii	Twinberry
Nightshade	Solanum umbelliferum	Nightshade
Pea	*Lupinus chamissonis	Chamisso's sand lupine
	*†Lupinus arboreus	Yellow bush lupine
Phlox	*Gilia chamissonis	Chamisso's gilia
	*Navarretia squarrosa	Skunkweed
Saxifrage	Ribes malvaceum	Wild currant
Spurge	*Croton californicus	Sand-croton

* Flowers still extant in the Presidio.
† Species previously described.

The Coast Redwoods

California's coast redwoods, *Sequoia sempervirens,* are unique in today's world, although in the course of their long, long history, species of redwoods have grown all the way across the United States, across all of Canada and Newfoundland, and across Europe and Asia—from France to Japan. Changes in climate, geological events— call them accidents of fate—gradually eliminated those great ancient forests. The coast redwoods, as it happened, made their last stand along a narrow strip (some 450 miles long) along the cool and moist Pacific coast of northern California. (Another species, *Sequoia gigantea,* the famous Big Tree, chose the southern slopes of the Sierra Nevada for its ultimate try for survival; and a third species, *Metasequoia,* which once flourished from the Black Sea to Greenland and was thought to have died out 25 million years ago, still grows in one small area in the Szechuan and Hupeh provinces of China.)

Redwoods are among the oldest species of trees that still exist. No one knows for sure when the first redwood thrust its way up through the primeval soils. But one day some 165 million years ago, a frond of redwood fell into the mud in what is now Manchuria and was sealed away to form a fossil record. Thus we know that there were redwoods long before there were mammals—and much, much longer before there were people. The trees are unusually well equipped for survival: their bark and their heartwood have an exceptionally high content of tannin, which makes the trees resistant to rot, dampness, fungi, and insects. And while it is true that redwoods produce only a

Redwood forest with sword ferns, Muir Woods National Monument. PHOTO BY RICHARD FREAR.

limited number of viable seeds, the trees do not die when they fall, but continue to live on by regenerating sprouts from their roots. This often results in a circular stand of redwoods: the young trees mark the girth of their parent tree, and so are sometimes referred to as a "family circle."

The Indian people, probably the first to come to live among the redwoods, respected the trees and were in awe of their dark and shadowy forests. The first white men who found the trees—the Spanish conquistadores of California—took only a few of the giants for their use. But when the Yankees arrived, they promptly fell to cutting the redwoods down. The trees they found were, in fact, incredible, taller than any they had ever seen before. (The tallest tree on record—anywhere in the world—is a *Sequoia sempervirens* 367 feet high that stands on a river flat of Redwood Creek in the Redwood National Park in northern California's Humboldt County.) When they got around to counting the rings in the huge stumps they left standing (people held dances on some of those stumps, so large were they), those early loggers found that the redwoods were extraordinarily tenacious of life: many had lived for 2,000 years or more. (There is a record of a Big Tree 4,000 years old; only the bristlecone pine is known to live longer.) Unrecognized by those early loggers was another remarkable feature of the redwoods; because they condense fog on their needles and let fall the drops of water so formed, they can add many inches to the annual rainfall of a region in which they grow.

The coast redwood (in contradistinction to the Big Tree, which shattered easily) also proved to be exceptionally valuable, its wood having many of the qualities of the living tree: its insect resistance extended even to termites, and its rot resistance enabled it to tolerate contact with earth and water. It turned out to be nonwarping as well, and it was comparatively light and easy to handle—and to fashion into boards, shingles and shakes, fence posts, wharf piles, matches, water tanks, pipelines and sluice boxes, cigar boxes, and coffins. Furthermore, it was beautiful, especially the heartwood. "The heartwood needs no coloring but its own natural soft rich hue," wrote Donald Culrose Peattie. "More, it has an inexplicable gloss of its own as delicate as the shimmer on a tress of blond hair." To top it all, one tree alone could contain enough board feet of wood to produce 15,000 shingles. And the supply of redwoods seemed to be endless. (There are estimated to have been, in fact, 2 million acres of redwood forests when logging first got under way.) What man in his right mind wouldn't profit from the redwoods? John Muir summed it up neatly: "As timber, the redwood is too good to live."

The California pioneers lost little time in claiming the redwood forests for their private land. Many of the forests were cleared for farmland and communities; more of them were harvested for their timber. This was especially true around the Bay Area, where the trees were easily accessed and the timber was easily brought to market. It took a team of men a week to bring down a redwood in the early days, and teams of oxen or bulls to "skid" the logs to the waterfront dump, or landing. But the introduction of steam machines (in particular the "Dolbeer Donkey," a one-cylinder contraption that hauled logs far faster than any beast) increased the speed and volume (and the destructive side effects) of logging. Despite this, it took a while to make a real dent in the total redwood resource. Many of the redwood forests to the north were inaccessible, and getting the timber to market was difficult. Thus it was that when the movement to "Save the Redwoods" finally began in the teens of the twentieth century, there were still magnificent park possibilities. (It is worth mentioning that redwoods were first christened "bastard cedars": imagine how different it would have been to try to "Save the Bastard Cedars"!) A few generous souls had given to the federal government (see Muir Woods) or to the state (see Big Basin State Park) the very few redwood parks there were at that time, and it immediately became clear that to gain more sizable redwood parks, the forests would have to be bought back from the (powerful and influential) lumber companies controlling the resource. Or that the public would have to depend upon the companies' generosity.

Gaining momentum during the twenties, the Save-the-Redwoods League did yeoman labor on behalf of the redwoods for decades. As a result, the California State Redwood Parks—to whom the league deeded the forests—ended up with some truly magnificent stands. But by the 1960s it was recognized that these were too few and far between—and some of the parks were almost as tall as they were wide. By this time, expanded and speeded-up logging of the redwoods had reduced park options drastically: of the original 2 million acres of redwood forest land, less than 10 percent—in bits and pieces—remained. At long last, the federal government entered the park picture seriously. The Sierra Club led the fight for a Redwood National Park large enough to afford real preservation for the species. (Edgar Wayburn initiated the battle and chaired the club's Redwood Task Force.) The park struggle was unusually tough, but unusually brief: in 1968, a Redwood National Park was established on Redwood Creek. Ten years later, it was expanded—largely because of the work of the late congressman Phillip Burton.

People in the Bay Area have only a few fragments of virgin redwood forest to visit: Big Basin State Park (the first of California's state parks, as well as, in part, a gift to the state) is the most distant (see The Parks of Santa Clara County) and has perhaps the most significant acreage. Butano State Park and Portola State Park down the Peninsula, Muir Woods in Marin County, and the Armstrong Grove in Sonoma County are also noteworthy. But the list is short. Second-growth redwoods stand along the crest of the East Bay hills, in places on Mount Tamalpais and its watersheds, and down the Peninsula and in the North Bay here and there, vivid reminders of the grand forests that preceded them.

But every redwood park and grove—large or small, second growth or no—in the Bay Area is a very special place, and one to be sought out and visited. For whenever you stand among these grand trees, survivors of untold millennia, you can, if you will, renew your ties to the primeval earth. You can sense the strength and the will to live that is epitomized in this remarkable species. And, perhaps you will, if you are fortunate, experience the wonder, the peace, and the beauty that are inherent in so much of the natural world around us.

Birding in the Bay Area

Some of the best birding in the United States occurs in the Bay Area. Not only does this lovely part of the earth lie along the Pacific Flyway, the well-traveled route of hundreds of thousands of birds, but it offers a wide variety of environments to an equally wide variety of species. From the pelicans gliding just above the waves, to the elegant egrets ornamenting the marshlands, to the shy wrentits carolling their bouncy song in the chaparral, and the kestrels hanging motionless above the mountain meadows, you will find an avian occupant of virtually every kind of landscape at every elevation. Add to this the hook of land thrust into the ocean by the Point Reyes Peninsula itself, and you have a birder's dream come true: migrants and vagrants as well are snagged in their overwater flight, and you can hope to enjoy rare as well as expected sightings there. For an update on which rare bird is where, you can call 415-681-7422.

The following list of Bay Area birds was prepared by ornithologist Dr. David DeSante. Not to worry if you don't sight every bird on this wonderfully comprehensive list of 479 species! Dave has sharp eyes: his "yard list"—birds seen from his former yard above Bolinas Lagoon—alone totals 171 species. (With Peter Pyle, Dave has published a definitive distributional checklist of North American birds—see Bibliography.)

Checklist of the Birds
of the San Francisco Bay Area
Compiled by David F. DeSante

Loons
Red-throated Loon
Pacific Loon
Common Loon
Yellow-billed Loon   V

Grebes
Pied-billed Grebe   B
Horned Grebe
Red-necked Grebe
Eared Grebe   b
Western Grebe
Clark's Grebe

Albatrosses
Wandering Albatross   V
Short-tailed Albatross   V
Black-footed Albatross
Laysan Albatross

Shearwaters and Petrels
Northern Fulmar   V
Mottled Petrel   V
Solander's Petrel   V
Murphy's Petrel   V
Cook's Petrel
Pink-footed Shearwater
Flesh-footed Shearwater
Buller's Shearwater
Sooty Shearwater
Short-tailed Shearwater
Black-vented Shearwater
Townsend's Shearwater   V

Storm-Petrels
Wilson's Storm-Petrel   V

Storm-Petrels (cont'd.)
Fork-tailed Storm-Petrel
Leach's Storm-Petrel   B
Ashy Storm-Petrel   B
Black Storm-Petrel

Tropicbirds
Red-tailed Tropicbird   V

Boobies and Gannets
Blue-footed Booby   V
Brown Booby   V
Red-footed Booby   V

Pelicans
American White Pelican
Brown Pelican

Cormorants
Double-crested Cormorant   B
Brandt's Cormorant   B
Pelagic Cormorant   B

Frigatebirds
Magnificent Frigatebird   V

Bitterns and Herons
American Bittern   B
Least Bittern
Great Blue Heron   B
Great Egret   B
Snowy Egret   B
Little Blue Heron   V, b
Cattle Egret
Green-backed Heron   B
Black-crowned Night-Heron   B
Yellow-crowned Night-Heron   V

B = Breeds in the San Francisco Bay Area; b = Formerly or rarely has bred in the area; V = Vagrant—out of its normal range or off its normal migration route; I = Introduced.

Ibises and Spoonbills

White Ibis	V
White-faced Ibis	

Storks

Wood Stork	V

Swans, Geese, and Ducks

Fulvous Whistling-Duck	V
Tundra Swan	
Trumpeter Swan	V
Greater White-fronted Goose	
Snow Goose	
Ross' Goose	
Emperor Goose	V
Brant	
Canada Goose	B
Wood Duck	B
Green-winged Teal	
Baikal Teal	V
Mallard	B
Northern Pintail	B
Blue-winged Teal	B
Cinnamon Teal	B
Northern Shoveler	B
Gadwall	B
Eurasian Wigeon	
American Wigeon	
Canvasback	
Redhead	B
Ring-necked Duck	
Tufted Duck	V
Greater Scaup	
Lesser Scaup	
King Eider	V
Harlequin Duck	
Oldsquaw	
Black Scoter	
Surf Scoter	
White-winged Scoter	

Swans, Geese, and Ducks (cont'd.)

Common Goldeneye	
Barrow's Goldeneye	
Bufflehead	
Smew	V
Hooded Merganser	
Common Merganser	B
Red-breasted Merganser	
Ruddy Duck	B

American Vultures

Turkey Vulture	B
California Condor	

Ospreys, Kites, Eagles, and Hawks

Osprey	B
Black-shouldered Kite	B
Mississippi Kite	V
Bald Eagle	b
Northern Harrier	B
Sharp-shinned Hawk	B
Cooper's Hawk	B
Northern Goshawk	V
Red-shouldered Hawk	B
Broad-winged Hawk	V
Swainson's Hawk	b
Red-tailed Hawk	B
Ferruginous Hawk	
Rough-legged Hawk	
Golden Eagle	B

Falcons

American Kestrel	B
Merlin	
Peregrine Falcon	b
Gyrfalcon	V
Prairie Falcon	B

B = Breeds in the San Francisco Bay Area; b = Formerly or rarely has bred in the area; V = Vagrant—out of its normal range or off its normal migration route; I = Introduced.

Partridges, Grouse, Turkeys, and Quail

Ring-necked Pheasant	B, I
Blue Grouse	B
Wild Turkey	B, I
California Quail	B
Mountain Quail	B

Rails, Gallinules, and Coots

Yellow Rail	V
Black Rail	B
Clapper Rail	B
Virginia Rail	B
Sora	B
Common Moorhen	B
American Coot	B

Cranes

Sandhill Crane

Plovers

Black-bellied Plover	
Lesser Golden Plover	
Snowy Plover	B
Semipalmated Plover	
Killdeer	B
Mountain Plover	
Eurasian Dotterel	V

Oystercatchers

Black Oystercatcher

Stilts and Avocets

Black-necked Stilt	B
American Avocet	B

Sandpipers and Phalaropes

Greater Yellowlegs
Lesser Yellowlegs
Solitary Sandpiper

Sandpipers and Phalaropes (cont'd.)

Willet	
Wandering Tattler	
Spotted Sandpiper	B
Upland Sandpiper	V
Whimbrel	
Long-billed Curlew	
Bar-tailed Godwit	V
Marbled Godwit	
Ruddy Turnstone	
Black Turnstone	
Surfbird	
Red Knot	
Sanderling	
Semipalmated Sandpiper	V
Western Sandpiper	
Little Stint	V
Least Sandpiper	
White-rumped Sandpiper	V
Baird's Sandpiper	
Pectoral Sandpiper	
Sharp-tailed Sandpiper	V
Rock Sandpiper	
Dunlin	
Curlew Sandpiper	V
Stilt Sandpiper	V
Buff-breasted Sandpiper	V
Ruff	V
Short-billed Dowitcher	
Long-billed Dowitcher	
Common Snipe	
Wilson's Phalarope	
Red-necked Phalarope	
Red Phalarope	

Jaegers, Gulls, Terns, and Skimmers

Pomarine Jaeger
Parasitic Jaeger
Long-tailed Jaeger

B = Breeds in the San Francisco Bay Area; b = Formerly or rarely has bred in the area; V = Vagrant—out of its normal range or off its normal migration route; I = Introduced.

Jaegers, Gulls, Terns, and Skimmers (cont'd.)

South Polar Skua
Laughing Gull — V
Franklin's Gull — V
Little Gull — V
Common Black-headed Gull — V
Bonaparte's Gull
Heermann's Gull — b
Mew Gull
Ring-billed Gull
California Gull — B
Herring Gull
Thayer's Gull
Iceland Gull — V
Western Gull — B
Glaucous-winged Gull
Glaucous Gull
Black-legged Kittiwake
Sabine's Gull
Caspian Tern — B
Royal Tern — V
Elegant Tern
Common Tern
Arctic Tern
Forster's Tern — B
Least Tern — B
Black Tern — B
Black Skimmer — V

Auks, Murres, and Puffins

Common Murre — B
Pigeon Guillemot — B
Marbled Murrelet — B
Xantus' Murrelet
Craveri's Murrelet — V
Ancient Murrelet
Cassin's Auklet — B
Parakeet Auklet — V
Least Auklet — V
Crested Auklet — V

Rhinocerous Auklet — B
Tufted Puffin — B
Horned Puffin — V

Pigeons and Doves

Rock Dove — B, I
Band-tailed Pigeon — B
White-winged Dove — V
Mourning Dove — B
Common Ground-Dove — V

Cuckoos, Roadrunners, and Anis

Black-billed Cuckoo — V
Yellow-billed Cuckoo — V
Greater Roadrunner — B

Barn-Owls

Common Barn-Owl — B

Typical Owls

Flammulated Owl — b
Western Screech-Owl — B
Great Horned Owl — B
Snowy Owl — V
Northern Pygmy-Owl — B
Burrowing Owl — B
Spotted Owl — B
Long-eared Owl — B
Short-eared Owl — B
Northern Saw-whet Owl — B

Goatsuckers

Lesser Nighthawk — B
Common Nighthawk — V
Common Poorwill — B
Whip-poor-will — V

Swifts

Black Swift — B
Chimney Swift — V

B = Breeds in the San Francisco Bay Area; b = Formerly or rarely has bred in the area; V = Vagrant—out of its normal range or off its normal migration route; I = Introduced.

Swifts (cont'd.) B
Vaux's Swift B
White-throated Swift

Hummingbirds
Ruby-throated Hummingbird V
Black-chinned Hummingbird b
Anna's Hummingbird B
Costa's Hummingbird B
Calliope Hummingbird
Rufous Hummingbird
Allen's Hummingbird B

Kingfishers
Belted Kingfisher B

Woodpeckers
Lewis' Woodpecker B
Acorn Woodpecker B
Yellow-bellied Sapsucker V
Red-naped Sapsucker V
Red-breasted Sapsucker B
Williamson's Sapsucker V
Nuttall's Woodpecker B
Downy Woodpecker B
Hairy Woodpecker B
White-headed Woodpecker V
Northern Flicker B
Pileated Woodpecker B

Tyrant Flycatchers
Olive-sided Flycatcher B
Greater Pewee V
Western Wood-Pewee B
Eastern Wood-Pewee V
Yellow-bellied Flycatcher V
Alder Flycatcher V
Willow Flycatcher b
Least Flycatcher V
Hammond's Flycatcher
Dusky Flycatcher

Tyrant Flycatchers (cont'd.)
Gray Flycatcher V
Western Flycatcher B
Black Phoebe B
Eastern Phoebe V
Say's Phoebe B
Vermilion Flycatcher V
Dusky-capped Flycatcher V
Ash-throated Flycatcher B
Great Crested Flycatcher V
Brown-crested Flycatcher V
Tropical Kingbird V
Cassin's Kingbird B
Thick-billed Kingbird V
Western Kingbird B
Eastern Kingbird V
Scissor-tailed Flycatcher V

Larks
Eurasian Skylark V
Horned Lark B

Swallows
Purple Martin B
Tree Swallow B
Violet-green Swallow B
Northern Rough-winged B
  Swallow
Bank Swallow B
Cliff Swallow B
Barn Swallow B

Jays, Magpies, and Crows
Steller's Jay B
Blue Jay V
Scrub Jay B
Pinyon Jay V
Clark's Nutcracker V
Black-billed Magpie V
Yellow-billed Magpie B
American Crow B
Common Raven B

B = Breeds in the San Francisco Bay Area; b = Formerly or rarely has bred in the area; V = Vagrant—out of its normal range or off its normal migration route; I = Introduced.

Titmice
Mountain Chickadee   V
Chestnut-backed Chickadee   B
Plain Titmouse   B

Bushtits
Bushtit   B

Nuthatches
Red-breasted Nuthatch   B
White-breasted Nuthatch   B
Pygmy Nuthatch   B

Creepers
Brown Creeper   B

Wrens
Rock Wren   B
Canyon Wren   B
Bewick's Wren   B
House Wren   B
Winter Wren   B
Sedge Wren   V
Marsh Wren   B

Dippers
American Dipper   B

**Old World Warblers,
Kinglets, Gnatcatchers,
Thrushes, and Babblers**
Dusky Warbler   V
Golden-crowned Kinglet   B
Ruby-crowned Kinglet
Blue-gray Gnatcatcher   B
Northern Wheatear   V
Western Bluebird   B
Mountain Bluebird
Townsend's Solitaire
Veery   V
Gray-cheeked Thrush   V

**Old World Warblers,
Kinglets, Gnatcatchers,
Thrushes, and Babblers**
(cont'd.)
Swainson's Thrush   B
Hermit Thrush   B
Wood Thrush   V
American Robin   B
Varied Thrush
Wrentit   B

**Mockingbirds and
Thrashers**
Gray Catbird   V
Northern Mockingbird   B
Sage Thrasher   V
Brown Thrasher   V
Bendire's Thrasher   V
California Thrasher   B

Wagtails and Pipits
Yellow Wagtail   V
Black-backed Wagtail   V
Red-throated Pipit   V
Water Pipit
Sprague's Pipit   V

Waxwings
Bohemian Waxwing   V
Cedar Waxwing   b

Silky-Flycatchers
Phainopepla   B

Shrikes
Brown Shrike   V
Northern Shrike
Loggerhead Shrike   B

Starlings
European Starling   B, I

B = Breeds in the San Francisco Bay Area; b = Formerly or rarely has bred in the area; V = Vagrant—out of its normal range or off its normal migration route; I = Introduced.

Vireos

White-eyed Vireo	V
Bell's Vireo	V
Solitary Vireo	B
Yellow-throated Vireo	V
Hutton's Vireo	B
Warbling Vireo	B
Philadelphia Vireo	V
Red-eyed Vireo	V

Wood-Warblers, Tanagers, Buntings, Sparrows, and Blackbirds

Blue-winged Warbler	V
Golden-winged Warbler	V
Tennessee Warbler	V
Orange-crowned Warbler	B
Nashville Warbler	
Virginia's Warbler	V
Lucy's Warbler	V
Northern Parula	V, b
Yellow Warbler	B
Chestnut-sided Warbler	V
Magnolia Warbler	V
Cape May Warbler	V
Black-throated Blue Warbler	V
Yellow-rumped Warbler	B
Black-throated Gray Warbler	B
Townsend's Warbler	
Hermit Warbler	B
Black-throated Green Warbler	V
Golden-cheeked Warbler	V
Blackburnian Warbler	V
Yellow-throated Warbler	V
Pine Warbler	V
Prairie Warbler	V
Palm Warbler	V
Bay-breasted Warbler	V
Blackpoll Warbler	V
Cerulean Warbler	V
Black-and-white Warbler	V

Wood-Warblers, Tanagers, Buntings, Sparrows, and Blackbirds (cont'd.)

American Redstart	V
Prothonotary Warbler	V
Worm-eating Warbler	V
Ovenbird	V
Northern Waterthrush	V
Kentucky Warbler	V
Connecticut Warbler	V
Mourning Warbler	V
MacGillivray's Warbler	B
Common Yellowthroat	B
Hooded Warbler	V
Wilson's Warbler	B
Canada Warbler	V
Painted Redstart	V
Yellow-breasted Chat	B
Hepatic Tanager	V
Summer Tanager	V
Scarlet Tanager	V
Western Tanager	B
Rose-breasted Grosbeak	V
Black-headed Grosbeak	B
Blue Grosbeak	
Lazuli Bunting	B
Indigo Bunting	V
Painted Bunting	V
Dickcissel	V
Green-tailed Towhee	
Rufous-sided Towhee	B
Brown Towhee	B
Cassin's Sparrow	V
Rufous-crowned Sparrow	B
American Tree Sparrow	V
Chipping Sparrow	B
Clay-colored Sparrow	V
Brewer's Sparrow	V
Field Sparrow	V
Black-chinned Sparrow	B
Vesper Sparrow	

B = Breeds in the San Francisco Bay Area; b = Formerly or rarely has bred in the area; V = Vagrant—out of its normal range or off its normal migration route; I = Introduced.

Wood-Warblers, Tanagers, Buntings, Sparrows, and Blackbirds (cont'd.)		Wood-Warblers, Tanagers, Buntings, Sparrows, and Blackbirds (cont'd.)	
Lark Sparrow	B	Western Meadowlark	B
Black-throated Sparrow	V	Yellow-headed Blackbird	B
Sage Sparrow	B	Rusty Blackbird	V
Lark Bunting	V	Brewer's Blackbird	B
Savannah Sparrow	B	Great-tailed Grackle	V, b
Baird's Sparrow	V	Common Grackle	V
Grasshopper Sparrow	B	Brown-headed Cowbird	B
Le Conte's Sparrow	V	Orchard Oriole	V
Sharp-tailed Sparrow	V	Hooded Oriole	B
Fox Sparrow		Northern Oriole	B
Song Sparrow	B	Scott's Oriole	V
Lincoln's Sparrow			
Swamp Sparrow	V	**Finches**	
White-throated Sparrow		Purple Finch	B
Golden-crowned Sparrow		Cassin's Finch	V
White-crowned Sparrow	B	House Finch	B
Harris' Sparrow	V	Red Crossbill	B
Dark-eyed Junco	B	Pine Siskin	B
McCown's Longspur	V	Lesser Goldfinch	B
Lapland Longspur		Lawrence's Goldfinch	B
Chestnut-collared Longspur	V	American Goldfinch	B
Snow Bunting	V	Evening Grosbeak	
Bobolink	V		
Red-winged Blackbird	B	**Old World Sparrows**	
Tricolored Blackbird	B	House Sparrow	B, I

B = Breeds in the San Francisco Bay Area; b = Formerly or rarely has bred in the area; V = Vagrant—out of its normal range or off its normal migration route; I = Introduced.

Monarch Butterflies

Should you decide to go hawk watching on a warm late September day, when the sun-filled sky is hazy with autumn, you may find smaller flying creatures caught in the view from your glasses. These are likely to be monarch butterflies (*Danaus plexippus*) arriving in the Bay Area to spend the winter. Their life cycle is as amazing as that of their avian contemporaries. The entire monarch population born west of the Rocky Mountains in the United States and Canada migrates to a few dozen chosen spots along a narrow strip of California's cool, moist coastline, there to spend the winter. (The northernmost wintering colony is presently believed to be in Mendocino County.) Congregating in great crowds, the tiny flyers huddle together for warmth and protection, attaching themselves to trees during the colder months. Come March or April, they will mate, and the females will then fly unerringly to a stand of milkweed (the ones you see may head for the Sierra foothills where the genus *Asclepias* is abundant), which provides the food necessary for the survival of the species. Depositing their pale green eggs on as many milkweed plants as they survive to find, some female monarchs may travel a thousand miles or more before they die, leaving their progeny behind them. Emerging as beautifully banded caterpillars, the new monarchs will feed on their special leaves until, in a couple of weeks, they metamorphose into chrysalises. These, in turn, will hatch lovely orange, black, and white butterflies in a matter of days; the whole process takes about a month. Able to mate at birth, the first generation insects will fly on (perhaps to Oregon) to find more milkweed leaves on which to lay their eggs. Their progeny—now second-generation butterflies—will know innately to fly to the cool, moist, California coast to winter in the same area that their forebears chose. This monarch migration is one of the wonders of the natural world; it is the only true migration known to take place among all the thousands of species of earth's butterflies.

Before the Bay Area was heavily populated and industrialized, it is believed that monarchs used California's native trees—such as the redwoods (*Sequoia sempervirens*) and the Douglas firs (*Pseudotsuga menziesii*) for their host trees. With the removal of many coastal forests of native trees and the introduction of the blue gum (*Eucalyptus globulus*), the monarchs made the best of it: now you are most likely to find them hanging on the swags of eucalyptus trees. Until recently, it was thought that monarchs returned year after year to the same trees, and organizations like Audubon Canyon Ranch acquired particular stands of trees to protect the species. It is now known that these beautiful travelers migrate to certain areas instead, choosing particular groves for their particular microclimates. Look for them beginning in late September and early October around Muir Beach (where construction of a hilltop recreation center changed the cold-air drainage below, causing the butterflies to move farther uphill, and out of Audubon Ranch's Terwilliger Grove); off Terrace Avenue in

Bolinas (where the falling of a major tree during a winter storm opened up the grove to the winds, causing the butterflies to move across the road, and out of another Audubon Ranch preserve!); and wherever you find eucalyptus stands along the Bay Area's coasts. A sunny winter's day will stir them to activity, and you may see thousands of them burst into the blue air in dazzling flight.

Bay Area Amphibians and Reptiles

Almost anywhere you travel in the Bay Area countryside, you will have the opportunity to see—and enjoy watching—one or another of the several species of amphibians and reptiles that make their homes here. These usually small and unobtrusive creatures belong to biotic families that date back deep into evolutionary time: some are believed to have crossed the Bering Land Bridge to establish populations in the New World; others are found in Europe and Asia (the Old World) as well as on the North American continent; and some occupy offshore islands, captured and contained in relatively small areas by the accidents of geology. Virtually all of them have developed interesting—and sometimes extraordinary—devices for survival. For example, some salamanders produce long-lived larvae (neotony) capable of breeding while still in the immature stage. Others, such as red-bellied newts, have been known to travel as much as 5 miles over rough and difficult terrain to return to their home—the place where they were born. (All newts are salamanders, but not all salamanders are newts.) The western fence lizard, on the other hand, will detach himself from his tail, when handled, and will then regenerate a replacement.

Herpetofauna—or herps, as their students call them—are highly adaptable. They exist successfully in a wide variety of environments: grassland, open meadow, moist woodland, coniferous forest, marsh, stream, river (even ocean), desert, farmland, city park (or backyard), vacant lot, sagebrush canyon, chaparral, rocky ledge, rockpile, dead or rotting log, riffle, flood plain—any or all of these may provide a habitat for one or more of these hardy creatures. Many require a running stream, a seasonal pond, or simply a damp place to breed and are most active during the wet months of the year. Most are shy and will go to great lengths to avoid encountering humans. And many are nocturnal or crepuscular. A surprising number, however, can be seen during the daytime if you keep your eyes open for them.

Only one Bay Area species of herps is venomous—the rattle-snake—and it is easily recognized and avoided. Although the newts are poisonous, they must be ingested in goodly numbers before they have serious effects. Folklore has it that a college freshman once was forced to eat a few newts in a fraternity initiation and subsequently died; however, under ordinary circumstances, newts are hardly apt to tempt even the hungriest person. Some biologists suggest that you wash your hands after handling newts. This writer suggests that you not handle these or any other of the herpetofauna that you find: several of the species are relatively easy to pick up, and many are enchanting enough to warrant a closer look or a touch. However, as the human population has grown in the Bay Area, these interesting animals have become increasingly pressured. Loss of habitat has been severe: many of these creatures have been killed through human carelessness; some of the reptiles, notably the rattlers, have been killed indiscriminately because of their supposed danger to people. As a result, some species are now listed by the federal government as being threatened or endangered. While you may want to look under a log or two, investigate a rockpile, or step aside to let a slow traveler cross your trail, please resist the impulse to pick up and fondle the charming little animal that you may see. If you must, turn it over gently to observe it and then help it right itself. But keep in mind that, no matter how carefully it is done, extensive handling is molesting.

Salamanders, toads, frogs, treefrogs, turtles, lizards, skinks, and snakes—all are represented in the Bay Area. Salamanders, however, are the most easily seen—especially during the rainy season. Here is what to look for and where to look for it. (*Note:* This is only a thumbnail field guide; these brief descriptions are taken from Stebbins's *Field Guide to Western Reptiles and Amphibians;* for more details consult this wonderful work—see Bibliography.)

Salamanders

You can hope to see as many as 11 species (and subspecies) of salamanders in the Bay Area. The most obvious way to enjoy watching these charming creatures is to take a walk after the first rain or two and see what crosses your path. A salamander is a delight to follow as it switches along a little clumsily, making its way with tiny-fingered arms and legs. It is easily distinguished from a lizard—

although both salamanders and lizards may make you think of miniature dinosaurs—since it has a soft, moist skin rather than a rough, dry one, and no scales. Following Stebbins, the measurements given are from the tip of the snout to the vent, a sort of all-purpose opening on the underside of the body—usually a little to the rear of the hind legs—that discharges urine and feces as well as serving as a breeding adjunct for both male and female: sperm as well as eggs are deposited via the vent.

There are two general categories of salamanders: those that have lungs and those that are lungless. The former are both aquatic and terrestrial; the latter, which breathe through their skin and must always be moist in order to obtain the requisite oxygen, are terrestrial.

Among the salamanders with lungs, look for:

California Tiger Salamander (*Ambystoma tigrinum californiense*). Size: large (3–6½ inches). Chunky; broad, rounded snout; small yellowish eyes; black ground color with large pale yellow or cream spots; well-defined costal grooves (furrows on sides); tail flattened vertically. Migrates during rainy season, breeding December through February. Look in pools and seasonal ponds in grasslands and open woodlands during the rainy months, and in rotten logs or other damp hiding places (animal burrows) in summer. An ancient species, the tiger salamander is highly adapted for survival and can produce neotenics, sexually mature larvae 7 to 15 inches long. These larvae (called axolotls, a Mexican Indian name meaning "water doll") ordinarily live and breed in the larval condition in the ponds in which they were born; however, if their pond dries up, they gradually lose their gills and fins while learning to breathe air at the surface and eventually emerge onto land as adult salamanders. A good place to look for this special salamander is in Contra Costa County.

Pacific Giant Salamander (*Dicamptodon ensatus*). Size: our largest salamander (2½–7 inches). Neotenic form (up to 14 inches) may persist to second or third summer. Smooth, dark brown skin mottled with black; large head; "formidable looking" (Stebbins); can climb; can give painful bite; low, rattling sound when alarmed. Breeds spring and fall. Look near springs, in headwaters of creeks and streams in damp forests, downwaters of pools, in moist shrubs, under logs, rocks, or bark in damp environments. Mount Tamalpais is a good place to look for this giant.

Pacific Newts (genus *Taricha*). Size: 2¼–3½ inches. Rough skinned, except breeding male is smooth; all dark above with red, orange, or yellow undersides (visible from top); no costal grooves; eggs, larvae, and body poisonous (same poison as Japanese puffer fish, tetrodotoxin, recently postulated as being used in Haiti to produce "zombies"); assumes rigid arched-back defense position, showing bright-colored underside, eyes closed. Three species are found in the Bay Area: the rough-skinned newt (*T. granulosa*); the California newt (*T. torosa*); and the red-bellied newt (*T. rivularis*).

The largest family of salamanders is the lungless Plethodontidae (meaning "many teeth"), with some 225 species worldwide; 6 species (or subspecies)—all terrestrial—are found in the Bay Area. These small salamanders are notable not only for breathing through their skin but for bearing fully formed young. Look for:

Ensatina (*Ensatina eschscholtzii*). Size: small (1½–3 inches). Smooth, moist skin; tail looks swollen, being indented at base; brownish, but color varies except base of limbs is usually orange or yellow; well-defined costal grooves; tiny furrow from nostril to upper lip. Generally woodland or forest dwellers. Breeds in spring and fall, the female brooding eggs inside decaying logs, under bark, or underground. Look also in nests of woodrats. There are three sub-species of *Ensatina* in the Bay Area: the yellow-eyed salamander (*E. e. xanthoptica*); the Oregon salamander (*E. e. oregonensis*); and the Monterey salamander (*E. e. eschscholtzii*).

California Slender Salamander (*Batrachoseps attenuatus*). Size: 1¼–1⅞ inches. This, the smallest salamander in the Bay Area, can be readily recognized by its slim shape, long tail (may be twice as long as its body), and its short, four-fingered arms and legs. Dark back with stripe that varies greatly in color in the Bay Area. Females may deposit eggs in a communal nest (November to April). May be found in leaf litter, usual places in grasslands and forests, and in suburban as well as chaparral communities.

Look for two representatives of the climbing salamanders:

Arboreal Salamander (*Aneides lugubris*). Size: 2¼–4 inches. Square jaws give triangular shape to the large, heavy head; projecting front teeth in males; obvious costal grooves; well-muscled legs; longish, squared-off toes; round tail; brown freckled with yellow; underside creamy white. Look in trees as well as on the ground; favors crevices and hiding places in and under logs, etc. When alarmed, can squeak and possibly bite. *Note:* This small creature can be found on South Farallon Island, more than 20 miles from Bay Area shores.

Black Salamander (*A. flavipunctatus*). Size: 2–3¼ inches. Has same overall characteristics as the arboreal, except climbs very little; rounded toes, head smaller; black or dark gray underneath, black on top; may be freckled with tiny white dots. Favors grassy land as well as deciduous and coniferous forest land. Look in the usual places.

Spadefoot Toads

Western Spadefoot (*Scaphiopus hammondii*). Size: 1½–2½ inches. Grayish or greenish, with tiny reddish or orange protuberances on skin; whitish underside. Has small, black earth-moving apparatus, or spade, on each of its hind legs. To dig a burrow, it works backward, twisting its body from side to side to shovel out the dirt with its spades. Its voice has great carrying qualities—a useful trait for locating a mate for breeding. Gives off a not unpleasant odor (roasted peanuts?) when handled and may cause sneezing, but not warts! Look along floodplains, grasslands, woods, and meadows in coastal region south of San Francisco.

True Toads

California Toad (*Bufo boreas halophilus*). Size: 2½–5 inches. Warty looking, toothless; usually walks rather than hops; grayish or greenish, with blotches surrounding its warts. Warts and parotid glands produce a sticky poison that may harm canines but rarely humans. Does not cause warts either!

Frogs

Pacific Treefrog (*Hyla regilla*). Size: ¾–2 inches. A pretty little frog, usually light, bright green, with a dark stripe across its eyes. Found (hopefully, it's numbers have recently decreased) around gardens and farms, in meadows, forests, and chaparral.

True Frogs

Three species (and subspecies) of these long-legged, smooth-skinned, and small-waisted frogs ornament the Bay Area. Look in Contra Costa County for:

California Red-legged Frog (*Rana aurora draytonii*). Size: 1¾–5¼ inches. Often reddish, or possibly gray or brown, with white-centered black spots. See note above.

Foothill Yellow-legged Frog (*R. boylii*). Size: 1½–2⅞ inches. Smaller than the red-legged frog; generally of same colors but in lighter shades. See note above.

Bullfrog (*R. catesbeiana*). Size: 3½–8 inches. Unmistakable, being largely aquatic and the Bay Area's largest frog. Its loud and cheerful *jug-o-rum* song can sometimes be heard in marshy places. Although not native here, it thrives in the region's quiet, plant-filled waters. *Note:* This large frog is good at pretending to be dead when picked up, a useful escape mechanism.

Note: The frog population of the world—including that of the Bay Area—is declining. Scientists conjecture that the thinning of the earth's protective ozone layer may be causing the decline.

Turtles

If you come across a turtle in your Bay Area travels, it will most likely be the:

Western Pond Turtle (*Clemmys marmorata*). Size: 3½–7½ inches. Very dark brown, usually with a pattern of dashed lines radiating from the center of the shields on its carapace.

Lizards

The Bay Area population of little dragons—more often called lizards—is intriguing. You may possibly encounter members of nine species (and subspecies).

The blue-bellied spiny lizards are among the most familiar lizards in the Bay Area. These are the gray or brown striped or patterned lizards that you may find basking in the sun on rocks, sides of buildings, or fence posts. Three species are found here:

Western Fence Lizard (*Scelopurus occidentalis*). Size: $2\frac{1}{4}$–$3\frac{1}{2}$ inches; tail longer than body. Rear of legs yellow; male has two blue throat patches with lighter blue band between them. (This is the fellow that can detach his tail.)

Western Sagebrush Lizard (*S. graciosus gracilis*). Size: $1\frac{7}{8}$–$2\frac{5}{8}$ inches. Unmistakable blue belly patches. Look for this one especially around Mount Diablo in Contra Costa County.

Coast Horned Lizard (*Phrynosoma coronatum*). Size: $2\frac{1}{2}$–4 inches. Equipped with almost a plethora of little horns or pointed scales; can, when frightened, squirt blood from its eyes.

The skink family is represented by the:

Skilton Skink (*Eumeces s. skiltonianus*). Size: $2\frac{1}{8}$–$3\frac{1}{4}$ inches. Slender, shiny scaled, with distinctive stripes running almost the length of its body. This quick little creature will also let go of its tail if grabbed by it. Look among rocks near streams; the East Bay is a good place to start.

The whiptails are represented in the Bay Area by the:

California Whiptail (*Cnemidophorus tigris mundus*). Size: $2\frac{3}{8}$–$4\frac{1}{2}$ inches. Dark spotted; brownish; slim; very active.

Two species of alligator lizards may be seen in the Bay Area. *Note:* Both of these lizards are found on islands offshore, and the San Francisco lizard is found on islands in San Francisco Bay.

San Francisco Alligator Lizard (*Gerrhonotus c. coeruleus*). Size: 2¾–5⅜ inches. Long bodied, short legged, long tailed; folds down sides of body. Bears young fully formed.

California Alligator Lizard (*G. m. multicarinatus*). Size: up to 7 inches. Long bodied, short legged, long tailed; folds down sides of body. Produces eggs.

The California Legless Lizards (genus *Anniella*) are very hard to tell from small snakes (they are about as big as a pencil: 4⅜–7 inches). Their distinguishing feature is their movable eyelids (not easy to see!). Look around beaches and other sandy spots. If you find a silvery or beige creature, shiny skinned, with a black line down its back, a rounded tail tip, but no visible ears, look closely to see if it blinks. If it does, it is a silvery legless lizard (*A. p. pulchra*). If you find a dark little creature resembling the above, it is a black legless lizard (*A. p. nigra*).

Snakes

Twelve species (and subspecies) of snakes make their home in the Bay Area—one member of them only tenuously: the San Francisco garter snake, which Stebbins calls "one of the most beautiful serpents in the Northern Hemisphere," is endangered.

Pacific Rubber Boa (*Charina b. bottae*). Size: large (14–33 inches). Smooth scaled; brown or olive; small eyes, vertical pupils; good climber, swimmer, burrower; when frightened, may roll itself into a ball, hiding its head.

Western Yellow-bellied Racer (*Coluber constrictor mormon*). Size: large (20–73 inches). Slim, smooth scaled; brown, bluish, or olive with whitish or pale yellow underside. Prefers open habitats, grassy places.

Alameda Whipsnake (*Masticophis lateralis euryxanthus*). Size: 30–60 inches. Smooth scaled; dark brown or black with broad orange stripe on each side, orange to pink underside; diurnal; travels with head high.

California Mountain Kingsnake (*Lampropeltis zonata*). Size: 20–40 inches. Beautiful; not venomous; scales glisten; black, white, and red crossbands; black head and nose; diurnal; likes moist woods and chaparral.

California Black-headed Snake (*Tantilla planiceps*). Size: small (5–15½ inches). Slim, smooth skinned; blackish; flat head with whitish collar; light brown back; wide reddish or orange stripe on underside. Look on roads on warm nights.

Pacific Ringneck Snake (*Diadophis punctatus amabilis*). Size: 8–30 inches. Slim, smooth scaled; brownish, blue gray, olive, or blackish. Shows bright underside of tail when alarmed.

Pacific Gopher Snake (*Pituophis melanoleucus catenifer*). Our largest snake (36–110 inches). Scales keeled on back; yellow or cream colored, splotched with brown to black. Look for in grassland, open brush. When alarmed, hisses, vibrates tail: *do not mistake for rattler.*

Sharp-tailed Snake (*Contia tenuis*). Size: small (8–18 inches). Smooth skinned; reddish brown, gray; tail tipped with sharp spine; secrctive.

Night Snake (*Hypsiglena torquata*). Size: 12–26 inches. Light-colored brown, beige; gray-splotched dark brown intensified on neck; vertical pupils; nocturnal, crepuscular. Look for it on roads on warm nights.

Garter Snake (genus *Thamnophis*). Size: medium (18–52 inches). Slim; keeled scales; usually a pale yellow to orange stripe down middle of back with set of pale stripes, one on each side, lower on body. Pattern reminded early snake-namer of a garter, hence name. A ubiquitous snake, it has the northernmost range of any Western Hemisphere reptile. Although beautiful, it has some unattractive aspects: it may empty its intestines and squirt an odiferous liquid from its anal glands when handled. The San Francisco garter snake (*T. sirtalis tetrataenia*)—green-yellow stripe down back; red, black-bordered stripe each side; red head; blue-green underside—is an endangered subspecies found in the western part of the San Francisco Peninsula, along the crest of the hills and along the coast, if you're very lucky.

Northern Pacific Rattlesnake (*Crotalus viridis oreganus*). The Bay Area's only viper. Size: 15–65 inches. Keeled scales; heavy bodied; blotched pattern of varying shades of brown; slender neck, wide jawed; well-defined triangular head. (Depressions in head are temperature-sensitive pits that help snake detect prey.) Its tail is barred: a rattle or horny button (not included in length given) is formed each time snake sheds its skin—perhaps three to four times a year in the young, and once a year or not at all in the old. Diet: prefers small mammals and birds, but will add amphibians and/or reptiles if hungry enough. Live bearing, with 1 to 25 (usually 4 to 12) young born, sometimes in large community den, August through October. Watch for rattlers in warm, sandy places, on rocks, ledges, and rocky stream beds.

The sound of this viper is unforgettable: you will be warned by rapid, sharp, dry-sounding clacks of its tail if you enter its territory, surprising it (its back-tingling rattle may surprise you instead!); if you come upon a rattler suddenly, it will not only shake its tail, but will probably burst into a loud, shrill hiss that might panic you. Don't let it. In either case, stand still, locate the animal, and withdraw quietly without harassing it. Avoid recently killed rattlers as well as live ones: a reflex action may set off its biting mechanism even after the animal is dead. (In attack, it swings out its pair of large, hinged upper fangs to stab its victim and inject its poison.) Should you, by remote chance, get bitten, seek medical attention immediately.

Parks, Museums, and Other Useful Information

Bay Area Parks

National Parks

Golden Gate National Recreation Area. Headquarters: Fort Mason, Building 201, San Francisco, CA 94123. 415-556-0560 or 0561.

GGNRA Units.
Cliff House, 415-556-8642.
Fort Funston, 415-239-2366.
Fort Mason Center, 415-979-3010.
Fort Point, 415-556-1693.
Marin Headlands, 415-331-1540.
Muir Woods, 415-388-2595.
Presidio, 415-561-4323.
Stinson Beach, 415-868-0942; call 415-868-1922 for weather.

Point Reyes National Seashore.
Headquarters: Bear Valley, Point Reyes, CA 94956. 415-663-1092.

Point Reyes National Seashore Units.
Drakes Beach, 415-669-1250 (weekends and holidays only).
Lighthouse, 415-669-1534.

San Francisco Maritime National Historical Park.
Headquarters: Building E, Fort Mason Center,
San Francisco, CA 94123. 415-556-3002.

San Francisco Maritime National Historical Park Units.
Hyde Street Pier; historic ships, foot of Hyde Street, 415-556-3002.
Maritime Museum, foot of Polk Street, 415-556-3002.
J. Porter Shaw Library, 415-556-9870.
Wapana, Bay Model Visitor Center, Sausalito, 415-332-8409.
Pampanito, Pier 45, 415-929-0202.
Jeremiah O'Brien, Pier 3, Fort Mason, 415-441-3101.

California State Parks

Advance campsite reservations for most state park facilities can be made through DESTINET; telephone 800-444-PARK (7275). For further information about the state parks and an updated list of state facilities, write: California State Parks, Department of Recreation and Parks, Box 942896, Sacramento, CA 94296; telephone 916-653-6995. There is a small fee for the list.

Angel Island State Park. By ferry from San Francisco, Tiburon, Oakland, Alameda, and Vallejo. 415-435-1915. *Environmental campsites.*

Annadel State Park. Channel Drive east off Montgomery Drive, Santa Rosa. 707-539-3911.

Año Nuevo State Reserve. 27 miles south of Half Moon Bay on Highway 1. 650-879-2025; 800-444-7275 for tours.

Armstrong Redwoods State Reserve. 2 miles north of Guerneville on Armstrong Woods Road. 707-869-2015.

Austin Creek State Recreation Area. 3 miles north of Guerneville on Armstrong Woods Road. 707-869-2015.

Bale Grist Mill State Historic Park. 3 miles north of Saint Helena on Highway 29/128. 707-942-4575.

Bean Hollow State Beach. 17.5 miles south of Half Moon Bay on Highway 1. 650-879-2170.

Benicia Capitol State Historic Park. First and G streets. Benicia. 707-745-3385.

Benicia State Recreation Area. 1.5 miles west of Benicia via Highway I-780. 707-745-3385.

Big Basin Redwoods State Park. 25 miles north of Santa Cruz on Highway 236. 408-338-8860. *Family, hikers, and/or bicyclists campsites.* (Included because it is a remarkable parkland directly south and contiguous with San Mateo County.)

Bothe-Napa Valley State Park. 4 miles north of Saint Helena on Highway 29/128. 707-942-4575. *Family, hikers, and/or bicyclists campsites.*

Brannan Island State Recreation Area. 3 miles south of Rio Vista on Highway 160. 916-777-6671. *Family, hikers, and/or bicyclists campsites.*

Burleigh Murray Ranch. 1.5 miles east of Half Moon Bay at Purisima Creek Road. 650-726-8819.

Butano State Park. 7 miles south of Pescadero on Cloverdale Road. 650-879-2040. *Family, hikers, and/or bicyclists campsites.*

Candlestick Point State Recreation Area. East of Highway 101 via Candlestick exit. 415-671-0145. *Advanced windsurfing.*

China Camp State Park. North of San Rafael via Highway 101 and North San Pedro Road. 415-456-0766. *Walk-in campsites.*

Cowell State Beach. South of Half Moon Bay. 650-726-8820.

Fort Ross State Historic Park. 12 miles north of Jenner on Highway 1. 707-847-3286. *Primitive campsites.*

Gazos Creek State Beach. Highway 1 south of Pigeon Point Lighthouse. 650-879-2025.

Gray Whale Cove State Beach. 9 miles north of Half Moon Bay on Highway 1. 650-728-5336. *Clothing optional beach.*

Half Moon Bay State Beach. 0.5 mile west of Highway 1 on Kelly Avenue. 650-726-8820. *Family camping.*

Henry W. Coe State Park. 14 miles east of Morgan Hill on East Dunne Avenue. 408-779-2728. *Family and/or backpackers campsites.*

Jack London State Historic Park. 1.5 miles west of Glen Ellen on London Ranch Road. 707-938-5216.

Montara State Beach. 8 miles north of Half Moon Bay on Highway 1. 650-728-7177. *Hostelling International, American Youth Hostel.*

Moss Landing State Beach. In Moss Landing, take Jetty Road from Highway 1. 408-384-7695.

Mount Diablo State Park. 5 miles east of Danville on Diablo Road. 510-837-2525. *Family campsites.*

Mount Tamalpais State Park. 6 miles west of Mill Valley on Panoramic Highway. 415-388-2070. *Family campsites.*

Olompali State Historic Park. 2.5 miles north of Novato on Highway 101. 415-892-3383.

Pescadero Marsh Natural Preserve. 14.5 miles south of Half Moon Bay on Highway 1. 650-879-2170. *Guided walks weekends.*

Pescadero State Beach. 14.5 miles south of Half Moon Bay on Highway 1. 650-879-2170.

Petaluma Adobe State Historical Park. 0.7 mile east of Petaluma on Highway 116, then 2.2 miles north on Casa Grande Road. 707-762-4871.

Pigeon Point Lighthouse. ¼ mile west of Highway 1 on Pigeon Point Road; 27 miles south of Half Moon Bay. 650-879-0633. *Hostelling International, American Youth Hostel.*

Pomponio State Beach. 12 miles south of Half Moon Bay on Highway 1. 650-879-2170.

Portola Redwoods State Park. Portola State Park Road. 6.5 miles west of Highway 35 on Alpine/State Park Road. 650-948-9098. *Family campsites.*

Robert Louis Stevenson State Park. 7 miles north of Calistoga on Highway 29. 707-942-4575. *Family campsites.*

Salt Point State Park. 20 miles north of Jenner on Highway 1. 707-847-3221. *Family, hikers, and/or bicyclists campsites.*

Samuel P. Taylor State Park. 15 miles west of San Rafael on Sir Francis Drake Boulevard. 415-488-9897. *Family campsites.*

San Gregorio State Beach. 10.5 miles south of Half Moon Bay on Highway 1. 650-879-2170.

Sonoma Coast State Beach. Bodega Dunes Campground, 0.5 mile north of Bodega Bay on Highway 1. Wrights Beach Campground, 6 miles north of Bodega Bay on Highway 1. Willow Creek and Pomo Canyon environmental campgrounds. 707-875-3483. *Family, hikers, and/or backpackers campsites.*

Sonoma State Historic Park. Spain Street at Third Street West, and at First Street East, Sonoma. 707-938-9559.

Sugarloaf Ridge State Park. 7 miles east of Santa Rosa on Highway 12, then north 3 miles on Adobe Canyon Road. 707-833-5712. *Family campsites.*

Tomales Bay State Park. 4 miles north of Inverness on Sir Francis Drake Boulevard. 415-669-1140. *Hikers and bicyclists campsites.*

Zmudowski State Beach. 1 mile north of Moss Landing on Highway 1; take Struve Road to Giberson Road and turn left. 408-384-7695.

County Parks

East Bay Regional Park District (Contra Costa and Alameda counties). 2950 Peralta Oaks Court, Oakland, CA 94605. 510-562-PARK (7275).

Marin County Department of Parks, Open Space, and Cultural Services. 3501 Civic Center Drive, San Rafael, CA 94903. 415-499-6387.

Midpeninsula Regional Open Space District. 330 Distel Circle, Los Altos, CA 94032. 650-691-1200.

San Francisco Recreation and Parks Department. McClaren Lodge, Fell and Stanyan streets, Golden Gate Park, San Francisco, CA 94117. 415-666-7201.

San Mateo Parks and Recreation Department. 590 Hamilton Street, Redwood City, CA 94063. 650-363-4020.

Santa Clara County Parks Department. 298 Garden Hill Drive, Los Gatos, CA 95030. 408-358-3741.

Solano County Parks. 512 Clay Street, Fairfield, CA 94533. 707-421-7925.

Sonoma County Regional Parks. 2300 County Center Drive, Suite 120-A, Santa Rosa, CA 95403. 707-527-2041.

Government Agencies

Association of Bay Area Governments, P.O. Box 2050, Oakland, CA 94604. 510-464-7900.

National Oceanic and Atmospheric Administration (NOAA). 3150 Paradise Drive, Tiburon, CA 94920. 415-435-3149.

National Park Service. Western Region Information Center, Building 201, Fort Mason, San Francisco, CA 94123. 415-556-0560.

San Francisco Bay Conservation and Development Commission (BCDC). 30 Van Ness Avenue, San Francisco, CA 94102. 415-557-3686.

U.S. Fish and Wildlife Service. 1 Marshlands Road, Fremont, CA 94536. 510-792-4275.

U.S. Forest Service. 630 Sansome Street, San Francisco, CA 94111. 415-705-2874.

U.S. Geological Survey. 345 Middlefield Road, Menlo Park, CA 94025. 650-853-8300.

Environmental Organizations

Bay Institute of San Francisco. 625 Grand Avenue, Suite 250, San Rafael, CA 94901. 415-721-7680.

Bay Keeper. Fort Mason, GGNRA, San Francisco, CA 94123. 415-567-4401.

California Alpine Club. Panoramic Highway, Mill Valley, CA 94941. 415-388-9940.

California Native Plant Society. 1722 J Street, Sacramento, CA 95814. 916-447-CNPS (2677). *Will provide information for Bay Area activities.*

Committee for Green Foothills. 3921 East Bayshore Road, Palo Alto, CA 94303. 650-968-7243.

Communities for a Better Environment. 500 Howard Street, San Francisco, CA 94105. 415-243-8373.

Earth Island Institute. 300 Broadway, San Francisco, CA 94133. 415-788-3666.

Environmental Defense Fund. 5655 College Avenue, Oakland, CA 94618. 510-658-8008.

Environmental Forum of Marin. P.O. Box 74, Larkspur, CA 94977. 415-479-7814.

Golden Gate Audubon Society. 2530 San Pablo Avenue, Berkeley, CA 94702. 510-843-2222. *Bird field trips listed in the* Gull.

Golden Gate National Parks Association. GGNRA, Fort Mason, Building 201, San Francisco, CA 94123. 415-776-0693. *One of the most effective park-support organizations in the country. Publishes* Gateways, *an excellent quarterly newsletter for members.*

Greenbelt Alliance. 116 New Montgomery Street, San Francisco, CA 94105. 415-543-4291. *Dedicated to preserving open space.*

Marin Audubon Society. Box 599, Mill Valley, CA 94942. 415-383-1770. *Bird field trips listed in the* Redwood Log.

Marin Conservation League. 55 Mitchell Boulevard, San Rafael, CA 94903. 415-472-6170.

The Nature Conservancy. 201 Mission Street, Fourth Floor, San Francisco, CA 94105. 415-777-0487.

Oceanic Society Expeditions. Building E, Fort Mason, San Francisco, CA 94123. 415-441-1104 or 1106. *Great whale-watching trips.*

Peninsula Conservation Center Foundation. 3921 East Bayshore Road, Palo Alto, CA 94303. 650-962-9876.

Peninsula Open Space Trust. 3000 Sand Hill Road, Building 4, Suite 135, Menlo Park, CA 94025. 650-854-7696. *Acquires open-space lands for transfer to public agencies.*

Save San Francisco Bay Association. 1736 Franklin Street, 4th floor, Oakland, CA 94612. 510-452-9261.

Save-the-Redwoods League. 114 Sansome Street, Room 605, San Francisco, CA 94104. 415-362-2352.

Sempervirens Fund. 2483 Old Middlefield Way, Mountain View, CA 94043. 650-968-4509.

Sierra Club. Main Office, 85 Second Street, San Francisco, CA 94105. 415-977-5500. *Library, bookstore.*

Sierra Club. Bay Chapter, 2530 San Pablo Avenue, Berkeley, CA 94702. 510-848-0800. *Hikes and outings. Bookstore* (6014 College Avenue, Oakland, CA 94618. 510-658-7470).

Sierra Club. Loma Prieta Chapter, 3921 East Bayshore Road, Palo Alto, CA 94303. 650-390-8411. *Hikes, outings, cabin.*

Sierra Club Legal Defense Fund. 180 Montgomery Street, San Francisco, CA 94104. 415-627-6700.

Tamalpais Conservation Club (TCC). 870 Market Street, San Francisco, CA 94102. 415-391-8021. *Devoted to the mountain.*

Trust for Public Land. 116 New Montgomery Street, San Francisco, CA 94105. 415-495-4014 or 5660.

Urban Creeks Council. 1250 Addison Street, Berkeley, CA 94702. 510-540-6669.

Natural History Museums and Botanical Gardens

Bay Area Discovery Museum. 557 East Fort Baker, GGNRA, Sausalito, CA 94965. 415-487-4398. *Great for inquisitive-minded children.*

California Academy of Sciences. Life Through Time Exhibit, Planetarium, Aquarium. Golden Gate Park, San Francisco, CA 94118. 415-221-5100. *A wonderful resource, open every day of the year.*

Coyote Point Museum. 1651 Coyote Point Drive, San Mateo, CA 94401. 650-342-7755. *Environmental hall with exhibit of Coast Range biotic zones; wildlife habitats exhibit with live animals. Highly recommended for family outings.*

The Exploratorium. 3601 Lyon Street, San Francisco, CA 94123. 415-563-7337. *Unique, hands-on scientific museum for children and adults.*

Marin Museum of the American Indian (formerly Miwok Museum). 2200 Novato Boulevard, Novato, CA 94948. 415-897-4064. *Films, lecture series, field trips, basketry, and other classes.*

Oakland Museum of California. Tenth and Oak streets, Oakland, CA 94607. 510-238-2200. *Ecology exhibit of California's biotic zones, wonderful California history section; weekend docent-led tours; California art gallery tours, Wednesday, 12:30 P.M.; other* *weekday tours by appointment (one architect considers this the finest building in the Bay Area).*

Presidio Museum. Lincoln Boulevard and Funston Avenue (in the Presidio), San Francisco, CA 94129. 415-561-4331. *Nostalgic exhibits of times past, plus two restored 1906 earthquake refugee shacks.*

Randall Junior Museum. 199 Museum Way, San Francisco, CA 94114. 415-554-9600. *Good resource for science-minded young people.*

Regional Park Botanic Garden. Tilden Regional Park, Berkeley, CA 94708. 510-841-8732. *Native plants, open 8:30 A.M.–5:00 P.M. daily, summer until 6 P.M.*

San Francisco Bay Model. 2100 Bridgeway Boulevard, Sausalito, CA 94965. 415-332-3871. *An excellent interpretive center for the bay; a must for any bay user.*

San Francisco Maritime Historical Park. Building E, Fort Mason Center, San Francisco, CA 94123. 415-556-3002. Hyde Street Pier, Hyde and Jefferson streets. *Historic ships; open daily, guided tours.* Museum, Beach Street at foot of Polk Street, *one of the country's few (and best) nautical displays; includes scrimshaw and artifacts.*

Strybing Arboretum. Golden Gate Park, San Francisco, CA 94122. 415-661-1316; tours, 661-3584. *Native plants; docent-led walks, Saturday–Sunday 1:30 P.M.*

University of California Botanical Gardens. Centennial Drive (Strawberry Canyon), Berkeley, CA 94720. 510-642-3343. *Native plants; docent-led walks, Saturday–Sunday 1:30 P.M.*

Nature Centers

Audubon Canyon Ranch. 4900 Shoreline Highway (Highway 1), Stinson Beach, CA 94970. 415-868-9244. *Heronry; trails; exhibit hall; bookstore. Open to public mid-March to mid-July, weekends and holidays, 10:00 A.M.–4 P.M.*

Lindsay Museum. 1931 First Avenue, Walnut Creek, CA 94596. 510-935-1978. *Outstanding exhibits (including living animals) and programs.*

Marine Mammal Center. Fort Cronkhite; west end of Bunker Road, Sausalito, CA 94965. 415-289-7325. *Marine mammal rehabilitation.*

Palo Alto Baylands. Lucy Evans Baylands Interpretive Center. East end of Embarcadero Road, Palo Alto, CA 94303. 650-329-2506. *Wetlands habitat; birding; walks and bicycle tours, weekends. Center open Tuesday–Wednesday 10:00 A.M.–5:00 P.M., Thursday–Friday 2:00–5:00 P.M., Saturday–Sunday 1:00–5:00 P.M.*

Point Reyes Bird Observatory (PRBO). 4990 Shoreline Highway (Highway 1), Stinson Beach, CA 94970. 415-868-1221; ext. 40 for birdwalks. *Annual Bird-a-thon.*

Point Reyes Bird Observatory (PRBO). Palomarin Banding Station. End of Mesa Road, Bolinas, CA 94970. 415-868-0655. *Early (dawn) morning bird banding demonstrations; summer, daily; winter, Wednesday, Saturday, and Sunday; small exhibit hall; self-guided nature trail.*

Point Reyes National Seashore. Bear Valley Headquarters, Point Reyes, CA 94956. 415-663-1092. *Outstanding visitor center and interpretive displays; Kule Loklo Coast Miwok Indian village; Morgan horse farm; earthquake trail; nature walks.*

Richardson Bay Wildlife Sanctuary. (National Audubon Society.) 376 Greenwood Beach Road, Tiburon, CA 94920. 415-388-2525. *Guided walks and lecture/slide show Sundays.*

San Francisco Bay National Wildlife Refuge. (U.S. Fish and Wildlife Service.) 1 Marshlands Road, Fremont, CA 94536. 510-792-4275. *Good interpretive display; nature walks.*

San Francisco Zoo. Forty-fifth Avenue and Sloat Boulevard, San Francisco, Ca 94132. 415-753-7061. *Penguins, koalas, and an outstanding primate house. Has more than three dozen endangered species, including snow leopards.*

Wildcare-Terwilliger Nature Education and Wildlife Rehabilitation. 76 Albert Park Lane, San Rafael, CA 94901. 415-456-7289. *Wildlife hospital, living animal display, classes, walks, and summer camps.*

Chamber of Commerce and Visitor Centers

Berkeley Convention and Visitors Bureau. 1834 University Avenue, Berkeley, CA 94703. 510-549-7040.

Fairfield-Suisun (Solano County) Chamber of Commerce. 1111 Webster Street, Fairfield, CA 94533. 707-425-4625.

Marin County Convention and Visitors Bureau. 30 North San Pedro Road, San Rafael, CA 94903. 415-472-7470.

Napa Valley Conference and Visitors Bureau. 1310 Napa Town Center, Napa, CA 94559. 707-226-7459.

Oakland Convention and Visitors Authority. 550 Tenth Street, Suite 214, Oakland, CA 94607. 510-839-9000.

Orinda Chamber of Commerce. 2 Theatre Square, Orinda, CA 94563. 510-254-3909.

Palo Alto Chamber of Commerce. 325 Forest Avenue, Palo Alto, CA 94301. 650-324-3121.

San Francisco Convention and Visitors Bureau. Lower Level, Hallidie Plaza, Powell and Market streets, San Francisco, CA 94102. 415-391-2000 or 415-974-6900; 24-hour recording of current events in the city: 415-391-2001.

San Jose Chamber of Commerce. 180 South Market Street, San Jose, CA 95113. 408-291-5250.

San Mateo County Convention and Visitors Bureau. 111 Anza Boulevard, Burlingame, CA 94010. 650-348-7600.

Santa Clara Convention and Visitors Bureau. 1850 Warburton Avenue, Santa Clara, CA 95052. 408-244-8244.

Santa Rosa Conference and Visitors Bureau. 637 First Street, Santa Rosa, CA 95404. 707-577-8674.

Sonoma Valley Visitors Bureau. 453 First Street East, Sonoma, CA 95476. 707-996-1090.

Walnut Creek Chamber of Commerce. 1501 North Broadway, Walnut Creek, CA 94596. 510-934-2007.

West Marin Chamber of Commerce. P.O. Box 1045, Point Reyes Station, CA 94956. 415-663-9232. (Visitor Center at The Creamery Building, 11431 Highway 1, Point Reyes Station.)

Some Other Helpful Names and Addresses

Redwood Empire Association. 2801 Leavenworth, San Francisco, CA 94133. 415-394-5991. *For a free "Redwood Empire Visitors Guide," send $3.00 for first-class postage, or stop by the REA for a copy.*

Sonoma County Farm Trails. P.O. Box 6032, Santa Rosa, CA 95406. 707-824-2060. *Send a stamped, self-addressed, legal-size envelope for map, updated yearly, of locally produced products. You can buy from the growers, have a firsthand "farm experience," or do some handcraft shopping.*

Wine Institute. 425 Market Street, San Francisco, CA 94105. 415-512-0151. *Trade association for northern California wineries. Call for a list of wineries.*

──────── Getting Around

Options

What to Do on a Rainy Day

Visit a Museum or Equally Interesting Place

Bay Area Discovery Museum, Sausalito

Bay Model, Sausalito

Beach Chalet, Golden Gate Park, San Francisco

California Academy of Sciences, Golden Gate Park, San Francisco: Life Through Time Exhibit; Steinhardt Aquarium; Planetarium

The Conservatory, Golden Gate Park, San Francisco

Coyote Point Museum, San Mateo

de Young Museum, Golden Gate Park, San Francisco

The Exploratorium, San Francisco

Lindsay Museum, Walnut Creek

Maritime Museum, or Mexican Museum, or African History Museum, GGNRA, Fort Mason, San Francisco

Mission in San Rafael, San Francisco, Sonoma, or Fremont

Musée Méchanique, Camera Obscura, Ocean Beach, San Francisco

Oakland Museum of California, Oakland

Palace of the Legion of Honor, San Francisco

Point Reyes National Seashore Visitor Center

Presidio Museum, San Francisco

Randall Junior Museum, San Francisco

San Francisco Museum of Modern Art, San Francisco

Stanford University Museum, Palo Alto

University of California Museum, Berkeley

Bundle Up and Walk in the Redwoods in
  Muir Woods, Marin
  Armstrong Grove, Sonoma
  East Bay Regional Parks, Alameda and Contra Costa
  Big Basin, San Mateo

What to Do on a Foggy Day

Any of the Above, Especially
  Walk in the redwoods
  Walk along Ocean Beach, or in Golden Gate Park, or in the Presidio in San Francisco

Bundle Up and Visit
  San Francisco Zoo (it's the very best time to see the animals)

Bundle Up and Photograph
  The flowers in Golden Gate Park
  The Berkeley Rose Garden (it's a very good time to get interesting flower shots)
  The fogfall from Vista Point, Marin, at the end of the Golden Gate Bridge (if the fog's cooperating; if it's not, continue to Muir Woods or the top of Mount Tamalpais)
  The trees in Lincoln Park, San Francisco

Carry a Jacket and Hike in
  Muir Woods or Bear Valley in Marin

Visit a Geological Site in
  San Francisco, San Mateo, or Marin

Escape the Fog—Visit
  The wine country, Sonoma and/or Napa—call Napa or Sonoma Visitors Bureau (see Chambers of Commerce appendix) to be sure the sun is out; it probably will be. You can enjoy the wineries, the historic buildings in Petaluma and Sonoma, Jack London State Park while you're there
  The top of Mount Tamalpais, Marin (call ranger at Pantoll to see if sun is out; it probably will be)
  Diablo State Park, Contra Costa (call ranger to see if sun is out; it probably will be)

Briones Wilderness Park, Contra Costa; take a hike or picnic (call
Diablo State Park ranger to see if sun is out)

Hike or Bicycle in Golden Gate Park
There are bicycles for rent on Stanyan Street

What to Do on a Scorcher

Take a Waterfront Walk—Try
The Golden Gate Promenade, GGNRA, San Francisco
Ocean Beach, San Francisco
Hayward Shoreline, Alameda
Carquinez Straits Shoreline, Crockett
San Francisco Wildlife Refuge, Newark, Alameda
Coyote Point or Palo Alto Baylands, San Mateo
Benicia State Recreation Area, Solano

Take a Swim—Try
Aquatic Park or China Beach, GGNRA, San Francisco
Stinson Beach, GGNRA, Marin
East Bay Regional Parks, such as Crown Beach, Lake Temescal,
etc., Alameda and Contra Costa
San Francisco's public swimming pools

Rent a Boat and Go Boating—Try
Lake Merced, San Francisco
Lake Chabot, Alameda
San Pablo Reservoir, Contra Costa

Go Kayaking or Sculling from
Marin, San Francisco, San Mateo, or Alameda County shores (see
Kayaking Rentals appendix)

Visit
Fort Point, GGNRA, San Francisco

Picnic at
San Mateo or Sonoma coastal park (see South Bay and North Bay
sections)

Take a Stroll in
Gerbode Valley, Marin Headlands, GGNRA, Marin

Take a Round-trip Ferry Ride Between
San Francisco and Larkspur or Tiburon or Vallejo

Take a Ferry Ride to
Tiburon and on to Angel Island; carry a picnic and/or bicycle

If You Have Only Half a Day in San Francisco

And You Enjoy the Urban Scene
Take Geary Walk from Market Street to Van Ness Avenue

And You Enjoy Things Maritime
Start GGNRA Waterfront Walk 1 at Hyde Street Pier, visit Maritime Museum and (have lunch at) Ghirardelli Square

And You Enjoy a Walk in a Park
Visit Golden Gate Park; pick up a map at McLaren Lodge headquarters

And You Enjoy the Ocean
Visit Ocean Beach, Sutro Gardens, and (have lunch at) the Cliff House

And You Enjoy Churches
Visit Mission Dolores or Saint Mary's Cathedral

If You Have Only One Day in San Francisco

And You Enjoy Exploring on Foot
Take Geary Street Walks and lunch at Japantown on the way

And You Enjoy Birding
Lunch in Sausalito, drive to Audubon Canyon Ranch in Marin, linger around Bolinas Lagoon, visit Point Reyes Bird Observatory's Palomarin Banding Station (mornings), dine in Olema

And You Have Children with You
Visit the merry-go-round and the buffaloes and the windmill in Golden Gate Park and have lunch and/or dinner on Geary Boulevard; or visit the Bay Area Discovery Museum in Sausalito

And You Have Children with You and It's Foggy
Visit the San Francisco Zoo and have lunch and/or dinner at
Leon's Bar-B-Q across the street from the main gate

And You'd Like a Country Picnic
Take your lunch to Point Reyes National Seashore and enjoy the
visitor center and other attractions around park headquarters

And You Want to See the Redwoods
Drive to Muir Woods and hike the Ben Jonson Trail to Pantoll and
back; carry your lunch
Drive to Olema Valley and take a trail to, and along, Bolinas
Ridge; carry your lunch

Nature Outings and Classes

Año Nuevo State Reserve. Questions: 415-879-0227. DESTINET
reservations: 800-444-7275. *Elephant seal tours, January–*
March.

California Academy of Sciences. Golden Gate Park, San Francisco,
CA 94118. 415-221-5100. *Local classes and foreign travel.*

College of Marin. College Avenue, Kentfield, CA 94904. 415-457-
8811. *Daytime and evening classes in natural sciences.*

Dolphin Charter. Ronn Patterson, 1007 Leneve Place, El Cerrito, CA
94530. 510-527-9622. *Natural expeditions on the water, whale-*
watching, and more.

East Bay Regional Parks. 2950 Peralta Oaks Court, Oakland, CA
94605. 510-562-7275. *Everything from bird-watching to sand*
castle building; several good visitor centers.

Environmental Forum of Marin. P.O. Box 74, Larkspur, CA 94939.
415-479-7814. *Training program aimed at increasing under-*
standing of basic ecology and environmental issues.

Golden Gate Audubon Society. 2530 San Pablo Avenue, Berkeley,
CA 94702. 510-843-2222. *Bird field trips listed in the* Gull.

Golden Gate National Recreation Area. Building 201, Fort Mason,
San Francisco, CA 94123. 415-556-0560 or 0561. *This park has*
a remarkably varied and informative monthly program, with
events scheduled for almost every day. You can get a copy of
ParkNews, *which contains an excellent quarterly calendar of*
park events, at park headquarters or any GGNRA visitor center.

Jasper Ridge Biological Preserve. Department of Biological Sciences, Stanford University, Stanford, CA 94305. 650-327-2277. *Docent-led tours; outstanding spring wildflowers.*

Marin Audubon Society. Box 599, Mill Valley, CA 94942. 415-383-1770. *Bird field trips listed in the* Gull.

Marin County Department of Parks, Open Space, and Cultural Services. Bob Stewart, naturalist. Marin Civic Center, San Rafael, CA 94903. 415-499-3647. *Bob is a fine interpreter of the local natural scene; leads wonderful free weekend walks.*

Marin Headlands Visitor Center. National Park Service, Golden Gate National Recreation Area, Building 948, Fort Berry, Sausalito, CA 94965. 415-331-1540. *Nature walks and more.*

Marin Museum of the American Indian. (Formerly Miwok Museum.) P.O. Box 864, Novato, CA 94948. 415-897-4064. *Films, lecture series, field trips, basketry, and other classes.*

The Nature Conservancy. 201 Mission Street, San Francisco, CA 94105. 415-777-0487. *Field classes and walks.*

Oceanic Society Expeditions. Building E, Fort Mason, San Francisco, CA 94123. 415-441-1104 or 1106. *Great whale-watching trips.*

Palo Alto Baylands. Lucy Evans Baylands Interpretive Center, 2775 Embarcadero Road, Palo Alto, CA 94303. 650-329-2506. *Wetlands habitat; birding.*

Point Reyes Bird Observatory (PRBO). 4990 Shoreline Highway (Highway 1), Stinson Beach, CA 94970. 415-868-1221; ext. 40 for birdwalks. *Annual Bird-a-thon; monthly birdwalks.*

Point Reyes Field Seminars. Bear Valley Road, Point Reyes, CA 94956. 415-663-1200. *Daylong and weekend seminars on subjects from photography to tidepools.*

Point Reyes National Seashore. Naturalist Activities Schedule, Point Reyes, CA 94956. 415-663-1092.

San Francisco Bay Model. 2100 Bridgeway Boulevard, Sausalito, CA 94965. Information: 415-332-3870; mailing list: 332-3871. *This exceptional exhibit is a hydraulic model of San Francisco Bay and the Delta.*

San Francisco State University. 1600 Holloway Avenue, San Francisco, CA 94132. 415-904-7700. *Wildlands field studies.*

Sierra Club. Bay Chapter, 2530 San Pablo Avenue, Berkeley, CA 94702. 510-653-6127. *Hikes and outings.*

Sierra Club. Loma Prieta Chapter, 3921 East Bayshore Road, Palo Alto, CA 94303. 650-390-8411. *Hikes and outings.*

Slide Ranch. Muir Beach, CA 94965. 415-381-6155. *Subsistence farm and environmental center; farm animals; great tidepools; weekend programs (reservations required).*

Sonoma State University. Biological Colloquia, Rohnert Park, CA 94928. 707-664-2189. *Public lectures, Tuesday noon during semester session, 108 Darwin Hall.*

Wildcare-Terwilliger Nature Education and Wildlife Rehabilitation. *Wildlife hospital; live animal display; hands-on wildlife exhibit; nature education; "Mrs. T" has even presidents making a V for vulture; a delightful teacher, especially for children.*

University of California Extension. Berkeley, CA 94720. 510-642-4111. *Natural history classes.*

Kayaking Rentals and Instruction

The following outfits can give you lessons, supply equipment, or take you out on a kayaking adventure.

Bluewaters Ocean Kayak Tours. Box 983, Inverness, CA 94937. 415-669-2600. *Tours and rentals.*

Sea Trek. Schoonmacher Point Marina, Sausalito, CA 94965. 415-488-1000. (Mailing address: Box 561, Woodacre, CA 94973.) *The first to take to the bay. Tours of San Francisco and Tomales bays and Drakes Estero.*

Note: There are new kayaking companies opening up in many parts of the bay. Look for them in the Yellow Pages of the San Francisco phone book, or the phone book of the city you're visiting.

Historic Bay Area Vineyards and Wineries

Several of the Bay Area counties have vineyards and wineries that date back well over 100 years. Many of these vineyards and wineries are presently in production and offer the pleasant opportunity to taste a bit of history along with a good California wine. Here's a list of vineyards. (Expect to pay a modest fee for tasting.)

Sonoma County

Buena Vista Winery and its vineyards, known as the birthplace of California wine, were started by Agoston Haraszthy, who, in 1857, oversaw the planting of his vines and the digging of storage tunnels in his limestone hills. On his European tour in 1861, he brought back the choice cuttings—for other California vintners as well as for himself—that helped establish California as a prime wine-producing state. Buena Vista Winery is 2 miles southeast of Sonoma at 18000 Old Winery Road; telephone 707-938-1266.

Sebastiani. In 1825, the Franciscan Fathers who established Mission Solano planted the first vineyard in Sonoma County to produce their sacramental wine. When the mission was secularized in 1835, General Mariano Vallejo took it over and went on (with the help of Dr. Victor J. Fauré, whose house still stands at 18 West Spain Street in Sonoma) to produce prize-winning wines under the Lachryma Montis label. Shortly after the turn of the century, the property was acquired by Samuele Sebastiani and his wife, Elvira, who carried on the tradition of turning out quality wines. Much of the vineyard is still in use and is still planted with fine wine grapes. You'll find it at Fourth Street East and Spain Street, Sonoma; telephone 707-938-5532.

Napa County

Beringer Brothers Winery has been in continuous operation since it was founded by Frederick and Jacob Beringer in 1876. The brothers employed Chinese labor to build their winery and excavate their storage tunnels in the limestone hills. The temperature in the tunnels is said not to vary more than a few degrees Fahrenheit throughout the year. Beringer is located at 2000 Main Street in Saint Helena and has daily tastings and tours; telephone 707-963-4812.

Charles Krug. This, Napa's oldest operating vineyard, was planted by Charles Krug in 1851. Seven years later, Krug was bottling and selling the county's first commercially produced wine. Located at 2800 Saint Helena Highway in Saint Helena, it turns out a million and a half cases of wine annually. The winery is open daily for tours and tastings; telephone 707-963-5057.

Schramsberg. In 1862, Jacob Schram planted the first hillside vineyard in Napa. This is the winery that was visited by Robert Louis Stevenson and that inspired him to write (in "Silverado Squatters") that "the wine is bottled poetry." Lily (the "Firebelle") Hitchcock

Coit and Ambrose Bierce were among other friends of Schram. Champagne from this vineyard has graced the White House table. The well-preserved Schramsberg operation is on Schramsberg Road, 3.8 miles south of Calistoga. Visiting hours and tours are by appointment; telephone 707-942-4558.

Alameda County

Concannon Vineyard. James Concannon found himself in the winemaking business at the urging of his San Francisco archbishop, who was seeking a reliable source for sacramental wines. Concannon did so well that between 1889 and 1904 he fathered Mexico's wine industry with cuttings from his vineyard. The vineyard is now owned by another company, but one of James's grandsons is one of its principals. Concannon's introduced the red wine Petite Sirah to the United States in 1964, and the winery is well known for its estate-bottled Sauvignon Blanc, Chardonnay, Cabernet Sauvignon, and Petite Sirah. Located at 4590 Tesla Road in Livermore (take I-580 east to North Livermore Avenue and drive south 3 miles), Concannon has weekend tours as well as tastings daily. It also has picnic grounds. Telephone 510-447-3760.

Wente Vineyards. For four generations, the Wente family has been producing wine in the Livermore Valley, where the soil is deep and gravelly—not unlike that of the Graves area of Bordeaux, France. Over the years, the family has acquired other equally historic neighboring vineyards—all noted for their good wine; Wente now incorporates some of the best-producing vineyards in the valley. There's a pleasant shady patio for picnicking at the Wente Estates Winery, 5565 Tesla Road, Livermore (510-447-3603). The Wente Vineyards restaurant and visitor center, and century-old caves—where the wine rests in tirage—are at 5050 Arroyo Road, Livermore (510-447-3694). (Summer concerts are held here.) Tastings and tours can be had at both historic winery sites.

Santa Clara County

Ridge Winery, located on a ridgetop of the Santa Cruz Mountains, is a turn-of-the-century winery that is listed on the National Registry of Historic Sites. It specializes in Cabernet, Zinfandel, and Petite Sirah, from vines well suited to the region. Tastings are held from 11:00

A.M. to 3:00 P.M. on Saturdays and Sundays. Ridge Winery is located at 17100 Monte Bello Road, Cupertino. Telephone 408-867-3233 or 3244.

Sunrise Winery, also on Monte Bello Road (13100), Cupertino, is a wonderful 1880s ranch, with a brick winery containing great old oak timbers and hand-carved vats. Planted by the Picchetti family, pioneer winemakers in the region, the vineyard is still producing grapes for good wine. Tastings are held on Friday, Saturday, and Sunday, from 11:00 A.M. to 3:00 P.M. Telephone 408-741-1310. (See also Los Trancos Earthquake Trail.)

See also California Wine.

Places to Stay and Places to Eat

San Francisco

Places to Stay

The Bed and Breakfast Inn. Four Charlton Court, San Francisco, CA 94123. 415-921-9784. *In a quiet nook off Union Street. Great for celebrity watching. Bed and breakfast. Expensive.*

The Mansion Hotel. 2220 Sacramento Street, San Francisco, CA 94115. 415-929-9444. *This Queen Anne Victorian went up in 1887. Bed and breakfast. Elegant and expensive.*

The Archbishop's Mansion. 1000 Fulton Street, San Francisco, CA 94117. 415-563-7872. *Built in 1904 for the archbishop himself. Spacious, stately, overlooking historic Alamo Square. Bed and breakfast. Expensive.*

The White Swan Inn. 845 Bush Street, San Francisco, CA 94108. 415-775-1755. Built in 1908. *A taste of old England with fireplace in each room. Bed and breakfast. Expensive.*

Places to Eat

Jack's. 615 Sacramento Street, San Francisco, CA 94111. 415-986-9854. *This more-than-a-century-old restaurant is near the financial center of the city. French cuisine (try any of the delicious lamb dishes). Moderate/expensive.*

Maye's Oyster House. 1233 Polk Street, San Francisco, CA 94109. 415-474-7674. *Since 1867. Nothing fancy. Good seafood. Moderate.*

Sam's Grill. 374 Bush Street, San Francisco, CA 94104. 415-421-0594. *Over a century old. Some say the best seafood in the city. A relaxing, unpretentious place. No reservations. Moderate.*

Tadich Grill. 240 California Street, San Francisco, CA 94111. 415-391-1849. *Excellent seafood. New menu every day. Bustling. No reservations. Moderate.*

North Bay

Places to Stay

MARIN COUNTY

Casa Madrona. 801 Bridgeway, Sausalito, CA 94965. 415-332-0502 or 800-567-9524. *Romantic hideaway tucked into the hills of Sausalito. Bay views. Moderate/expensive.*

The Olema Inn. 1000 Sir Francis Drake Boulevard at Highway 1, Olema, CA 94950. 415-663-9559. *Restored 1876 country inn. Bed and breakfast. Garden restaurant.*

The Pelican Inn. 10 Pacific Way, Muir Beach, CA 94965. 415-383-6000. *Comfortable rooms with a great English pub and restaurant below. The beach down the road is a local favorite. Expensive.*

Ten Inverness Way. 10 Inverness Way, Inverness, CA 94937. 415-669-1648. *A quiet, restful place near Point Reyes National Seashore in West Marin. Built in 1904. Bed and breakfast. Moderate.*

THE WINE COUNTRY

The Burgundy House. 6711 Washington Street, Yountville, CA 94599. 707-944-0889. *Built in 1870 as a brandy distillery, this two-story stone building, furnished with antiques, is full of charm. Bed and breakfast. Moderate/expensive.*

Mount View Hotel. 1457 Lincoln Avenue, Calistoga, CA 94515. 707-942-6877. *Small hotel in a Victorian garden setting; three cottages. Spa and pool. Bed and breakfast. Moderate.*

The Sonoma Mission Inn. 18140 Sonoma Highway (Highway 12), Sonoma, CA 95416. 707-938-9000. *A full-service resort with European-style spa. Built in 1927. In the heart of the wine country. Expensive.*

SOLANO COUNTY

The Union Hotel. 401 First Street, Benicia, CA 94510. 707-746-0100. *A taste of the nineteenth century in a town that was once the state capital. Moderate.*

Places to Eat

MARIN COUNTY

The Alta Mira Hotel. 125 Bulkley, Sausalito, CA 94965. 415-332-1350. *Locally famous for its Sunday brunch on the deck overlooking the bay. If you're curious about decadent Marin, start here. Moderate/expensive. (Also a good place to stay.)*

Station House Cafe. Main Street, Point Reyes Station, CA 94956. 415-663-1515. *Relaxing. Unpretentious. Excellent food. Garden seating. Live music on weekends. Inexpensive/moderate.*

The Sand Dollar. 3458 Shoreline Highway, Stinson Beach, CA 94970. 415-868-0434. *A favorite local hangout. Good seafood. Good people watching. Relaxing in the distinctive West Marin mode. Inexpensive/moderate.*

THE WINE COUNTRY

Domaine Chandon. California Drive, Yountville, CA 94599. 707-944-2892. *French/California cuisine. Elegant dining. The winery is famous for its champagne. Expensive.*

Mustards Grill. 7399 Saint Helena Highway, Yountville, CA 94558. 707-944-2424. *They call the cuisine American Grill, and the local reputation of this wonderful place is soaring. Moderate.*

The Calistoga Inn. 1250 Lincoln Avenue, Calistoga, CA 94515. 707-942-4101. *The building dates from the turn of the century and is beautifully restored. Fresh, simply prepared food. Generous portions. Highly recommended. Moderate/expensive.*

The Restaurant at Meadowood. 900 Meadowood Lane, Saint Helena, CA 94574. 707-963-3646. *Wine country cuisine with a*

French flair, featuring locally grown produce and game. Expensive.

SOLANO COUNTY

Mabel's Cafe. 2034 Columbus Parkway, Benicia, CA 94510. 707-746-7068. *California cuisine. Delicious, innovative, and fun. Inexpensive/moderate.*

Remark's Harbor House. Harbor Way on the Municipal Marina, Vallejo, CA 94590. 707-642-8984. *In a Victorian house overlooking the marina. Fresh seafood. Moderate.*

East Bay

Places to Stay

Gramma's Rose Garden Inn. 2740 Telegraph Avenue, Berkeley, CA 94705. 510-549-2145. *Three converted 1905 Tudor-style homes, appointed with overstuffed, finely carved furniture. Also garden house and cottage. Moderate.*

Hotel Durant. 2600 Durant Avenue, Berkeley, CA 94704. 510-845-8981. Close to the University of California campus. *Comfortable. Moderate.*

East Brother Light Station. 117 Park Place, Point Richmond, CA 94801. 510-820-9133. *On a bay island in a lighthouse that dates from 1873. Period-piece decor. Good dining. North of Berkeley. Unusual. Run as a nonprofit operation.*

South Bay

Places to Stay

Sanborn Park Hostel (Welch Hurst). 15808 Sanborn Road, Saratoga, CA 95070. 408-741-9555. *The redwood building dates from 1908. In Sanborn County Park, surrounded by forest. Inexpensive.*

The Victorian on Lytton. 555 Lytton Avenue, Palo Alto, CA 94301. 650-322-8555. *The house dates from 1890, and the rooms are furnished in antiques. Bed and breakfast. Expensive.*

The Cowper Inn. 705 Cowper, Palo Alto, CA 94301. 650-327-4475. *The house dates from 1896 and is attractively restored. Antique furniture. The living room is really grand. Bed and breakfast. Inexpensive/moderate.*

Places to Eat

Beauséjour. 170 State Street, Los Altos, CA 94022. 650-948-1382. *Elegant California cuisine. Expensive.*

Chez T. J. 938 Villa, Mountain View, CA 94041. 650-964-7466. *Innovative, modern French cookery. Prix fixe. Expensive.*

Campgrounds

National Park Campgrounds

Golden Gate National Recreation Area. Headquarters: Fort Mason, Building 201, San Francisco, CA 94123. Reservations: 415-331-1540 (call between 9:30 A.M. and noon, 7 days a week). *Walk-in campsites; reservations issued no more than 90 days in advance, except for Kirby Cove. Permits required, issued at Marin Headlands Visitor Center; 3-day limit per campground per year.*

Point Reyes National Seashore. Headquarters: Bear Valley, Point Reyes, CA 94956. Reservations: 415-663-1092 (call between 9 A.M. and noon, weekdays). *Hike-in campsites; reservations issued no more than two months in advance; permits required, issued at Bear Valley Visitor Center; 4-night limit per camper per visit.*

State Park Campgrounds

Reservations for most California state park campgrounds are made through DESTINET, either by telephone or by mail, and are available up to seven months in advance. There is a modest reservation fee. Cancellations may be made by telephone; again, there is a modest fee. Phone-in reservations (on Visa or MasterCard): 800-444-PARK (7275). For reservation form by mail, write to DESTINET, 9450 Carroll Park Drive, San Diego, CA 92121. Payment in advance is required.

The exceptions to this reservation system are Austin Creek State

Recreation Area, Half Moon Bay State Beach, and Henry W. Coe State Park. These are primitive, first-come, first-served campgrounds. Registration is required (see individual listings below). Reservations are required in some parks year-round, others only during their most popular season. A few parks close during the rainy season.

Note: State park campgrounds are very popular; stays are limited. All charge reasonable fees. Dogs, on leash, are allowed in state park campgrounds and picnic areas, but not on trails or most beaches. For more information, contact the Bay Area district office of California State Parks, 250 Executive Park Boulevard, Suite 4900, San Francisco, CA 94134. 415-330-6300.

Marin County

China Camp State Park. North San Pedro Road, San Rafael, CA 94901. 415-456-0766. *Walk-in campsites, some wheelchair-accessible; showers; picnic facilities; reservations required year-round.*

Mount Tamalpais State Park. 801 Panoramic Highway, Mill Valley, CA. 415-388-2070. *Walk-in ¼ mile; showers; reservations year-round.*

Samuel P. Taylor State Park. P.O. Box 251, Lagunitas, CA 94938. 415-488-9897. *Reservations; seasonal; showers; wheelchair-accessible campsites.*

Sonoma County

Austin Creek State Recreation Area. Registration: Armstrong Redwoods State Reserve, 17000 Armstrong Woods Road, Guerneville, CA 95446. 707-869-2015. *About two dozen primitive campsites at Bullfrog Pond Camp; four hike-in sites. All first-come, first-served. Not recommended during the rainy season.*

Salt Point State Park. 25050 Coast Highway 1, Jenner, CA 95450. 707-847-3221. *Walk-in; hike or bike in; wheelchair-accessible campsites; trailers; also car camping; reservations seasonal. May close during the rainy season.*

Sonoma Coast State Beach. Bodega Bay, CA 94923. 707-875-3483. *Two campgrounds, one with showers; reservations year-round. Two hike-in campgrounds, open April 1–November 30, are first-come, first-served.*

Sugarloaf Ridge State Park. 2605 Adobe Canyon Road, Kenwood, CA 95452. 707-833-5712. *Car and tent camping; trailers; one mile of steep, narrow, winding road; reservations seasonal.*

Napa County

Bothe-Napa Valley State Park. 3801 Saint Helena Highway North, Calistoga, CA 94515. 707-942-4575. *Car camping; trailers; wheelchair-accessible campsites; showers; reservations year-round. (Note: the Napa Fairgrounds, owned by the state, are pressed into service for car camping during the tourist season; they are located at 575 Third Street in Napa, CA 94559. For information, telephone 707-253-4900.)*

Solano County

Brannan Island State Recreation Area. 17645 Highway 160, Rio Vista, CA 94571. 916-777-6671. *Boat berths; car camping; showers; trailers; wheelchair-accessible campsites; reservations seasonal.*

Contra Costa County

Mount Diablo State Park. P.O. Box 250, Diablo, CA 94528. 510-837-2525. *Car and tent camping; trailers (over 20 ft. not advised); showers; winding mountain roads. Fire restrictions June 1 to September 30; contact park for information; park entrance gates closed from sunset to 8:00 A.M. Reservations seasonal.*

San Mateo County

Butano State Park. P.O. Box 9, Pescadero, CA 94060. 415-879-0173. *Drive-in and walk-in campsites; trailers; reservations seasonal.*

Half Moon Bay State Beach. 95 Kelly Avenue, Half Moon Bay, CA 94019. 650-726-8820. *Car camping; trailers; one wheelchair and one hike-in, bike-in campsite; outside cold showers; all campsites first-come, first-served.*

Portola Redwoods State Park. Box F, Route 2, La Honda, CA 94020. 650-948-9098. *Car camping; trailers (no hookups); walk-in campsites; showers; reservations seasonal.*

Santa Clara County

Henry W. Coe State Park. Information: Box 846, Morgan Hill, CA 95038. 408-779-2728. *Many backpacking sites in this 80,000-acre wilderness; some 20 drive-in campsites on Pine Ridge close to headquarters (where you register) and museum. All campsites first-come, first-served.*

Santa Cruz County

Big Basin Redwoods State Park. 21600 Big Basin Way, Boulder Creek, CA 95006. 408-338-6132. *Drive-in and walk-in campsites; one wheelchair-accessible site; showers; trailers; reservations year-round.* (Included because this is an exceptional parkland, contiguous with San Mateo County.)

County Park Campgrounds

Sonoma County

Doran Park. Doran Park Road, P.O. Box 372, Bodega Bay, CA 94923. 707-875-3540. *Showers; car camping; trailers; wheelchair-accessible campsites; 140 units, all first-come, first-served.*

Gualala Point Park. Highway 1 at Gualala River, P.O. Box 95, Gualala, CA 95445. 707-785-2377. *Sonoma County's northernmost coastal park. Car camping; walk-in; first-come, first-served.*

Spring Lake Park. 5390 Montgomery Drive, Santa Rosa, CA 95409. 707-539-8092. *County's most developed recreation area; swimming; Parcourse; 30 campsites; showers; reservations seasonal; open weekends only, Oct. to May.*

Stillwater Cove Park. 22455 Highway 1 (3.5 miles north of Fort Ross), Jenner, CA 95450. 707-847-3245. *Coastal pleasures; diving; tidepool viewing; plus a redwood canyon; camping, first-come, first-served.*

Solano County

Lake Solano Park. Off Highway 128, Pleasant Valley Road, Winters, CA 95694. 916-795-2990. *Near Winters; 90 sites; hot showers; trailer facilities; fishing. Reservations seasonal; open year-round.*

Sandy Beach Park. P.O. Box 312, Rio Vista, CA 94571. 707-374-2097. *On the Sacramento River; 42 sites; hot showers; trailer facilities; reservations year-round.*

Alameda County

Anthony Chabot Regional Park. Redwood Road between Oakland and Castro Valley (off Marciel Gate entrance to park). Information: East Bay Regional Park District, 2950 Peralta Oaks Court, Oakland, CA 94605. 510-635-0135. Reservations: 510-562-CAMP. *75 trailer; tent and walk-in campsites; showers; dogs allowed.*

Del Valle Regional Park. 10 miles south of Livermore. Information: East Bay Regional Park District, 2950 Peralta Oaks Court, Oakland, CA 94605. 510-635-0135. Reservations: 510-562-CAMP. *150 sites; 21 with water and sewage hookups (no electrical); dogs allowed.*

Sunol Regional Wilderness. Geary Road off Calaveras Road, 5 miles south of Sunol (near park headquarters). Information: East Bay Regional Park District, 2950 Peralta Oaks Court, Oakland, CA 94605. 510-562-0135. Reservations: 510-562-CAMP. *Small walk-in campground; backpack sites; permit required; parking fee; dogs allowed.*

San Mateo County

Pescadero Park. 9500 Pescadero Road, La Honda, CA 94020. 650-879-0212. *See Peninsula Parklands.*

Joseph D. Grant Park. Mount Hamilton Road, San Jose, CA 95140. 408-274-6121. *See Peninsula Parklands.*

Sanborn Skyline Park. 16055 Sanborn Road, Saratoga, CA 95070. 408-867-9959. *Walk-in sites; RV sites; first-come, first-served. See Peninsula Parklands.*

RV Campgrounds

San Francisco

Golden Gate Trailer Park. 7321 Mission Street, Daly City, CA 94014. 415-994-6758. *26 sites; RV facilities; Laundromat; showers; pets okay on leash.*

San Francisco RV Park. 255 Townsend Street, San Francisco, CA
94107. 415-986-8730. *200 sites; RV facilities; Laundromat;
game room; showers.*

Marin County

Golden Gate Trailer Court. 2000 Redwood Highway, Greenbrae,
CA 94904. 415-924-0683. *40 sites; RV facilities; showers; pets
okay on leash.*

Olema Ranch Campground. Highway 1, Olema, CA 94950. 415-
663-8001. *150 tent and 75 RV sites (32 spacious acres); post
office; gas station; general store; Laundromat; weekend programs in summer; dogs okay on leash.*

Sonoma County

KOA San Francisco North Petaluma. 20 Rainsville Road, Petaluma,
CA 94952. 707-763-1492. *300 sites; RV facilities; Laundromat;
store; showers; recreation room; spa; pool; pets okay on leash.*

Alameda County

*See County Park Campgrounds, Alameda County. Both Anthony
Chabot and Del Valle Regional parks have hookups for RVs.*

San Mateo County

Trailer Villa. 3401 East Bayshore Road, Redwood City, CA 94063.
415-366-7880. *40 sites; RV facilities; pets okay on leash.*

Santa Clara County

Saratoga Springs Picnic and Campgrounds. 22801 Big Basin Way,
Saratoga, CA 95070. 408-867-3016. *1 hour south of San Francisco; trailers and tents; swimming; pets okay on leash.*

Youth Hostels

There are more than a half dozen hostels in the Golden Gate Council of Hostelling International, American Youth Hostels, all superbly
located—two are in old lighthouses, two in the heart of San Francisco—and all with comfortable (sometimes dormitory-type) facilities. You bring your own sleeping bag (most have linen rental) and

share a communal (completely equipped) kitchen and comfortable common room. (Some even have hot tubs!) Some have wood-burning fireplaces, and you may find laundry facilities. A few-minute household chore may be requested. No alcohol or cigarettes, please.

Hostels offer a unique chance to get acquainted with fellow travelers from all over the world. Rates are extremely modest. You won't find a better lodgings buy anywhere in the Bay Area. You can telephone or write for more information, reservations, and instructions on how to reach them. Here's where they are:

Marin Headlands Hostel. Building 941, Fort Barry, Sausalito, CA 94965; telephone 415-331-2777. Five miles from San Francisco, 4 from Golden Gate Bridge. An army historic landmark in the GGNRA's Marin Headlands; spacious and homey; lovely setting. Has a piano, hot showers, laundry, bicycle storage; super-reasonably priced, as are the other hostels outside the city. Private rooms are available for couples and families. Accommodates 103 guests.

Pigeon Point Lighthouse Hostel. 210 Pigeon Point Road/Highway 1, Pescadero, CA 94060; telephone 650-879-0633. Fifty miles south of San Francisco. In one of the tallest lighthouses in the United States; close to elephant seal colony (at Año Nuevo State Reserve); near tidepools and redwoods. Has four modern bungalows, each with a fully equipped kitchen (formerly Coast Guard family residences). Private rooms available for couples and families. Accommodates 52 guests.

Point Montara Lighthouse Hostel. Sixteenth Street/Cabrillo Highway (Highway 1), P.O. Box 737, Montara, CA 94037; telephone 650-728-7177. Off Highway 1, 25 miles south of San Francisco. Has spectacular views of the Pacific Ocean, outdoor hot tub, volleyball court, private beach, information desk. Wheelchair-accessible; never closed. Accommodates 45 guests in a modern seven bedroom duplex, with two kitchens. The Fog Signal Building houses a spacious common room with a wood-burning stove. Private rooms can be reserved for couples and families.

Point Reyes Hostel. P.O. Box 247, Point Reyes Station, CA 94956; telephone 415-663-8811. Fifty miles north of San Francisco. Formerly a working ranch house in the middle of a field of daffodils. Has a patio and wood-burning stove. Accessible by car, foot, or bicycle. (Recommended for individuals, especially on weekends. However, a family room can be reserved for families with children under five.) Accommodates 44 guests.

San Francisco—Fisherman's Wharf Hostel. Building 240, Fort Mason, San Francisco, CA 94123; telephone 415-771-7277. In GGNRA and close to the San Francisco scene. Historic, Civil War vintage–building with lovely bay view. This is understandably one of the most popular hostels in the country, so make your reservations early. Accommodates 150 guests.

San Francisco—Downtown Hostel. 312 Mason Street, San Francisco, CA 94102; telephone 415-788-5604. This remarkably situated downtown former hotel has numerous urban amenities, including vending machines and access to public transportation to all parts of the Bay Area. Two to six people in a room; in some cases two rooms share a bath. You can't get much closer to the action than this comfortable hostel, and you certainly can't beat the price anywhere in the city! Early reservations are essential. Accommodates 234 guests.

Hostels are open to everyone, for a modest fee you can join the Hostelling International, American Youth Hostels, and get an international hostel pass and a free United States/Canada Hostel Handbook; this will give you access to more than 5,000 hostels in 77 countries. Write Hostelling International, AYH, 425 Divisadero Street, Suite 307, San Francisco, CA 94117; telephone 415-863-1444. AYH in San Francisco will also send you a free folder on northern and central California hostels; write at the above address and enclose a self-addressed stamped envelope.

Note: There are two beautiful American Youth Hostels down the Peninsula that are not administered directly by the Golden Gate Council. One is **Hidden Villa Ranch,** 26870 Moody Road, Los Altos Hills, CA 94022; telephone 650-949-8648. This is within the Golden Gate Council but is administered by the Trust for Hidden Villa; it is closed from June 1 to August 31. Another is the **Sanborn Park Hostel** (Welch Hurst), 15808 Sanborn Road, Saratoga, CA 95070; telephone 408-741-0166. It is open all year. (The Sierra Club's Loma Prieta Chapter's hikers' hut in Sam McDonald Park is also available to energetic hostelers who don't mind a 1½ mile walk from their cars. Contact Sierra Club, Loma Prieta Chapter, 3921, East Bayshore Boulevard, Palo Alto, CA 94303; telephone 650-390-8411.)

┌──── Public Transportation

Buses and Trains

AC Transit. Serves San Francisco to the East Bay and the East Bay. 510-817-1717.

Bay Area Rapid Transit (BART). Serves San Francisco–East Bay (Concord and Fremont and points between) and northern Peninsula (Colma). 510-464-6000.

Caltrain. Serves San Francisco and Peninsula counties. 800-660-4287.

Golden Gate Transit Bus Service. Serves San Francisco to Marin and Sonoma counties and within Marin and Sonoma counties. 415-923-2000 from San Francisco; 415-455-2000 from Marin; 707-541-2000 from Sonoma.

Municipal Railway of San Francisco (MUNI). Serves city of San Francisco. 415-673-MUNI (6864). Free *Timetable Booklet* available from above number; full-color street map of San Francisco with MUNI routes for sale at MUNI, 949 Presidio Avenue, and Information Booth at City Hall—also bookstores.

San Mateo County Transit District (SAMTRANS). Serves San Francisco and Peninsula counties and San Francisco International Airport. 800-660-4287.

Ferries

Alameda-Oakland Ferry. Serves Oakland, Alameda, and San Francisco. Weekend service from Oakland to Angel Island. 510-522-3300.

Angel Island–Tiburon Ferry Service. Serves Tiburon to Angel Island. 415-435-2131.

Blue and Gold Fleet. Serves San Francisco and Vallejo. Bus connections at Vallejo for Marine World and the wine country. Bay cruises. Dinner dance cruises. 415-705-5555.

Red and White Fleet. Serves San Francisco, Sausalito, Alcatraz, Angel Island, and Tiburon. Bus connections at Tiburon for Muir Woods and the wine country. Bay cruises. 415-546-2628.

Maps

Most National Park Service visitor centers sell or supply trail maps for their particular parks. Bay Area bookstores also carry local maps. For topographic maps, call, write, or visit the U.S. Geological Survey at 345 Middlefield Road, Building 3, Menlo Park, CA 94025 (telephone 800-223-8081). The USGS is open 8:30 A.M.–4:00 P.M. weekdays.

Local map publishers include the following; call them for a complete list of the recreational maps they produce: Olmsted Brothers Maps, 9 Plaza Drive, Berkeley, CA 94705; telephone 510-658-6534. Thomas Brothers Maps, 550 Jackson Street, San Francisco, CA 94133; telephone 415-981-7520.

Bibliography

Adams, Gerald. *A San Francisco Neighborhood Guide.* San Francisco: California Living Books, 1980.

Allen, Hayward. *Great Blue Heron.* Minocque, Wisc.: Northward Press, 1991.

Arrigoni, Patricia. *Making the Most of Marin.* Novato, Calif.: Presidio Press, 1981.

Bagwell, Beth. *Oakland: The Story of a City.* Novato, Calif.: Presidio Press, 1982.

Bay Area Runners Guide. San Francisco: BARGE Publications, 1978.

Bennett, Ben. *Oceanic Society Field Guide to the Gray Whale.* San Francisco: Legacy Publishing, 1983.

Block, Eugene B. *The Immortal San Franciscans for Whom the Streets Were Named.* San Francisco: Chronicle Books, 1971.

Boden, Clive, and Angus Chater. *The Windsurfer Funboard Handbook.* Woodbury, N.Y.: Barron's, 1984.

Boutelle, Sara Holmes. *Julia Morgan, architect.* New York: Abbeville Press, 1995.

Caldeway, Jeffrey. *Wine Tour: Napa Valley.* San Francisco: Wine Appreciation Guild, 1984.

Chapman, Jean. *Exploring Benicia State Recreation Area.* Suisun City, Calif.: Solano Community College, 1977.

Clary, Raymond H. *The Making of Golden Gate Park.* San Francisco: Don't Call It Frisco Press, 1985.

Cole, Tom. *A Short History of San Francisco.* San Francisco: Lexicos, 1981.

DeSante, David, and Peter Pyle. *Distributional Checklist of North American Birds.* Lee Vining, Calif.: Artemisia Press, 1986.

Dillon, Richard. *Great Expectations.* Benicia, Calif.: Benicia Heritage Books, 1980.

Doss, Margot Patterson. *The Bay Area at Your Feet.* San Rafael, Calif.: Presidio Press, 1981.

————. *Paths of Gold*. San Francisco: Chronicle Books, 1974.

————. *San Francisco at Your Feet*. San Rafael, Calif.: Presidio Press, 1981.

Dowd, John. *Sea Kayaking*. Seattle: University of Washington Press, 1970.

Ferris, Roxana S. *Flowers of Point Reyes National Seashore*. Berkeley and Los Angeles: University of California Press, 1970.

Gilliam, Harold. *Between the Devil and the Deep Blue Bay*. San Francisco: Chronicle Books, 1969.

————. *Island in Time*. San Francisco: Sierra Club Books, 1967.

————. *San Francisco Bay*. Garden City, N.Y.: Doubleday, 1957.

————. *Weather of the San Francisco Bay Region*. Berkeley and Los Angeles: University of California Press, 1962.

————and Ann Lawrence. *Marin Headlands*. San Francisco: Golden Gate National Park Association, 1993.

Gudde, Erwin G. *California Place Names*. Berkeley and Los Angeles: University of California Press, 1969.

Hansen, Gladys. *San Francisco Almanac*. San Rafael, Calif.: Presidio Press, 1980.

Hart, John. *Farming on the Edge: Saving Family Farms in Marin County, California*. Berkeley and Los Angeles: University of California Press, 1991.

————. *Muir Woods*. San Francisco: Golden Gate National Park Association, 1991.

————. *Wilderness Next Door*. San Rafael, Calif.: Presidio Press, 1979.

Herron, Don. *The Dashiell Hammett Tour*. San Francisco: City Lights Books, 1991.

————. *The Literary World of San Francisco and Its Environs*. San Francisco: City Lights Books, 1985.

Holliday, J. S. *The World Rushed In*. New York: Simon and Schuster, 1981.

Hopper, James, and Leon Dorais, eds. *WPA Guide to California*. New York: Pantheon Books, 1984.

Howell, John Thomas. *Marin Flora*. Berkeley and Los Angeles: University of California Press, 1970.

Hubbard, Doni. *Favorite Trails of Northern California Horsemen*. Redwood City, Calif.: Hoofprints, 1980.

Hutchison, Derek. *Sea Canoeing*. London: Adam and Charles Black, 1976.

Kahn, Edgar M. *Cable Car Days*. Stanford, Calif.: Stanford University Press, 1963.

Kaufmann, Paul. *Paddling the Gate*. Santa Monica, Calif.: Mara Publishing, 1978.

Kemble, John Haskell. *San Francisco Bay: A Pictorial Maritime History*. New York: Bonanza Books, 1978.

Leschoier, Ruth. *The Coast Miwok People*. Novato, Calif.: Nova-Albion-ko Press, 1984.

Liberatore, Karen. *The Complete Guide to the Golden Gate Recreation Area*. Fairfax, Calif.: Goodchild Jacobsen, 1982.

Livingston, Kimball. *Sailing the Bay*. San Francisco: Chronicle Books, 1981.

Lowenstein, Louis K. *Streets of San Francisco: The Origins of Street and Place Names*. San Francisco: Lexicos, 1984.

McClintock, Elizabeth; Walter Knight; and Neil Fahy. *A Flora of the San Bruno Mountains*. San Francisco: California Academy of Sciences, 1968.

Margolin, Malcolm. *The East Bay Out*. Berkeley, Calif.: Heyday Books, 1974.

———. *The Ohlone Way*. Berkeley, Calif.: Heyday Books, 1978.

Noble, John Wesley. *Its Name Was M.U.D.* Oakland, Calif.: East Bay Municipal Water District, 1970.

Petersen, Grant, with Mary Anderson. *Roads to Ride, A Bicyclist's Topographic Guide to Alameda, Contra Costa, and Marin Counties*. Berkeley, Calif.: Heyday Books, 1984.

Pratt, Helen. *Herons and Egrets of Audubon Canyon Ranch*. 1993. May be purchased at Audubon Canyon Ranch, Stinson Beach.

Reeves, Randall R. *The Sierra Club Handbook of Whales and Dolphins*. San Francisco: Sierra Club Books, 1983.

Robbins, Chandler S.; Bertel Bruun; and Herbert S. Zim. *Birds of North America*. Racine, Wis.: Western Publishing, 1983.

Rubissow, Ariel. *Cliff House and Land's End*. San Francisco: Golden Gate National Park Association, 1993.

Rusmore, Jean. *The Bay Area Ridge Trail, Ridgetop Adventures Above San Francisco Bay*. Berkeley, Calif.: Wilderness Press, 1995.

———, and Frances Spangle. *Peninsula Trails*. Berkeley, Calif.: Wilderness Press, 1982.

Scanlan-Rohrer, Anne, ed. *San Francisco Peninsula Birdwatching*. Burlingame, Calif.: Sequoia Audubon Society, 1984.

Scott, Mel. *The Future of San Francisco Bay*. Berkeley: University of California Press, 1963.

Shanken, Marvin R., ed. *Wine Maps: Wineries, Restaurants, Lodging*. San Francisco: The Wine Spectator, 1986.

Sharsmith, Helen K. *Spring Wildflowers of the San Francisco Bay Region*. Berkeley and Los Angeles: University of California Press, 1965.

Shuford, W. David. *The Marin County Breeding Bird Atlas: A Distributional and Natural History of Coastal California Birds*. Bolinas, Calif.: Bushtit Books, 1993.

———, and I. C. Timossi. *Plant Communities of Marin County*. Sacramento, Calif.: California Native Plant Society, 1992.

Spangle, Frances, and Jean Rusmore. *South Bay Trails*. Berkeley, Calif.: Wilderness Press, 1984.

Stebbins, Robert C. *A Field Guide to Western Reptiles and Amphibians*, 2d ed., rev. Boston: Houghton Mifflin, 1985.

Taber, Tom. *The Expanded Santa Cruz Mountains Trail Book*. San Mateo, Calif.: Oak Valley Press, 1982.

Van der zee, John. *The Gate: The True Story of the Design and Construction of the Golden Gate Bridge*. New York: Simon & Schuster, 1986.

Wahrhaftig, Clyde. *A Streetcar to Subduction*. Washington, D.C.: American Geophysical Union, 1984.

Waldhorn, Judith Lynch. *A Gift to the Street*. New York: St. Martin's Press, 1982.

Walker, Theodore J. *Whale Primer*. Point Loma, Calif.: Cabrillo Historical Association, 1979.

Weir, Kim. *Northern California Handbook*. Chico, Calif.: Moon Publications, 1994.

Whitnah, Dorothy L. *Guide to the Golden Gate National Recreation Area*. Berkeley, Calif.: Wilderness Press, 1978.

———. *Guide to Point Reyes National Seashore*. Berkeley, Calif.: Wilderness Press, 1981.

———. *An Outdoor Guide to the San Francisco Bay Area*. Berkeley, Calif.: Wilderness Press, 1984.

Wurman, Richard Saul. *Wine Country Access Guide*. Dunmore, Penn.: HarperCollins, 1992.

Index

Numbers in italics indicate photographs.

About the Author

PEGGY WAYBURN is an avid hiker, river runner, outdoor photographer, and lifelong environmental activist, and the author of *Adventuring in the San Francisco Bay Area*. She lives with her husband in San Francisco.